UNDERSTANDING HOMELESSNESS IN IRELAND SINCE INDEPENDENCE
Decades in the Making

Eoin O'Sullivan, Mike Allen and Sarah Sheridan

First published in Great Britain in 2026 by

Policy Press, an imprint of
Bristol University Press
University of Bristol
1-9 Old Park Hill
Bristol
BS2 8BB
UK
t: +44 (0)117 374 6645
e: bup-info@bristol.ac.uk

Details of international sales and distribution partners are available at policy.bristoluniversitypress.co.uk

© Bristol University Press 2026

DOI: 10.51952/9781447378761

British Library Cataloguing in Publication Data
A catalogue record for this book is available from the British Library

ISBN 978-1-4473-7873-0 hardcover
ISBN 978-1-4473-7874-7 paperback
ISBN 978-1-4473-7875-4 ePub
ISBN 978-1-4473-7876-1 ePdf

The right of Eoin O'Sullivan, Mike Allen and Sarah Sheridan to be identified as authors of this work has been asserted by them in accordance with the Copyright, Designs and Patents Act 1988.

All rights reserved: no part of this publication may be reproduced, stored in a retrieval system, or transmitted in any form or by any means, electronic, mechanical, photocopying, recording, or otherwise without the prior permission of Bristol University Press.

Every reasonable effort has been made to obtain permission to reproduce copyrighted material. If, however, anyone knows of an oversight, please contact the publisher.

The statements and opinions contained within this publication are solely those of the authors and not of the University of Bristol or Bristol University Press. The University of Bristol and Bristol University Press disclaim responsibility for any injury to persons or property resulting from any material published in this publication.

Bristol University Press and Policy Press work to counter discrimination on grounds of gender, race, disability, age and sexuality.

Cover design: Liam Roberts Design
Front cover image: RTÉ Stills Department/Corporation Place, Dublin city (1972)

Contents

List of figures and tables	iv
Acknowledgements	vi
Timeline	vii
Introduction: Colonial inheritances	1
1 Poor Laws, the family economy and housing policy, 1922–1948	15
2 The end of the Poor Laws, economic development and modernisation, 1948–1963	41
3 Housing policy, housing agitation and the emergence of the homelessness sector, 1964–1981	58
4 Two housing bills and one act, 1981–1988	83
5 From the implications of the Housing Act to local partnerships on homelessness, 1989–1997	111
6 A decade of strategies, the Celtic Tiger and austerity, 1997–2011	131
7 From austerity to economic recovery, 2011–2016	153
8 Homelessness becomes a 'national crisis', 2016– 2020	180
9 Pandemic, migration and a housing crisis, 2020–2024	208
Conclusion: Reflections on Homelessness in Ireland	232
Appendix 1: Measuring homelessness in Ireland	254
Appendix 2: Recent trends in homelessness in Ireland in comparative perspective	258
Notes	262
References	265
Index	298

List of figures and tables

Figures

0.1	Number of casuals or night lodgers in Irish workhouses, 1869–1914	4
0.2	Dwellings built by local authorities, 1880–1922	12
1.1	Social housing output, 1923–1948	29
1.2	Net migration (,000), 1926–1948	37
2.1	Net migration (,000), 1926–1963	43
2.2	Social housing output, 1923–1963	54
3.1	Social housing completions, 1923–1981	75
3.2	Net migration (,000), 1926–1981	81
4.1	Social housing completions, 1923–1988	90
4.2	Net migration (,000), 1926–1988	108
5.1	Social housing output, 1923–1996	118
5.2	Net migration (,000), 1926–1996	125
6.1	Social housing output, 1923–2011	135
6.2	Net migration (,000), 1926–2011	150
7.1	Social housing output, 1923–2016	161
7.2	Net migration (,000), 1926–2016	178
8.1	Social housing output, 1923–2020	185
8.2	Adults in families and adult-only households in Local Government emergency and temporary accommodation, June 2014–December 2019	197
8.3	Unsheltered point-in-time count Dublin, 2014–2019	198
8.4	Number of new adults entering Section 10 funded emergency and temporary accommodation, 2014–2019	199
8.5	Adults' exits from emergency accommodation to housing, 2014–2019	200
8.6	Net migration (,000), 1926–2020	205
9.1	Number of new adults entering Section 10 funded emergency and temporary accommodation, 2014–2024	213
9.2	Adults' exits to housing from emergency accommodation to housing, 2014–2024	214
9.3	Adults in families and adult-only households in Local Government emergency and temporary accommodation, June 2014–December 2024	214
9.4	Unsheltered point-in-time count in Dublin, 2014–2024	217
9.5	Expenditure on services for households experiencing homelessness by local authorities Dublin/outside Dublin, 2009–2024	219
9.6	Social housing output, 1923–2024	221

9.7	Net migration (,000), 1926–2024	223
A.1	Index of homelessness at a point-in-time in selected countries, 2008–2024	259
A.2	Households experiencing homelessness and staying in temporary and emergency accommodation in Denmark, Finland and Ireland, 2008–2024	260
A.3	Households experiencing homelessness and staying in temporary and emergency accommodation in Denmark, Finland and Ireland per 1,000 households, 2008–2024	260

Tables

6.1	Breakdown of the category homeless in the Assessment of Housing Need, 2005	148
6.2	Accommodation needs of homeless households, 2005	148

Acknowledgements

We would like to thank colleagues who read and commented on the draft versions of this book, in particular Aidan Culhane, Tony Fahey, Mary Higgins, Carole Holohan, Tony McCashin, Mary Murphy and Michelle Norris. We would also like to thank the anonymous referees who provided invaluable feedback at the formative stages of writing this book.

Timeline

This timeline, starting from pre-Independence through to the present day, shows how each chapter chronologically covers the journey.

Pre-Independence

1824 *Act for the Punishment of Idle and Disorderly Persons, Rogues and Vagabonds* (later extended in 1871)

1883 *Labourers (Ireland) Act*

1890 *The Housing of the Working Classes Act*

1906 Report of the *Departmental Committee on Vagrancy* – Appendix XIV 'Vagrancy in Ireland'

1906 Report of the *Vice-Regal Commission on Poor Law Reform in Ireland*

1908 *Housing of the Working Classes (Ireland) Act* (or 'the Clancy Act')

1909 *Royal Commission on the Poor Laws and Relief of Distress (Ireland report)*

Chapter 1: Poor Laws, the family economy and housing policy, 1922–1948

1923 *The Land Act* and establishment of Land Commission

1924 *Housing (Building Facilities) Act* and the 'Million Pound Scheme'

1925 Establishment of 'The Commission on the Relief of the Sick and Destitute Poor, including the Insane Poor'

1932 *The Housing (Financial and Miscellaneous Provisions) Act*

1936 *Labourers' Acts* and provision for sale of rural cottages

1938 *Report on Slum Clearance in Dublin*

1939–1943 *Report of Inquiry into the Housing of the Working Classes*

1939 *Public Assistance Act*

1939 Establishment of the 'Dublin Housing Inquiry Commission'

1948 *White Paper on Housing*

Chapter 2: The end of the Poor Laws, economic development and modernisation, 1948–1963

1951 Inter-Departmental Committee report on county homes (unpublished)

1951 *White Paper on the Reconstruction and Improvement of County Homes*

1952 Circular 7/52 to local authorities on future of county homes

1952 *Report on Rent Control* report by Rents and Leaseholds Commission

	1953 *Health Act* – Section 54 and provision of 'institutional assistance'
	1957 Second report of Capital Investment Advisory Committee (housing)
	1958 *Programme of Economic Expansion* and *Economic Development*
	1958 *Housing (Amendment) Act*
	1960 *Rent Restrictions Act*
Chapter 3: Housing policy, housing agitation, and the emergence of the homelessness sector, 1964–1981	**1964** *White Paper on Housing: Progress and Prospects*
	1966 *White Paper on The Health Services and their Further Development*
	1966 *Housing Act*
	1966 Report from the *Commission of Inquiry on Mental Illness*
	1967 Establishment of Dublin Housing Action Committee (DHAC)
	1968 *Interdepartmental Committee on the Care of the Aged*
	1969 *White Paper on Housing in the Seventies*
	1973 National Tenant Purchase Scheme was introduced
	1974 Establishment of Task Force on Child Care Services
	1979 *The Management of Local Authority Housing, Renting Subsidy and Sales, Policy and Practice*
Chapter 4: Two housing bills and one act, 1981–1988	**1982** *Housing (Private Rented Dwellings) Act*
	1983 Private Members' Bill: *Housing (Homeless Persons) Bill 1983* (rejected by government)
	1984 The establishment of the *Ad-Hoc Committee on Homelessness*
	1984 Establishment of National Campaign for the Homeless
	1984 Surrender Grant Scheme
	1985 *In Partnership with Youth: The National Youth Policy*
	1985 *Housing (Miscellaneous Provisions) Bill*
	1985 Establishment of Focus Point (later Focus Ireland)
	1988 *Housing Act*
Chapter 5: From the implications of the Housing Act to local partnerships on homelessness, 1989–1997	**1991** *The Child Care Act*
	1991 *A Plan for Social Housing*
	1991 *Review of the 1998 Housing Act* and revised N9/91 Circular for local authorities
	1992 *Housing (Miscellaneous Provisions) Act 1992*
	1992 *Memorandum on the Preparation of a Statement of Policy on Housing Management*

Timeline

	1993 Lord Mayor's Commission on Housing in Dublin
	1995 *Social Housing – The Way Ahead*
	1996 Establishment of the Homeless Initiative, Dublin
	1997 S.I. No. 236/1997 Social Welfare (Rent Allowance) (Amendment) Regulations
	1999 Land Commission dissolved
Chapter 6: A decade of strategies, the Celtic Tiger and austerity, 1997–2011	2000 *Planning and Development Act*
	2000 *Homelessness – An Integrated Strategy*
	2002 Introduction of Part V in the *Planning and Development Acts*
	2002 *Homelessness Preventative Strategy*
	2004 Introduction or Rental Accommodation Scheme (RAS)
	2004 *Residential Tenancies Act* and establishment of Residential Tenancies Board
	2006 Social Partnership's fifth report *Towards 2016*
	2006 Establishment of MakeRoom NGO coalition
	2006 Establishment of the National Homeless Consultative Committee (NHCC)
	2007 *Delivering Homes, Sustaining Communities: Statement on Housing Policy*
	2008 *The Way Home: A Strategy to Address Adult Homelessness in Ireland 2008–2013*
	2009 *Implementation Plan for The Way Home*
Chapter 7: From austerity to economic recovery, 2011–2016	2011 Dublin Housing First Demonstration Project
	2013 *Housing Policy Statement*
	2013 Establishment and first report of Homeless Oversight Group
	2013 Pathway Accommodation and Support System (PASS) rolled out nationally
	2014 *Housing (Miscellaneous Provisions Bill)* and introduction of Housing Assistance Payment Scheme
	2014 *Implementation Plan on the State's Response to Homelessness*
	2014 *Homeless Action Plan 2022–2024: A Framework for Dublin*
	2014 *Social Housing Strategy 2020*
	2015 *Stabilising Rents, Boosting Supply: A Package to Deliver Rent Certainty and Housing Supply*

Chapter 8: Homelessness becomes a 'national crisis', 2016–2020	2016	Oireachtas Committee Report on *Housing and Homelessness*
	2016	*Rebuilding Ireland: Action Plan for Housing and Homelessness*
	2016	Inclusion of Approved Housing Bodies under regulatory remit of Residential Tenancies Board
	2017	Establishment of Homelessness Inter-Agency Group
	2018	*Housing First Implementation Plan 2018–2021*
	2018	Establishment of Raise the Roof coalition
Chapter 9: Pandemic, migration and a housing crisis, 2020–2024	2020	*Emergency Measures in the Public Interest (COVID-19) Act 2020*
	2021	*Housing for All: A New Housing Plan for Ireland*
	2021	*Lisbon Declaration on the European Platform on Combatting Homelessness*
	2021	Establishment of the National Homeless Action Committee (NHAC)
	2021	*Affordable Housing Act* 2021
	2022	*Housing First National Implementation Plan 2022–2026*
	2022	*Youth Homelessness Strategy 2023–2025*

Introduction: Colonial inheritances

This book tells the story of how Ireland tackled the challenges of homelessness in the century following the foundation of the Independent Irish State. When the first Irish Government met in September 1922 it did not, of course, start with a blank slate. When they sat down to look at what was to be done, they had an inheritance of centuries of legislation governing the poor, the indigent and vagrants and recently published reviews of that legislation, and a wide range of inherited attitudes to vagrancy and poverty, some of which had been challenged in the nationalist movement while others remained unexamined. They also inherited a set of institutions – both in the sense of abstract ways of doing things and in the sense of actual buildings – tenements, cottages, workhouses and an array of other institutions for the management of marginality in both rural and urban areas. In order to set the scene for the story of what happened after Independence it is useful to look at some of those legacies from the earlier era.

'Homelessness' prior to Independence

In the century before Independence – and indeed for almost 50 years after Independence – the term 'homelessness' had not been coined. People who experienced the sort of conditions which we would now term homelessness were referred to in legislation and policy documents as 'vagrants' and 'vagabonds' and even in formal communications as 'down-and-outs', 'tramps' and 'casuals' (that is non-resident users of workhouses), and were provided with accommodation and services in workhouses and a range of shelters provided by charitable bodies, largely religiously motivated.

The *Irish Poor Law Act, 1838* provided for a system of State-funded and managed workhouses, operating on the principle of 'less eligibility', and in a relatively short period of time after the passing of the legislation, 130 workhouses were constructed to a uniform design, each with a capacity for between 500–900 inmates (Crossman, 2006a). The 1838 legislation was modelled on English 'new poor law' legislation of 1834, the objective of which was 'to deter applications for assistance by making the nature of the relief and the conditions under which it was given repugnant' (Brundage, 2002, 66), with the workhouse the primary means to achieve these objectives. Unlike England, Ireland did not have a legacy of a statutory 'old poor law' provision that was deemed to require reform, rather poor relief was provided by a 'complex mix of systems of relief' (Cousins, 2015, 36) prior to the introduction of a national Poor Law. The impetus for the introduction of a national Poor Law to Ireland was both to alleviate the widespread poverty experienced by a large swathe of the population (and the extent of poverty was contested by the two official inquiries discussed next), and to curtail the migration of Irish paupers to Britain (Crossman, 2006a).

Workhouses in Ireland were constructed despite the recommendations of the voluminous *Royal Commission of Inquiry into the Conditions of the Poorer Classes in Ireland*, which concluded its deliberations in 1836. Methodologically innovative and ambitious in scope, the 1836 Poor Law Inquiry aimed to provide an analysis of Irish society in totality, on the basis that in their view the vast majority of the population of Ireland were impoverished, and did so by garnering expert opinion from the landowners and clerics via a questionnaire and from the poor themselves, via oral testimony gathered at public meetings (Ó Ciosáin, 2014). Chaired by the Church of Ireland Archbishop of Dublin, Richard Whately, and reporting in 1836, the Commission argued against the introduction of a workhouse system to Ireland, similar to the system constructed in Britain due to differing social and economic conditions in Ireland (Burke, 1987). Rather they proposed a 'bold and constructive' scheme (McDowell, 1964, 175) to alleviate poverty. The scheme, in essence, was provision of State-assisted emigration schemes for able-bodied paupers, various charitable or voluntary inspired institutions supported by donations from the public with support from the State if necessary for the largely dependent destitute such as orphans and the aged, and a network of hospitals and specialist medical facilities for those paupers physically and mentally afflicted (Gray, 2009, 118–119).

Rejecting the recommendations of the Whately Commission, Westminster instead dispatched George Nicholls, an English Poor Law Commissioner, with a mandate to explore 'the erection and maintenance of Workhouses' in Ireland, and in three relatively short reports, he concluded 'that the workhouse system, which has been successfully applied to dispauperize England, may be safely and efficiently applied, as a modicum of relief, to diminish the amount of poverty in Ireland' (Nicholls, 1836, 27). Initially concerned that given the 'proneness of the Irish peasantry to outrage and insubordination' (1836, 22) the workhouse would be unable to discipline the Irish paupers; however, 'if no out-door relief whatever be allowed', Nicholls anticipated 'no difficulty in establishing an efficient system of discipline and classification' as it would not be in the interests of the Irish paupers to damage their only source of material aid (1836, 22).

His recommendations were accepted in Westminster and were legislated for in the *Irish Poor Law Act, 1838*. For Nicholls, '[t]he governing principle of the workhouse system is this: – that the support which is afforded at the public charge in the workhouse, shall be, on the whole, less desirable than the support to be obtained by independent exertion' (1838, 23). This principle of less eligibility, allied to the absence of Outdoor Relief; relief could only be obtained in-doors in the workhouse, resulted in Crossman's judgement that the 'relief system established in Ireland was harsher than that in England, adhering much more closely to the principles of the New Poor Law than the English system did in practice' (2006b, 11).

The introduction of the Poor Law in Ireland in 1838 resulted in a new tax or rate on landlords, often absentee, to fund the Poor Law (Gray, 2012, 25). Given that the landlord class both funded and largely managed the workhouse system during the first 40 years of their existence, and was not prone to extravagance in relieving destitution, it is not surprising that those who were forced to use the workhouses experienced them as 'grim bastilles of despair' (Mahoney, 2016). Hence, the workhouse system was, in the words of O'Neill (2024, 44), 'forever tainted … and hated in Ireland – hated by its occupants, hated by the ratepayers, whose own parsimony and derision towards their fellow subjects in the decades that followed were regrettably consistent'.

Forever associated with the famine period (1845–1849), nonetheless, as the governance structure of the workhouses shifted in the late 19th century, from landlord classes to increasingly nationalist control, by the early 1880s, there were more recipients of Outdoor Relief than Indoor Relief in the workhouse. Prior to 1847, only 'Indoor relief' was permitted, but under the immense strain of the Great Famine on workhouses, 'Outdoor relief' was permitted (Ó Cinneide, 1969). Dismantling the workhouse system was to become a key demand of nationalists, but as we will see in later chapters, despite pious post-Independence declarations that Poor Law had been abolished, the workhouse (or County Home as it was re-named post-Independence) remained a punitive and degrading feature of the lives of the destitute until the late 20th century.

Both Poor Law Inquiries left significant legacies; in the case of the *Three Reports by George Nicholls, Esq* (1838) published between 1836 and 1837, a physical legacy of bleak institutions that provided rough care for the homeless and other impoverished groups until late into the 20th century, and from the *Royal Commission of Inquiry into the Conditions of the Poorer Classes in Ireland*, an ideological legacy that saw the provision of services for the homeless and other impoverished groups as being more suitably provided by the voluntary efforts of charitable and religious bodies rather than State bodies.

Vagrants and the workhouse

Unlike the workhouses in England, Scotland and Wales, no separate provision within the workhouse, known as Casual Wards, was made for vagrants in Ireland during this period (Cossman, 2013; Crowther, 1992), and as a result they were 'subject to the same rules as ordinary inmates' (Local Government Board, 1906, xv), but as we will see in later chapters, separate institutional provision was made for vagrants in many of the County Homes that replaced workhouses after Independence. As shown in Figure 0.1, the numbers of 'casuals or night lodgers' entering workhouses over the period of a week between 1872 and 1914 increased steadily, peaking at over 1,000 in the first decade of the 20th century.

This was despite Boards of Guardians 'taking strenuous steps to discourage these people from resorting to their workhouses for temporary refuge' (Local Government Board, 1908, xxi). However, as Crossman (2013) argues, the reason for the increase was the growing reluctance of workhouse masters and relieving officers not to allow the able-bodied access workhouses other than as casuals allowing them only temporary access to relief. Thus, the patterns observed in Figure 0.1 'were rooted not in individual need but in the structures of the relief system: the kind and amount of relief that was on offer' (Crossman, 2013, 225).

The introduction of Outdoor Relief in 1847 facilitated the introduction of specific legislation to repress vagrancy in the context of the workhouse system. Legislation to punish vagrants and beggars existed prior to 1847, but as McCabe (2018, 82–83) notes the numbers prosecuted were miniscule with only 1,464 convictions between 1805 and 1831. In the absence of Outdoor Relief 'it was felt that direct legal sanctions against vagrancy could not be justified' (Crossman, 2018a, 269). The legislation, *An Act to make Provision for the Punishment of Vagrants and Persons offending against the Laws in force for the Relief of the destitute Poor in Ireland, 1847*, provided that:

Figure 0.1: Number of casuals or night lodgers in Irish workhouses, 1869–1914

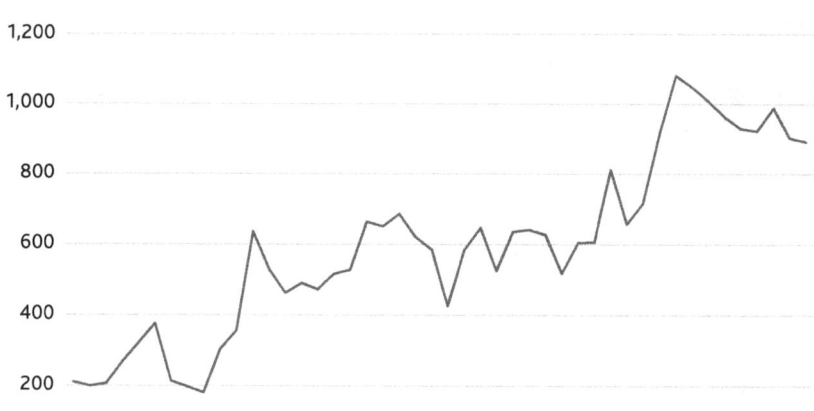

Source: Annual Report of the Local Government Board for Ireland (various years)

Every person wandering abroad and begging, or placing himself in any public place, street, highway, court, or passage to beg or gather alms, or causing or procuring or encouraging any child or children so to do, and every person who, having been resident in any union in Ireland, shall go from such union to some other union, or from one electoral or relief district to another electoral or relief district in Ireland, for the purpose of obtaining relief in such last-mentioned union or district, shall on conviction thereof before any justice of the peace, if such justice shall think fit, be committed to the common gaol or house of correction, there to be kept to hard labour for any time not exceeding one calendar month.

This comparatively narrow prohibition of actives was extended in 1871, when key provisions of the earlier, more comprehensive *Vagrancy Act, 1824*, which applied only to England, were extended to Ireland via the *Prevention of Crimes Act, 1871*. This targeted '[n]ot just people without money but those who seemed to be about to gain money by illegal means' (Clear, 2007, 130), including 'every person having in his or her custody or possession any picklock, key, crow, jack, bit, or other implement with intent feloniously to break into any dwelling house, warehouse, coach-house, stable or outbuilding'.

The numbers prosecuted under the Vagrancy Acts were relatively modest, fluctuating between 3 and 4,000 per annum from the 1880s to the cusp of the First World War, and nationally never more than 2 per cent of total non-indictable offences per annum (Clear, 2007, 178–179). This association of vagrancy with crime and disorder predated the Vagrancy Acts of the 19th century, but the legislative framework was substantially modified in the 19th century to regulate those who threatened social order, particularly tramps and beggars, with the key objectives of regulating the migratory patterns of those tramping from place to place in search of shelter and work. As we will see in later chapters, this association of vagrancy with disorder remained a feature of institutional provision for those of no fixed abode well into 20th-century Ireland and the provisions in the legislation on 'wandering abroad', that is without fixed abode, was only removed in 1988 with the passing of the *Housing Act, 1988* as detailed in Chapter 4 of this book.

The vagrant question

The question of how to respond to poverty, destitution and vagrancy was a significant political issue across Britain and Ireland (and indeed across Europe and North America, see Althammer, 2014) in the years prior to the First World War (1914–1918), with numerous different commissions or committees reporting on subjects which, either fully or incidentally, related to Ireland. In 1906 the British Government published the three-volume *Report of the Departmental Committee on Vagrancy* (1906) which, although not dealing specifically with Ireland, contained a memo, Appendix XIV to the Report, from the Local Government Board for Ireland on *Vagrancy in Ireland*.

The memo noted that in the year from April 1904 to April 1905, there was a daily average of 745 'casuals', 'tramps' or 'night lodgers' in Irish workhouses, with the 'number of males usually from four to five times that of females'. The memo noted that strict rules were in place in relation to discipline, work tasks, cleaning, searching and so on, but that:

> These rules are, we regret to say, very often not adhered to. The regulation regarding the giving of baths is evaded in every possible way, on the plea of ill-health, etc., and the porters appointed in many workhouses are often physically unfit to adopt stringent measures with this troublesome class of inmate. The male tramps are generally required to perform a certain task of work, such as stone breaking, before leaving. The female tramps are sometimes required to pick oakum, but generally it has been found impossible to put them to any kind of work beyond cleaning up their ward ... The amount of work these tramps are called upon to perform depends entirely on the energy and strictness of the master. (1906, Vol. 3, 85)

The 1906 *Report of the Vice-Regal Commission on Poor Law Reform in Ireland* also provided a detailed analysis of 'Casuals and Ins-and-Outs'. The Commission drew a distinction between 'casuals' and 'vagrants', with casuals being those who were 'frequently in receipt of indoor relief in the same workhouse, who have usually or for a considerable time resided within the Poor Law Union', with a vagrant (or tramp or night lodger) being one 'who wanders about from Union to Union, very frequently obtaining in a workhouse a bed for the night and a meal or two before resuming his journey' (1906, 52).

The Vice-Regal Commission estimated that there were 813 casuals and 878 vagrants in Workhouses in Ireland on 11 March 1905, but observed that while the number of vagrants overall were low, they resulted in very high numbers of admissions to workhouses, concluding that '[a]ny statistics that could be collected about Vagrants would show clearly how apposite is the comparison of the Vagrant class in Ireland to a *stage army* that passes and repasses the line of vision in such a way as to convey the idea of multitudes far in excess of the actual number concerned' (1906, 53 – emphasis added). Acknowledging that the number of vagrants in the workhouses did not include all vagrants in Ireland, the Commission suggested that a figure of 2,000 'seems not improbable to us, and the official estimate is that there are four or five males for every female' (1906, 54).

Introduction

The evidence given to the *Departmental Committee on Vagrancy* was highly hostile to vagrants, as was the evidence given to *Vice-Regal Commission* (see Cousins, 2011, 238), with '[w]itnesses, almost without exception, in favour of depriving this class of their liberty to march around the country terrorizing women while men are in the fields, and collecting food and money to enable them shirk work and to escape any regular exertion for self-support' (1906, 54).

The Commission agreed with this assessment of vagrants and therefore recommended that vagrants should be brought before a Court of Justice, and where they could not provide evidence that they were 'habitually hard working and self-supporting', they could be 'sent for a term of from one to three years to a Labour House', and that four disused workhouses should be converted into such labour houses (1906, 5).

The *Royal Commission on the Poor Laws and Relief of Distress* in their 1909 Report on Ireland recommended 'the introduction into Ireland of modified labour colonies which have proved to some extent successful in England and on the Continent. Some such systems should be inaugurated if adequate provision is to be made for the able-bodied, casuals and tramps' (1909, 59). They also recommended the establishment of 'one or more compulsory detention colonies'. These would be under the supervision of the General Prisons Board, and under certain conditions vagrants could be detained for between 6 months and three years. The recommendation was for such colonies to be established for men, but the Report noted that it 'may be found necessary to organise similar colonies for women' (1909, 59).

The provision of such labour colonies for vagrants were particularly popular at that time in Holland, Belgium, Germany and Switzerland, and despite numerous visits to these colonies by various commissions and policy advocates, they had only a very limited impact in North America, England, Scotland and Wales and none in Ireland (see O'Sullivan, 2023 for a more detailed discussion of the development of these continental labour colonies). In a paper read before the *Statistical and Social Inquiry Society* in April 1906, on the 'inefficiency and extravagance of the Poor Law systems in Ireland and Great Britain', Charles Dawson, Dublin businessman and former MP, called for 'labour stations be established to indicate employment to the "want works." Let the "won't works" be sent to forced labour farms to make them work' (1906, 438). Equally, Fr Gerald O'Donovan, chaplain in the workhouse in Loughrea in Co. Galway, argued in favour of the introduction of labour colonies for vagrants and tramps (1899; see also Clear, 1997 and Ryan, 2022). Several years after Independence, in a further paper read before the *Statistical and Social Inquiry Society* in January 1928, Charles Eason, director of the stationer and bookseller of the same name, made reference to the 1906 and 1909 inquiries, before ruefully noting that '(n)othing was done to give effect to the recommendations of these reports' (Eason, 1928, 17).

Hostility towards vagrants was particularly prevalent in rural areas and during the war of Independence they were 'significantly overrepresented among the civilians killed by the IRA from 1919 to 1921, and, even when they were not shot, vagrants were often harassed by republican gunmen' (Griffin, 2024, 114). In his detailed study of the activities of the Irish Republican Army (IRA)in County Cork, Hart (1998, 304) showed that, at a minimum, 8 per cent of those shot by the IRA during the period 1919–1923 for allegedly informing were 'tinkers/tramps'.

The institutionalisation of marginality

In addition to the provision of workhouses, a range of other institutions were opened in the 19th century to manage marginality. For example, *Reformatory Schools* were established by statute in 1858 for young offenders over the age of 12. The first one opened in early 1859, and by 1870, ten had been certified throughout the country, five each for girls and boys. *Industrial Schools*, whose objective was to inculcate children with habits of 'industry, regularity, self-denial, self-reliance and self-control' (Barnes, 1989), were legislated for in 1868. The first industrial school was certified in 1869 and by 1871 there were 51, growing to 70 by 1900 with a capacity for nearly 8,000 children. *District and Auxiliary Mental Hospitals* were established in the early 19th century and were entirely managed and funded by Central Government unlike other countries where the provision of private asylums was considerably greater (Kelly, 2022). The *Irish Lunatic Asylums for the Poor Act, 1817* allowed for the provision of public district asylums and by the middle of the century, ten hospitals were open containing 3,000 inmates, a figure that grew to 16,000 by the end of the century contained in 22 different hospitals. Thus, workhouses, mental hospitals, reformatory and industrial schools, alongside Magdalen Asylums and prisons provided a dense inter-locking range of coercive institutions in every county in Ireland (O'Sullivan and O'Donnell, 2012).

None of the institutions were uniquely Irish. However, the pattern of institutional usage may have been distinctive in Ireland. By the mid-1920s there were more children held within the industrial school system in the 26 counties of the Irish Free State than in Northern Ireland, Scotland, England and Wales combined. Similarly, the mentally ill were confined in comparatively unusually large numbers (Brennan, 2014).

Charitable organisations

Charitable organisations providing accommodation and other services which we would broadly recognise as the ancestor to the 'homeless NGOs' of today started to emerge in Dublin from the second half of the 19th century.

Introduction

Most of these organisations had an explicit religious affiliation and motivation for their work, Dublin Corporation being the only State body providing shelter-type accommodation through the Model Lodging House in Benburb Street on the North Quays, which opened in 1887 (Cullen, 2011) and still operates today, but which has been managed by the Dublin Simon Community, an NGO, since 2015.

A 200-bed night refuge for women and children, St. Joseph's, off Cork Street, in the South Inner City opened in 1861 and was managed by the Sisters of Mercy from 1871 (Gahan, 1942–1943; O'Brien, 1982, 169–170). St Joseph's Night Shelter closed between July and September each year, and during this period, a night refuge in Henrietta Street run by the Daughters of Charity of St. Vincent de Paul, which opened in 1913, provided shelter (O'Neill, Devlin and Prunty, 2014).

The Salvation Army, founded in the UK in 1878, operated in Ireland from the 1880s onwards and opened its first shelter in Peter Street, also in the South Inner City of Dublin, until it closed in 1943, when they opened a new shelter in nearby York Street, off St Stephens Green. The Dublin Shelter for Men was opened in 1884 by a number of Dublin businessmen, only closing in the 1980s. The Iveagh Hostel with 508 cubicles, as part of the wider social housing provision of the Guinness/Iveagh Trust, opened in 1905 (Aalen, 1990; King, 2015) and the Society of St. Vincent de Paul opened a night shelter adjacent to the Iveagh Hostel in 1915 (Ni Chearbhaill, 2008), both operating in 2024. A night refuge for 'sober, destitute and friendless men, women and children, without religious distinction' in Bow Street in the Smithfield district of the North Inner City which had opened in 1834, closed its doors for the last time in 1917, and had provided 'neither food nor beds', only benches and a 'wooden ledge served as a pillow for the sleepers on the floor' (Barrett, 1884, 24).

Alongside these various providers of shelter, other charitable bodies provided food, clothing and other forms of relief to indigents (those experiencing extreme poverty) and mendicants (those engaged in begging), such as the Sick and Indigent Roomkeepers Society established in 1790 (Lindsay, 1990) and the Mendicity Institution established in 1818 (Woods, 1998), both still operating in 2024.

Those who desired more permanent accommodation and could not afford an established residence were forced into the privately owned common lodging houses (McManus, 2018). These had a notorious reputation as centres of disease, congestion and immorality. Keepers often divided the rooms into pens by erecting wooden partitions and allocating up to three persons per bed. Not until the adoption of a Bylaw by the Corporation in 1917 was the letting of a bed in a common lodging house to two or more males over ten years of age prohibited (O'Brien, 1982, 169–190).

Housing

A lack of housing, and the poor quality of much of what did exist, along with chronic overcrowding were persistent problems in Ireland in the years prior to Independence, contributing to social unrest in both rural and urban communities. While housing problems existed both in the cities and rural areas, there were significant differences in nature and the policy response, with these differences continuing to have an impact well after Independence. The provision of public rental housing in Ireland dates from the late 19th century and followed a somewhat divergent path from that of public housing in other European countries. This was due to the political demands of the Irish Party and the desire of the British Conservative party to contain unrest resulting in unprecedented financial resources directed towards the provision of State housing.

The motive for the development of large-scale public housing in rural Ireland was generated more by the need to calm and control agrarian unrest than necessarily a desire to alleviate the acknowledged wretchedness of the existing labourers' cabins (Fraser, 1996). As Potter (2018) has argued, it wasn't simply the objectively appalling housing conditions they were so comprehensively documented in various Parliamentary enquiries, rather the particular political situation in Ireland was the driver of the development. Furthermore, as Fahey notes: '[p]ublic housing in Ireland was ... remarkable for its essentially agrarian origins' (2002, 60) and unlike other jurisdictions where social housing was predominantly an urban development, Ireland's public housing was mostly concentrated in rural areas. This unrest resulted in rural Ireland being 'transformed from a teeming mass of impoverished labourers, small cottiers, and very small tenant farmers, into a stable, conservative, land owning peasantry' (Hannan and Breen, 1987, 43). The consequences of rural unrest, and the demand by tenant farmers to acquire land and for labourers to acquire cottages was to persist into the 20th century and the new State, and had long-term consequences, not just on the shaping of social housing, and housing more generally, but on the social structure of rural Ireland and consequently urban Ireland and political priorities after Independence. The establishment of the Land Commission in 1881 and the Congested Districts Board in 1891 were the key institutional mechanisms for the redistribution of land in Ireland.

The *Labourers' Ireland Act, 1883* provided one of the first major public house building projects in Western Europe and by 1900, over 15,000 labourers' cottages had been built, compared to only 14 cottages built in England and Wales (Aalen, 1992, 138), by the outbreak of the First World War, over 45,000 labourers' cottages were constructed (Crossman, 2006a, 144). The 'labourers' in question were agricultural labourers, who neither owned nor rented land themselves, but worked for landowners or tenant farmers.

The housing that was subsequently provided in an urban context was associated with the various 'Housing of the Working Classes' Acts. This legislative distinction between rural and urban housing therefore reflected political histories and continued until the 1960s.

The objectives of the 1883 Act and subsequent *Labourers' Acts* were to provide cottages for landless labourers on half-acre sites, improving existing dwellings, and introducing rent controls on the dwellings. As Aalen has summarised, 'In Ireland more was done by the government and local authorities for the housing of rural labourers than in England, Scotland or other European countries. On the other hand, less was accomplished by private enterprise and nothing by housing associations' (1992, 146).

The large-scale provision of public housing in urban areas was to take longer to develop, as the political pressure to ease unrest was less urgent in urban areas. From 1870s onwards, non-government bodies such as the aforementioned Guinness/Iveagh Trust and the Dublin Artisans Dwellings Company (Cullen, 2011; King, 2015) emerged, building 4,500 homes and accounting for 15 per cent of Dublin's housing stock by the outbreak of World War I (Norris, 2003).

The first significant step by the State to assist local authorities in the provision of housing for the urban working classes was *The Housing of the Working Classes Act, 1890*. This act gave power to local authorities to improve sanitary conditions in urban areas. However, due to the poor borrowing terms given to the local authorities, it didn't prove possible to provide large-scale public housing schemes, and it was not until the provision of a housing subsidy under the *Housing of the Working Classes (Ireland) Act, 1908* that a structure was established for the provision of public housing in urban areas.

Under the terms of the 1908 act, direct subsidies were given to local authorities to provide housing, almost a decade ahead of Britain. With the introduction of the act, the provision of public rental housing became almost the sole preserve of the local authorities, and the existing philanthropic organisations either ceased operation or continued in a very minor way. These developments were significant as by the end of the 19th century, the State had invested heavily in the provision of subsidised housing, particularly in rural areas. The extent of this activity in both rural and urban areas is shown in Figure 0.2.

Urban housing conditions

Housing conditions in Dublin had declined during the 19th century, primarily through a process through which the large, single family Georgian housing in the centre of the city were converted into buildings where many families rented individual rooms in what became known as tenements (Brady and McManus, 2021). A housing inquiry in 1885, the *Third Report of the Royal*

Figure 0.2: Dwellings built by local authorities, 1880–1922

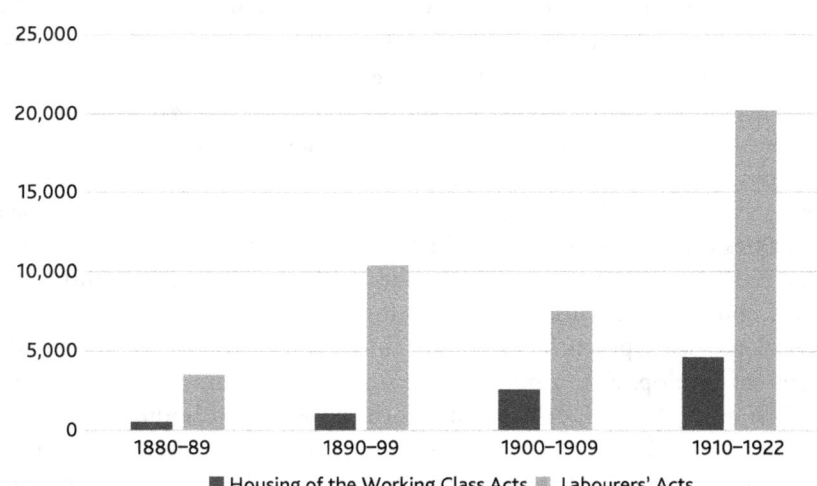

Source: Minister for Local Government (1964) Housing – Progress and Prospects (Dublin, Stationery Office), p 35

Commission on the Housing of the Working Classes, covering Ireland, showed that conditions in Dublin were not a lot different than in other cities in the UK at that time, but the scale of the problem was much greater in Dublin. Housing conditions in the rest of Ireland that was to form the Free State were also poor. Thirty-five years before Independence, the Commissioners found that 'the poverty of the labouring classes in most towns in Ireland is extreme; that nothing could be more miserable than the conditions of many dwellings and surroundings in the towns'. The Report noted that wages were low, and rents were high so that 'the depressed conditions under which people live lower their wage-earning power and deprive them of the chance of making for themselves more favourable surroundings' (pp vi and vii). The first scheme of housing for the very poor rather than artisans by Dublin Corporation was Corporation Buildings constructed in 1905 in the North Inner City with 480 units consisting of 'barracks-style flats of five stories with interconnecting balconies' (O'Brien, 1982, 143). Demolished in 1972, the cover picture of this book Corporation Buildings immediately prior to their demolition.

Dublin Corporation launched a substantial building programme in the years that followed, prompted by the Report of the Departmental Committee appointed by the Local Government Board for Ireland to Inquire into the Housing Conditions of the Working Classes in the City of Dublin (1914). The committee had been established after the collapse of two tenement houses on Church Street in Dublin's North Inner City in September 1913, which claimed seven lives (Corlett, 2008). The report set out the scale of the poor housing conditions in Dublin (MacManus, 2003; Murtagh, 2020). That the collapse occurred during the bitter industrial dispute between workers and employers, in what was known as the Dublin Lockout of 1913, further confirmed the intolerable housing conditions of the Dublin working classes (Yeates, 2000, 110–111). The *Report* identified three classes of tenements – those that were in good structural condition and in need of some improvement; those that were so decayed that they were approaching a state where they were not fit for human habitation; and those which were already deemed to be unfit for human habitation and not capable of being brought up to a habitable standard. Almost one fifth of the population of the County Borough (18,000 families, comprising 60,000 people) lived in one of these types of tenements and urgently required rehousing; 1,518 houses fell into the most extreme category, with 6,831 families comprising 22,701 people living in homes that were unfit for human habitation and beyond repair (see Prunty, 1998; Carroll, 2011; and Murtagh, 2023 for further details on slum conditions in Dublin at the end of the 19th and beginning of the 20th century).

The other major cities, in particular Cork (Dwyer, 2013) and Limerick (Potter, 2018), had similar large-scale and severe urban housing problems, as did the provincial towns (McManus, 2019; Connell, 2023) reflecting years of neglect, and in the words of the 1885 Report, 'the profits ... often go to the enrichment of the middle-men or house-farmers' and not to the upkeep of the dwellings.

Conclusion

Thus, by the time of Independence, Ireland had a comparatively large stock of public housing in comparison with neighbouring Great Britain. Some 8,861 houses were provided under the *Housing of the Working Classes Acts, 1890* and 41,653 under the *Labourers' Acts, 1893*, a total of 50,514. From 1906, in addition to the borrowings by local authorities for the cost of constructing labourers' cottages, an exchequer contribution based on a percentage of the loan charges was introduced, and in 1908, a similar exchequer contribution was provided to the urban local authorities. Thus, a financing model that combined borrowings by local authorities and an exchequer or Central Government subsidy was to provide a template for financing social housing in Ireland until the late 1980s. In addition, Ireland had a comparatively advanced welfare system as a consequence of welfare initiatives in the industrialised British State, which also applied to Ireland, resulting in a welfare system that had a 'comparatively generous but narrowly focussed coverage' (Cousins, 2005, 29).

In the half-a-century or so prior to Independence, the broad structures of the infrastructure, institutions, ideologies and practices in relation to responses to poverty, poor housing conditions and marginality were established.

These structures remained largely in place for the first half-a-century after Independence, but were gradually dismantled, physically and ideologically, from the 1960s onwards, although as we highlight in later chapters, shelters for the homeless have not only survived, but have thrived and remained as the default response to the growth of homelessness at the beginning of the 21st century.

1

Poor Laws, the family economy and housing policy, 1922–1948

Introduction

This chapter covers the period followed independence and the Civil War, starting from the first national government under Cumann na nGaedheal (the victors in the civil war), through the ten years of Cumann na nGaedheal-led governments until 1932 and then through the 16 years of government by Fianna Fáil (the vanquished in the civil war). The chapter will describe the services available to people experiencing homelessness in Ireland during this period, the failed attempts to reform the workhouse system in a new 'County Home' system reflecting 'native' values of 'gratitude and consideration'. During this period homelessness was seen as being of little importance politically or administratively; rather it was considered either a health or criminal justice matter, as opposed to a matter requiring a response from housing authorities. The chapter will also look at the way in which rural housing policy continued to develop on the path set out since the 1870s and the limited beginnings of an urban housing policy. The chapter notes a number of policy decisions taken at this time – including social housing rent setting and tenant purchase schemes – that were to fundamentally shape the evolution of social housing policy in subsequent decades.

Political and economic context

The Dáil elected in June 1922 (3rd Dáil) formed the first Government of the Irish Free State but most of its energies were taken up with the Civil War concerning acceptance or rejection of the Anglo-Irish Treaty which had ended the War of Independence six months earlier. The Civil War came to an end in May 1923 and was followed by a General Election in August that year. Pro-treaty Sinn Féin (Cumann na nGaedheal from April 1923) were the largest party after both elections and had a majority due to the non-attendance of the Anti-Treaty Sinn Féin (largely Fianna Fáil from 1926). While the period running up to independence had been characterised by high aspirations for national development and progress, 'the 1920s were not the most opportune decade for a newly independent nation' (Daly, 1992, 13) with the economic damage done by World War I, the War of Independence and the Civil War, agrarian agitation before, during and after both the War of Independence and civil war, along with the death and division in the political leadership, presented a bleak outlook. Furthermore, as Garvin (1987, 167) has argued the revolutionaries had not given much thought to 'the actual practical problems of governing a country, as distinct from the imaginings of the ideal conditions which the citizens of the country would eventually enjoy under the benign governance of patriots'.

The Cumann na nGaedheal administration, which John A. Murphy, in one of the earliest appraisals of 20th century Ireland, described as having "lacked any real social and economic policy" (1975, 64), has been re-evaluated more favourably in recent scholarship (Dolan, 2018; Barry, 2024). Barry (2024, 16), for example, observes that the Irish Free State emerged amid a severe economic downturn and that, having inherited old-age pension rates set by the Westminster Parliament that were relatively generous in the Irish context, 'social spending was high by international standards'. It is estimated that the cost of the civil war was £50m or nearly one-third of estimated national output (Kenny and McLaughlin, 2022, 55), and in 1922 and 1923, nearly 30 per cent of voted expenditure was on defence and between 12–13 per cent in 1924 and 1925 before dropping to 6.6 per cent in 1930 (Bewley and Barbieri, 2022). This expenditure on defence was a result of rapid recruitment by the Cumann na nGaedheal administration of a National Army to defeat those who opposed the Treaty, increasing in strength from 33,000 men in 1922 to 55,000 in 1923, before rapidly declining to 5,000 by the early 1930s (Kinsella, 2023, 14). This mass demobilisation resulted in a 'whole new layer of impoverished men', with some sleeping out in public parks in Dublin (Ferriter, 2021, 128).

Cumann na nGaedheal remained in Government after two elections in 1927, though under increasing pressure from Fianna Fáil who had taken up their Dáil seats from 1927. Fianna Fáil formed a government for the first time after the election in 1932, with Labour Party support. They were re-elected at the five subsequent elections until losing office in 1948, after 16 years in power. Given the political and military context that led to the formation of Cumann nGaedheal and Fianna Fáil, one of the striking features was the 'resilience of parliamentary democracy' and administrative stability which McGarry attributes to 'high levels of land ownership and mass emigration' (2016, 120). Recent assessments of the Irish economic performance over this period argue that Ireland was not comparatively unusual in the economic and fiscal policies adopted in that 'Irish politicians were relatively liberal during the 1920s and were protectionist like everybody else from 1932 onwards' (O'Rourke, 2017, 30). The Cosgrave administration provided a 'political stability in a country that badly needed it, not only in the context of the instability from which it emerged, but in a Europe where stability, not least in new states, was a scarce commodity' (Lee, 2017, 788–789).

Those in power ensured that that the interests of the owners of private property were secure and 'the interests of this class were protected (and furthered) while tight books were balanced, unforgiving ideology was cemented in legislation and limited welfare provision was pruned and depleted to survive the economic reality of political independence' (Earner-Byrne, 2017, 20). The view in the Department of Finance, according to Lee (2008, 36), at the time of Independence was that 'the role of the state was to keep out of the way of private enterprise and to keep taxation as low as possible, and therefore, at least in the short term, social services as meagre as possible', and that it wasn't until the election of Fianna Fáil in 1932, with the support of the Labour Party, with their the plans for the industrialisation of Irish society that also saw the gradual emergence of State welfare services with 'improved employment benefits, pensions for the blind, and the launch of an ambitious slum-clearance campaign and house-building programme' (Lee, 2008, 37; Dunphy, 1995), policies also advocated by the Labour Party (Puirseil, 2007, 44).

Further incremental changes in the provision of social security in the 1930s and 1940s, including the unemployment assistance in 1933, a widows and orphans pension in 1935 and introduction of children's allowances in 1944 (Cousins, 1999), and generally increasing benefits (O Grada, 1997, 91) was to lead to the introduction of a comparatively comprehensive social security code by the early 1950s administered by a newly established Department of Social Welfare in 1947 (Cousins, 2003; Carey, 2007). Similarly incremental improvements in health care services and administrative reform led to the establishment of a separate Department of Health at the same time (Robins, 1997).

Land and the family economy

The response to housing and homelessness during this period, and the wider development of social policy, needs to be understood in the context of Ireland's predominantly rural nature at this time. Fahey (2002) has argued that standard interpretations of the development of welfare states, which stress the role of organised urban labour movements, downplay the extent to which rural interests, directed at land distribution for farmers and the provision of cottages for agricultural labourers, provided an alternative form of social protection *via* self-sufficiency on the land from the 1870s to the 1940s – what Norris has termed 'a property-based welfare state' (2016).[1] In a context where agriculture accounted for over a third of national income and, in 1926, more than half of the working population was working directly in agriculture (Dooley and McCarthy, 2015, 134), economic and social policies that supported agriculture, and in particular production and exportation of cattle, were to the forefront of the new political administration of the Irish Free State, leading Oliver (2025, 3) to describe the Irish economy in this period as a 'bovine economy'.

The energetic first Minister for Agriculture and Lands in the Free State, Patrick Hogan, was of the view that 'agriculture was and would remain by far the most important industry in the Free State, and that the touchstone by which every economic measure must be judged was its effect on the prosperity of the farmers' (O'Brien, 1936, 255). This was a view endorsed by the leading Irish economist of the period, George O'Brien who argued that '[i]n the Free State the interests of the farmers and the nation are, at least *prima facie*, identical, and the best utilisation of the resources of the country is that which maximises the prosperity of the farming classes' (O'Brien, 1936, 356).

There was also mounting pressure on the new administration to resume the work of the Land Commission, and the Congested Districts Board whose work in dividing and redistributing land was largely paused during the period 1914–1918, particularly in a context when emigration was substantially reduced, thus swelling the numbers seeking land (Donnelly, 2023). It is estimated that 'there were more than 57,000 large farmers with between 50 and 100 acres, and over 33,00 graziers and land monopolists who boasted more than 100 acres and generally lived off the fat of the land' (Donnelly, 2023, 178–179). In contrast there were 113,000 holdings of less than one acre and a further 173,000 with between 1 and 15 acres, the former 'lived on the very edge of existence' and the latter lived 'an impoverished life' (Donnelly, 2023, 178).

Ideologically, the new Irish State inherited what Hannan and Commins call 'powerful strains of rural fundamentalist ideology' (1992, 101).

> Irish rural fundamentalism, like that found in other largely agrarian societies, was expressed through a set of values and beliefs which stressed (i) the advantages of family-owned, family farms and of a numerous class of landholders; (ii) the healthy nature of farming as an occupation, and open country farming communities as ideal settlement models; and (iii) agriculture as the basis for national prosperity. Support for the family farm ideal, as well as for having as many people as possible working on the land, was even inserted into the Irish Constitution. (1992, 101)

The political concerns of rural Ireland were also imposed on the political system more generally leading to what Garvin (1974) described as the 'periphery-dominated centre', whereby key positions in the State apparatus in Dublin were filled by those whose values, ideology and interests were those of the rural periphery. These concerns were also largely the same concerns of the clerical members of the Catholic Church who were the 'kith and kin' of the original tenant farmers of the 19th century who became proprietors of the land by the 20th century and 'who were the bastions of this church spiritually and financially' (O'Shea, 1983, 232).

In what two early historians of the programme described as a 'bloodless revolution' (Kolbert and O'Brien, 1975, 62), the reconstituted Land Commission and the *Land Act, 1923* (which allowed for the compulsory acquisition of Land) benefited close to a quarter of million families between 1923 and 1987 by distributing land acquired by the Land Commission to them in various forms (Dooley, 2004b, 183). When Fianna Fáil entered Government in 1932, following on their election promises, the *Land Act, 1933* gave the Land Commission further powers of compulsory acquisition, to realise their vision of a self-sufficient rural family economy by maximising the number of family farms. These distributive policies directed at ensuring the maximum number of small family farms allied to distinctive inheritance practices that emerged in the post-famine period, with single heir inheritance the norm, resulted in 'a relatively comfortable small farmer class', but also 'large-scale outmigration of the "surplus" population on farms' (Hannan and Commins, 1992, 96).

A particular bone of contention in the run up to the election of Fianna Fáil in 1932 were land annuities – repayment to the British Government by farmers for lands acquired under the various Land Acts prior to independence, aptly described by McMahon (1984, 38) as having 'a complicated and controversial history'. Amounting to £5m per annum, this was a significant sum of money given that the total revenue collected in 1931/2 was €25.5m (Johnson, 1985, 15), both Fianna Fáil in opposition and other more left-wing groups had opposed the payment of these annuities. On election, Fianna Fáil ceased the transfer of the payments, which had been collected by the Land Commission, to the British Government. However, rather than returning the payments to those who had made them, the Irish Government held onto them, albeit having reduced the amounts payable by up to 50 per cent. This significantly boosted the exchequer allowing for additional spending on social infrastructure, in particular housing. The withholding of the payments resulted in the Anglo-Irish economic war, which was eventually resolved by 1938, with a one-off payment of £10m to the British Government or 10 per cent of what was estimated to be the value of these loans (O'Rourke, 1991).

However, by this stage, it was becoming increasingly recognised, politically and administratively, that there was simply an insufficient supply of land to satisfy the demand from both the landless and those whose holdings were uneconomic and needed expansion, and that many of those who were allocated land did not possess the agricultural skills to make productive use of their holdings (Gahan, 2024). Nonetheless, despite concerns by some Fianna Fáil ministers from the early 1940s, in particular Sean Lemass, in relation to the inefficiencies of small-scale farming resulting from the programme of redistribution and the negative financial impact resulting from a reduction in cattle exports as grazing land was acquired (Jones, 1997, 133; see also Jones, 2001) argued 'the economic argument did not really win the day and that the policy of land distribution continued largely unabated'. The transfer of land 'led to the metamorphosis of the impoverished tenant farmers of the post-famine period almost entirely into peasant proprietors … and to the emergence of a new stratification order dominated by "middle peasants"' (Hannan and Commins, 1992, 95) or family farms that did not employ labour outside the family. Agricultural labourers remained part of the rural landscape, but were increasingly locked out of acquiring land, and the failure until the 1970s to extend benefits that were provided to non-agricultural workers, such as minimum wages and holiday legislation, 'exacerbated their poverty and low status in Irish society' (Curtis, 2024, 243) for the first 50 years after independence.

Although no accurate figure is available on the total cost of the programme of land acquisition and distribution, at the time of the introduction of the *Land Act, 1923*, the Minister for Agriculture and Land Paddy Hogan estimated the cost of the programme would be in the region of £30m. Later estimates are significantly higher but, whatever the final cost, it was undoubtedly in Dooley's assessment (2004a, 58) 'a truly colossal figure of the implementation of any social policy, and undoubtedly one that constrained the political ambitions of Cumann nGaedheal, and indeed, their expenditure in other areas of social policy'.

There was no space in the Free State for the various radical ideas on the reorganisation of society on vocational lines in the Papal encyclicals *Rerum Novarum* (1891) and *Quadragesmio Anno* (1931) and that 'it would have been reasonable to expect that in a country, which was predominantly Catholic, that Catholic social teaching would have powerful impact – but this did not happen' (O'Leary, 2000, 188). Despite the energetic pamphleteering by a number of Catholic clerics and lay people (Curtis, 2008) promoting a social, economic and financial 'third way' between capitalism and socialism, these energies were subsumed into a *Commission of Inquiry into Banking, Currency and Credit* (1934–1938) (O'Driscoll, 2000) and a *Commission on Vocational Organisation* (1939–1943) (Lee, 1979) whose lengthy deliberations ensured that *status quo* favoured by the civil service, the major political parties, and indeed the majority of the Catholic Hierarchy prevailed.

Homelessness, public assistance and institutional provision after Independence

Despite the pre-Independence social movements and the rhetoric of the Programme of the First Dáil, for most of the period immediately after independence, what we now consider 'homelessness' rarely arises as a policy issue. Most people who were homeless were accommodated in temporary accommodation units (Casual Wards) in County Homes. The 1919 Democratic Programme of the First Dáil had committed to 'abolishing the present odious, degrading and foreign Poor Law System, substituting therefore a sympathetic native scheme for the care of the Nation's aged and infirm, who shall not be regarded as a burden, but rather entitled to the Nation's gratitude and consideration'. In a similar fashion, in a memo from the Republican Local Government Department, dated 30 September 1920, to all public bodies in Ireland, following a *Dáil Eireann Commission of Enquiry into Local Government*, the Department declared that '[t]he Workhouse is an evil institution' and [i]t is the intention of this Department to work towards complete abolition through amalgamation on large scale ... All children should be boarded out. The aged, infirm and feeble minded should be boarded out whenever possible ... Sane epileptics could be boarded out in Rural Districts where suitable employment is procurable (1920, 3).

In the first annual report of the Department of Local Government and Public Health, the 'official view' of the workhouse was articulated, whereby:

> The associations connected with Workhouse relief were seldom desirable. The Poor Laws were introduced when the Country was passing through the great famine, and the workhouse became associated in the minds of the people with the hardships and sufferings of that period. The feelings of objection to the Workhouse arising from historic reasons remained long after the causes which produced them had passed. The Workhouse was the sole refuge of vagrants, and of the physical wreckage of the population, and being largely availed of by these classes came to be regarded with abhorrence by the respectable poor, amongst whom relief in a Workhouse carried with it an enduring stigma. (Department of Local Government and Public Health, 1927, 52)

In this articulation, the homeless were clearly a class apart, a theme we return to on many occasions in the course of this book. Similar perspectives were also articulated by witnesses to the first Commission on Inquiry into the operation of the Poor Laws established in 1925, on how to provide relief to the respectable and decent poor without aiding 'undesirables' (Lucey, 2015, 55).

Despite these denunciations of the workhouse system, in the acerbic view of Lee, the new government substituted the existing system with 'an odious, degrading and native system' (1989, 124). Following Independence, local authorities were requested to draw up schemes to make provision for those classes previously dealt with under the Poor

Law and to reorganise the administration of the relief of the poor. The majority of the workhouses that survived the War of Independence and Civil War, when 22 workhouses were substantially damaged (Lucey, 2024), were either closed, or converted into hospitals. In all counties, with the exception of County Louth, a single workhouse was retained to cater for those in the population who did not require hospital or other treatment. They were now to be known as the 'County Home' (O'Connor, 1995). County Homes were effectively 'catch-all' institutions managed by local authorities catering for the aged and infirm, the chronically sick, children, unmarried mothers, mental defectives and epileptics, in addition to the homeless. They provided what, some 30 years after independence in the 1950s, the Department of Health termed 'rough care' for the destitute (Department of Health, 1953, 8).

The Census of 1926 recorded 12,823 adults (6,291 men and 6,532 women) accommodated in County Homes, a figure which includes both Casual Wards and other residents. The nature of this accommodation remained primitive. In a paper on 'The Improvement of the County Homes' at a conference in the Mansion House in Dublin in July 1930, A. P. Delany, an Inspector of Local Government, bluntly stated that '[w]ith the establishment of Saorstat Eireann the workhouse disappeared, at any rate in name. It is now the County Home. I fear that the change of name is the principal change that has occurred, and that characteristics are largely unaltered' (1930, 86). He went on to argue that 'A County Home should not be a continuation of the Workhouse which it replaced; it should not be a compound where poor are herded like cattle; it should not have the primitive horrors of a prison. If a County Home is any of these things the schemes introduced nine or ten years ago have to that extent failed' (1930, 86–87).

The other main change in relation to the Poor Law after independence was to remove restrictions on outdoor relief, that is relief outside of the workhouse. This was legislated for under the *Local Government (Temporary Provisions) Act, 1923* with the objective of having 'a system of poor relief conforming to the wishes and sentiments of the people and providing efficiently and sympathetically for the needs of the poor' (Department of Local Government and Public Health, 1927, 52). This had the effect of gradually decreasing the numbers required to enter a County Home to receive assistance, but increased the number of recipients of outdoor relief, which was now termed Home Assistance.[2] *The Commission of the Relief of the Sick and Destitute Poor* reporting in the 1927 (see further details next) noted that in the absence of the workhouse test, applications for Home Assistance 'requires careful scrutiny of each applicant's case and courage and determination to resist undue pressure to afford relief under circumstances that may not altogether warrant its being given'. The Commission noted that many witnesses put forward the view that 'the removal of the restrictions in regard to Home Assistance had led to great extravagance and that the cost of Home Assistance was now altogether excessive' (1927, 53).

Home Assistance provided considerable discretion to what were termed Home Assistance Officers in providing assistance, with 'no detailed regulations determining who should receive assistance, nor what means are to be taken into account nor are there any assistance scales' (Kaim-Caudle, 1967, 68), and criticism of this discretion became a longstanding feature of the scheme until its abolition in the 1970s (see Chapter 3). Such fears of extravagance as voiced by *The Commission of the Relief of the Sick and Destitute Poor* may have been misplaced, as the initial *Rules and Regulations for the Administration of Home Assistance* in 1924 devoted more space to outlining the reasons why Home Assistance should not be allowed to the 'able-bodied' rather than allowed. For those for whom assistance was allowed, the regulations prescribed that

> one-half at least of such assistance shall be given in articles of food or fuel, or in other articles of absolute necessity, and the Board of Health may, at their discretion, require such person as a condition of the granting of such assistance to perform such suitable task or work as the Board may determine so long as such person shall continue to receive home assistance. (1924, 3)

A further element of discretion was the absence of a uniform rate of home assistance. For the period in which home assistance operated,

> [i]n practice, the authorities determine, each for its own area, what is regarded from time to time as the minimum income required to maintain an individual living on his own or as a member of a household and, on the basis of these amounts, Assistance Officers recommend whether assistance should be paid and, if so, the amount. (Farley, 1964, 6–7)

The demand that the able-bodied be required to work for assistance remained a constant feature of public assistance and resurfaces again in discussions on the provisions for casuals in County Homes in the course of debates on the *Health Act, 1953* as detailed in the Chapter 2. This concern by Poor Law administrators that they be vigilant in identifying a class of people who were in their view, either habitually conditioned or deliberately manipulative, in seeking State or charitable support, is a constant theme in understanding responses to homelessness, and as we identify in Chapters 8 and 9, 'gaming the system' was the contemporary manifestation of this viewpoint as homelessness increased from 2014 onwards, whereby an 'official' viewpoint put forward the view that households were deliberately becoming homeless in order to accrue a State benefit that they were entitled to.

Nonetheless, on balance, the changes to the Poor Law were progressive. John Collins, a senior official in the Department of Local Government and Public Health, in his assessment of the changes that took place in the provision of public assistance in the first two decades after independence, in particular with the passing of the *Public Assistance Act, 1939*, which brought together the various Poor Law legislation since the 1838 into one comprehensive statute, argued:

> Many of the harsher features of poor relief have been removed from public assistance. The workhouse test has gone with the workhouse, which has been replaced by institutions managed on more humane principles and aiming at higher standards. The growth of other social services has made it unnecessary for many who would formerly have had to seek relief to resort to the public assistance authorities but nevertheless the public assistance organisation must continue in existence whilst there are gaps in the specialised service. (1942–1943, 115, see also Garvin, 1944)

On the other hand, the Bishop of Clonfert, the Rev John Dignan, in his proposed scheme of National Health Insurance published in 1945, argued that in the health and social services inherited by the Irish State at independence, 'no great change, at least no essential change, has taken place since then and even to-day the taint of pauperism and destitution clings to many of them' (1945, 7).

In addition to these Casual Wards in the County Homes, the range of congregate shelters provided by religiously inspired non-State bodies discussed in the Introduction continued to operate and expand. They were supplemented with the provision of an additional three shelters for men and women experiencing homelessness in Dublin in the late 1920s and early 1930s operated by the newly established Catholic lay organisation, the *Legion of Mary* (Ó Broin, 1982; Kennedy, 2011, 86–99). The two main shelters, the Regina Coeli for women and the Morning Star for men, which still operate today, are situated in a part of the original North Dublin Union Workhouse complex, which in turn was part of the site which had housed the Dublin House of Industry, opened in 1773 and were part of a larger complex that included the Richmond Penitentiary in 1802 and later the Richmond Asylum, a remarkably dense network of institutions for marginal populations (Fennelly, 2020).

A range of Magdalen Refuges or Asylums also provided accommodation to women experiencing homelessness and other issues (O'Sullivan, 2016). For example, the Sean McDermott Street Magdalen in the North Inner City of Dublin, '[p]rovided what could be termed emergency accommodation for a wide range of categories – former prisoners, women on route to or from England, girls found sleeping rough and brought by Gardaí, social workers and members of the Legion of Mary' (Prunty, 2017, 518). Contrary to popular perception only a small minority, approximately 5 per cent, of those who entered this asylum stayed on a long-term basis. In addition, as noted in the Introduction, to the County Homes and Magdalen Asylums, there were a range of other institutions for managing marginality including four reformatory and 52 Industrial Schools for children, 19 District and Auxiliary Mental Hospitals, and 12 prisons, with approximately 31,500 adults and children coercively confined in these institutions in 1926 or 1,060 per 100,00 population (O'Sullivan and O'Donnell, 2012).

The Commission on the Relief of the Sick and Destitute Poor, including the Insane Poor

In 1925, the Government established *The Commission on the Relief of the Sick and Destitute Poor, including the Insane Poor*. Chaired by Charles O'Connor, a former member of the Local Government Board, and reporting in 1927, the Commission noted that following schemes of Poor Relief that each Local Authority was obliged to provide under the *Local Government (Temporary Provisions) Act, 1923*, one workhouse in each county had been designated a County Home. In the County Homes, the Commission reported finding 'aged and infirm of both sexes; lunatics, idiots and imbeciles of both sexes; unmarried mothers and their children, in some cases married mothers and their children; and orphan and deserted children' (1927, 17). However, the Commission concluded that there was a 'want of uniformity in the institutional relief provided and the classes for whom it is provided', and in particular, 'that in no single case is any institutional relief contemplated to be given to or provided for the destitute poor able-bodied of any sex' (1927, 12). This conclusion was supported by their observation that

> (t)here is one class common enough in the old workhouses which did not come under our observations in the County Homes – tramps, casuals or night lodgers. There are no provisions in the Schemes for the reception into institutions of casuals of any description. In a few Homes they appear to have been received occasionally, but except in the South Cork County Home, provision was not made for them and the number seeking admission was small even in Cork. (1927, 17)

However, the Commission did observe that, while Casuals were not evident in the County Homes, 'we know that they exist'. The Commission reported that Casuals were 'now relieved by the Home Assistance Officer by the method either of giving them the price of a night's lodging and food or finding and paying for a night's lodging for them. We understand that sometimes cases of hardship arise through the difficulty of obtaining lodgings' and that they believed 'that it may be necessary in Cork, Dublin, Waterford, and Limerick to set aside special accommodation for this class (1927, 61).

At the request of the Commission, 'the Garda Siochana made a census of homeless persons observed wandering on the public highways in a single night in November 1925' (1927, 17). The Garda observed 1,719 men and 686 women, with the majority observed outside of Dublin. Just over 1,000 (652 men and 416 women and a further 614 children) were described as 'habitual tramps' and Bhreatnach (2006, 9) has suggested that those counted certainly would have included Irish Travellers, particularly those with children.

The lack of attention to Casuals in the Commission's Report was somewhat surprising because, as we have seen in the Introduction, a number of detailed reports on the operation of the Poor Law in Ireland, and a detailed report on Vagrancy in the period prior to independence, devoted considerable space to exploring this issue. In addition to the detailed discussions in previous reports on the operation of the Poor Laws in relation to vagrants, the Commission received a detailed memorandum from Frank Duff,[3] founder of the aforementioned Legion of Mary, who also gave oral evidence to the Commission on 21 January 1926. The Commission noted that a 'scheme for dealing with the class of derelict men in Dublin who ordinarily resort to the casual ward, the free shelters, or inferior lodgings and who usually live by odd jobs on the streets was put before us' (1927, 86), but did not specify that it was Duff who put forward the proposal.[4]

Duff estimated that there were 'at least 600' of the 'Down and Out Class' in Dublin and '[g]enerally their life is shocking in its hardship'. Clearly familiar with the discussions on how to manage vagrants in the various Poor Law commissions and committees of inquiry, Duff argued against the role of the State in providing services to the 'down and out class' and that the Commission should 'not think that the State does better in other countries', arguing that '[w]e see that the more enlightened (according to secular ideas) becomes the Poor Law, the more severe become its methods towards this particular type of man. Read any literature on the subject'. He went on to state:

> The idea of all those that are esteemed authorities is that of scientifically dividing up the Down and Out Class into its constituent parts, ranging from the temporarily unemployed at the end of their resources to the vicious and criminal type. The treatment then proposed roughly boils down to a two-fold classification corresponding to the above-mentioned extremes, the former to be left very much as is; the latter being dealt with along lines of punishment; a very doubtful course

and one to be resorted to only when it is very certain that a given individual is harming the community, a thing hard to define.

His two-fold solution was that

> (i) the remedy is not within the reach of the Poor Law or other secular administrative machinery; and (ii) a lodging house of some kind or another is manifestly indicated. The latter, therefore, under the management of some voluntary body, animated by religious ideals, is the basis of the solution I propose for the Down and Out Problem.

The lodging house would not be free: admission would involve a test to identify those who could afford to pay, while those without money would work for their admittance by making firewood. The Morning Star Hostel, opened in 1927 for men, and the Regina Coeli Hostel, opened in 1930 for women both still operate today without direct State financial support.

There are a number of possible reasons why there was little discussion about vagrancy in the first decades after independence. First, for much of this period, in Norris's (2019) term, it was the 'Golden Age of Irish Social Housing'; second, the new Independent State had inherited a large number of institutions which O'Sullivan and O'Donnell (2012) argue managed marginality by coercively confining up to 1 per cent of the population in the first three decades after independence; and third, high rates of emigration helped dispose of those who were neither attached to land nor employed.

Both emigration and the institutions of coercive confinement were means of managing marginality through banishment, whereas the provision of social housing was a means of inclusion. In comparative terms, both the provision of social housing, primarily in rural areas, and the provision of an array of institutions of confinement are unusual: the provision of social housing and the establishment of institutions such as mental asylums and reformatory/industrial schools and social housing are generally seen as resulting from the displacements and disturbance following industrialisation and urbanisation. In the Irish case, they resulted from a uniquely interventionist State, as a consequence of political concerns about unrest in Ireland, whereby 'the middle of the nineteenth century Ireland possessed a range of institutions and services that had no parallel in other parts of the United Kingdom' (Crossman, 2018b, 542).

Public rental housing post-Independence

As we have seen in the Introduction, the new Irish State inherited a large stock of social housing in comparison with neighbouring Great Britain, with a total of 50,514 houses constructed by public authorities, predominantly in rural areas (Fahey, 2002). However, despite the comparatively high rate of public housing provision, poor housing conditions in urban and rural areas ensured that housing remained a pressing issue for the newly independent State. The first phase of State activity directed investment to social housing with the introduction of the 'Million Pound Scheme', through which the exchequer provided £500,000 with the balance coming from local authorities themselves (12.5 per cent) and from bank borrowings (Norris 2003). As a result of this programme, almost 1,000 new homes were built by 1924, mostly in urban areas. This scheme also funded Dublin's Marino Garden suburb which comprised over 1,200 homes laid out in an innovative radiating pattern with green areas (McManus, 2002). However, after the General Election of 1923, a shift of priorities which was reflected many times over the coming century, with the new Cumann na nGaedheal shifting its emphasis away from public housing towards private housing output, introducing substantial public subsidies for the construction of private homes under the *Housing (Building Facilities) Act 1924*. This led Philip Monahan, the then Cork County Manager, to conclude that 'the houses provided under the Housing Acts 1924–30 did not cater for the casual worker nor did their provision make any impression on the problem of the slums' (1959, 175).

Housing supply was falling well behind need in urban areas, with local authority surveys estimating the need for an additional 40,000 homes in 1929. In response the Cumann nGaedheal Government introduced the *Housing (Miscellaneous Provisions) Act 1931*, but before this could fully come into effect, the government fell and was replaced in 1932 by the first government led by Fianna Fáil (as noted earlier which was formed from the politicians who had taken the anti-treaty position in the Civil War) and supported by the Labour Party. This new government rapidly introduced the *Housing (Financial and Miscellaneous Provisions) Act, 1932* which resulted in a substantial increase in social housing in both rural and urban areas, and also an increase in subsidised private building, which Tom Johnston of the National Housing Board attributed to the 'simplified and expeditious procedure under the Act of 1931, and the financial assistance obtainable under the Act of 1932' (1944, 202). This legislation also provided funding for local authorities to assist with the clearance of slums and the demolition of unhealthy houses, but as we will see, progress was slow on this front.

This substantial increase in public housing under Fianna Fáil had two long-term consequences: first, the public housing programme not only provided housing for labourers and the working classes alike, but also provided a source of employment during the 1930s depression, garnering support for Fianna Fáil from these two constituencies; second, 'new house construction enhanced Fianna Fáil's relationship with another important group – property speculators and builders' (O'Connell and Rottman, 1990, 232–233). The decade from 1933 until 1943 was the only period in which more public housing was constructed than private housing with a total of 48,875 public homes constructed compared with 9,994 public homes during the earlier decade (Norris, 2003).

By 1948, the new Irish State had provided 43,113 homes under the *Housing of the Working Classes Acts* and a further 21,340 under the *Labourers' Acts*, a total of 64,633 houses (Department of Local Government, 1948, 35). As shown in Figure 1.1, output was not consistent, with a pattern of peaks and troughs evident (a pattern we will see again in the second half of the 20th and early part of 21st century).

Local authorities were not the only State agencies building public housing and, in addition to local authority housing, 6,344 houses were erected or reconstructed by the Department of Lands and the Gaeltacht (Irish language speaking areas) and the Land Commission (discussed previously, see Dooley, 2004b) erected or reconstructed a further 14,764 houses between 1932 and 1946 (Department of Local Government, 1948, 5–6), and were also responsible for planned internal migration schemes, establishing Irish language 'Colonies' in the fertile East midlands, providing 20 plus acres of land, with livestock, and a house for Irish-speaking farming families from the congested West of Ireland (Whelan, Nolan and Duffy, 2004; O'Halloran, 2020).

The key funding mechanism for local authorities, with exception of Cork and Dublin, during this period was borrowing from the Local Loans Fund which was funded through central government borrowing. The size of this

Figure 1.1: Social housing output, 1923–1948

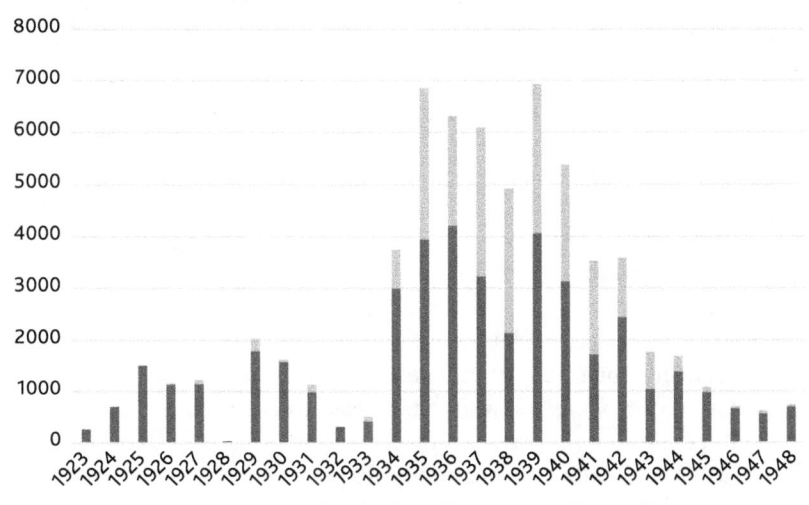

Source: Minister for Local Government (1964) *Housing – Progress and Prospects*. Stationery Office, 36

fund was regularly expanded and this funding, alongside central government direct subsidies, facilitated the substantial housing output over this period (with the exception of the war years) (see Daly, 1997 and Norris, 2019 for further details).

The shifting pattern of housing construction just outlined reflects a specifically Irish debate about the relative demands of rural and urban populations. But it also reflects a more prevalent debate about the extent to which the State should direct its resources to providing social housing or to supporting private owner-occupation. This debate is underpinned by the question of how this building should be funded and what should be the relative responsibilities of local and national government in relation to this. This question of funding is partly driven by political ideology but also reflects what is considered possible under the prevailing economic conditions of the time. For instance, Fianna Fáil's decision to cut expenditure on social housing during the period of World War II was driven by an effort to control spending during the war-time recession, but nevertheless reduced housing output from more than 6,000 in 1938 to just 744 in 1947.

As a neutral country, Ireland did not participate in World War II (the period was known as 'The Emergency' in Ireland). As a result, aside from a small number of occasions where the Luftwaffe accidentally bombed a village in County Wexford and the North Inner City of Dublin, Ireland did not experience the widespread destruction of housing and other infrastructure that occurred in combatant nations, nor did it require the extensive rebuilding programmes which characterised those economies in the post-war period. However, Ireland did experience significant economic challenges due to the effects of the war, and this resulted in a slow-down in the construction of public housing from the late 1930s into the early 1940s.

Private rented housing post-Independence

The Census of 1926 recorded 583,537 inhabited houses in Ireland, a figure that had declined continuously since the Census in 1841 which recorded just over one million inhabited houses. The 1946 Census provided information on the nature of housing occupancy for the first time. There were 662,654 private dwellings and nearly 41 per cent of households lived in private rented dwellings which had been let as unfurnished, with just under 2 per cent living in furnished private rented dwellings. In the major cities, over 70 per cent of households were living in the private rented sector. 'Unfurnished dwellings' was a proxy for private rented tenancies that were rent controlled, with 'furnished dwellings' having no regulation of rent levels (from the 1960s onwards, this distinction became blurred). Rent control for private rented dwellings was introduced in 1915 as a temporary war-time measure, but was extended in 1923, 1926 and 1928 via specific pieces of legislation which were then extended on an annual basis until 1946 when a new consolidating piece of legislation, the *Rent Restrictions Act, 1946* was passed (Coughlan, 1950): 193,237 or 29 per cent of private dwellings were owned, and a further 155,500 were in the process of being purchased from local authorities. In addition, 44,844 people (25,887 men and 18,957 women) were recorded as being in 'Boarding-houses, lodging-houses or Hostels' with a further 64,594 in 'Other types of institutions'.

Urban slums

As noted in the previous section, the provisions of the *Housing (Financial and Miscellaneous Provisions) Act, 1932* provided financial assistance to local authorities for slum clearance and the demolition of unhealthy houses, by the early 1940s, just over 11,000 houses were demolished, the majority in slum areas. However, as noted before, the pace of improvements to housing was reduced dramatically during the war years and by the late 1940s 'the poverty of the housing conditions of the great majority of people can hardly be exaggerated. Lack of amenities, insanitary conditions, crumbling dwellings in rural areas combined with wide scale tenement living in the cities comprised a grim situation' (Kennedy, 1972, 373). In one of the few first-hand accounts of life in a Dublin slum, an anonymous contributor to the *Bell* magazine in 1940 reported '[t]here are fifty-six of us all told in one house. There is one water tap and one lavatory. There was gas some years ago but it was taken out. All cooking has to be done on the fire' (anonymous, 1940, 46; see also Fagan, 2013 and Kearns, 1994 for oral histories of slum conditions in Inner City Dublin).

Following a series of articles in the *Irish Press* newspaper on slum housing in Dublin and other cities and towns in 1936, a Citizens Housing Council was established in Dublin (Murphy, 1984). It produced the *Report on Slum Clearance in Dublin* in 1938 which noted that '9,500 dwellings are required immediately to re-house people actually living in houses condemned as unfit for human habitation' (1938, 9). Membership of the Citizens Housing Council was largely made up of members of religious orders and others involved with various charitable bodies such as Sir Joseph Glynn of the Society of St Vincent De Paul. The Chair of the co-ordinating Committee was the Jesuit Fr J.E. Canavan, and the Honorary Secretary was Robert (or Bob) Collis, a well-known paediatrician. Collis had authored a play in 1943 on slums in Dublin, entitled *Marrowbone Lane*. The play concludes with the death of the child of the main character, Mary, who lives in a tenement house with her husband and his extended family, having made endless attempts to find suitable accommodation from Dublin Corporation, but being told she was not a priority case. The play was described by Wills (2007, 260) as 'poor drama but good socialist-realist propaganda'.

The Council noted that despite the considerable efforts of Dublin Corporation in building houses for rent, 'the central slum problem in Dublin is almost unchanged' (Citizens Housing Council, 1938, 12). This the Council argued was because of a false assumption that the slum dwellers would occupy the new houses, when in practice the slum dwellers couldn't afford the rents on these dwellings. The Council argued that 'it is impossible to borrow money at current rates, clear slum sites, rebuild and let the new flats, or build dwellings in the suburbs and provide transport, and then pay the interest on the loan out of rents. *It can't be done*' (1938, 12, emphasis in original).

The *Report of Inquiry into the Housing of the Working Classes of the City of Dublin, 1939–43* (1943, 17), established by the Minister for Local Government and Public Health, Fianna Fáil's Sean T.O Ceallaigh detailed that in 1938 there were still 28,210 families living in 37,848 rooms in 6,307 tenement houses, an increase from the previous survey in 1913 (albeit that the 1913 survey excluded Rathmines and Pembrooke) when there were 25,822 families in 35,227 rooms in 5,322 tenement houses. Equally, the Rev R. J. Dalton (1945) describes the appalling conditions in Cork during the 1930s. Despite the poor housing conditions in urban areas in particular, the Irish Government was slow to make improvements, with May (1944, 356) caustically observing in relation to two Dublin slums that 'only one change has occurred in these slums since we got our own government ... the names of the alley and the street have been changed from English into Irish'. The reluctance of the native government to tackle the wholesale urban slum clearance and the provision of new homes has been described by Aalen as resulting from the many

> conflicting demands upon scarce resources which rendered the government reluctant to undertake extended and expensive programmes of slum clearance which required massive, long-term subsidies. Additionally, many of the new political elite came from rural backgrounds and had limited sympathy with or interest in urban problems and development. (1992, 158)

This rural fundamentalism noted earlier by Aalen is echoed in other historical analyses with Dickson (2014, 482) arguing that funds that 'could have supported a more muscular urban agenda' were diverted to the provision of labourers' cottages and private housing reflecting what Daly (1984, 319) describes as 'an undefined feeling that urban Ireland was somewhat alien to the true Irish identity'. In addition, a further contributory factor was that both Dublin and Cork Corporations were not allowed to borrow from the Local Loans Fund and as Norris (2019, 11) notes as a result of this exclusion, 'fundraising crises were a regular occurrence, particularly in Dublin which achieved only half its target social housing output during the 1930s'. Despite these constraints, Dublin Corporation, via the housing architect's department under the leadership of Herbert George Simms, provided not only a significant output of housing units, but also architecturally innovative flat complexes that are in the main tenanted to this day (Ó Broin and McCann, 2025).

Differential rents in public housing

A significant development in the 1930s in relation to public rented housing was the introduction of a differential rent for local authority tenants, whereby the rent for local authority housing was based on the household income rather than servicing the cost of constructing and maintaining the housing. Introduced initially in Cork in 1934 and in 1950 in Dublin City and County and 19 other authorities, by 1963, 64.1 per cent of local authority rented dwellings were on graded or differential rents, compared to 16 per cent in 1947 (Government of Ireland, 1964, 20). From 1967, following the *Housing Act, 1966*, differential rents applied to all new local authority dwellings for rent. The rationale for the introduction of differential rent was that providing the accommodation on the basis of the cost of constructing the dwelling resulted in some households in need of housing being unable to afford the rent (Quinlivan, 2006, 142–145) with households on the lowest incomes being confined to the cheapest – and lowest quality – homes.

As noted previously, the Citizens Housing Council also identified fixed rents as a barrier to slum clearance. They reported that

> It was alleged in the course of the evidence that indifference or incompetence on the part of the Corporation or its officials was responsible for the undue preference being given to the better-off families, and that allocations were made in an irregular fashion. After careful enquiry we are satisfied that these allegations had no substantial basis. (1943, 56)

Rather they found that:

> the great and all powerful cause was that the Corporation, under its existing regulations and system, could not freely give houses to families under the £2 to £3 income category, without facing the fact that a few weeks or months later they would have to bring Court proceedings to evict many of them for non-payment of rent, thus leaving them eventually in a worse position than that in which they had found them. (1943, 56)

Having discussed the various pros and cons of introducing a differential rent, the Report concluded that although it would

> not solve the Housing problem, but we are of the opinion it will place the Corporation renting system on a more equitable basis for all tenants, will permit the re-housing of persons not at present dealt with by the Corporation, and at the same time require those in a position to pay, to contribute on a scale commensurate with their means towards the cost of the houses allocated to them. (p 73)

The Report also examined the system of differential rents introduced in Cork and noted that 'Mr. Philip Monahan, City Manager of Cork, gave us some very interesting detailed information on the Cork experiment' (1943, 77):

> Certain objections were raised at the outset, amongst others, that people would not agree to pay 8/- for a house for which their neighbours were only paying 3/- or 4/-; that it would involve undesirable investigations into families; that it would lead to spying on one another by the tenants and the writing of anonymous letters. None of the theoretical objections were realised. No difficulties of administration occurred, and no marked increase of staff was required. (1943, 78–79)

The national differential rent system also received support from the three-person *Housing Board* which was established by the Minister for Local Government in November 1932 to 'examine housing conditions thoroughly, and to advise and assist the minister in the solution of the present housing shortage' (Daly, 1997, 234).[5] The Board was dissolved in August 1944 on the advice of the Board itself to the Minister, largely as a result of the lack of authority given to it by successive Ministers (Gaughan, 1980, 356). The chairman, Michael P. Colivet, in a brief article describing the work of the Board noted that

> [a]fter an exhaustive examination of the subject the Board advised the Minister of the necessity of adopting some form of differential rent rebates. In 1939 the Dublin Housing Inquiry Commission was set up, Messers Colivet and Johnson serving on it, the former as Chairman. This Commission, inter-alia, also recommended the introduction of this form of rent-fixing. (1954/55, 85)

The adoption of the differential rent played a crucial role in reducing slum conditions in Dublin because a key criterion for allocation of a local authority house was the ability to pay the fixed rent and as 'those inhabiting the vilest slums had the lowest family income' (Dillon, 1945, 18) and so were least likely to obtain the new dwellings.

However, in achieving the positive outcome that families would be able to afford their rent, little attention was given to the long-term implications of setting rents at a level that would not cover the cost of providing and maintaining local authority housing, when rents remained unaltered for long periods of time and where other costs were rising. Nor was consideration given to where the local authorities were to find the resources to fund the difference between the rent level and the cost of maintaining the dwelling. This was to have long-term implications for public housing in Ireland and the people who were to live in it.

Tenant purchase schemes

Provision for the sales of public housing to the tenants existed in Ireland before independence, albeit at a small scale and confined to rural housing. Prior to 1936, local authorities could, at their own discretion, apply to the Central Government to establish schemes to sell rural labourers' cottages to their tenants. In 1932, Fianna Fáil established a *Commission of Inquiry into the Sale of Cottages and Plots provided under the Labourers' Acts*, and its recommendations were broadly accepted by the Government and legislated for in the *Labourers Act, 1936* (Hayden, 2025). The majority report of the Commission concluded that

> (1) a general demand for vested ownership existed amongst tenants of labourers' cottages. (2) a general scheme of sale acceptable to the general body of tenants was practicable without placing an unreasonable burden on the ratepayers or increasing the liability of the State. (3) the sale of the cottages and plots to the occupying tenants would be advantageous to the agricultural labourers as a class, and, with adequate provisions against alienation outside the class, need not lead to a housing shortage. (4) the average present tenant was in a position to maintain his property in addition to paying purchase charge and rates.

Despite some reservations from John Collins, from the Department of Local Government and Public Health, whom Roche, in his history of local government in Ireland, noted 'argued with admirable courage the case against sale' (Roche, 1982, 226), a purchase scheme was introduced with the terms providing for annuities equalled initially to 75 per cent of existing rents, over the balance of the repayment period of the loan raised for the cottages. In addition, cottages for purchase were to be repaired by the local authority before sale, with the purchaser to bear the cost of all future repairs. The demand for a purchase scheme came from the local authorities rather than tenants, as they were concerned with the cost of maintaining the cottages and the cost of the building schemes on the rates and therefore proposed a purchase scheme whereby tenants would have responsibility for the maintenance of the dwelling (Daly, 1997; Walsh, 1999, 60–61).

Purchase Schemes for 51,680 cottages were prepared at a local level and approved by the Minister for Local Government and Public Health by 1938, but initial take up was low until changes were introduced by the Labour Party in the early 1950s that reduced the annuity, detailed in the following chapter. Described by P.J. Meghan in the first account of housing policy in Ireland in 1963 as 'very great social experiment' (1963, 53), the introduction of a tenant purchase scheme would eventually shape the development of social housing in Ireland in a significant way by facilitating the majority of tenants in publicly owned housing to purchase their dwellings at a substantial discount (Walsh, 1999). De Bromhead and Lyons (2023, 4) have argued that this 'set a precedent that all social housing would come with an expectation of discounted tenant purchase'.

Emigration and homelessness

Figure 1.2 shows net migration in Ireland between 1926 and 1948, with only in 1939 and 1940 showing a positive net inward flow.

Britain was the primary destination for Irish emigrants during the 20th century, particularly from the 1920s when emigration to the United States was restricted. The 'vast bulk of migrants hailed from lower-class, Catholic backgrounds in rural parts of independent Ireland, and had been educated to only primary level' (Swift and Campbell, 2017, 524). Conrad Arensberg in his pioneering ethnographic study of rural Clare described the system that generally held for much of the West of Ireland until the 1950s as: 'Usually, only the heir and one daughter are married and dowered, the one with the farm, the other with the fortune. All the rest, in the words of the Luogh residents, "must travel"' (Arensberg, 1937, 79). In the words of Hannan (1979, 39) '[w]hen the system worked effectively it simultaneously guaranteed inheritance, marriage of the successor and dispersal of the non-inheritors'. Hannan notes that with farmers having an average of six of children, '[e]ven with one son inheriting, one daughter being "dowered off" and perhaps one other son or daughter being provided for locally, still over half the children born to farm families would have to emigrate' (1979, 40). Seeking non-institutional sources of support for unmarried mothers and services that allowed mother and child to remain together after birth was a further significant driver of emigration as women eschewed the punitive institutional services available in Ireland (Earner-Byrne, 2004).

Figure 1.2: Net migration (,000), 1926–1948

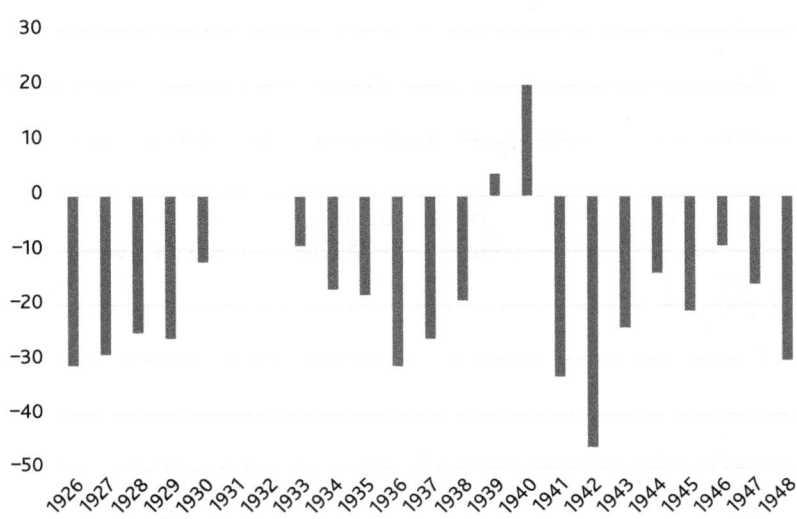

Source: Central Statistics Office – https://datasalsa.com/dataset/?catalogue=data.gov.ie&name=c0401-components-of-population-change-since-1926

During 'The Emergency' around 50,000 Irish people left the country to volunteer to fight for the allied forces, with an impact both on housing demand and building labour. Nevertheless, for a variety of internal and international reasons, Irish emigration from independence until the end of the war was relatively low in comparison with earlier and later periods. The profile of those who emigrated, it is argued, ensured the dominance of a conservative mindset as those most likely to seek radical change and better their lot were those who emigrated (Delaney, 2005, 50). Daly, in her demographic history of Independent Ireland, notes the complex relationship to emigration with 'the Irish state and its people took pride in the large numbers of men and women of Irish birth or descent scattered throughout the world' and in particular 'their contribution to bringing Catholicism to Britain, the United States and Australia (2006, 257). Whatever was said about Irish emigrants' contribution to spreading Catholicism and pride in their achievements,

> emigrants also supported families who remained in Ireland, and by doing so reduced the incidence of poverty, they injected valuable money into the economy of the most deprived parts of Ireland, they reduced the burden on Irish charities and taxpayers, and they made a significant contribution to the balance of payments. (Daly, 2006, 258)

Surveys of the homeless in the countries traditionally associated with Irish emigration show high percentages of Irish persons included in their statistics on homelessness. For example, in a census of tramps in the United States in 1893, 'in order of nativity, America leads the list with 56.1 percent; Ireland is next with 20.3 percent' (McCook, 1893, 756). Over 60 years later, a study of homeless men in the United States found that

> 25 percent of the men were born in Ireland; 42 percent of their fathers and 44 percent of their mothers were also born in Ireland. We do not know how many second or third generation Irish Americans were in our sample ... an estimated guess would be at least one third of them were of Irish descent. (Levinson, 1966, 168)

Similarly high numbers of Irish born males are found in various surveys of homelessness in England and Wales. For example, in a study of London's Skid Row, the single largest ethnic group in their sample were Irish at 37 per cent (Edwards et al, 1966, 449). Washbrook in his survey of 200 homeless offenders in London observed that 24 per cent were Irish (1970, 178), and Lodge-Patch, in a survey of a London lodging house, found that 25 per cent of his sample were originally Irish (1970, 314). Daly (2006, 310) cites an article in the Irish Independent newspaper reporting that there were approximately 5,000 Irish people homeless in London in 1961.

The 1948 White Paper: *Housing: A Review of Past Operations and Immediate Requirements*

In 1948, the first White Paper on housing was published which noted that *via* 'various forms of assistance, new homes have been provided in the past 50 years for more than one-fourth of the population' (Government of Ireland, 1948, 5). The White Paper estimated that 100,000 new dwellings were required to meet existing need: 44,511 of these were required in urban areas to house the working classes but as a consequence of the priority given to providing housing for agricultural labourers since the late 19th century, just over 16,000 dwellings were required in rural Ireland. The White Paper also acknowledged that 'Dublin City's housing problem is by far the greatest in any single area in the country' (1948, 14) with 23,346 dwellings required, or 38 per cent of the total number of dwellings required for the entire country.

The Paper set out the challenge ahead, cautioning that, in addition to delivering housing to meet immediate needs, the

> long-term objective of the housing programme must be the achievement of a rate of house output which will not alone make

good our immediate wants, but will supply the deficiency arising from year-by-year obsolescence of existing dwellings, changes in population structure, migration, elimination of overcrowding, rising standards of accommodation and other causes. (1948, 7)

Conclusion

During the period from independence until the end of the 16 years under the power of Fianna Fáil, much was achieved in building on the legacy of the late 19th century in providing subsidised housing to both agrarian labourers and the urban working classes, but the positive bias towards rural Ireland ensured that housing conditions in urban areas, and in particular Dublin, remained acute. Toward the later part of the period, the gradual introduction of various social security measures such as widows' pensions and children's allowances improved the conditions of those they were targeted at. But for the most impoverished and those without family support, the Poor Law institutions, alongside the institutions ostensibly for those with mental illnesses, operated much as they had operated prior to independence, providing a grim existence for those dependent on them, regardless of the legislative framework that was in part modernised. Two key policy developments in the 1930s – the introduction of a differential rent scheme in Cork that was eventually adopted nationally and a tenant purchase scheme that would grow and become ever more generous in the decades that followed – had immediate positive effects on their beneficiaries and would shape social housing for the following 90 years.

The basic template for the provision of specific services for those experiencing homelessness was that of encouraging either non-State entities, preferably religiously inspired, to provide accommodation and related services with minimal regulation or funding from the State. As noted in the Introduction, an ideology had emerged in the mid-19th century by exponents of a laissez-faire ideology, but could also be justified by Catholic social teaching on subsidiarity, which advocates the provision of welfare services by local non-State actors rather than by central State services. What funding was made available tended to be ad hoc: as in the example of Minister for Health James Ryan immediately pledging £30,000 of public money when he was appalled by conditions during a visit to the Legion of Mary Hostel for women, the Regina Coeli, in the late 1940s (Deeny, 1989, 161). This understanding of the appropriateness of the role of non-state bodies providing services and support to marginal populations were undoubtedly also shaped by the fact that many civil servants in post-independent Ireland were committed Catholics and active in Catholic societies such as the Society of St Vincent de Paul (Daly, 2016, 57) and the Legion of Mary (Kennedy, 2011), with both organisations operating shelters for the homeless in Dublin and elsewhere. Thus, although Catholic social principles were never formally adopted in the organisation of politics, economy and society in independent Ireland, the delivery of 'good works' at the individual level outside of the workplace was a notable feature of homelessness services in post-independent Ireland.

2

The end of the Poor Laws, economic development and modernisation, 1948–1963

Introduction

This chapter covers the period between 1948 and 1963 when a coalition (or inter-party) government temporarily disrupted the hegemony of Fianna Fáil in government. As a neutral country, the Irish experience after the World War II (Emergency) had been distinct from most other European countries. After the significant drop in social housing output during the war years, large-scale social housing resumed in the early 1950s. The chapter relates how a further review of the Poor Law institutions in 1949 led to the eventual demise of Poor Law institutions for those experiencing homelessness. Debates on the role of the State in the provision of housing in the 1950s were linked with the late modernisation and industrialisation of the Irish economy. The late 1950s saw the publication of a *Programme of Economic Development* and the gradual transition from an agrarian to an industrial economy and ideology, with the gradual ending of the protectionism that characterised economic policy for the first 30 years of Independence to policies that favoured free trade, and by extension, the first steps towards entry to the European Economic Community created in 1957. By the early 1960s, while housing needs in rural Ireland had been largely met, the housing of the working classes in urban areas, and particularly in Dublin, remained largely unmet. Responsibility for meeting the needs of the 'homeless', largely understood as single men, was the legislative responsibility of health services who provided 'rough care' alongside a range of religiously inspired NGO providers. Despite emigration, the housing needs of families were unmet, particularly in Dublin, and this was becoming increasingly a political priority. This led to experiments in providing large-scale high-rise social housing. Symbolically, this era closes with the collapse of a number of tenement buildings in Bolton Street and Fenian Street in Dublin in the summer of 1963 resulting in the deaths of a number of children.

Political and economic context

After Fianna Fáil's 16 years in power, they were challenged by a newly founded political movement, *Clann Na Poblachta* which advocated full employment, increased social provision, particularly in health and housing. There were expectations that Clann Na Poblachta would become the largest party but in the event, they only elected ten TDs. After much negotiation they were able to form a 'makeshift majority' coalition with four other parties and independents, led by a nominee of Fine Gael (formerly Cumann na nGaedheal), John A. Costello (McCullagh, 1998). The Minister for Housing was Tim Murphy from the Labour Party, and the Minister for Health was a radical doctor Noel Browne, who had been elected for Clann Na Poblachta. This Government lasted until 1951, collapsing over a dispute with the Catholic Church and the medical profession concerning Browne's health scheme for mothers. In 1951, Fianna Fáil regained a majority until, at the election of 1954, a new coalition government was elected. In the 1957 election, Fianna Fáil again took power, the last government to be led by Eamonn De Valera, who stood down in 1959, to be replaced by Sean Lemass, who was determined to 'bring Ireland into the promised land of economic development, where it would share the prosperity apparent in Western Europe' (Murphy, 2009, 306).

Emigration

Emigration from Ireland continued at a rapid pace during the post-war/post Emergency years, as the Irish economy lagged behind the rapid growth rates experienced in many of the economies in combatant countries (see Figure 2.1). There was net emigration of over half a million people during this period. With the election of the Inter-Party Government in 1948, the Minister for Social Welfare and leader of the Labour Party, William Norton, established a *Commission on Emigration and Other Population Problems* which reported six years later in 1954 (Connolly, 2004). Identifying the 'fundamental cause of emigration' as economic, that is 'the absence of opportunities for making an adequate livelihood, and a growing desire for higher standards of living on the part of the community, particularly the rural community' (1954, 134–135). The Commission's report was a significant contribution to what was to emerge by the end of the decade of a fundamental re-orientation of the Irish economy, given the 'all-too-prevalent mood of despondency about the country's future' (Department of Finance, 1958, 4–5).

While the drivers of emigration during this period were largely to do with economic conditions and employment opportunities in particular, the impact on housing need was significant. The fact that it was younger adults who were most likely to emigrate accentuated the impact on family formation and substantially reduced the level of growth in housing need which would have otherwise occurred. The widespread view that housing needs had been 'virtually satisfied' was strongly related to the fact that so many people were now being housed in the countries that they had emigrated to for work.

Figure 2.1: Net migration (,000), 1926–1963

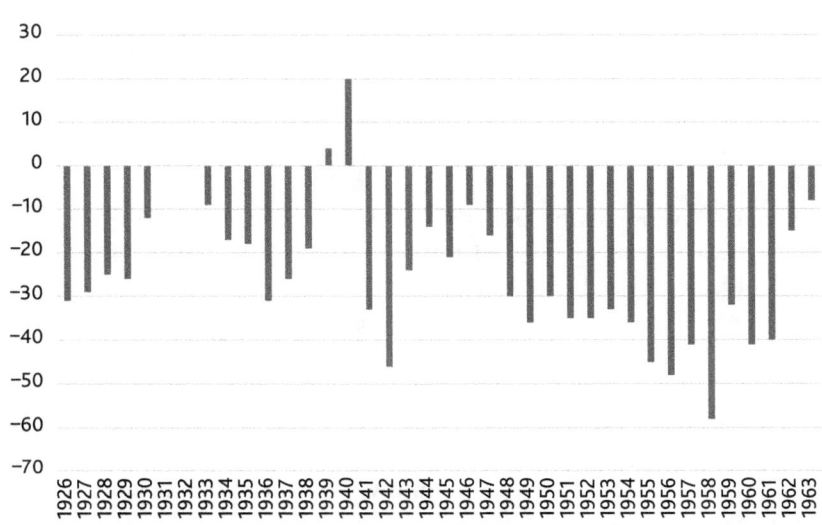

Source: Central Statistics Office – https://datasalsa.com/dataset/?catalogue=data.gov.ie&name=
c0401-components-of-population-change-since-1926

The year 1951 was one of the lower years for migration during this period with net outward migration of around 35,000 people. In contrast it was the very best year for social housing construction during the period, but this amounted to just under 9,000 homes being completed. Emigration began to decline towards the end of the period as the various measures to promote economic growth began to lead to increases in job opportunities in Ireland and the impact of this on housing demand and homelessness will be discussed in the next chapter.

Casuals and the *Inter-Departmental Committee on County Homes*

Although this period saw determined attempts to reform the County Homes, the broad pattern of provision for homeless people continued largely unchanged: some, despite the absence of any formal provision, continued to be accommodated in the Casual Wards of the County Homes with others by largely faith-based non-governmental organisations. Attempts to reform the County Homes were driven by the new Clann Na Poblachta Minister for Health, Noel Browne. Browne visited a number of the County Homes and was 'greatly shocked by unsatisfactory conditions of the buildings and the primitive conditions under which the inmates are in many cases maintained'. In a memorandum to the Government in February 1949,

Browne sought exchequer funding towards the cost of reconstructing or replacing County Homes.

Speaking in a debate in Dáil Éireann on 1 July 1949, Browne signalled his concern that what was available fell 'far short of minimum standards of comfort'. In his autobiography, Browne provides a description of the Longford County Home where:

> an open sewer ran through the recreation grounds. The food was cooked, as it was in most of the workhouses, in a large vat which had a block and tackle to open and close the vast lids in the open-air kitchens. Whatever was to be stewed for the inmates was poured into these enormous stew pans. The wards were long, the walls had no pictures, the floors were bare and the sky was frequently visible through the broken slates on the roof. The beds were on raised platforms to accommodate straw-filled paliasses, long lines of them on either side of the room, occupied by pale, mummy-like human beings lying semi-comatose, apathetic and completely uninterested in their surroundings. (1986, 199–200)

Browne is primarily remembered for his reforms in tackling TB and his proposed Mother and Baby Scheme – and the fierce resistance to it from the medical profession and the Catholic Church. However, he faced similar resistance to his aspirations for the County Homes, first through a decision to establish an inter-departmental committee rather than agree to new funding, and later through the suppression of the report when it was completed.

In 1949, rather than investing in reconstruction in response to Browne's concerns, the government established an inter-departmental committee consisting of representatives of the Department of Health, Social Welfare, Local Government and Finance to examine the issue and to report to the Minister for Health. After the inter-departmental committee had finalised its report, a dispute emerged as to whether or not it should be published. The Department of Finance wanted the section describing a typical County Home omitted 'as undesirable use might be made of this extract by certain propagandists', with the Department of Health of the view that 'there would not seem to be any justification for understating the unpleasant facts as recorded by the Inter-departmental Committee'.[1] The offending section broadly matched the description of the County Homes by Browne, with the Inter-departmental Committee providing the following account:

> No description of a County Home would be complete without some reference to the residents, who often seem such a part of their environment that it is difficult to decide whether they looked as they

did because they lived in County Homes or whether County Homes take the tone and appearance of the inmates. The ambulant men, dressed in suits of almost uniformly drab grey, are most in evidence. The majority look apathetic and listless. The women are poorly clothed but the sense of drab uniformity is less evident in their attire. They also seem to lack interest in their surroundings. They sit in the day room motionless and often silent waiting for the next meal or for bedtime. The unmarried mothers generally look rather slatternly; they, of course, do a large part of the domestic work of the institution. The children are often bright and cheerful, in poignant contrast with their environment. The chronic sick need no special comment. They, too, are apathetic; few make any effort to read. In most chronic wards wireless has been installed and this helps to pass the time.

The view of the Department of Finance prevailed, and the report was not published, but is available in the National Archives of Ireland. Instead, a White Paper, '*On the Reconstruction and Improvement of County Homes*', based on the inter-departmental report, was published by the Department of Health in 1951.

The Report of the Inter-Departmental Committee had noted that the pre-Independence reports had recommended that County Homes be reserved for the aged and infirm poor and chronic invalids only. They had recommended that separate arrangements should be made for the care of other classes of inmates such as 'unmarried mothers' and 'mental defectives'. The Committee reported that '[a]s a general rule the recommendations have not been carried out. Individual Homes have been improved but the underlying defects persist. The Homes are residual institutions and types of classes, for which nothing better in the way of institutional treatment can be found, drift there and remain there' (1949, 4).

In relation to people who were homeless, the Inter-Departmental Committee recommended that 'as far as possible accommodation for casuals should be provided in a section of the home removed from the main building'. The rationale for this recommendation was that '[i]f County Homes are to be improved, the presence of these casuals will become more and more incongruous and embarrassing' (1949, 27). The White Paper, although omitting the descriptions of conditions, made the same recommendation as the Inter-Departmental Committee and noted that of the 8,585 individuals accommodated in County Homes on 31 March 1950, only 139 were 'casuals', whereas in Dublin alone, the Legion of Mary and the Society of St Vincent de Paul operated four shelters with a capacity for nearly 400. The number of 'casuals' in the majority of the County Homes on 31 March were in single figures, with only Galway and Athy having double figures of 20 and 14 (seven men and seven women) respectively.

However, the Inter-Departmental Committee concluded that, in the long run, alternatives to the County Homes for casuals would be required and they suggested that '[c]ollaboration between local authorities and voluntary bodies concerned with the welfare of destitute and indigent persons might provide a solution'. They were particularly impressed by the Morning Star Hostel in Dublin and the 'achievements of the Legion of Mary in this thorny field' (1949, 27), and recommended that

> the local authorities in Dublin, Cork and Galway responsible for the provision of accommodation for casuals should approach the Legion of Mary or other voluntary bodies interested in this type of work with a view to ascertaining whether accommodation on the lines provided in the Morning Star Hostel could be provided by such voluntary bodies. (1949, 27)

A year after the publication of the White Paper, the Department moved to implement these recommendations, issuing a circular to local authorities which requested the preparation of a scheme for the future of the County Homes. It was stressed that 'the first aim should be to remove to Special Homes, or suitable Institutions, Unmarried Mothers and Children, Mental Defectives, Blind, Deaf and Dumb, etc ... and that the removal of all children from the County Home is a fundamental part of the Scheme of Improvements' (Circular, 7/52, 28 January 1952).

As discussed in the Introduction and Chapter 1, the removal of these classes from the workhouse/County Home had been recommended as far back as 1906 in the Report of the *Vice-Regal Commission on Poor Law Reform in Ireland*, and again in the report of the *Commission on the Relief of the Sick and Destitute Poor, including the Insane Poor* in 1927. However, 30 years after Independence, a different approach was proposed for accommodating people who were homeless – the 'casuals'. In contrast to the 1923 Schemes, casuals were now to be explicitly catered for within the new County Homes scheme, with the 1952 Circular noting that 'It is considered that it will be possible to reserve a suitable small section of the County Home Building for Casuals'. For example, in the case of Athy, when devising their scheme of improvements, it was noted that in respect of 'casuals' that they

> are few and far between as far as County Home, Athy, is concerned. The average number over 11 years is five, three men and two women. It is suggested that provision should be made, in some segregated section of the County Home, for them. I suggest that provision is made for 10 beds, six for men and four for women.

The number of beds for men was revised upwards to 8 in 1955 but revised downwards to five in 1960.

Plans for the Reconstruction and Improvement of County Homes were paused during the balance of payments crisis of the mid-1950s which we discuss later in this chapter, and did not resume until the early 1960s, at which point a further Inter-departmental Committee had been established to look (again) at the future role of the County Homes. In 1958, the Department of Health had commented that, as a consequence of the pausing of funding for the reconstruction, 'conditions in some of these institutions are still intolerable' with 'disgraceful conditions' in many of the Homes.

Composition of those experiencing homelessness

It is difficult to determine who the people experiencing homelessness at this time were. Whether they were in the County Home system or accommodated by faith-based charities, their pathways into homelessness are largely unknown, nor do we know about their pathways out, or if such pathways existed to any extent. In a memo to the Department of Health, on 22 March 1950, Frank Duff, the aforementioned founder of the Legion of Mary, based on his experience of running shelters in Dublin, was of the view that Industrial Schools were a significant contributor to those entering the Legion of Mary Shelters:

> One figure at least can be given with authority in this connection. It is that one out of three of the street girls dealt with in our hostel, No. 76 Harcourt Street., are ex-Industrial School Girls. ... A formidable proportion of the men resident in the Morning Star are of the same class, the ex-Industrial School child. Therefore the action of any society which deliberately breaks up the union of child and mother is one to be seriously viewed and if at all possible checked. (Frank Duff, memo to the Department of Health, 22 March, 1950, not published)

The *Health Act, 1953* and Casuals

In 1951, Dr Noel Browne resigned as Minister for Health and from his party Clann Na Poblachta in protest over the lack of support for his Mother and Baby Scheme in the face of hostility from the Catholic Church and the medical profession. The Inter-Party Government collapsed a few months later and the subsequent election returned Fianna Fáil to power, with Dr James Ryan, who had been Minister for Health and Social Welfare in the previous Fianna Fáil administration, returning to that post.

In further proposed reforms of the County Home system, Ryan seemed to signal a significant shift in the approach to people who were homeless and accommodated as casuals in the County Homes. When introducing the provisions of what became the *Health Act, 1953* in the Dáil (Parliament),

Dr Ryan sought to legislate that able-bodied Casuals (alongside other able-bodied residents of County Homes) would be obliged to 'perform such work as the authority consider suitable to his sex, age, strength and capacity' when in the County Home. Many members of the Dáil argued the provisions relating to the obligation to work reflected 'the continuance of the workhouse mentality as well as the continuance of the workhouse atmosphere'. Noel Browne, who had returned to the Dáil as an Independent TD but joined Fianna Fáil in October 1953, put forward an amendment to remove this section on 8 July 1953. The amendment was accepted by the Minister and no work conditionality was introduced for people experiencing homelessness or other 'able-bodied' people accommodated in County Homes.

Ryan's Bill also aimed to create the offence of behaving in a 'disorderly manner in such home or institution, or cause[ing] unreasonable disturbance to other persons maintained in such home or institution or to persons therein'. People found guilty of this offence were to be 'liable on summary conviction thereof to a term of imprisonment not exceeding twenty-one days' (Harvey, 1984). In the debates on the Bill, the Minister for Health made it clear that this provision was only intended to apply to casuals, not to any of the other inmates of the County Homes. This provision too met with a concerted and lengthy critique from the opposition, particularly from members of the Labour Party and Clann Na Poblachta. Browne described the provision as the 'retention of the old pauper type of legislation imposed on this nation in bygone years'. The Minister argued that, without this provision, there would be no remedy to deal 'with blackguards who kick up a row at night'. Nevertheless, he did agree to modify the original provisions and remove the sections relating to insubordination and being drunk and disorderly as grounds for an offence. Despite the opposition, this provision was passed as part of the Act.

A more positive element of the 1953 Act was found in Section 54 which would provide the only statutory basis for the provision of 'institutional assistance' to people who were homeless. Significantly, it was in a Health Act that a statutory basis was established for the provision of shelter and maintenance in a County Home for persons 'unable to provide shelter and maintenance for himself or his dependants'. However, as we will see in the following chapter, following the passing of the *Housing Act, 1966*, there emerged considerable disagreement between health authorities and housing authorities as to where statutory responsibility lay.

Thus, from 1953, it was envisaged that provision for those experiencing (what we now consider) homelessness would remain a residual function of the County Homes supplemented by voluntary organisations such as the Society of St Vincent de Paul and the Legion of Mary where required. This was built on ideologies, both Catholic and Laissez-faire, whereby denominational voluntary bodies and agencies and congregations /orders of the main churches provided the bulk of health, educational and social services in Ireland, with varying degrees of financial support from Central and Local Government (Binchy, 1967).

'Blackguards' and the law

Despite the lengthy debates on what became Section 54 of the *Health Act, 1953*, there is no record of any 'casual' being convicted and committed to prison for behaving in a disorderly fashion or causing an unreasonable disturbance in a County Home or ancillary institution. It may be that the perception of casuals as 'blackguards' was misplaced, and as Dr Ryan acknowledged in his contribution, the sections relating to work and behaviour were continuations of earlier legislation and hence his willingness to remove and modify the sections. It may also reflect that the Gardaí already had considerable powers under the Vagrancy Acts to manage the behaviour in casuals, inside or outside the County Homes, the number of offences under the Vagrancy Acts in which proceedings were taken, averaged at just under 1,000 per annum between 1927 and 1963.

From the publication of the first Garda Annual Report in 1947 until 1958 (when detailed data on the implementation of the Vagrancy Acts was discontinued), data is provided on the outcome of proceedings taken under the Vagrancy Acts. For example, in 1951, 472 persons were prosecuted under the Vagrancy laws and 291 were convicted. The offence of begging accounted for 358 prosecutions, and 159 of the total arrested were female. Of those convicted, 197 were given a prison sentence of less than one month, 36 were given a prison sentence of more than one month, two were committed to a reformatory school with three given the Probation Act. Others were fined or had the charge dismissed. Only during this period is data provided on the number of offences under Section 4, that is the offence of sleeping out. Between 1924 and 1963, for the majority of years, the number of committals averaged between 150 and 200 per annum.

Social security and public assistance

The first significant output from the newly established Department of Social Welfare in 1947 was a *White Paper on Social Security* in 1949. Focused primarily on social insurance rather than social assistance, many of its recommendations were legislated for in the *Social Welfare Act, 1952*, but only after much debate and a change of government. The Act provided the basis for the future development of the social security system in Ireland but did not expand until the 1960s and was described by McCashin (2019, 57) as 'an attenuated version of the Beveridge Plan', the well-known plan in the UK that laid the basis for the post-war welfare state in Britain. This gradual development of a comprehensive social security system in Ireland was a further step towards ending the Irish Poor Law, but as we will see in later chapters, there were still a number of steps left in this particular journey.

It is also of note the scheme of social security developed by the Department of Social Welfare 'repudiated two Catholic corporatist initiatives' (McCashin, 2019, 56). These were the aforementioned *Commission on Vocational Organisation* and Bishop Dignan's *Scheme of National Health Insurance*, and in the case of the social welfare system as opposed to the health and education system, the Catholic Church 'had very little direct impact on the social welfare system' (Cousins, 2003, 196). In the case of Bishop Dignan's *Scheme of National Health Insurance*, the Minister for Local Government and Public Health, Seán McEntee established a departmental committee to examine the scheme 'which anatomised it with an almost sadistic attention to detail' (Riordan, 2000, 48) with a view to undermining the scheme. However, the Government legislation did maintain the ideological and practical benefit to rural Ireland by providing a particular generous State subsidy to those working in the agricultural sector (Carey, 2005).

Housing policy, the *Capital Investment Advisory Committee* and economic development

In 1956, in the face of a budgetary crisis brought about by a balance of payments deficits (Honohan and O Grada, 1998), a *Capital Investment Advisory Committee* was established

> which should be small in numbers and expert in equality to survey, analyse and evaluate by sectors the existing capital structure of the economy and to consider and – with full regard to the interests of the national economy – advise the government on the volume of public investment from time to time desirable, the general order of priority appropriate for the various investment projects, and the manner in which such projects should be financed. (Quoted in Fanning, 1978, 506)

The second report of this committee, published in 1957, was devoted to housing on the basis that 'it forms roughly one-third of the whole State capital programme and because policy decisions are now presumably imminent since, taking the country as a whole, the wartime arrears of housing have been largely met' (Capital Investment Advisory Committee, 1957, 3).

This belief, that the housing needs of the 'county as a whole' were met, informed the key recommendations of the majority report, whose signatories included two influential economists, Louden Ryan and Patrick Lynch.

Their recommendations, in brief, were that rent control and restrictions on repossessions in the private rented sector should be phased out; that grants be made available to landlords to maintain their properties; that all subsidies for new housing, other than for slum clearance, should be abolished; that local authorities apply differential rents to all tenants, loans for house purchase be extended and the expenditure saved on housing used to 'promote productive projects'.

A minority report written by M.J. Costello, general manager of the Irish Sugar Company, and Ruaidhri Roberts, general secretary of the Irish Trades Union Congress, critiqued the assumptions of the majority report and strongly argued for a substantial building programme, but the signatories of the majority report defended their analysis, noting 'that expenditure on housing is of a most desirable character from the social point of view, always provided that social desirability is related to economic feasibility' (1957, 35). Daly (1997), in her history of the Department of the Environment, notes that the Departments of Finance, Local Government and the Gaeltacht were tasked with coming up with a set of agreed recommendations given the divisions on the Committee and some opposition from the Department of Local Government on some of the recommendations of the majority report, but no report was ever produced. Daly notes that the *Housing (Amendment) Act, 1958* increased housing subsidies and grants rather than reducing them, which 'suggests that Fianna Fáil were not wholly committed to implementing the recommendations of the Capital Investment Advisory Committee' (1997, 437).

The views expressed in the majority report were also reflective of the views of the Department of Finance, with T.K. Whitaker, the Secretary of the Department of Finance, arguing in a paper read to the influential Statistical and Social Inquiry Society of Ireland that there was a 'preponderance of housing' in the country as a consequence of high levels of capital devoted to social investment, and over the period 1949–1954 'dwellings alone formed as high a proportion of gross domestic capital formation as agriculture, mining, manufacturing and other construction combined' (1956, 193). Equally, Ó hUiginn (1960, 61–63; see also Meagher, 1959) in a relatively rare comparative analysis of social and economic aspects of housing in Ireland, noted that three-quarters of capital invested in the new dwellings in Ireland came from public funds, compared to half in the majority of Western European countries, resulting in lower rents for local authority housing and more preferential purchase terms for owner-occupiers than was the case in other countries in Western Europe.

The belief that the housing needs of the country and other social needs 'are virtually satisfied over wide areas of the State' (1958a, 4), that 'an extensive social infrastructure has been provided' (1958a, 19) were reiterated in *Economic Development* and even more bullishly in the *Programme for Economic Progress*

(1958b, 8) where it was stated that '[t]he social capital investment of the past years has given us an "infrastructure" of housing, hospitals, communications etc., which is equal (in some respects, perhaps, superior) to that of comparable countries'. As summarised by Kennedy (1972, 375), 'in 1948, there was a general consensus on top priority for housing, by 1958, there appeared to be a widespread consensus, among the policy makers and in documents which must have exerted important influence on the policy makers, that housing should have a low priority'. Peter Kaim-Caudle, a lecturer in social administration in the University of Durham, in the first textbook on social policy in Ireland acknowledged this consensus on housing, but argued that the findings of the majority report 'were supported by plausible and logical deductions rather than a survey of the facts' (1967, 93) and that they 'seemed in large measure to share Adam Smith's faith in the invisible hand of God, the conviction that it was best not to interfere with the forces of the market' (1967, 94).

The evidence for these assertions that housing need was met will be discussed in further detail in the following chapter, but it clearly reflected a dominant view among the Department of Finance and other influential economists, that capital should be devoted to 'productive' investment in agriculture, fisheries, industry and tourism rather than 'social' investment in housing and other social amenities in order to 'provide self-sustaining and permanent employment' (1958a, 4). Both *Economic Development* written by key civil servants in the Department of Finance and the Government's *Programme for Economic Expansion*, described by Daly as a 'watered down version of Economic Development that expunged or diluted many of the tougher, politically unacceptable recommendations' (2016, 23), nonetheless moved Ireland from a policy of self-sufficiency to an open economy. This process culminated in membership of the EEC in 1973, a policy shift for which Daly (2016, 4) argues there was 'no alternative if the nation was to survive in world where international trade and economic integration were seen as prerequisites for economic growth'.

Local authority housing

While the approach to the treatment and accommodation of people who were homeless was being debated in health legislation, there were initial signs that significant change was taking place in the provision of social housing. Noel Browne's period as Minister for Health is remembered not just because of the controversy surrounding his Mother and Baby Scheme but also for the significant changes in public health where he introduced mass free screening for tuberculosis sufferers and launched a program to build new hospitals and sanitoria. While these responses to TB were primarily through the health system, the prevalence of the disease in Ireland was also closely related to the poor housing and overcrowded housing conditions that continued for many people.

As noted in the earlier chapter, when the 1948 Government took power, social housing output had been in decline for several years, largely due to reductions in investment arising from the economic pressures of World War II. The election of the Inter-Party Government led to a rapid growth in public expenditure on housing in Ireland and a consequent increase in the construction of public rental dwellings. Local authority housing completions jumped from 729 completions in 1948 to 7,486 in 1952. However, despite several changes in government, this turned out to be the only phase of increasing social housing construction during the period covered in this chapter. The collapse of the first Inter-Party Government and the re-election of Fianna Fáil resulted in a decline in social housing in the decade from 1952. When the Fianna Fáil Government itself fell in 1954 and was replaced by the second Inter-Party Government, the decline in social housing output was not reversed. Reflecting the budgetary situation discussed earlier, the re-election of a Fianna Fáil Government in 1957 saw even further decline in social housing output. Between 1948 and 1963, 38,787 dwellings were constructed under the Housing of the Working Class Acts and a further 24,487 constructed under the *Labourers' Acts*, a total of 63,274 dwellings as shown in Figure 2.2.

Tenant purchase

As noted in the previous chapter the *Labourers Act, 1936* allowed for a tenant purchase scheme in rural areas under which tenants could purchase based on an annuity equivalent to 75 per cent of existing rents, paid over the balance of the repayment period of the loan which had been raised to construct the cottages. Initially there was only limited interest in the scheme, with only 8,209 cottages sold or vested by 1950. The initial terms of the scheme for purchase of dwellings (75 per cent) were compared unfavourably with the annuity terms received by farmers under the Land Acts, which led to pressure from the Labour Party, as a member of the Inter-Party Government between 1948–1951, to deliver similar concessions to agricultural workers. A reduction from 75 per cent of existing rents to 50 per cent in March 1951 resulted in a significant increase in purchases with approximately 60,000 sold over the following 16 years.

Housing tenure in Ireland, the decline of private rented housing and ending rent control

The Census conducted in 1961 showed a modest increase in the number of private households from 1946, from 662,654 to 676,402, but also revealed the growing dominance of homeownership with nearly 60 per cent of

Figure 2.2: Social housing output, 1923–1963

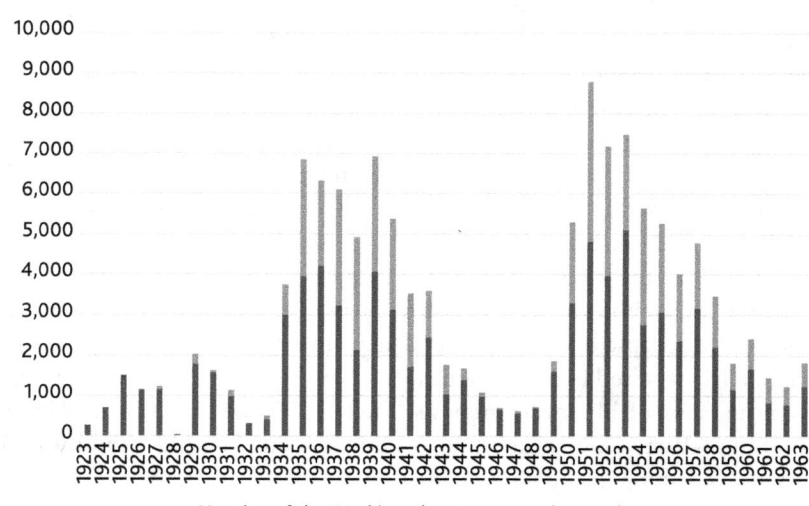

■ Housing of the Working Class Acts   ■ Labourers' Acts

Source: Department of Local Government and Public Health Annual Report (various years) (Dublin: Stationery Office)

private households in that tenure compared to nearly 53 per cent in 1946. The changes in the Tenant Purchase Scheme noted in the previous section, under which 41,960 households had purchased their dwelling from their local authority by 1961, were partly responsible for this increase in the number of owner-occupiers and would continue to swell the number in this tenure in future censuses. Those in local authority housing increased modestly while the number of households in private rented dwellings declined from 26.1 per cent to 17.2.

This decline in households who were renting in the private market was particularly strong for unfurnished private rented dwellings (essentially rent controlled dwellings) in urban areas (Baker and O'Brien, 1979; O'Brien and Dillon, 1982). The *Rents and Leaseholds Commission*, chaired by Judge John Conrey, issued a detailed report on *Rent Control in 1952*, with the Commission recommending that 'rent control be continued' and that they saw 'no reasonable likelihood of the need for rent control ceasing in the foreseeable future', on the basis 'that the discontinuance of rent control would lead to substantial increases in rents and to the ejectment of tenants either because they could not pay increased rents or because the owner wanted to get possession to sell at an inflated price with resultant hardships to large numbers of tenants' (1952, 19).

Five years later, in 1957, the majority of the aforementioned *Capital Investment Advisory Committee* in their second report, which was devoted to housing as discussed before, argued that the justification for the Rent Restrictions Acts 'has disappeared with the substantial new building since 1948' and continuing with rent restrictions was 'indefensible'. However, they noted that 'a sudden and complete repeal of these Acts, however, would cause hardship' (1957, 8) and argued instead for a repeal of both rent control and restrictions on repossession over a 10-year period, with rent control phased out over the first five years and restrictions on repossession over the next five years.

Both *Economic Development* (1958a) and the *Programme for Economic Expansion* (1958b) endorsed the views of the *Capital Investment Advisory Committee* in relation to Rent Control, with *Economic Development* (1958a, 47), arguing the '[p]reservation of the national stock of houses would be greatly helped by the progressive abolition of rent control over private dwellings', with the *Programme for Economic Expansion* also arguing for the gradual phasing out of rent control 'to avoid hardship for existing tenants' (1958b, 8).

The legislative response to both reports was the introduction of the *Rent Restrictions Act, 1960*, whereby new tenants, by and large, did not enjoy the protections of the earlier acts (Coughlan, 1979; de Blacam, 1984). The rationale for this shift in policy was given by Parliamentary Secretary to the Minister for Justice, Charles Haughey, who told the Seanad that '[c]onditions have altered materially since the Conroy Commission reported' and 'the Government have decided that no further extensions of control can be justified in present circumstances and that the public interest requires such relaxations of control as can be effected without imposing hardship on tenants' (Seanad Éireann debate, Wednesday, 1 June 1960, Vol 52, No 12).

Conclusion

Despite the continued inadequacy of housing for many people in Ireland, it is important to take measure of the progress that had been in force in providing housing either directly by the State or indirectly via grants and subsidies in the first 40 years since Independence. This was remarkable in the context of the relatively restricted role of the State in the development of other welfare and social services. Although clearly there were a number of deficiencies in the system, the State had demonstrated its ability and desire to meet a basic welfare need. Paul Pfretzschner, a visiting American academic in Trinity College Dublin, argued in 1965 that

> [t]here is no question that the housing policy prescribed by the law has been of profound consequence to the nation and its people. Of the approximately 650,000 dwellings now standing in Ireland, probably more than half were aided in some way by at least one of the programs established since 1890. (1965, 37)

However, this period also saw the gradual decline of local authority housing output relative to private output, a trend that continued in subsequent decades, leading to the growing residualisation of local authority housing, as housing for a minority of citizens rather than a majority as was the case until the 1950s.

Despite these achievements, the belief among key policy makers that housing needs of the country 'are virtually satisfied over wide areas of the State', was largely underpinned by levels of emigration unprecedented since Independence. In the view of Kam-Caudle (1967, 95) the belief 'was not supported by any evidence and is difficult to reconcile with the facts', with housing conditions in some parts of the country, and in particular in parts of Dublin, substandard. This became tragically evident on Sunday, 2 June 1963, when Leo and Mary Staples, two elderly residents of 20 Bolton Street in North city centre Dublin, were killed as a result of the collapse of their tenement. Just ten days later the collapse of tenements at 2a, 3, and 4 Fenian Street in the south city centre resulted in the deaths of Linda Byrne and Marion Vardy, two young girls who lived locally and happened to be passing the buildings when they collapsed.

These shocking events echoed the collapse of the Church Street tenements 50 years earlier, leading to what was known as the 'dangerous buildings scare' (Hanna, 2013, 113) as a further 900 houses were identified by Dublin Corporation as 'dangerous', that is, liable to collapse (Kaim-Caudle, 1965, 15), and according to Hanna (2013, 115) in 1963 and 1964 'around 1,200 of Dublin's Georgian terrace houses and mews were destroyed' and just over 1,800 families were displaced from these 'dangerous buildings' (Brady, 2016, 198). The families displaced by the demolitions were in some cases rehoused by Dublin Corporation, but some were temporarily placed in Griffith Barracks (women and children only) with the men placed in shelters, particularly the Model Lodging House run at the time by Dublin Corporation.

The official inquiry by Colm Condon SC into the collapse of the buildings concluded that there was no connection between the events (the collapse in Bolton Street the result of demolition works in adjacent buildings and in the case of Fenian Street, adverse weather conditions triggered the collapse). The inquiry exonerated Dublin Corporation in relation to their responsibility under the Dangerous Buildings legislation but noted that the Fenian Street buildings were deemed 'not fit for human habitation' (1963, 21) when inspected by Health Officers of Dublin Corporation earlier in the year.

Both families displaced by the 'dangerous buildings scare' which were privately owned, and other families on housing waiting list often turned down offers of housing in Dublin Corporation schemes, particularly 'Keogh Square, Benburb Street, Mount Pleasant Buildings and Corporation buildings, which were all well known for the substandard quality of the accommodation provided and social problems' (Hanna, 2013, 118). Michael Viney, the Irish Times investigative journalist, writing in 1966, suggested that Dublin Corporation were in effect dumping 'problem families' in one of the three Dublin ghettos (Keogh Square, Corporation Place or Mount Pleasant Buildings) and these housing complexes were largely demolished in the 1970s. Keogh Square, colloquially known as 'the Dungeons' (Sweetman, 1972), was repurposed as housing in 1924/5 from the Richmond Army Barracks in Inchicore (O'Meara, 2014; Fallon, 2021); Corporation Place or Buildings in the North Inner City, colloquially known as 'the Cages' was completed 1905, and Mount Pleasant Buildings in the suburb of Rathmines opened in 1931. Keogh Square was demolished in 1970, Corporation Buildings in 1972 and Mount Pleasant in 1977. These complexes, along with the other 'dump estates', the Marshalsea Barracks/Prison complex off Thomas Street, originally constructed in 1775, and Holyfield Building in Rathmines, constructed in 1903, were demolished respectively in 1975 and 1978.

Like the 1913 tenement collapse and symbolic failures in years to come, the 1963 collapses opened up an opportunity for reflection and the possibility of a new direction. In response to poor housing conditions, a National Building Agency was established in 1963 'to goad local authorities to build on an expanding scale' and their 'first and most significant jobs was the construction of the only large, high-rise estate in Ireland – Ballymun' (Power, 1993, 333–334). Constructed between 1966 and 1969, Ballymun comprised 2,621 flats and 400 houses, including seven 15-storey towers named after Irish republicans executed in the immediate aftermath of the 1916 rising.

3

Housing policy, housing agitation and the emergence of the homelessness sector, 1964–1981

Introduction

This chapter covers the period from 1964, when the *Programme for Economic Development* (1958) was beginning to impact on the economy through to a period of economic prosperity to the debt crisis of the early 1980s. The chapter covers a further round of reform in the County Homes along with efforts to close the Casual Wards, and the impact of deinstitutionalisation from psychiatric hospitals on homelessness. The period saw the publication of two *White Papers* on housing in 1964 and 1969, with the first one preparing the ground for the first national framework for delivering social housing, the *Housing Act, 1966*. The chapter will explore the role played by civil society organisations from the political movement, Dublin Housing Action Committee, to the new 'homeless sector', comprising NGOs that both provided services and agitated for changes in policy and provision. The chapter charts the most sustained period of social housing construction since the foundation of the State and sets it in the context of new, more generous schemes for the sale of social housing to tenants, resulting in a net reduction in the total social housing stock.

Political and economic context

This period covers five governments, four of which were single party Fianna Fáil administrations led by three different leaders, and one a Fine Gael/Labour Coalition (1973–1977). The period covers the opening up and growth in the Irish economy following the first *Programme for Economic Expansion* (1959–1963). The first period of three Fianna Fáil Governments ran from 1961–1973, led by Sean Lemass and then Jack Lynch. The 1973–1977 Fine Gael/Labour Coalition under Liam Cosgrave was followed by a further Fianna Fáil administration, the first to be led by Charles Haughey. The OECD in their 1964 report on Ireland noted that the previous five years 'witnessed Ireland's period of fastest economic growth in the century' (1964, 5), however along with economic and social progress, the period also saw a number of periods of recession and cutbacks. Ireland joined the European Economic Community (EEC) in 1973 (along with Denmark and Britain), a decision which was to have profound, largely positive, social and economic benefits for Ireland over the next 50 years (O Cinneide, 1992; O'Donnell, 2000; FitzGerald and Honohan, 2023); and in 1979, broke the historic link with sterling and joined the European Monetary Union (EMU) (O'Hagan, 2018).

Closing the Casual Wards

Despite the exhortations to reserve the County Homes for the aged and chronically sick as outlined in the Interdepartmental Committee Report of 1951, and the debate around the *Health Act 1953*, the use of County Homes for people who were homeless continued through to the early 1980s. In 1966, a White Paper on *The Health Services and their Further Development* noted that improvements had only taken place in nine of the County Homes (Government of Ireland, 1966, 47). On 31 March 1966, there were 214 'casuals' accommodated in the County Homes, with 120 over the age of 65. It was clearly envisaged that casuals would no longer be catered for in the County Homes noting that '[i]n the past, provision was made in them for the institutional shelter and maintenance of persons, not ill, but unable through social incompetence to provide for themselves' (Government of Ireland, 1966, 47). In an important shift in administrative responsibility and public policy, it was argued the County Homes should be reserved only for those requiring medical or nursing care but others, particularly elderly inmates not requiring such care, should be provided with housing by the local authorities rather than institutional care by the health authorities. It was noted that:

> The number of persons in County Homes at present who do not require medical and nursing care at hospital level is estimated at about 5,000. In present circumstances it would be unrealistic to ask housing authorities to build specifically for such large numbers in order that they could be taken out of County Homes as an immediate prospect. The intention is, however, that housing policy development of the future will pay special attention to the needs of the aged – This is dealt with in the recent White Paper on Housing and in the draft Housing Bill, 1965. Voluntary agencies will specifically be encouraged to play an active role. Pending the realisation of this policy approach, it is essential to humanise the existing conditions under which the 'social' cases live in County Homes without at the same time spending extravagantly on new buildings that should not be required as the housing policy approach materialises.[1]

Two years later an *Interdepartmental Committee on the Care of the Aged*, which recommended transforming the County Homes into geriatric homes, noted that while the casuals constituted a 'social problem' (Inter-Departmental Committee on the Care of the Aged, 1968, 87) it was not in their terms of reference to make any recommendations in relation to them. However, State policy, such as it was, still saw the provision of services for those experiencing homelessness as requiring the rehabilitative and reformative input of charitable bodies, rather than being a function of Local Government. The acknowledgement that elderly people should be provided with their own dwellings by local authorities was to pave the way to the gradual inclusion of groups, other than traditional families with children, to be provided with State funded housing rather than institutional provision.

Deinstitutionalisation and homelessness

The gradual closure of the County Homes, Psychiatric Hospitals and Reformatory and Industrial Schools were part of a wave of deinstitutionalisation that occurred across the Global North in the 1950s and 1960s. In terms of sheer number of inmates, psychiatric hospitals (or mental asylums) were a distinctive feature of the institutional landscape and Ireland had the highest number of inmates in the world, with a commission established in the 1960s to explore the system. In their report, the *Commission of Inquiry on Mental Illness* (Government of Ireland, 1966, 24–25) commented that 'Statistics in respect of different countries may not be directly comparable, but, even if allowance is made for this, the number of in-patients in Ireland seems to be extremely high – it appears to be the highest in the world. It is hard to explain this.'

More recent scholarship has argued that 'despite a high rate of psychiatric hospitalisation, there is insufficient evidence to conclude that Ireland ever had a higher rate of mental disorder than elsewhere', rather 'Ireland had an epidemic of mental hospitals rather than an epidemic of mental illness' (Kelly, 2022, 123). Following Independence from Britain and the partition of Ireland, the asylum system continued to operate much the same as it did in the pre-Independence era. Despite the loss of six district asylums following partition, the number of inmates rose continuously from the foundation of the State and reached a peak of 20,046 in 1958 or 742 per 100,000 population distributed across 22 institutions. From the mid-1960s, the psychiatric hospital population gradually began to decline, prompted by the publication of the *Commission on Mental Illness* in 1966 (Walsh and Daly, 2004). By the early 1980s, the psychiatric hospital population was half what it had been in the early 1960s and again, following on the publication of a review of psychiatric services in 1984 – *The Psychiatric Services: Planning for the Future* – the population continued to decline to just over 2,000 patients in 2024 (Daly, Lovett and Lynn, 2025).

The voluminous literature on psychiatric deinstitutionalisation in the United States suggests there was direct correlation between rising homelessness and psychiatric deinstitutionalisation. In contrast, although the psychiatric in-patient population declined from just under 19,000 in 1964 to just under 14,000 in 1981, there appears to have been no noticeable impact on homelessness services in Ireland. More recent research on deinstitutionalisation in the United States has also argued that it is difficult to make 'empirical connections between deinstitutionalization and homelessness' (Montgomery et al, 2013, 61). This also applies to the Irish case with no evidence to suggest that the dramatic decline in the psychiatric hospital population resulted in an increase in homelessness either as a result of discharging patients or individuals accessing homelessness services in the increasing absence of psychiatric hospital beds.

Mother and Baby Homes and Magdalen Asylums or Laundries were also in terminal decline by the end of the 1960s, although they continued to operate until the 1990s. Earner-Byrne (2023, 276) argues that this came about because

> adoption was more accessible and acceptable, and social attitudes to sexuality and single mothers were changing. Crucially, the availability of legal abortion in England forced contemporaries to re-evaluate the impact of a hostile climate for single mothers in Ireland leading, among other things, to a welfare payment for single mothers.

Magdalen Asylums in particular provided accommodation to women experiencing homelessness (O'Sullivan, 2016; Prunty, 2017). The numbers of children in residential Reformatory and Industrial Schools were also in terminal decline (O'Sullivan, 2014), but in this case, the emergence of youth homelessness in 1970s is attributable in large part to the closure of these institutions (O'Sullivan and Mayock, 2008) and is discussed in great detail later in the chapter.

Attitudes to homelessness, vagrancy and the law

Homelessness in this period was still associated, in the media at least, with dysfunctional alcoholic men. In an article in the magazine *Nusight*, Feeney, Ruddy and Browne (1969) wrote that:

> The weaknesses of vagrants are unattractive. They may drink methylated spirits, petrol, embalming fluid, even take boot polish, for a mental escape from the harshness of their condition. Their failings

ensure that they do not live far beyond the line of survival, and their isolation renders them as incapable of enjoying any provision made for their betterment as they were of preventing their decline. The problem is psychological and social, and while the mechanics of modern society do not allow for the heterodoxy of the inadequate, it is a problem that will endure.

In more general terms, the article stated that:

In terms of vagrancy Ireland has a dismal record. The extensive social displacement that has been inflicted on succeeding generations of Irish families has increased the likelihood of vagrancy amongst them and the less competent have fallen by the wayside. No one knows how many vagrants there are in Ireland. The Society of St. Vincent de Paul, which is one of the most active organisations in this field, believes that there are in the region of 1,000 homeless men sleeping rough in Dublin each night. These would by no means all be vagrants, and the process of natural selection probably ensures that for the majority their ill-fortune is transitory.

As we shall see, this period is characterised by demands from civic society organisations and commentators for greater State intervention to assist people who were homeless, however, as O'Brien (1979, 7) noted, one of society's few concrete attempts to intervene in the lives of the homeless was the arrest of homeless people by the Gardaí, and sometimes their imprisonment. As noted in the previous chapter, sleeping rough or 'wandering abroad' and 'not giving a good account of himself or herself' were offences under Section 4 of the *Vagrancy Act, 1824*, as applied to Ireland under the *Prevention of Crimes Act, 1871*, as were begging, frequenting or loitering in certain places. Offences under the Vagrancy Acts, primarily for the offence of begging, continued during this period, but a steady reduction in the number of offences recorded is evident from the mid-1970s onwards. Equally, the number of committals to prison per annum declined steadily over this period, and from 1980, the numbers committed under the Vagrancy Acts are not recorded in the Annual Prison Statistical Reports, presumably due to the very small number of committals. From the 1960s onwards, the majority of the committals were for begging.

Given the relative invisibility of homeless women over this period, it is of note that 27 per cent of all prison committals under the Vagrancy Acts were women. However, it is likely that a significant number were members of the Traveller community. Based on fieldwork conducted in Dublin in the early 1970s, American anthropologists George Gmelch and Sharon Bohn Gmelch (1978) concluded that the vast majority of beggars observed were female members of the Traveller community, with an American geographer, Kearns (1977, 542), noting that Traveller men refrained from begging, because it reflected badly on 'their masculine pride rather than a disapproval of the activity itself' and 'a practical recognition that women and children can better elicit sympathy and compassion from the settled population'.

This echoed the Government appointed *Report of the Commission on Itinerancy*, which reported in 1963 that men did not beg 'partly due to masculine pride but mostly due to the fact that the women are more successful at it owing to their greater persistence and their control over the younger children whom they use with great skill in the begging operations' (1963, 91). More generally, it appears that members of the Traveller community were disproportionately represented in the prison population. For example, The Commission on Itinerancy reported that 154 'itinerants' were committed under sentence of imprisonment in 1961 and 357 in 1962 (1963, 157). This represented 9.6 and 22.4 per cent of total committals in these years and 5.5 and 12.9 per cent of the total Traveller population over the age of 14, based on the Census of Travellers in 1961.

The emergence of youth homelessness

The recognition of youth homelessness as a distinct category of homelessness can be traced to 1966, when a category 'homeless' appeared in the annual reports of the Department of Education as a reason for committal to an Industrial School (this section and material on youth homelessness in Chapter 4 draws largely on O'Sullivan and Mayock, 2008). This situation does not reflect an absence of children who were without accommodation prior to this period; rather, the Industrial, alongside Reformatory Schools effectively absorbed such children, but labelled them as 'wandering abroad' from the mid-19th century. They maintained this role until the system gradually reshaped itself as small-scale residential care units some 100 years later in the 1970s (for further details, see O'Sullivan, 2009).

In 1974, the Minister for Health at that time, Brendan Corish, established a *Task Force on Child Care Services*. Within a year of its establishment, the Task Force issued an interim report stating that they had been able to isolate a number of major gaps in the existing range of services requiring attention as a matter of great urgency. In relation to homeless children, the interim report argued that additional accommodation was needed for 'older boys who have no fixed abode', with the Task Force estimating that, in addition to those boys residing in the available hostels, a further 30 had no fixed abode and, on this basis, concluded that additional hostel accommodation was required.

In 1975, a new lay voluntary organisation was established to provide accommodation for young people, particularly boys, who were sleeping rough. HOPE was founded by a German student Win Schickle who, when visiting Dublin, was struck by the number of children sleeping rough (Harvey and Menton, 1989). The founders of HOPE estimated that there were at least 60 under-18s sleeping rough in Dublin every night based on a relatively crude assessment of the extent of youth homelessness.

Social movements and civic society

Until this point, the primary response of what we would now call civic society, was the provision of emergency accommodation by faith-based organisations to people who were 'down-and-out'. As we have seen, the development of such responses was encouraged – if not funded – by the State. While many County Homes continued to provide shelter for people who were homeless, public policy clearly favoured a position where this form of voluntary organisation provided support for the homeless.

From the mid-1960s we saw, for the first time, a different form of social movement which did not seek to provide services but mobilised to challenge Government policy on housing and homelessness (Acheson et al, 2004). Appalling housing conditions had been an issue in urban and rural areas since before the foundation of the State, and while this had been a concern of the Labour Movement, Republicanism and other social movements, it had never before been the primary focus of any social movement. This was to change from the mid-1960s.

In addition, parallel developments by civic society organisations such as Cherish and the Women's Liberation Movement were responsible for the introduction of an unmarried mother's allowance in 1973 (Richards, 1998; Grimes, 2023). Significantly improved services for those with an intellectual disability (Kilgannon, 2023) for example, ensured a more favourable political and social environment for those campaigning on behalf of those experiencing homelessness. More generally, in this period civil society organisations such as *Tuairim* produced a series of influential pamphlets which prompted debate on topics such as residential child welfare services and the aims of social policy (Finn, 2012). Campaigning journalists such as Michael Viney were providing in-depth articles in the *Irish Times* on topics previously barely discussed in public, such as mental illness (1962), the situation of unmarried mothers (1964), young offenders (1966) and marriage breakdown (1970).

In addition, within the Catholic Church 'the emphasis on charity of earlier decades was replaced by one of active participation. Activist priests and religious figures such as Austin Flannery, Kevin Crowley, and Michael Sweetman – were instrumental in raising awareness of social justice issues in the 1960s and 1970s, often drawing the ire of government ministers' (O Corrian, 2024, 157). Ironically, the greater involvement of Catholic clerics in social issues was at a time when the number of vocations to Catholic Congregations and Dioceses was plummeting, from 1,409 vocations in 1966 to 560 in 1978 (Inglis, 1979). More institutionally, the Catholic Hierarchy were responding to the challenges posed by *Economic Development* by developing a distinctive social science perspective on development (Murray and Feeney, 2017) and engaging with the newly established *Raidió Teilifís Éireann* (RTÉ) in 1960 *via* a documentary programme *Radharc*. Radharc produced a documentary on homelessness entitled 'Down and Out in Dublin' in 1964 – as part of the broader impact of the Second Vatican Council on shaping Catholic ideas on poverty and welfare (Keogh, 1994; Holohan, 2020; Earner-Byrne, 2024).

Politically, during this period Fine Gael partially and temporarily endorsed a broadly social democratic approach to social policy under the banner of a *Just Society* (Meehan, 2013), where their 1965 election manifesto *Towards a Just Society* noted the 'very wide areas in our society where great poverty exists, poverty which is degrading and capable of remedy, to appalling social conditions. We are not living in a just society' (Fine Gael, 1965, 3). The Labour Party was also moving to the left and advocating welfare reform and 'Fianna Fáil responded to increased electoral competition over social issues by emphasising its own commitment to social spending and reform of social welfare programmes' (O'Connell and Rottman, 1992, 235). The Sinn Féin party was also focusing on social issues during this period, rather than simply the National Question and partition; hence, it was a period of unparalleled social activism and debate in Ireland.

Dublin Housing Action Committee

The most prominent expression of this activism that addressed the issue of housing (and homelessness) was the Dublin Housing Action Committee (DHAC) which was founded in 1967 (McEneaney, 2019). According to Hanley and Millar, the DHAC emerged from the work of Sinn Féin, in particular 'from the work of the citizens' advice bureau and the IRA's general strategy, the DHAC sought to bring together republican activists and other radicals in a campaign involving the homeless themselves' (2009, 88).

They suggest that Prionsias de Rossa (then a Sinn Féin activist and later in the 1990s, the Minister for Social Protection) was the 'prime mover' (2009, 89) in establishing the DHAC, and that most prominent actors were members of Sinn Féin. But DHAC also included members of various Communist organisations including Michael O'Riordan, General Secretary the Communist Party of Ireland and Denis and Mary Dennehy from the Irish Communist Organisation.[2] The aforementioned Jesuit priest, Fr Michael Sweetman, who was known for his work with young offenders and young people leaving care, was also actively involved as was a Dominican Priest, Fr Austin Flannery, described by the then Minister for Finance, Charles Haughey, as 'a gullible cleric'. This was in reaction to a late-night television programme, *Outlook*, in which Fr Flannery departed from the usual devotional format to involve Fr Michael Sweetman and Michael O'Riordan in discussing the housing crisis in Dublin. To the accusation of being a Communist, Fr Flannery would retort that sitting down with Michael O'Riordan no more made him a Communist than sitting down with Michael Sweetman made him a Jesuit. Equally, more secular documentaries like *7 Days* addressed topics such as 'emigration, homelessness, discrimination against Travellers and the plight of unmarried mothers' (Holohan, O'Connell and Savage, 2021, 283) and contributed to a heightened awareness of these social issues, gradually leading to what McCashin (1982, 211) argues was the increasing universalism of social provision and the growing professionalism of social services.

More generally, Holohan (2016, 40) argues that the housing issue 'made for a highly visible manifestation of poverty in this period. Sustained media coverage was given to Dublin's crumbling tenements, the use of army barracks and caravans to house those displaced, and the plight of the increasing number of young married couples who could not find a first home.' Both Holohan (2016) and Earner-Byrne (2017) note the number of letters to Archbishop McQuaid on housing conditions in Dublin, with Holohan (2016, 47) noting that '[p]oor living conditions, exorbitant rents, eviction, homelessness, condemned buildings, squatting and emergency accommodation all feature in the charity letters sent to McQuaid'.

By 1968,

> the DHAC had brought together members of the Communist Party, the Labour Party, Sinn Féin, the Citizens Advice Bureau, Maoists, Trotskyites, members of the Salvation Army, members of the St. Vincent de Paul Society, members of the Irish Student Movement, students in Trinity College and University College Dublin Republican Clubs, a member of the Catholic clergy, and Hilary Boyle, an eccentric heiress. (Keenan-Thomson, 2006, 131–132)

DHAC explicitly linked their demand for affordable housing with the problem of homelessness – but they set out a much broader concept of homelessness than casual residents of County Homes and 'down-and-outs'. In the first explicit definition of homelessness in Ireland, the DHAC regarded as homeless:

- Split families: father and mother and children unable to live together.
- The severely overcrowded.
- Married couples living in property where children are not allowed.
- Families obliged to live with their parents-in-law.
- Families obliged to pay rent excessive in relation to their income.

- Fatherless families: mothers and children with no male support, for example widows and deserted wives.
- The statutory homeless, who have been taken into local authority reception centres.
- Most caravan-dwelling families.
- Squatting families who have been forced to squat on either private or Corporation property.

The DHAC published at least two editions of their magazine *Crisis*, both published in 1969, and at least one edition of a short bulletin entitled *Squatter*.[3] The magazines provided updates on the various campaigns, interviews, letters to the editor and occasional 'warnings'. For example, in Crisis No. 2:

> The Dublin Housing Action Committee hereby issues a warning to Mr. John Fearon, 28, Dolphins Barn, that if he ever again engages in the wanton destruction of facilities which are being used by the homeless of Dublin, or if he interferes with, or tries to intimidate members of this Committee, as he did on the 18th of July '69, he can expect to suffer the consequences for such inhuman acts. (1969, 2)

The editorial in Crisis No. 1, sets out the agenda for the DHAC as seeking to 'organise all the homeless people in Dublin into a mass militant body to agitate against the appalling housing situation that now exists'. It stated that the DHAC is

> a non-political and non-sectarian organisation of homeless people that to date has had limited successes in focusing public attention on the housing shortage, in stopping evictions and in protecting tenants from the arrogance of extremist landlords. However, we realise that as yet we have only scratched the surface but, judging from the response to our recent demonstration we believe that the potential for the future is enormous.

By 1970, according to Hanley and Scott, the DHAC was in decline 'due to a combination of activists' concentration on Northern issues and the Gardaí's adoption of a more belligerent approach' (2009, 238), and that a siege in a property in Pembroke Road in May 1970 'marked "the last hurrah of the squatter"' (2009, 239; see also Kenny, 2023). It also reflected the divisions between the Irish Communist Organisation, Sinn Féin and the Irish Workers' Party on the involvement of political activists in the DHAC. The Irish Communist Organisation (ICO) (later the British and Irish Communist Organisation), in a detailed 40-page pamphlet entitled *The Housing Crisis and the Working Class*, argued that they in fact had established the DHAC not Sinn Féin, stating that they had 'been working since 1965 to develop an organisation of the homeless (as distinct from a bourgeois organisation for the homeless), through which the homeless could take direct action relevant to their situation' (1970, 34). The ICO saw the role of Sinn Féin and the Communist Party of Ireland as merely opportunistic, and in the view of ICO, 'the efforts of these opportunists to tame the DHAC and make it non-political have recently been successful' (ICO, 1970, 34–35). As a result, ICO resigned from the DHAC.

Campaigning for the single homeless

While the DHAC included 'the statutorily homeless' in their concerns, their primary focus was on the situation of families that were in various forms of homelessness. From the late 1960s, other newly formed non-governmental bodies, particularly the Simon Community, repeatedly highlighted the limited range of services available for people experiencing homelessness, particularly the single homeless, and specifically the absence of clear statutory responsibility between housing and health authorities for assisting people experiencing homelessness (Harvey, 1985), and the impact of this campaign on housing legislation will be discussed in the next chapter.

The Simon Community, named after Simon of Cyrene who carried the cross of Jesus of Nazareth as he was taken to his crucifixion, was established in England in 1963 by Anton-Wallich-Clifford, a probation officer, with the dual objectives of 'creating an experimental venture in care and being an alerting body concerned to draw the attention of the public and the Government to the homeless problem' (Wallich-Clifford, 1976, 19). The Simon Communities in England were avowedly Christian in philosophy, however, the Simon Communities in Ireland were avowedly secular, with the first community founded in Dublin in 1969 following a visit to Dublin by Wallich-Clifford where he addressed a public meeting in Trinity College (see Hart, 1978 and Coleman, 1990 for the origins of the Simon Community in Dublin). Operating a soup-run initially (which still operates today), Jim Murray, the first full-time worker, recollected remonstrating with representatives of the Legion of Mary Hostel for women, the Regina Coeli, about their admittance policy, to be told 'that "we were helping people long before you were heard of", which was true but irrelevant. It was experiences like that which heightened our already well-developed sense of seeing ourselves as a new and radical alternative to existing organisations and indeed to the existing order' (Murray,1989, 3).

Adult homelessness in the early 1970s: extent and service provision

The first survey of services for people experiencing homelessness was conducted by the aforementioned newly formed Simon Community in Dublin in 1971, funded by the Medico-Social Research Board (Ó Cinneide and Mooney, 1972). The survey identified 14 shelters/hostels providing just over 1,300 beds for adults experiencing homelessness, with one hostel, the Iveagh, having 408 beds.[4] Seventy-five per cent catered for men. Less than 10 per cent were provided by statutory health or Local Government providers and the majority were closed during the day. They also identified 196 rough sleepers, either on the streets, or who were intermittently using shelters, of whom 16 were female.

By 1977, the number of rough sleepers had declined to 20 according to Hart (1978), which he attributed to the provision of shelter and other residential services by the Simon Community. Hart also conducted a survey of 82 residents of the Simon Community services, the majority of whom were male: nearly half had never married, nearly two-thirds had no contact with family and two-thirds had spent time in prison, a psychiatric hospital, a children's home or a County Home. The *National Economic and Social Council*[5] estimated that the 'number of people who are homeless, including those squatting in local authority premises, is likely to be at least 2,000–3,000' (NESC, 1976a, 110), but did not provide a source for this estimate.

In a relatively uncommon, nuanced analysis of the question of the extent of homelessness in Dublin, Leahy and Magee (1976, 8–9) argued that:

> This we feel is an impossible question to answer no matter how many surveys one might carry out. At the very best, one can only give a very rough estimate. There are many reasons for this:
>
> a. Within any large centre of population, there is a constant movement in and out of the homeless situation. Thus, the number of homeless people at any one time depends on such factors as the overall economic situation. This relates more specifically to employment – the unskilled labour market, e.g. building industry, the casual labour market and seasonal employment. The state of the traditional labour market in the United Kingdom is also a factor.
> b. The price and availability of cheap accommodation is also a factor
> c. The rate of movement of population from rural to urban areas is relevant
> d. There is also a migration of single homeless people from one centre of population to another. We have noticed recently the reappearance of old faces in the city after an absence of many months.
> e. There are also a number of people both single and married who live in intolerable permanent accommodation. These people live in dreadful conditions under severe pressure and are constantly on the brink of total breakdown. When this happens, they very often enter the homeless circuit for varying periods of time. We would estimate, taking into consideration the number of different people

we have seen, that the average numbers staying in hostels, sleeping rough and in 'skippers', to be between 1,200 and 1,500.

In the mid-1970s, a dedicated health service was being provided to people experiencing homelessness in Dublin by a newly established voluntary body called Trust (Leahy, 1974; Leahy and Dempsey 1995, Leahy, 2018), and a Programme for the Homeless was established in the St. Brendan's Psychiatric Hospital in North Dublin (Fernandez, 1995). A day centre also opened in Bow Street in the late 1960s under the auspices of the Capuchin Franciscan Friars and still operates today, as does Trust. The number of hostel beds available in Dublin were deemed sufficient by the Dublin Diocesan Welfare Committee in a Report on Vagrancy in 1974, but the Committee noted that there were approximately 40 males and 10–12 females who regularly slept rough but were well known to services and did periodically use the hostels. The Committee were of the opinion 'that the time is opportune to establish some form of structure involving voluntary and statutory agencies to implement a gradual rationalisation and co-ordination of services' (Dublin Diocesan Welfare Committee, 1974, 6).

Facilities in the hostels in Dublin ranged from 'good to primitive' according to Leahy in her survey of the medical services available to those who were homeless in Dublin (1974, 8). A broadly similar assessment was provided in an *Economic and Social Research Institute* monograph on housing in Ireland where the authors noted that 'hostels appear to offer sufficient quantity of crude shelter on a day-to-day basis, but neither the physical conditions of this shelter nor its organisational arrangements make it acceptable as a stable living environment to its occupants' (Baker and O'Brien, 1979, 143). In addition to the various night shelters, those experiencing homelessness also spent spells in the various psychiatric hospitals, with nearly 500 termed as *No Fixed Abode* (NFA) admissions in 1974. Over 80 per cent were male admissions and three-quarters were recorded as single and two-thirds under 45 years of age (Medico-Social Research Board, 1979, 33).

O'Brien (1979, 2) provides an evocative description of homelessness in Dublin in the 1970s. Those experiencing homelessness were single and

> chronically poor. Most are unemployed and some unemployable. They are usually unskilled workers who stand little chance of employment in our modern, consumer society, and their ill-health and personal disabilities reduce their chances even more. Consequently, they have to depend almost exclusively on State welfare benefits to survive … For such a person to survive in Dublin means sleeping in one the 9 hostels (seven of which are run by voluntary groups, one by the Iveagh trust, and one by the Corporation). Hostel living entails sharing a room with others like yourself or paying extra for a cubicle if you can

afford it. It means being out by 9 a.m. and sometimes having to be in by 7.30 p.m. The cost of a night's stay varies from being free of charge to £1.70, so there is little left for food, and penny dinners, usually provided by religious orders, have to fill the gap.

For a number of the hostels, 'the nineteenth century idea of moral defectiveness is still attached to the single homeless' (O'Brien, 1981, 90). Nationally, there were 25 hostels operated by voluntary bodies and 13 institutions, mainly Casual Wards, operated by the regional Health Boards by the early 1980s (Housing Centre, 1986).

Outside of Dublin, little was known about homelessness, but Simon Communities were established in Cork in 1971, Dundalk in 1973 and Galway in 1979.[6] In the case of Galway Simon, the Community conducted a survey of the extent of single homelessness in the city and the services available to them. Only two shelters, both run by the Legion of Mary, with nine beds for males and six for females, provided temporary accommodation for casuals. However, it was estimated that there were 25 males in need of nightly accommodation in Galway. Those who could not access the Legion of Mary Shelters slept rough (Galway Simon Community, 1980). In response, the Simon Community sought to establish a shelter for those men. However, it was to take over three years to establish a 15-bed prefabricated shelter, which was to be run in conjunction with the Galway Social Service Council (see Mac Riocaird, 1989 for a detailed account of the extraordinary barriers that the Simon Community faced in attempting a establish a shelter in Galway).

Housing policy

As noted earlier, the 1966 report on the *Future of Health Services* concluded that 'little point in spending extravagantly on new buildings that should not be required as the housing policy approach materialises'. Although the primary reference is to older people in the Causal Wards of County Homes, this represents not only one of the first statements in public policy of the link between homelessness and housing but was also a strong expression of optimism about the delivery of housing and its impact on homelessness.

White Paper: *Housing – Progress and Prospects*

In 1964, the Fianna Fáil Minister for Local Government, Neil Blaney, published a new White Paper on Housing, *Housing – Progress and Prospects*. It noted that between 1880 and 1964, 178,368 dwellings had been built by local authorities, considerably exceeding the 126,191 dwellings built by private enterprise over the same period. Government grants provided for the reconstruction of a further 126,501 dwellings. The White Paper also highlighted the age of the Irish housing stock, with 300,000 dwellings over 60 years old and 160,000 over 100 years old out of a total stock of only 676,000. Curiously, in light of the collapse of the tenement buildings in the year previous to its publication, no mention of this is made in the White Paper.

The White Paper estimated that 14,000 new dwellings were required per annum and while recognising that private building (albeit with substantial public subsidies) would now provide more dwellings than local authorities, the White Paper reaffirmed the centrality of the role of local authorities in housing provision, stressing that

> [t]o meet the needs of those unable to house themselves even with the assistance of grants and loans, and particularly to eliminate unfit housing and overcrowding, which must be a first charge on any housing programme, local authorities will be encouraged to increase their output of dwellings substantially, their level of output being reviewed periodically in light of the progress being made. (Government of Ireland, 1964, 26)

It also noted that the legislative basis for housing policy was contained in over 50 acts, many dating back to the 19th century, and proposed new comprehensive legislation to govern the provision of housing. Arising from this recommendation and reflecting the increasing prominence of housing on the public agenda, the *Housing Act, 1966* was passed which repealed in whole or in part 60 previous acts. This legislation stressed the key role of the local authorities in providing, managing and funding housing for those unable to provide housing from their own resources; providing a scheme of financial assistance to individuals to enable them to purchase their own homes, and financial assistance to sitting tenants to purchase their own homes. It was this act that provided the basis for the optimism that new housing would obviate the need for the construction of temporary accommodation for people who were homeless.

While there was a strong commitment to delivering social housing, it is important to note that the primary focus of housing policy continued to be to increase private owner-occupancy. Writing in the mid-1960s, Peter Kaim-Caudle (1965, 16) observed that:

> The major objectives of government housing policy have remained virtually unaltered since the foundation of the State. They can be summarised under four headings: to encourage owner-occupation, to maintain and improve the stock of dwellings, to increase the number of dwellings and to keep rents down to such levels as tenants are willing and able to pay. All the various measures adopted – grants for

owner-occupiers of new dwellings; rate remissions; grants for supply of water, sewerage and for general improvements; subsidised rents for Local Council tenants; rent restrictions - were directed to achieve these objectives and on balance, did so successfully.

White Paper: *Housing in the Seventies*

Five years after the publication of the 1964 White Paper, a further one, *Housing in the Seventies*, was published in 1969 by the subsequent Fianna Fáil Government with Kevin Boland as Minister for Local Government. Over the five years between 1964 and 1969, just over 18,000 local authority and 39,000 private households had been constructed, and 86,000 houses were reconstructed or improved with State grants. For the first time, the White Paper articulated the overall objectives of housing policy which they viewed as ensuring 'that, as far as the resources of the economy permit, every family can obtain a house of good standard at a price or rent they can afford' (1969, 3). The White Paper noted the shift from the position where local authorities had provided the majority of new dwellings: by the end of the 1960s, private provision of housing, with State aid, was producing considerably more housing units than local authorities. The shift was brought about, the paper suggested, by greater prosperity allowing more households to purchase their own dwellings; the demand to replace unfit and overcrowded accommodation had become less important over time for local authorities. The paper somewhat downplays the role of State subsidies in achieving this shift and promoting homeownership. By the early 1980s, Baker (1984, 88–89) noted no less than 15 specific financial forms of encouragement for homeownership, which he described as 'an impressive, and not necessarily exhaustive list of inducements to owner-occupation'.

Kenny Report

In January 1971, the Minister for Local Government, Bobby Molloy of Fianna Fáil, established a *Committee on the Price of Building Land* chaired by John Kenny, a Judge of the High Court. The impetus for the establishment of the Committee was 'that between the beginning of 1963 and the end of 1971 the average price of serviced land in County Dublin increased by 530%. In the same period the consumer price index increased by about 64%' (Committee on the Price of Building Land, 1973, 3). Reporting in 1973, the Majority report of the Committee recommended that local authorities should be able to compulsorily acquire undeveloped lands at existing use value plus 25 per cent which they argued was 'a reasonable compromise between the rights of the community and those of the landowners' (Committee on the Price of Building Land, 1973, 40). The Minority report, authored by the two representatives of the Department of Local Government on the Committee, argued that it was not justifiable 'that land should be made available for development by taking it from its owners and paying them a price which is less than its market value' (Committee on the Price of Building Land, 1973, 84). For the past 50 years, and somewhat simplifying complex discussions in both the Majority and Minority Reports, despite repeated calls to implement the key recommendations of the Majority Report, which as O Broin (2019, 39) has observed, 'have been quoted as much as they have been ignored', the view of the Minority report has prevailed (see Mansergh, 2024, 39–54 for a more detailed discussion of the report and various debates on iterations of the key recommendations).

Local authority housing

With the passing of the *Housing Act, 1966*, local authorities had embarked on the most sustained programme of large-scale building in the history of the State that saw 91,172 units constructed in the 14 years between 1967 and 1981 (see Figure 3.1). Nearly 4,000 units were built in 1967, rising to just under 9,000 in 1975, with between 6,000–7,000 units completed each year until 1981. This allowed for nearly 86,000 lettings by local authorities to be made between 1966 and 1981 with a record 8,079 lettings in 1975 alone.

Despite this substantial increase in provision, problems remained. In 1974 a number of pilot schemes to combat poverty were established, covering the period from 1974–1980. In the final report from the National Committee appointed to oversee the projects, it was observed that

> It is particularly significant that in practically all the projects and the urban ones in particular, problems relating to housing arose; long waiting periods for local authority housing, difficulty in getting maintenance and repairs carried out, the complexities of the local authority 'points system'. the specific problems of single parents and women not legally separated, the inadequacies of inner-city housing, the lack of security and rights of private sector tenants etc. (1980, 250)

In addition, in a pioneering study of a local authority housing estate completed in the 1950s in Limerick to house families who were living in slum conditions in the city, Ryan (1967), based on field work carried out in the mid-1960s, provided a prescient account of the difficulties encountered in such estates in the absence of community and social facilities, poor management and maintenance of dwellings, high rates of unemployment and early school leaving.

The emergence of the homelessness sector, 1964–1981

Figure 3.1: Social housing completions, 1923–1981

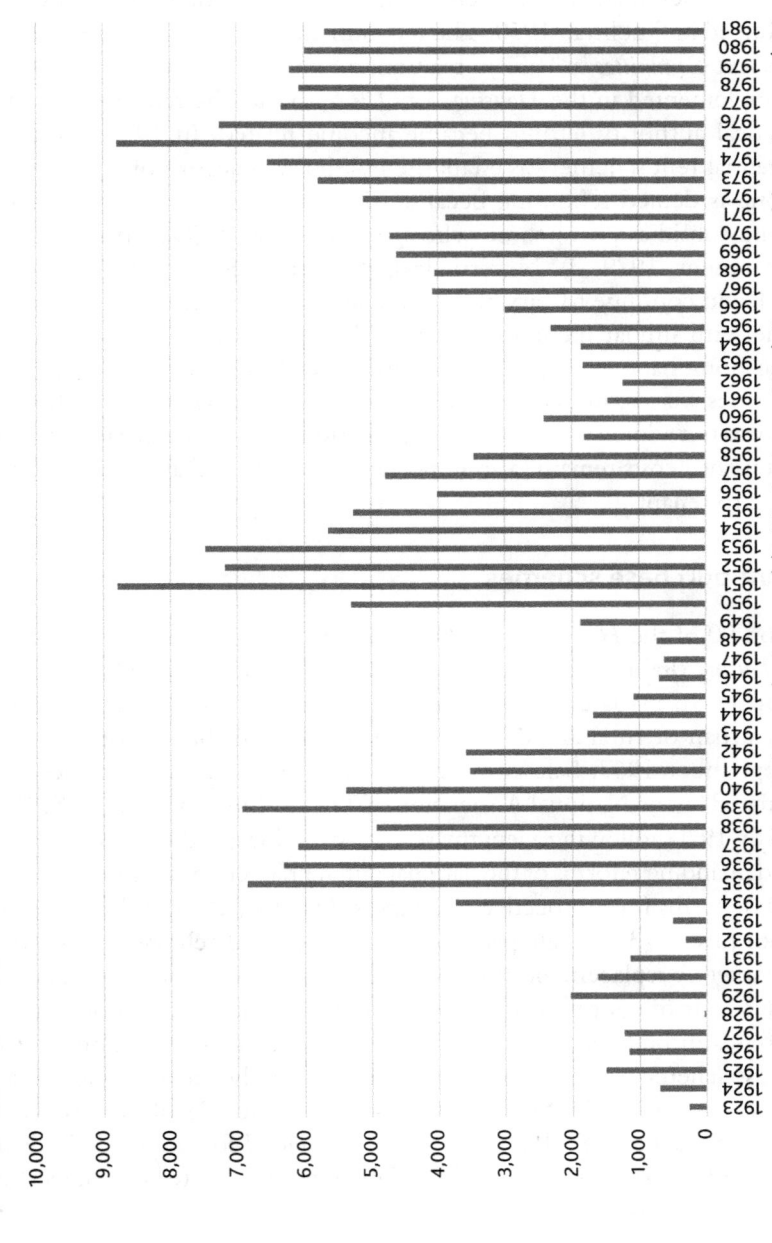

Source: Department of Local Government and Public Health Annual Report (various years) (Dublin: Stationery Office). Department of the Environment (various years): Annual Housing Statistics Bulletin (Dublin: Department of the Environment).

Differential rent

As noted in Chapter 1, differential rent, that is rent based on household income rather than a fixed rent, originated in Cork in 1930 and was introduced in Dublin in 1950. The recommendation of the *Capital Advisory Investment Committee* in 1957 in relation to rents for local authority housing was implemented in the *Housing Act, 1966*, so that the rent payable on all new local authority lettings became income related. In 1973, a national differential rent scheme was established with the objective of ensuring that 'no one is denied rehousing because of an inability to pay rent and that housing subsidies go to those who need them most' (Department of the Environment, 1979, 3). Nevertheless, the exact details of the means test varied, and continue to vary, from local authority to local authority so that people with similar incomes are charged quite different levels of rent for similar homes across different local authorities. The question of how local authorities were to fund the construction and maintenance of their housing stock was not addressed in these policy decisions, and avoidance of the future maintenance costs remained an important factor in local authority attitudes to sales to tenants.

Tenant purchase schemes

Section 90 of the *Housing Act, 1966* replaced the provisions for sale under the *Housing (Ireland) Act, 1919* and the *Labourers Act, 1936*, allowing local authorities to prepare a scheme for the sale of their houses to tenants in either urban or rural areas. This provision was brought into operation on 30 September 1967. Sales were modest until revised sales schemes were negotiated by the National Association of Tenants Organisations (NATO) in the early 1970s following a lengthy rent strike by local authority tenants who were demanding reforms of the national differential rent system and improved purchase terms for prospective purchasers (Hayden, 2014; Tubridy, 2024).

Until July 1973, the sale price of local authority dwellings was based on the market or replacement value of the houses less a discount of 3 per cent for each year of continuous tenancy, subject to a maximum of 30 per cent for houses in built-up areas and 45 per cent elsewhere. A national tenant purchase scheme was introduced in July 1973, mainly due to strong reaction from tenants and public representatives against the sale of houses on the basis of 'market value'. The new scheme provided for the sale of existing houses to tenants on the basis of the following general terms, subject to a minimum sale price of £100:

- the original all-in cost of the house updated to current money values by use of a Central Statistics Office Value of Money Table;

- a discount of 3 per cent per annum for length of tenancy up to a maximum discount of 30 per cent in built-up areas and 45 per cent in other areas; and
- a discount of £900 representing the ordinary State and supplementary new house grants and the capitalised value of a remission of rates over nine years.

Not surprisingly, the number of sales rose rapidly, with nearly 12,000 in 1974 alone. The National Economic and Social Council (NESC) in their report on *Housing Subsidies* (1976b, 21–22) noted that this rate of sales could result in local authorities being 'left managing the most unattractive portion of the dwelling stock'. Significantly, for the first time the sales policy was criticised by NESC as 'short-sighted' on the basis that 'the State is disposing of its dwelling stock on very concessionary terms' (1976b, 22), a criticism that was to become a constant refrain by NESC in their observations on housing policy in subsequent decades. Equally the *Economic and Social Research Institute* in their overview of the Irish housing system (Baker and O'Brien, 1979, 241) argued trenchantly that the subsidy available to tenant purchasers under the 1973 scheme 'is impossible to justify and that a substantial reduction in the level of point-of-sale subsidy would improve both the equity and the efficiency of the housing system, while releasing considerable funds for redeployment within or beyond the field of housing.'

In 1974, the peak point of social housing construction was reached with just under 9,000 units completed, while in the previous year the peak point of tenant purchases saw almost 12,000 units sold, resulting in a substantial fall in the total social housing stock. In July 1978 the terms of the national tenant purchase scheme were revised, providing for a discount of £1,300 in every case in lieu of the new house grant of £1,000 payable to first-time owner occupiers (replacing the existing State and supplementary house grants) and £300 in respect of rates paid by tenants. Various new schemes were introduced in subsequent years which largely updated the CSO Value of Money Table.

Abolition of domestic rates

In 1977, the incoming Fianna Fáil Government implemented one of their election promises, the full abolition of domestic rates, which was legislated for in the *Local Government (Financial Provisions) Act 1978*. The previous Fine Gael-Labour Coalition had promised to phase out domestic rates, and hence, were not ideologically opposed to the proposal from Fianna Fáil, although critical of the methods (Roche, 1982, 157). Popular with ratepayers who had seen significant increases in domestic rates from the 1960s, due primarily to a rise in health expenditure, the income that was derived from domestic rates was replaced by a grant from Central Government. Local Government revenues from rates declined 34 per cent in 1977 to just over 22 per cent by the late 1980s (Ridge, 1992, 58), resulting in an increasing dependence on Central Government exchequer sources to fund Local Government services. Furthermore, as revenues from the sale of social housing were split 60:40 between Local and Central Government, in the absence of domestic rates, this revenue became an increasingly important source of funding for Local Government and incentivised increased sales of housing stock (O'Sullivan, Palcic and Reeves, 2025).

Private rented housing

As noted in Chapter 1, in 1946 nearly 43 per cent of households had lived in the private rented sector, the vast majority of them in unfurnished or rent-controlled private rented dwellings. The 1964 White Paper on Housing observed that both positive financial incentives to support homeownership and rent control had 'probably inhibited the building of housing to rent' (Government of Ireland, 1964, 12). On the basis that the various restrictions had been removed for various types of dwellings in 1960, it was hoped that the decline of the rent-controlled private rented sector would be halted, but the Census of 1971 showed an ongoing steady decline, dropping to 8.4 per cent nationally and just under 15 per cent in the major cities, and declined further a decade later to just under 4 per cent nationally.

The 1969 Housing White Paper had simply noted the gradual unwinding of rent control, concluding that 'the law on rent restrictions should not now have any inhibiting effect on the provision from private sources of accommodation for renting' (Government of Ireland, 1969, 42). However, Census 1981 showed an ongoing decline in the number of private rented dwellings (both controlled and uncontrolled), accounting for 10 per cent of the national housing stock in 1981 compared to 26 per cent in 1946.

However, it was not only the decline in the quantity of private rented dwellings that was of concern, but also the quality of the accommodation and the terms and conditions of renting, both in the controlled and increasingly the uncontrolled dwellings. The *Dublin Flatdwellers Association*, established in 1968, and *Threshold*, established a decade later, emerged to campaign for better conditions in the private rented sector: for example, the Dublin Flatdwellers Association campaigned to establish a Rent Tribunal to determine rents, the provision of rent books, legislation to control deposits, the registration of tenancies and the adequate maintenance of private rented dwellings (1973, 32). ALONE, founded in 1977, also highlighted the appalling housing conditions of some elderly people in Dublin, particularly those in dilapidated, rent-controlled private rented dwellings (Bermingham and O Cuanaigh, 1978).

Thus, from being the dominant tenure in urban areas in particular in the first three decades after Independence, by the early 1980s privately rented dwellings had faded into insignificance in absolute and relative terms due to the growth of homeownership and local authority provision of rental dwellings.

Rent control, originally introduced in 1915 and gradually dismantled from the 1960s, was dealt a final blow in two related constitutional cases in 1980. In *Blake v AG* and *Madigan v AG*, the Rent Restrictions Acts then in force were found to be unconstitutional, primarily due to the arbitrary effect of the legislation. Rent-controlled tenancies lost both security of tenure and low rents as a result.

In response, the Government at that time introduced *The Housing (Private Rented Dwellings) Act, 1982* which established a *Rent Tribunal* to regulate rents in such tenancies (de Blacam, 1984). There were just over 1,300 households who qualified for a *Rent Allowance* (as distinct from the separate *Rent Supplement* introduced in 1977 and discussed next) from the Department of Social Welfare, which mitigated the impact for tenants of moving from a controlled rent to a market rent. The number of recipients gradually decreased as no new tenants were eligible for the allowance (with the exception of a small number of successor tenants) and the existing tenants passed away – by 2024 there were 33 remaining recipients of this allowance (Department of Social Protection, 2025, 71).

The late 1970s also saw the final abolition of income support provisions derived from the Poor Law and the introduction of a Rent Supplement scheme, as part of a Supplementary Welfare Allowance legislation, which would play a substantial role in subsidising the rent of low-income households living in the private rental sector for several decades. Earlier legislation, The *Public Assistance Act, 1939*, had merely tidied up the various Poor Law legislation, rather than bringing about any fundamental change, and included a discretionary Home Assistance scheme which had originated in the *Poor Relief (Ireland) Act, 1847*, and had been originally entitled Outdoor Relief (as discussed in Chapter 1).

In the only detailed study of the operation of the Home Assistance scheme, Ó Cinneide (1970, 106) argued that although some might think that:

> home assistance is very different from the outdoor relief given under the Poor Law from 1847 but the facts contradict this. Now, as then, persons in need have no right to assistance; they are dependent on the goodwill of the authority which gives assistance and cannot have recourse to any appeals machinery, including the courts. Now, as then, no great effort is made to seek those in need and the public image of the service is forbidding. Now, as then, the emphasis is on saving the ratepayer's money. Now, as then, the method by which assistance is

given is inconvenient and compromising of the self-esteem of those who must avail themselves of it.

Frank Cluskey of the Labour Party, who introduced The *Supplementary Welfare Allowance Act (1975)*, claimed that it achieved 'the removal from our social welfare legislation of the remaining vestiges of the poor law'. The legislation, which was enacted in 1977, ensured that for the first time, households with insufficient means to meet their needs would be *entitled* to supplementary welfare allowances or 'a statutory guarantee of a minimum income below which no citizen is expected to fall' (Mills et al, 1991, 25). The scheme was funded by the Department of Social Welfare and administered by the Regional health authorities. As part of the Supplementary Welfare Allowance scheme, provision was made for regular income supplements for households whose income was insufficient to meet the cost of renting in the private sector. There were 1,316 recipients of a rent supplement in 1980, and this number rose to just over 6,500 by 1990 (Commission on Social Welfare, 1986, 369).

Emigration

While net emigration continued during the first part of this period, albeit at declining rates, the situation reversed from the early 1970s as, with the economy growing, former emigrants began to return to Ireland. This shift began to add greater pressure on all aspects of the housing system as returning workers sought housing and younger people were no longer seeking homes elsewhere. However, the shift was not to last and towards the end of the period, as Government debt rose to unprecedented levels and unemployment went above 120,000 for the first time, net outward migration began to re-emerge (Figure 3.2).

Conclusion

The period from 1963 to 1981 was characterised by a number of significant and contradictory developments, perhaps the most paradoxical being the longest sustained period of construction of social housing, yet delivering a net decline in social housing stock due to the scale of the tenant purchase schemes. The *Housing Act, 1966* also extended succession tenancies, whereby tenants could pass on their tenancy to members of their families, subject to certain criteria, further encouraging local authorities to sell the dwellings as the majority of houses would not return to the stock available for renting (Lewis, 2019, 30). Furthermore, the period saw the decided shift from a long period in which most homes had been constructed by local authorities to a situation where private developers, supported by a range of public subsidies,

The emergence of the homelessness sector, 1964–1981

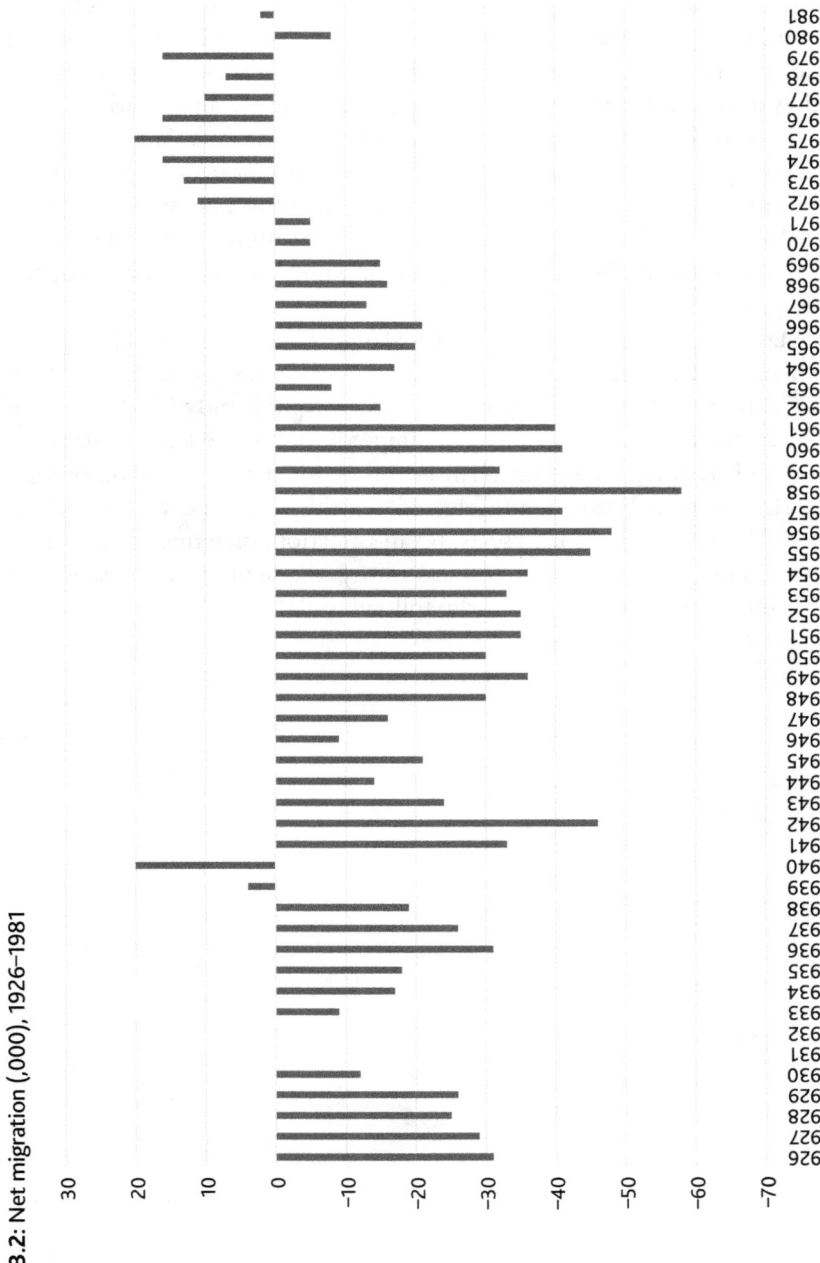

Figure 3.2: Net migration (,000), 1926–1981

Source: Central Statistics Office – https://datasalsa.com/dataset/?catalogue=data.gov.ie&name=c0401-components-of-population-change-since-1926

became the largest providers of new homes. Private rented housing was increasingly a residual sector, memorably termed 'the forgotten sector' in the first detailed analysis of the sector (O'Brien and Dillon, 1982).

Homelessness became the subject of a new level of public concern and activism, with in particular the Dublin Housing Action Committee setting out for the first time a much broader concept of homelessness, involving families in insecure and overcrowded accommodation, and clearly linking homelessness with inadequate and unaffordable housing. While historic charitable approaches to homeless provision persisted, along with perceptions of the homeless as 'inadequate', there were also the first signs of a new critical evidence-based understanding of the different experiences of homelessness for families, young people and those with addiction or mental health problems.

In May 1981, the Taoiseach, Charles Haughey, called a general election, which resulted in the Fianna Fáil Government being replaced by a Fine Gael Coalition led by Garret FitzGerald. More significantly for the story of homelessness, the 1981 election to the upper house of the Irish Parliament, the Seanad, resulted in a long-term activist with the Simon Community in Cork, Brendan Ryan, being elected for the first time to one of the National University of Ireland seats. Ryan's election, bringing his articulate commitment to tackling homelessness into parliamentary debates, was to significantly shape the debate for the following decade.

4

Two housing bills and one act, 1981–1988

Introduction

This chapter explains how a unique set of circumstances – high outward migration, continued social housing construction and a grant to encourage tenants to move out of social housing – resulted in homeless households receiving an unprecedented number of social housing allocations, resulting in a decline in homelessness. It also reports on increased awareness of how homelessness impacts women. The chapter describes the political deliberation behind the series of legislative proposals put forward by an independent senator and by two successive political coalitions in the 1980s, culminating in the *Housing Act, 1988* which established the foundation stone for homelessness policy over the succeeding decades. The *Housing Act, 1988* recognised homelessness as fundamentally a housing issue by allocating to local authorities the responsibility for supporting those experiencing homelessness but did not establish a right to housing. Rather, the legislation provided housing authorities with a broad range of discretionary powers, including the provision of emergency shelter. The introduction of this legislation coincided with changes in the funding model for social housing, with social housing now financed entirely from exchequer funding rather than by local authority borrowings, a policy that was to have significant implications on social housing output in the following years.

Political and economic context

The first years of the period covered by the chapter were characterised by political instability and a continuation of the severe problems in the State finances which had shaped the final years of the earlier chapter. A series of short-lived governments rotated into and out of office, swapping places with their former opposition, starting in June 1981, again months later in February 1992 and yet again, just seven months later, in November 1982. The Government elected in November 1982 was a Fine Gael/Labour Coalition led by Garret FitzGerald. The coalition governed until January 1987, when the Labour Party withdrew its support over tensions related to public finances and the 1987 budget, as a result of which the Housing Bill which had been prepared, fell. The February 1987 election resulted in a minority Fianna Fáil Government, led by Charles Haughey, which continued until 1989, passing the *Housing Act, 1988* which provides the legislative framework for responses to homelessness up until the present day. During most of the period the economy struggled with high levels of Government debt, constraints on public expenditure, high unemployment and a return to high levels of new outward migration.

The level of homelessness and conditions in residential services for those experiencing homelessness

Although no robust data exists for this period, campaigning groups and other commentators usually gave an estimate of between 3,000 and 5,000 people experiencing homelessness in the early part of this period, the majority being single males (O'Brien, 1981). One estimate of homelessness in Dublin in the mid-1980s indicated that 620 people were sleeping in shelters on any given night (point-in-time), with approximately 2,000 adults using the services over a year. There were approximately 1,500 shelter beds available nationally for adults experiencing homelessness. More than half of these were in Dublin, with just under 80 per cent for males (Housing Centre, 1986). An unpublished joint survey of rough sleepers in Dublin conducted by the Dublin Simon Community and Focus Point in April 1986 to coincide with that year's census identified 33 men and four women sleeping rough.

While the data for the level of homelessness and the number of shelter beds over this period is inconsistent, there was remarkable consistency in the nature of the service provided: in the main they were large congregate facilities where shelter users had to vacate the premises during the day. Conditions in hostels in Dublin had not improved since Leahy observed in the early 1970s, as noted in the previous chapter, that conditions ranged from 'good to primitive'. If anything, they appear to have deteriorated with a visiting American academic describing the physical conditions of hostels in Dublin in the early 1980s as ranging from 'primitive to appalling', 'managed by kind, but often inexperienced, volunteers and are typically understaffed, under-financed, and poorly equipped' (Kearns, 1984, 226), with Harvey and Higgins (1988, 33) noting that '[t]he Dublin Simon shelter is a converted, old, disused fire station, where 45 men and women sleep each night in dormitories'. With the exception of one shelter operated by Dublin Corporation, the Model Lodging House, all residential services for those experiencing homelessness in Ireland were provided by a range of not-for-profit non-government organisations, of varying ideological dispositions (O'Brien, 1981). Services were funded to varying degrees on a discretionary basis by local authorities and/or health boards, but with no statutory entitlement to funding.

In a survey of residential services for people experiencing homelessness in Dublin in the mid-1980s, the authors noted that 'statutory funding to hostels varies from none at all to different amounts of annual block grants which pay staff salaries and general upkeep to different amounts of weekly capitation fees, with some receiving £11 per week and others receiving £30 per night' (Murphy and Kennedy, 1988, 8). The majority of these residential services were for single men, with a very limited range of services for single women or families experiencing homelessness (Carlson, 1990). There was only one hostel for single women and women with children in Dublin, the Regina Coeli run by the Legion of Mary, which in early 1988 had 90 residents (Murphy and Kennedy, 1988, 17). This reflected the relative invisibility of women sleeping rough and in shelters and a perception that homelessness was primarily a male phenomenon.

However, in a pioneering study of homeless women in Dublin by Sr Stanislaus Kennedy (1985), a one-night census identified 384 women in the various hostels. The primary reasons identified for women becoming homeless were severe family disruption, often involving violence and sexual abuse. She argued that

> [o]nce homeless, the women tend to get trapped in a cycle of homelessness that is very difficult for them to break. There are many factors militating against their breaking this cycle, the main one being their poverty: they have access to neither adequate income, housing, emergency accommodation, information, advice nor creative activity centres. (Kennedy, 1985, 174–175)

The study also estimated, based on a range of secondary sources, that there were upwards of 9,000 'hidden' homeless women, the majority of them on the housing waiting lists. As Kennedy noted: 'The idea of women being homeless seems a paradox. Throughout history, the role of the women has been as a homemaker, harbour, resting place' (1985, 72). Describing homeless women as in the main the 'hidden homeless', Kennedy demonstrated that homeless women were less likely to be counted in surveys of the homeless, because of the lack of adequate facilities for them and their tendency to double up with friends and relations rather than utilise emergency hostel accommodation.

A short survey of the users of the Brú Chaoimhín shelter for homeless women in Dublin was published in 1989 (Bell, 1989). Opened in 1978, the shelter consisted of two wooden prefabs at the rear of the old Fever Hospital in South inner-city Dublin. The report gave an account of the daily regime in the shelter and policies that it operated. Data was collected on the users of the shelter from June 1987 to June 1988, which showed there were 259 individual entries to the shelter during the time period, with traveller women representing 93 of the cases. The ages of the users ranged from 12 to 70, with those aged 22 to 30 the most frequent users. The conditions in the shelter were castigated by both the author and by the *National Campaign for the Homeless* who sponsored the report. A number of years earlier, in a debate on the shelter in the Seanad, Mary Robinson, later President of Ireland, then a senator provided a graphic description of conditions in the shelter:

> Some 25 to 30 residents, on average, are in the prefab on any given night. The facilities where they live are very primitive indeed. When I visited the prefab, which was open during the day time this week, there was an open dormitory area with 11 beds and two cots in it. There was no privacy whatsoever, no curtains or partitioning between the beds. In a small room beside the dormitory there were three lavatories, two of them installed relatively recently, one of them out of order, and a small bath which is used by the women for washing their clothes, because they have no other laundry facilities, as well as bathing.
>
> There are six tall rather unsafe lockers in the dormitory. There are no keys to them and they are structures which cause problems with children when playing because if they fell on a child they could cause some injury. There are no washing facilities. There is no clothes line. There is no office where families could be spoken to individually by a social worker. One-third of the prefab structure, unit five as it is called, is used as a shelter for the women and children and two-thirds of it is a sacristy and chapel which is used once a week. So more than two-thirds of the space of this long prefab is empty and yet devoted to Christianity. In the other third is the reality of a very urgent human situation involving very vulnerable families. If Christ had visited Brú Chaoimhín He would have had something to say about this strange sense of priorities. It appeared that it would be very valuable to Brú Chaoimhín to have more space and particularly more privacy. (Seanad Éireann debate – Thursday, 7 July 1983, Adjournment Matter – Cork Street (Dublin) Shelter)

Shortly before the report was published, the shelter was closed and a new shelter was constructed adjacent to the Regina Coeli shelter on Morning Star Avenue.

A survey of hostels in Dublin in 1991 found that only just over 20 per cent of all hostel residents were female (131 women without children and 75 with children). The reasons for the relatively low number of women in the hostels were, first, that much of women's homeless was hidden in that they tended to stay with friends or other forms of temporary accommodation rather than accessing hostels; second, that the availability of places did not match demand, particularly for women escaping domestic violence. The age profile of those in the women's hostels tended to be lower than the population in the male hostels and their usage of the hostels tended to be of shorter duration than those in the male hostels. However, the authors point out that 'many women prefer to stay with friends or in dangerous and violent homes rather than to stay in hostels. This means that women's homelessness is often concealed or hidden and is therefore not reflected in hostel numbers' (Kelleher, Kelleher and McCarthy, 1992, 58).

Over this period a number of different factors in the housing system, combined with high levels of emigration arising from high unemployment and prolonged recession, resulted in an unprecedented – and unrepeated – availability of social housing, some of which was allocated to enable people to move out of homelessness, with those who were homeless getting priority from Dublin Corporation. The policy outlined next dramatically highlights the impact of the sustained local authority construction programme, alongside substantially reduced demand, on lettings policy.

> (a) The policy of Dublin Corporation to house homeless persons, including single persons, as a priority. The Corporation has, at present, a surplus of accommodation which it is anxious to have occupied.
> (b) Rent supplements are available under the Supplementary Welfare Scheme. This means that many people, who would otherwise be homeless, can afford to live in private flats.
> (c) Persons approaching the Board for accommodation are discouraged from using hostel accommodation where local authority or private accommodation is a practical alternative. Many persons who otherwise enter the hostel system are, at that point, persuaded and assisted to remain in the community.
> (d) the standard of accommodation in many hostels is poor. (Donohue, 1988, 97–98)

Social movements and civil society

Wider public involvement in campaigning about poor housing and homelessness came to an end with the winding up of the Dublin Housing Action Committee in the early 1970s, but groups with a more specific focus on homelessness, in particular the Simon Communities of Ireland, continued to campaign for changes in legislation and practice. In 1984, Focus Point (later Focus Ireland) was established by Sr Stanislaus Kennedy to follow up on the issues which emerged from her research on women and homelessness, as discussed (see Focus Ireland, 2011 for a history of this organisation). In the same year, a number of different homeless organisations, activists and academics came together to establish the *National Campaign for the Homeless*. This group convened a number of significant conferences and commissioned a number of pieces of important research over a decade of activity and were particularly influential and active in the period up to the passing of the *Housing Act, 1988*. Perhaps the most lasting impact of the *National Campaign for the Homeless* was the convening, in September 1985, of the first ever seminar exploring aspects of homelessness in Europe, which was held in Cork (National Campaign for the Homeless, 1986). One of the recommendations of the seminar was that:

> the European Commission fund an association of organisations working with homeless people in the member states so that they may consult regularly on issues affecting homeless people, on methods that will secure improvements in the conditions of homeless people and advise the Commission on policy that will improve the conditions of homeless people.

This recommendation led to the establishment of the Fédération Européenne d'Associations Nationales Travaillant avec les Sans Abris (FEANTSA) in 1989. In 1991, the European Observatory on Homelessness was established by FEANTSA. Both FEANTSA and the European Observatory on Homelessness remain active and are integral to the European Commission's strategy to end homelessness by 2030, which will be discussed in later chapters.

Growing visibility of youth homelessness in the 1980s

A national survey of youth homelessness conducted by the National Campaign for the Homeless in 1985 identified over 800 young people between ten and 30 years and proposed that 'the Health Board take the leading role in providing accommodation for all homeless people aged 16 to 40' (National Campaign for the Homeless, 1985, 15). Explicit recognition by the Government of the problem of youth homelessness, and an apparent willingness to tackle the situation, came in 1985 in the form of a National Youth Policy entitled, *In Partnership with Youth* (Government of Ireland, 1985). This document contained the clearest articulation to date that youth homelessness was viewed by the State as an area distinct from adult homelessness requiring specific attention (Government of Ireland, 1985, 34–35), when it stated that: 'The Government accept that it is the responsibility of the health boards to provide for long-term and short-stay accommodation for homeless young people incapable of independent living and in need of special care.'

The document further noted that new legislation was in preparation that would address many of the unmet needs of homeless children, *The Children (Care and Protection) Bill, 1985* which eventually emerged as the *Child Care Act, 1991*. In March 1987, to mark the *International Year of Shelter for the Homeless*, a conference entitled 'Streetwise' was organised by Focus Point and UNICEF to highlight the plight of young homeless people both in Ireland and internationally. Kennedy (1987) noted that although only fragmentary evidence was available, it did suggest that youth homelessness was a growing issue attributable in part to changes in the nature and provision of residential care. Residential places for older children had decreased since the 1970s and, according to Kennedy (1987, 67), '[p]reventative services have not been developed to provide support for families in their local communities'. Arising from this conference, a relatively short-lived umbrella group to highlight the issue of youth homelessness, the *Streetwise National Coalition*, was established and conducted a national survey of youth homelessness in 1987 which estimated that in one week in November 1987 just over 600 young people aged 18 or under were homeless or at risk of homelessness (McCarthy and Conlon, 1988).

Housing supply and allocations

As noted in the previous chapter, the number of social housing lettings or allocations per annum had been increasing steadily from the passing of the *Housing Act, 1966*, and reached a historic high of nearly 12,000 lettings in 1986. There were a number of reasons for this increased availability of social housing.

First, there was the aforementioned substantial increase in the number of new local authority units being built following the *Housing Act, 1966* and the sustained period of social housing construction continued on well into the mid-1980s. While the peak in housing delivery came in the mid-1970s, the 1980s continued to see between 6,000 and 7,000 units completed each year until the mid-1980s before completions began to fall with only 1,450 units completed in 1988, as shown in Figure 4.1.

Second, in 1984, direct Government funding for voluntary housing agencies, or what are currently referred to as Approved Housing Bodies, was introduced. Although various schemes had been funded prior to this scheme, this was the first time that a significant role was envisaged for such bodies, initially for the provision of housing for those with specific needs such as those experiencing homelessness or the aged (National Economic and Social Council, 1988), but over time to provide general needs social housing and hence providing an additional supply of social housing.

Third, in addition to the supply of new units, an increased number of existing units were becoming vacant due to the combined impact of tenants emigrating and tenants availing of a Surrender Grant Scheme. The Surrender Grant (a grant of £2,000 and a £3,000 mortgage subsidy provided to local authority tenants to allow them to purchase in the private housing sector) operated between late 1984 and early 1987, resulting in just over 7,700 local authority tenants surrendered their social housing tenancy hence further boosting the stock of local authority housing available for letting (Threshold, 1987).

Figure 4.1: Social housing completions, 1923–1988

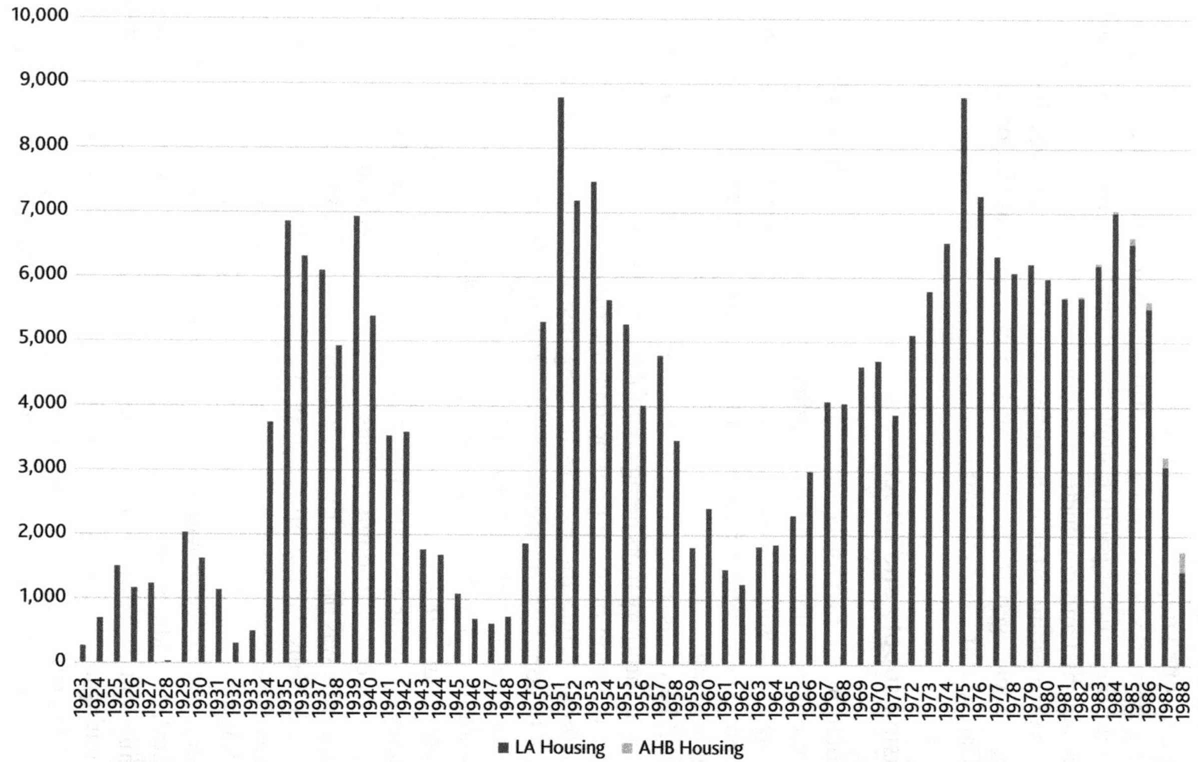

Source: Department of Local Government and Public Health Annual Report (various years) (Dublin: Stationery Office). Department of the Environment (various years): Annual Housing Statistics Bulletin (Dublin: Department of the Environment).

Fourth, net outward migration increased steadily during the 1980s from -1,000 in 1981 to -43,900 in 1989, the highest rate of net migration since the 1950s. In 1989 alone, 70,600 people emigrated from Ireland and this contributed to both the increase in casual vacancies in the local authority stock and to a reduction of the waiting list. The number of local authority allocations from 'casual vacancies', that is, units of housing that become available when the existing tenants vacate, increased from just over 2,000 vacancies in 1981 to nearly 6,000 in 1988 and just over 5,000 in 1989.

As a consequence of these factors, the number of households on the local authority waiting list dropped from nearly 30,000 in the early 1980s to just under 18,000 by 1988. In Dublin, for example, the numbers fell by more than half from a waiting list of 6,732 in 1981 to 3,093 in 1988. The average waiting period on the list over the same time period also declined from 3.2 years to 1.2 years (Lord Mayor's Commission on Housing, 1993, 84).

Increased housing supply and homelessness

In the case of Dublin, the high level of vacancies in the public housing stock resulted in 'an increased capacity by the Corporation to deal with marginal cases, particularly those classed as "homeless"' (Morrissey, 1988, 80). In Dublin, between May and December 1986, 472 families, 316 single parents, 349 single persons (mainly men) and 35 senior citizens who were homeless were housed. The housing co-ordinator for Dublin city and county described this as 'a most remarkable achievement' (Morrissey, 1988, 80). Indeed, in the case of homeless families in Dublin, by the mid-1980s it was noted that 'the Corporation has quite a number of vacant dwellings available and any family which is homeless can be accommodated quickly' (O'Sullivan, 1988, 87).

A similar picture existed in the rest of the country. In 1987, 9 per cent of all local authority lettings nationally were allocated to homeless households (631 singles and 239 families), up from 363 in 1983 (National Economic and Social Council, 1988, 150) (data for other years is not available). The increased allocations to homeless households were matched with increased allocations to single parent households (which increased from 2,818 allocations in 1983 to 3,931 or just over one in five of all allocations in 1987).

This rapid increase in social housing allocations to households which would not previously qualify was not without potentially problematic consequences. This led John Blackwell, a noted housing economist and contributor to many official reports on housing, to note that '[t]his trend may lead to a perpetuation of housing problems in estates that are becoming increasingly stigmatised' (1987, 14). This was also the view of Threshold, the voluntary organisation set up to address problems in the private rental sector. Threshold argued (1987, ix) that although the Surrender Grant had the positive impact of reducing waiting lists, the households that benefited were frequently unemployed and, in some cases, already marginalised. The overall effect, they argued, was to encourage existing employed tenants to vacate their tenancies and purchase in private estates. Indeed, such were the rates of vacancies in certain low-demand estates that Dublin Corporation had to expend £1 m (million) in securing vacant properties (NESC, 1988, 189).

There is some evidence of this socially polarising effect, with the number of Local Authority tenants who were dependent on social welfare payments increased from 51 per cent in 1983 to 70 per cent in 1987 (Blackwell, 1990, 112), although this period also experienced a high level of factory closures and redundancies which would also partially explain this trend (Allen, 1998, 77). Between 1987 and 1994, the odds of local authority renters being poor in Dublin increased from 25 to 35 times greater than for owner-occupiers (Nolan, Whelan and Williams, 1998). For Higgins (1988, 34), while welcoming the increase in allocations to single parent families, the allocations were usually in 'low-demand areas' and as a consequence 'the problems facing these families may only have been transformed not resolved, with a new set of problems arising'.

The negative impact of these interrelated changes was most visible in the Ballymun complex estate built between 1966 and 1969 as noted in the previous chapter (Somerville-Woodward, 2002). By the mid-1980s, nearly 70 per cent of allocations to Ballymun were to single persons and lone parents and with the flats proving unpopular, many tenants immediately placed themselves on the local authority 'transfer list' seeking a house rather than a flat. Power, in her analysis of Ballymun, argued that '[i]nvariably the priority for houses went to the more established, more stable tenants. As people moved out, empty flats became harder and harder to let. The people left behind in this process were poorer and less favoured economically and socially' (1997, 245). On top of this, the surrender grants had a disproportionate impact on Ballymun with 10 per cent of tenants applying for the grant and vacating their dwelling and by 1989 there were 450 boarded up flats in Ballymun (Power, 1997, 246). As a consequence, 'the rapid change in the composition of the population, the dramatic rise in the number of empty dwellings, the loss of confidence generated by the Surrender Grant take-up, and the rapid rehousing of single, homeless people, many of whom could not cope with flat living in Ballymun, all created an atmosphere of mayhem on the estate' (Power, 1997, 246).

'The most significant scheme of privatisation to date since the formation of the State'

While the policies and demographic factors as outlined were combining to increase the amount of social housing available during this period, this was the closing point of these trends with new policies with long-run effects of reducing the supply of social housing beginning to come into effect. As noted earlier, schemes for allowing social housing tenants to purchase their dwellings had existed in rural areas since before the foundation of the State, with less favourable schemes for urban housing being introduced from the 1930. The number of social houses purchased by their tenants peaked in 1975 at just below 12,000 and had fallen to just a third of that level by 1982.

From 1983 onward, a series of Tenant Purchase Schemes were introduced which removed the distinction between urban and rural areas and provided for successively more attractive terms for tenants. It is significant that there were limitations to this policy of aligning rural and urban schemes – although it has been legally possible to purchase flats since 1979, technical difficulties have prevented the completion of any sales. In February 1988, the Minister announced the *Millennium Tenant Purchase Scheme* (colloquially known as the 'sale of the century'), which aimed to significantly expand the tenant purchase scheme by selling 40,000 dwellings (a third of the social housing stock), on terms that were described by the department with responsibility for devising the scheme as 'particularly generous' and, not surprisingly, there was an 'unprecedented response' (Department of the Environment, 1989, 42) with over 40,000 applications to purchase dwellings were received before the scheme concluded in February 1989.

Since the overwhelming supply of social housing flats are in the large urban areas, the social impact of tenant purchase has continued to be distinct in different environments. While in the United Kingdom, tenant purchase of social housing is seen as a highly politicised policy identified with Margaret Thatcher, in the Irish context Hayden argues that '[n]o political party at any point disputed in any sense the principle of tenant purchase, and by 1988 there was a universally shared drive to offer even more generous terms for purchase to tenants' (2014, 118).

Concerns were expressed from outside the political system. In December 1988, the National Economic and Social Council (NESC) review of housing policy repeated its warnings from a decade earlier (see Chapter 3), arguing that '[t]he main impacts of the sales scheme have been to effect a change of ownership – essentially the most significant scheme of privatisation to date since the formation of the State' (1988, 181). The detailed critique of the sales scheme concluded that the 'sales scheme should be revamped so that dwellings are sold at replacement rate, without any discount for length of tenancy' (1988, 266). NESC recommended, on the grounds that the sales schemes had 'little financial justification', that they 'should be reformed to ensure that the schemes better meet their social objectives, if reform is not possible then the schemes should be abandoned' (1988, 62). In 'A Strategy for the Nineties' (NESC, 1990) the Council noted that while they approved of tenant purchase in principle, they regarded the 'terms of the schemes as inappropriate' (1990, 246). They further noted that, despite their earlier recommendation that the schemes should be reformed or abandoned, no reform had occurred, and the schemes had continued.

The path towards the *Housing Act, 1988*

The question of whether homelessness should be seen as a housing problem or a health problem has been a theme in this story from the beginning, but from the early 1980s it began to crystallise into the question of which public authority should have the statutory responsibility for those experiencing homelessness. The view that homelessness should be seen primarily as a housing problem and therefore fall under the remit of the Department of Environment and local authorities, became a focal point of the early campaigning work of a range of civic society organisations and committed individuals over the next decade.

The policy debate about the link between housing and homelessness was played out over that decade and interacted with a particularly unstable political period, so that a number of different governments with different perspectives proposed quite different legislative responses without passing legislation until almost the end of the decade. The political and policy debate is well recorded in departmental files in the National Archives of Ireland and Dáil records and is worth exploring in some detail.

Under the *Health Act, 1953* and the *Housing Act, 1966*, the respective statutory responsibilities of health authorities and local councils were ambiguous. The 1953 Act made health authorities responsible for providing 'institutional assistance' to people experiencing homelessness and for providing funding to voluntary bodies aiding the homeless, while the 1966 Act gave responsibility to municipal authorities for providing housing for those 'in need of it or who were unable to provide it from their own resources'. Different health and municipal authorities adopted varying levels of responsibility, resulting in 'homeless people being shunted from health board to local authority and vice-versa' (Shannon, 1988, 136; see also O'Brien, 1981; Harvey, 1985; Kennedy, 1985).

For the National Economic and Social Council (1988, 287):

> The persistent nature of homelessness has brought into sharp relief the lack of clarity in regard to dealing with this issue which has existed between the housing authorities and the health boards. The Health Boards have often found that they were in disagreement with housing authorities over respective responsibilities for dealing with homelessness. As a result, there was a continuous referral of people backwards and forwards between Health Boards and housing authorities, each of which was either reluctant or unable to deal effectively with the problem.

A number of different factors came together to drive this debate at this time. One factor was the gradual closure of the Casual Wards (Doherty, 1982) along with the gradual dismantlement of the vast in-patient psychiatric hospital network from the early 1960s, which at its peak in 1958 held over 21,000 patients (Walsh, 2015) which had provided institutional accommodation for marginal populations for the first 50 years after Independence. The displacement of families due to the clearance of slum tenements also formed part of this backdrop.

A further factor was the increased campaigning activities of civic society organisations. Of particular significance was the Simon Community and the influential work of the 'Simon Senator', Brendan Ryan, a long-standing member of the Cork Simon Community. In addition, long-standing organisations such as the Society of St. Vincent de Paul (1981, 23–34) were attracting increased political and public policy attention to homelessness and the aforementioned National Campaign for the Homeless served as a mechanism to coordinate much of this increasing campaigning energy and demand for change.

It is also notable that this increased political momentum for legislation to improve homelessness services, and civic society's urgency to push that forward, comes at a time when the actual number of people who were homeless was falling and, as we have seen, homeless individuals and families were increasingly likely to be provided with public housing.

Brendan Ryan's *Housing (Homeless Persons) Bill, 1983*

To address these pressures, two significant developments were initiated in 1983. The first was a Private Members Bill encapsulating the aspirations of the civic society organisations, and the second was the establishment by the Department of Health of an *Ad-hoc Committee on the Homeless* chaired by one of the Department's senior officials.

As noted in the previous chapter, in 1981, after a long period of activism with the Simon Community in Cork, Brendan Ryan was elected to one of the National University of Ireland seats in the upper House of the Irish Parliament, the Seanad. Given the political instability at this time, he had to be successfully re-elected twice in just two years before he was able to introduce a Private Members Bill, the *Housing (Homeless Persons) Bill, 1983*. This Bill proposed to define homelessness for the first time in Irish legislation and included provision for those threatened with homelessness. It would also place a legal duty on local authorities to provide 'accommodation of a reasonable and suitable type' for people experiencing homelessness, thus ending the confusing division of responsibility between health and municipal authorities. It would also oblige municipal authorities to make provision for people experiencing homelessness, particularly single people.

The definitions of homelessness set out in the Bill were:

a. he or any person who might reasonably be expected to reside with him (i) has no accommodation and is vulnerable as a result of old age, mental illness, handicap or physical disability, pregnancy or other special reason and/or (ii) has no fixed abode and/or (iii) is usually resident in common lodging houses, refuges, night shelters or hostels and/or (iv) solely because of having no alternative accommodation, is forced to continue to reside in a general or psychiatric hospital, a County Home or other such institution; or
b. he has accommodation but he cannot secure entry to it or it is probable that occupation of it will lead to violence from some other person residing in it; or
c. his accommodation consists of a moveable structure, vehicle or vessel designed or adapted for human habitation and there is no place where he is entitled or permitted both to place it and to reside in it.

Where a local authority was satisfied that a person met these criteria but were not immediately in a position to provide them with a home ('accommodation of a reasonable and suitable type'), the local authority was required to 'arrange temporary accommodation with all deliberate speed'. An important provision, recognising the risk of long-term 'warehousing' of homeless people in shelters, was that the homeless person 'shall not be obliged to spend a certain period in interim accommodation as a matter of policy on the part of the housing authority'. Persons threatened with, and likely to experience, homelessness within the next 28 days were also to be owed a duty by the local authority to provide 'accommodation of a reasonable and suitable type'. If the local authority determined that an applicant did not meet the criteria, an applicant was entitled to appeal that decision to the Circuit Court. The Bill also required that an Annual Report on the operation of legislation be published.

The drafting of the Bill was strongly influenced by the *Housing (Homeless Persons) Act, 1977* in the United Kingdom (see Crowson, 2013) which was enacted following classic BBC drama on homelessness, *Cathy Come Home* (Fitzpatrick and Pawson, 2016), but excluded the controversial provisions of 'intentional homelessness', and the 'local connection rule' and did include single persons as a 'priority', which they were not in the UK (Maher, 1989).

The Bill was rejected by the Government of the time, a Fine Gael/Labour Coalition, on the advice of the Deputy Prime Minister and Minister responsible for housing policy, Dick Spring, of the Labour Party. Spring argued in a memo[1] to Government that:

(i) the definitions of homelessness and threatened homelessness are much too broad and include many currently on the local authority waiting list; (ii) it would seriously interfere with established practice in regard to housing priorities by creating two different routes to rehousing; (iii) it implies the provision by the Government of substantial financial and staffing resources; (iv) the bill would do nothing to solve the complex medico-social problems which give rise to some of the worst cases of homelessness; and (v) it would give rise to extensive and costly litigation.

It also noted that the Bill 'contains no safeguards against abuses such as intentional homelessness'. Observations from the Department of Justice included possible 'scope for collusion under section 4(1)(b) of the Bill which would regard as homeless a person who cannot gain entry to any accommodation he may have or can do so only at the risk of violence'. Ultimately, the memo concluded that as there was no likelihood of the additional funding and resources required to realise the objectives of the legislation, 'the enactment of this Bill would bring the law and local authorities into disrepute and cause serious embarrassment to the Minister'.

However, it was accepted that clarification was required on the issue of statutory responsibility, and that Spring was 'anxious to see everything possible done to ameliorate the plight of the homeless'. Observations on the Bill from the Department of Health clearly stated that, in their view, 'homelessness is essentially a housing problem and that many of the residents of hostels, night shelters etc. are houseable and do not require special support services and as such should be provided with housing by local authorities'.

The memorandum concluded that the promoter of the Bill, Senator Ryan, would be requested to withdraw the Bill as the Government would not support it, asked to await the findings of the *Ad-Hoc Committee on the Homeless*, and to be given assurances 'that the matter will be given further consideration in light of the findings of the committee'.

On 7 November 1983, Senator Ryan was informed of this decision but following intensive lobbying of Government backbenchers and public support for the Bill by a range of civil society actors, the Government announced it would allow for a reading of the Bill. Following a detailed rationale for the Bill by Senator Ryan, the Minister of State in the Department of Environment, Ruairi Quinn, also of the Labour Party, outlined his opposition to the Bill on the grounds that

> in its present form it would not contribute to the achievement of the ideals to which the Senator and I – and indeed the Tánaiste and the Government as a whole – are fully committed. It would, on the contrary, tend to frustrate those ideals by upsetting traditional and well-established policies of ensuring that local authority housing

is allocated to those whose need is most acute, in accordance with recognised criteria.

He argued that:

> To enact this legislation in its present form would be bordering on irresponsible because it would impose a duty on local authorities that could not be discharged within the resources likely to be available to them. To do so would bring the law into disrepute, probably lead to expensive litigation seeking to secure the performance by local authorities of the duty imposed on them, and be most unfair to families who have been deservedly placed on approved waiting lists.

However, Minister Quinn stated that the Government would introduce its own legislation, 'framed after reasoned and mature consideration of all the possibilities and implications' as a matter of urgency which would 'clearly define who is responsible for the homeless, to clearly define what constitutes being homeless, and also clearly define, if we can, the border line between being homeless and being made homeless or being threatened with homelessness'.

He also noted that earlier in the year the Minister for Health had established an *Ad-Hoc Committee on the Homeless* and that they would 'take a fairly fundamental look at these important aspects of the homelessness problem and that they will come up with recommendations that will be clearcut, practical and, hopefully, effectual'.

The *Ad-hoc Committee on Homelessness*

The *Ad-Hoc Committee on Homelessness* was chaired by a senior civil servant in the Department of Health but included officials from both housing and health authorities at Central and Local Government level. The rationale for the establishment of the Committee by the Department of Health was 'primarily because Health Boards reported finding an increasing "housing" element in the problems coming before them when dealing with homeless people'. The health boards also found themselves in disagreement with the housing authorities over their respective responsibilities and the objective of the Committee 'to examine and issue guidelines on the respective responsibilities as between health boards and local authorities for providing accommodation for homeless people' (1984, 1).

In December 1984, the *Ad-hoc Committee* published their report. It noted that under the arrangements for allocation of social housing operated by local authorities at that time, 'the single homeless person who is not elderly or disabled will normally have a low priority and consequently have little chance of obtaining permanent or temporary accommodation from a housing authority' (1984, 12–13). The response of the health boards to those experiencing homelessness, the report noted, took 'a number of forms' including the provision of Casual Wards and funding various non-governmental agencies.

The Committee considered the provisions of Ryan's Housing (Homeless Persons) Bill, 1983, and it is unclear if the paragraphs rejecting the principles in the Bill are a summary of the Government position or the views of the Ad-hoc Committee, but if the former, the Ad-hoc Committee certainly did not contradict the Government position. The Ad-hoc Committee stated that:

> The Bill would place a statutory duty on housing authorities to provide permanent accommodation for a broadly and loosely defined category of persons. The provisions of the Bill could discriminate against many people already on housing authority waiting lists and would cause confusion and inequity in providing alternative routes to housing by housing authorities. A specific duty on housing authorities to house all those within the scope of the Bill would leave housing authorities in an impossible position. Long established practices for allocating houses on the basis of relative need would be disrupted and preference would accrue to persons whose needs might not by any means be the most acute. There would be an incentive for ordinary applicants to have themselves classified as homeless or so threatened to gain priority over others. It would be impossible to impose an enforceable duty on housing authorities which they could not discharge within the resources likely to be available to them. (1984, 24)

Nonetheless, having recognised that single homeless persons were unlikely to obtain social housing under the existing arrangements, and rejecting a statutory basis for prioritising single homelessness, the Ad-hoc Committee recommended clarifying the respective responsibilities of local and health authorities. It recommended that the local authorities should have responsibility for housing those persons in hostels that were capable of independent living, those facing homelessness due to emergency circumstances and 'victims of family violence' who had received 'appropriate care and counselling' (1984, 32). Those who were deemed not capable nor desirous of independent living in permanent housing, or those requiring short-term emergency accommodation, 'victims of family violence' who had not received 'appropriate care and counselling', and homeless children, they would be the responsibility of the health authorities.

This, the Ad-hoc Committee noted, would require a new legal framework, and while the Committee envisaged both authorities playing a role in providing services to different categories of people experiencing homelessness, the recommendations of the Committee signalled a distinct policy shift, clearly identifying local authorities as the primary State body with responsibility for responding to people experiencing homelessness. In terms of the role of health authorities, the view of the Committee was that the function of the health authorities:

> in the care of homeless persons should diminish. Ultimately the responsibilities of health boards would be confined to accommodating in hostel-type or institutional accommodation persons with health and social problems requiring special support services and persons who are not capable of managing independent accommodation. (1984, 34)

To give effect to the recommendations of the Ad-hoc Committee, a circular was issued by the Department of the Environment to each local authority in February 1985 requesting each authority to 'nominate an officer (preferably the housing officer) to liaise with health boards and voluntary bodies on individual cases of homelessness. (This arrangement should ensure that a homeless person is referred from one agency to another only on the basis of a prior agreement between the authorities.)' The Committee recognised that if their recommendations were to be implemented, it would require 'a new legislative framework which permits a redirection of priorities within the housing authority programme' (1984, 2).

The Fine Gael/Labour *Housing (Miscellaneous Provisions) Bill, 1985*

In January 1985, a memo for the Fine Gael/Labour Government outlined the general scheme of a Bill to address the issues highlighted in the *Housing (Homeless Persons) Bill, 1983* and to respond to the recommendations of the Ad-hoc Committee. The proposed Bill would impose two duties on local authorities. In the first instance, local authorities would have a statutory duty to 'take steps to ensure that accommodation is available for any homeless person who is capable of maintaining an independent tenancy and is unable to provide accommodation from their own resources'. However, in contrast to the Ryan Bill, the Government Bill included a provision that, if the person was deemed to be homeless intentionally, there would be no duty to provide accommodation. Secondly, where a person was 'likely to become homeless within 28 days', local authorities would be enabled to provide financial assistance (rather than accommodation as envisaged by Ryan) to prevent homelessness.

Acknowledging that these new duties would have a considerable cost for local authorities, it was proposed that 80 per cent of their expenditure on housing or otherwise assisting homeless persons could be recouped from

Central Government. In addition, local authorities would be required to conduct an annual assessment of housing needs, and homeless persons would be included in these assessments. The Minister, Liam Kavanagh of the Labour Party, noted in his memo to Government that these duties are:

> breaking new ground as far as the housing functions of the authorities are concerned. It is impossible to predict what the ultimate consequences might be from a cost point of view. There is a risk that action in the courts could lead to liberal interpretation and extensive use of the provisions which could have far reaching repercussions both in terms of cost and otherwise. These could arise not directly from the duty of local authorities to homeless persons but also from pressure to expand the local authority housing programme to ensure that the prospects of persons in need of housing are not diminished by reason of homeless persons being given local authority homes. The Minister is, however, of the view that, if there is to be legislation to deal with the problem of the homeless, it cannot do less than the General Scheme proposed if it is to be seen as a worthwhile measure.

In June 1985, a revised memo to Government was submitted which dealt with three substantive issues raised at the Cabinet meeting in January. These were concerns in relation to the duty imposed on local authorities to house homeless people; how the provision of financial assistance to homeless persons, or those threatened with homelessness, by local authorities would interact with the social welfare system; and how to prevent 'queue jumping' for local authority housing.

On the first issue, the Minister considered replacing the statutory obligation placed on local authorities to provide accommodation for those experiencing homelessness with an enabling provision, but concluded that

> if there is to be legislation to deal with homelessness, it cannot do less than the Bill provides and that, in particular, to remove the statutory obligation referred and replace it with an enabling power, even if it were to give greater priority to homeless persons, would be ineffective as a means of improving the situation of homeless persons.

Further, he was of the view that there were sufficient safeguards in the legislation to 'deal with any possible abuse'.

On providing financial assistance to homeless people and those threatened with homelessness, the Minister concluded that the overlap between the role of local authorities and broader income support services were complex and decided to remove this provision. To deal with concerns over 'queue jumping' for social housing, the Minister reiterated his view that the provisions whereby 'an applicant has either deliberately occupied unsuitable accommodation or failed to occupy suitable accommodation which was reasonably available to him, the authority may disregard his present accommodation for the purpose of determining his priority for a tenancy of a local authority house'.

In October 1985, the Government published the *Housing (Miscellaneous Provisions) Bill, 1985*, which had its second reading on 3 December. Many of the recommendations of the Ad-hoc Committee, and indeed certain aspects of Ryan's *Housing (Homeless Persons) Bill, 1983*, were incorporated into the Bill.

It defined homelessness as:

> a person who has no accommodation available to him or who lives in a hostel, night shelter or other such institution because he has no other available accommodation is regarded as homeless; gave local authorities primary responsibility for meeting the needs of homeless people, provided that they were 'capable of living independently'.

It required local authorities to include homeless people when determining the need for social housing in their area and extended a scheme of funding not-for-profit bodies providing rented accommodation for people experiencing homelessness, among others.

Significantly, the Bill contained provision that

> A person shall not be regarded as homeless ... if the housing authority are of the opinion that he has deliberately or without good or sufficient reason done or failed to anything (other than an action or omission in good faith) in consequence of which accommodation is not available for him which it would have been, or would be, reasonable to occupy.

This, it was pointed out, was similar to Section 17(1) of the *Homeless Persons Act, 1977* in Britain and this 'intentionality clause' drew the ire of the Simon Community who described it as 'fundamentally wrong, psychologically unsound, legally catastrophic and must be deleted' (Simon Community, 1986, 10). However, the Bill made no progress through Parliament and fell with the dissolution of the Parliament in January 1987, when the Labour ministers resigned over a budget dispute.

In June 1985, in preparation for the expected operationalisation of this new legislation, a Working Group on the Implementation of the Provisions relating to the Homeless, chaired by a senior official in the Department of the Environment (which was responsible for issues concerning local authorities and also for housing) had been established. Three members of the group also visited the United Kingdom to gain first-hand knowledge of the implementation of the *Housing (Homeless Persons) Act, 1977*. The group produced a 56-page report, in December 1986, but as the legislation fell with the Fine Gael/Labour Government, the report was never published or circulated to the local authorities.

Fianna Fáil's *Housing Act, 1988*

The February 1987 election resulted in the return of a Fianna Fáil Government in the midst of severe economic circumstances of recession, high unemployment and emigration. Later that year, in October 1987, a further memo was brought to Cabinet to prepare legislation to replace the former Government's *Housing (Miscellaneous Provisions) Bill, 1985*. This new legislation proposed to delete some of the remaining provisions of Ryan's 1982 Bill. In particular, the provision placing a statutory duty on local authorities to provide accommodation for homeless people was to be replaced with 'more discretionary provisions which would not give homeless persons a right to accommodation superior to that of all other persons in need of housing'. The rationale for this policy change was that the Minister, Padraig Flynn, did not:

> regard as prudent to impose a statutory obligation on housing authorities to secure accommodation for homeless persons when the resources necessary to discharge that obligation would not be available to the authorities. In addition, with reduction in the availability of local authority accommodation, a statutory obligation to secure accommodation for homeless persons would create a premium on being adjudged homeless. This could result in applicants who are frustrated at delays in securing accommodation seeking to be housed as homeless persons with the likely outcome that few, if any, applicants would ultimately be rehoused from the normal waiting lists.

On the other hand, as the statutory duty on local authorities to provide accommodation for homeless people was replaced with a broad range of discretionary powers, the Minister also proposed to delete the intentionality clause, which was central to the 1985 Bill, as it would 'be extremely difficult to administer and as such would represent undesirable additions to the housing code'.

Flynn acknowledged that these new proposals would be met with criticism, outlining:

> Notwithstanding that the Minister's proposals should represent an improvement in the lot of homeless persons compared with the present position and an improvement in certain provisions of the 1985 Bill,

it can be expected that the lobby on behalf of the homeless will be severely critical of the dropping of the obligation contained in the earlier Bill that local authorities should act to secure accommodation for homeless persons. There is likely to be pressure to restore to the Bill a clear-cut obligation on local authorities to cater for the housing needs of the homeless since the other provisions of the Bill designed to help the homeless will not be seen by some as an adequate response to the problem.

It was also proposed to repeal the offence of 'wandering abroad' (which in effect criminalised homelessness) under Section 4 of the *Vagrancy Act, 1824*, an issue that many NGOs had campaigned for, and was also recommended by the Law Reform Commission in their report on *Vagrancy and Related Offences* (1985) and by the *Parliamentary Committee on Crime, Lawlessness and Vandalism* in their Ninth Report on certain offences under the Vagrancy Acts (1986).

The Bill progressed quickly and was signed into law as the *Housing Act, 1988* in July and the sections relating to people experiencing homelessness commenced at the beginning of 1989. As predicted by the Minister, '[r]eaction to the new Bill has been universally critical … described as "disappointing" both by Sr Stanislaus Kennedy, Director of Focus Point and Ms Mary Higgins, chairperson of the National Campaign for the Homeless' (Simon Community, 1988, 1), and by the Simon Community, primarily for not imposing a duty on local authorities to house those experiencing homelessness.

In brief, Section 2 of the Act defined a homeless person in very broad terms, Section 9 required local authorities to conduct periodic assessments of the needs of people experiencing homelessness, Section 10 set out the responsibilities of housing authorities to people experiencing homelessness and allowed them to recoup 80 per cent of their expenditure from Central Government (it was increased to 90 per cent in 1993), and Section 28 repealed the 'wandering abroad' section of the *Vagrancy Act, 1824*.[2]

The Act gave local authorities significant discretion in determining if a person is homeless under the terms of the Act and broad options for how they should address the housing needs of homeless people and guidelines were issued by the Department of the Environment in May 1989.

As Harvey notes, the *Housing Act, 1988* rejected placing a statutory obligation on local municipalities to house people experiencing homelessness and this 'obligation was replaced by expectation, assessment and enablement' (2008, 12). Reflecting on the limitations of the legislation, the 'Simon Senator', Senator Brendan Ryan, mused that 'In some ways the tragedy is that some of the development of the publicity by the voluntary sector about homelessness is perhaps at the root of some of the problems in this Bill'.

He went to state that:

> When I and other people like me become involved with the problem of homelessness – in my case 16 or 17 years ago and in the case of many other people 20 or 25 years ago – we used particularly lurid imagery to draw people's attention to the problem of homelessness – lurid imagery of the dosser, the down and out, the wino and the alcoholic. In that process we created an image of the homeless which has never been got rid of.

He concluded that: 'In a way we had sown the seeds of many of the problems I now see with this Bill, by feeding to public opinion, in particular to those who have a major influence in determining public policy, a prejudiced perception of who the homeless are.'

Unfortunately, no amount of subsequent research has entirely rid us of that image' (Seanad Éireann debate – Wednesday, 22 June 1988, 120(7)).

Financing for social housing construction

From the foundation of the State in 1922 to the late 1980s, social housing provision in Ireland was delivered directly and largely exclusively by local authorities through newly constructed homes. The number of new builds varied significantly by decade, but between 1923 and 1990 just over a quarter of a million houses/apartments were constructed for letting (or sale) by local authorities. This model continued until the late 1980s but, without any formally or explicitly announced change of policy, from the early 1990s we see the emergence of a different 'mixed economy' of social housing in terms of providers, financing and schemes. This broad shift in approach can be explained by multiple factors and specific policy decisions. These include spending cuts during the recession of the late 1980s, and a change in the funding model for social housing (Norris, 2016, 182–183).

Until 1987, the provision of social housing by local authorities was funded by borrowing by local authorities at rates which were subsidised by Central Government, with the loans repaid using the rental income. In 1987 the Government had changed this system to one in which construction of social housing would be funded by capital block grants from Central Government. This change went largely unremarked and undebated at the time but would prove to have a number of unanticipated consequences. Allied to the abolition of domestic rates in 1978 as discussed in the previous chapter, the dependence of local authorities on Central Government grants to provide social housing and other services was further exacerbated by this decision.

Norris and Fahey define the mid-1980s as a 'critical juncture' in social housing policy in Ireland; as the economy began to struggle at this time, an ideological shift within broader policy making occurred towards lower taxes and lower spending. The authors also note that, at the time, there was relatively little ideological debate about these spending cuts (Norris and Fahey, 2011). This decline in State spending also applied to the provision of social housing and new builds fell sharply from 7,002 units in 1984 to 768 in 1989 (Norris and Fahey, 2011).

At the same time, the income that local authorities received from rents had been steadily falling from the 1960s, as rents calculated on the basis of the income of the tenant ('differential rents') gradually replaced 'cost rents', arising from an even earlier Government decision. The differential rent model is effective at ensuring that social housing is affordable for low-income tenants, but from a housing management perspective, where tenant incomes are low, it leaves a gap between rental income and the cost of upkeep of the housing units. As a result, ongoing maintenance can be delayed and other the quality and extent of housing services can be limited (Coates and Norris, 1996; Norris, 2001; Norris and Hayden, 2018). Furthermore, as noted earlier, from the middle of the 20th century, differential rents had the benefit of allowing lower income families to access social housing which they could not otherwise afford, thus creating a social mix with higher income working families. However, as these higher income working families left social housing, either through purchase or surrender grants, social housing tenants became less socially mixed, with the remaining tenants increasingly paying the lowest level differential rent. While these changes can be understood as part of an international trend towards the marketisation of social housing, it is also worth noting that, for Byrne and Norris, a desire from Central Government to reduce local authority borrowing 'rather than any overt political hostility to the sector, drove the relative reduction in funding and output from the late 1980s' (2022, 189).

Social partnership: 'the Irish Experiment'

Another development from this time that was to have long-run implications on economic and social policy was the Fianna Fáil Government's engagement with the employers, farmers and trade unions to agree a framework to tackle the vicious circle of inflation, wage demands, high levels of taxation and economic stagnation (O'Donnell and O'Reardon, 1996). The agreement, reached in 1987 and entitled the *Programme for National Recovery*, was the start of what was to become the Social Partnership process which was to shape economic and social development for the next two decades, with successive governments involving all the main parties of the time. Under these arrangements, the 'social partners' – employers, trade unions, farmers and (from 1996) anti-poverty NGOs – came together every three years to negotiate a strategic consensus on economic and social policy. A further 'environmental pillar' was added to the process in 2009.

These negotiations were underpinned by a review of economic and social policy by the NESC, which incorporates all the key social partners. Social Partnership in Ireland is best described by one of its key architects as:

> [p]artnership involves the players in a process of deliberation that has the potential to shape and reshape their understanding, identity and preferences. This idea, that identity can be shaped in interaction, is important. It is implicit in NESC's description of the process as 'dependent on a shared understanding', and 'characterised by a problem-solving approach designed to produce consensus'. (O'Donnell, 1998, 20)

The first Social Partnership Agreement, the *Programme for National Recovery* (1987–1990) had remarkably little to say about homelessness beyond a reference to the fact that the 1988 Bill was to be enacted and had nothing to say on social housing except that capital funding would be used to meet the housing needs of 'disadvantaged groups'.

In fact, housing and homelessness featured very little in the first four partnership agreements until the *Programme for Prosperity and Fairness* in 2000. It is widely recognised that the policies pursued over the two decades of social partnership brought profound economic and social change, such as effective full employment and sharp decreases in the rate of consistent poverty. As we shall see, after the turn of the century critics of the 'Celtic Tiger' economy argued that social policies became subordinate to economic policies and deepening inequalities have characterised Irish society over the later decade. A review of these debates can be found in O'Riain (2014), but in relation to homelessness the important point is that, while homelessness did not feature at a national level until the turn of the century, starting at a national level, new forms of governance emerged from the late 1980s, which gradually filtered down to local areas and concerns.

As a consequence, a focus on shared understanding and problem solving permeated the majority of policy areas, and homelessness was no exception. This generalised partnership approach in which State and non-State bodies worked together to solve particular social problems was adopted outside the formal structures and was to influence the next phase of policy in relation to homelessness and will be discussed in the next chapters.

Migration

As noted earlier, net outward migration returned during this period, as shown in Figure 4.2, as a result of the severe recession in Ireland and greater

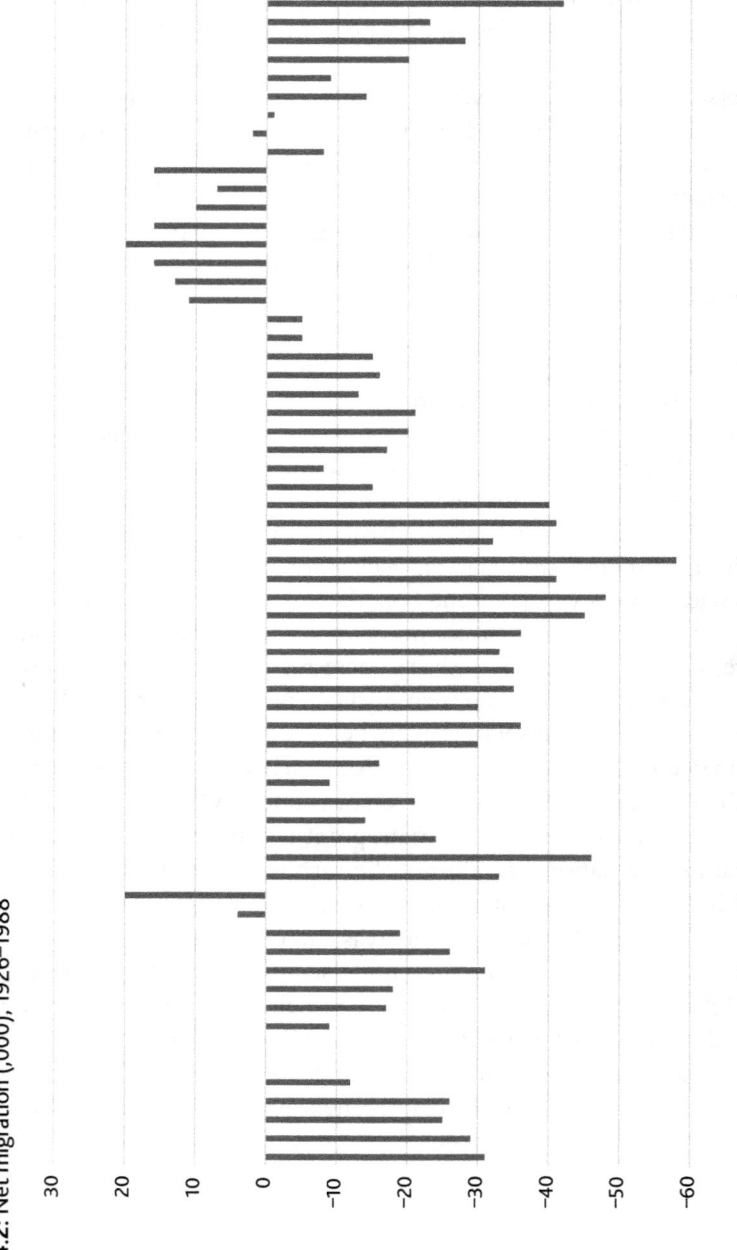

Figure 4.2: Net migration (,000), 1926–1988

Source: Central Statistics Office – https://datasalsa.com/dataset/?catalogue=data.gov.ie&name=c0401-components-of-population-change-since-1926

employment prospects elsewhere. In earlier periods, net emigration has reduced the pressure to build more homes, but during this period, given the extent of housing construction in the earlier period, it resulted in, for the first time, a period where housing supply could match the demand for housing from those who remained.

Conclusion

While the 1980s were extremely difficult years economically and socially for Ireland in general, with high levels of unemployment and poverty, they were also years where housing was more readily available, and the foundations were laid for a new way of addressing homelessness. It was also the period where, as Norris and Byrne (2021, 505) persuasively argue, that the property-based welfare system, which was the defining feature of housing and welfare policy in the first six decades after Independence 'was almost entirely abolished and replaced with a strongly marketized and financialised model'. This new model saw Government grants and access to mortgages for homeowners replaced by the newly deregulated banking sector lending and a fundamental change in how social housing was funded, as discussed earlier. This shift arose from the logic of the model of economic development embarked on in the late 1950s from protectionism to internationalism as discussed in Chapter 2, and the increasing adoption of social security and social services more typical of the urban societies of the other members of the European Community that Ireland was now an integral part.

In the next chapter, we will look at the implications of the *Housing Act, 1988* for homeless services and people who experienced homelessness, in the context of a paradigm change in housing policy, but it is relevant to note the closing of one long-running theme in this story at the same time as the new Act was passed. As we have seen, proposals to close the Casual Wards in the County Homes had been made from the start of the century. Even the reiteration of this proposal in the 1968 Interdepartmental Report on the Care of the Aged did not bring the practice to an end. In the early 1980s the Simon Community reported that nearly three-quarters of County Homes still made provision for casuals, albeit often on a reduced scale (Doherty, 1982). By the late 1980s, only eight units remained for 'casuals' in four health board areas, three of which were 'locked', where the casuals were locked into the unit at night.

In a recurring feature of policy on housing and homelessness, it took a fatality to end the practice of accommodating homeless people in these former workhouses. The death of John Broderick in a 'locked casual unit' in the grounds of the former County Home, now the Hospital of the Assumption, in Thurles, Co. Tipperary, on 1 June 1988 led to this casual unit being closed in November. John, who was born in Limerick in 1925, later emigrated to England where he had worked as a coal miner, before returning to Ireland. He became ill during the night, but help could not be summoned as the unit was locked and at a distance from the main hospital. The remaining units quickly followed suit and closed (O'Sullivan, 2020), bringing to an end the long history of using workhouses and their successor institutions as accommodation for homeless people.[3] The legacy of the County Homes as a response to homelessness lives on in legislation, as the current definition of homelessness, contained in the *Housing Act, 1988*, includes a person living in the County Home, despite that ironically the last County Homes were closing as the legislation was enacted.

5

From the implications of the Housing Act to local partnerships on homelessness, 1989–1997

Introduction

The previous chapter closed with the introduction of the *Housing Act, 1988* and this chapter will explore the consequences of its enactment. In 1991, the first statutory national Assessment of Homelessness since 1925 took place and more detailed data on homelessness started to be available from this point. The chapter will set out our knowledge of the extent and nature of homelessness during this period. There were important developments in how homelessness was thought about and responded to in Europe and the US during this period, and this chapter will provide a brief comparative account of these.

In the later part of this period, Ireland was comparatively one of the earlier adopters of integrated strategies to organise statutory and non-governmental responses to homelessness, including the prevention of homelessness. This chapter will explore the motivation underpinning these strategies, and their effectiveness.

The role of what are now termed Approved Housing Bodies (not-for-profit housing providers) was significantly expanded and given explicit policy recognition during this period with the first ever *Plan for Social Housing* published by the Department of Housing in 1991, and a further elaboration in 1995 with the publication of *Social Housing – The Way Ahead*. The chapter will also explore the origins of the *Homeless Initiative* in Dublin in 1995, an initiative that formally integrated statutory health and housing services, while also considering its impact on strategic thinking on homelessness nationally during this period.

Political and economic context

This period is unusual in seeing two General Elections but three Governments. Despite the significant changes in political leadership over the time, the period shows a consistent development of homelessness and housing policy as the implications of the 1988 Act are played out and a national strategic approach begins to emerge. After the June 1989 general election, Fianna Fáil was returned to office but this time requiring a coalition with the Progressive Democrats to form a government. In February 1992, Charles Haughey resigned as Taoiseach and was replaced by Albert Reynolds, who called an election by the end of the year. This November 1992 General Election resulted in a finely balanced Dáil which ultimately ratified two successive Governments: a Fianna Fáil/Labour Coalition led by Albert Reynolds from 1992 to 1994 and, after that fell in 1994, a Fine Gael/Labour/Democratic Left Government – the so-called Rainbow Coalition – under John Bruton which ran until May 1997. The period, particularly the later part, was characterised by greater economic stability and growth, with unemployment peaking at 21 per cent of the labour force in 1993 (Kennedy, 1993) but falling over the following years.

Impact of the *Housing Act, 1988* on homeless households

Despite the relatively far-reaching reforms in the 1988 Act, it took several years for the new legislation to have any real impact on the practice of local authorities or the experiences of people who were homeless. This delayed impact led to a number of reviews being conducted, in the first place primarily by the homeless NGOs, to ascertain the extent to which homeless persons were being accommodated by the local authorities. In a report commissioned by Focus Ireland, Kelleher (1990) provided an initial overview of the services available to homeless people in Dublin in the period after the implementation of the Act. The report rather bleakly argued that any changes that were of direct benefit to people who were homeless were minimal. In particular, the report recommended that greater coordination between the State agencies should be developed and that a 'housing forum' comprising members of voluntary and statutory bodies be inaugurated.

Two years later, Murphy-Lawless and Dillon (1992) in a national survey of housing authorities, commissioned by the National Campaign for the Homeless, showed that, at the time of the research, only five authorities had staff specifically trained to deal with the needs of homeless clients. None of the larger authorities had appointed specific staff to deal with homelessness and six authorities did not recognise those sleeping rough as homeless, as had been defined by the 1988 Act.

Providing basic shelter was the main response reported by the majority of local authorities which responded to the researchers, with other forms of support being minimal or non-existent. The researchers concluded that the Act did have some positive impact on local authorities but that it was ultimately disappointing, particularly in light of the expectations of voluntary bodies. This was a consequence, they argued, not only of the permissive nature of the Act, but also of the wider structural changes taking place in Ireland. In a similar vein, Leonard (1992a) argued that despite the promise of consultation in the Act, the experience of the Simon Communities showed that, in practice, little formal consultation on local issues was apparent and that local authorities, without any significant input from voluntary agencies, were still operating on their own in deciding policy towards the homeless.

In 1991 the Department of Environment also conducted a review of the implementation of the Act. The Department noted that 'the basic legislation and guidelines are generally satisfactory, where they are implemented in a flexible and sympathetic manner by local authorities'. However, the review found that the 'concern expressed about the manner of implementation of the guidelines by some local authorities was justified' (1991a, 15). As a result of the review, Minister Padraig Flynn – who had been responsible for the 1988 Act in the previous Government and been re-appointed as Minister for the Environment in the 1989 Fianna Fáil/Progressive Democrat Government – issued a revised circular to local authorities (Circular N9/91). This stressed that the relevant sections of the Act should be implemented in a 'flexible and sensitive manner' and that the 'Minister views as totally unacceptable the failure of any housing authority to respond, to the full extent of its powers and capacity, to the deprivation that homelessness represents'. In November 1991, Minister Flynn was sacked from Cabinet after voting no confidence in his party leader, Charles Haughey, during internal party conflicts which dominated Fianna Fáil during that period. He was succeeded in quick succession by two Ministers before the Government fell in early 1992.

The policies of local authorities for allocating social housing ('Schemes of Letting Priorities') prioritised the needs of families and the elderly, so that working-age single homeless persons were unlikely to be offered local authority homes. Thus, despite the aspirations of the 1988 Act, the structural constraints faced by local authorities in the period immediately after its enactment made the prioritisation of single homeless people unlikely. Where urban local authorities did offer accommodation, the homes tended to be in difficult-to-let flat complexes, many of which had been ravaged by the opiate epidemic that had emerged, particularly in Dublin, from the early 1980s (Butler, 1991).

At the end of 1992, the Fianna Fáil/Progressive Democrats Government fell, and the November election resulted in a finely balanced Dáil, with initially no clear government emerging. Negotiations for a new coalition – which would eventually result in a Fianna Fáil/Labour Coalition with Albert Reynolds continuing as Taoiseach – continued for several weeks after the election.

The extent of homelessness in the 1990s

Although a number of estimates of the extent of homelessness had been produced during the 1970s and 1980s, they were either localised (Farrell, 1988; Bell, 1989; Dillon et al, 1990) or 'guesstimates' (Harvey and Higgins,

1988; National Economic and Social Council, 1988; Daly, 1990). The figure of 5,000 homeless persons nationally was the one most commonly cited by voluntary and campaigning agencies in the late 1980s and early 1990s. However, in 1991, as a consequence of the *Housing Act, 1988*, the first national assessment of the extent of homelessness since 1925 took place. The assessment included those on local authority housing waiting lists *plus* those residing in various hostels but not on the waiting list. This was in contrast to the Assessment of Housing Needs, which only included those on the waiting list.[1] The results of this 1991 survey indicated that there were 2,751 homeless households in Ireland. This exercise was repeated in 1993 and saw a slight decrease in the number of homeless households to 2,667 with the number decreased again in 1996 to 2,501.

The initial figures produced by the Assessment of Homelessness from 1991 were considerably lower than the estimates put forward by the voluntary sector, and the sector was not slow in criticising the methodology and administration of the assessment (Leonard, 1992b, 1994). In light of these criticisms, and of the housing assessment methodology more generally, the Department of the Environment, recognising the 'difficulties in quantifying the true extent of homelessness' (Department of Housing, 1995, 16) commissioned the Economic and Social Research Institute (ESRI) to explore the meaning and adequacy of these assessments. The ESRI concluded that 'some undercount has taken place' (Fahey and Watson, 1995, 104) but that they were not in a position to quantify the degree of undercount. They also highlighted the inconsistencies in recording homeless persons between different local authorities.

The ESRI report highlighted two aspects of the local authority approach to housing that militated against responding effectively to homelessness: the tendency to provide long-term accommodation primarily to families, and the lack of expertise by the local authorities in dealing with households with psychiatric or addiction problems. The authors recommended greater coordination between the health boards and voluntary agencies in meeting the needs of the homeless, in particular in enhancing the possibility of moving them to permanent housing. It also recommended that the policy regarding the eligibility of one-person households for local authority housing be clarified. Collins and McKeown (1992) had raised this issue earlier in their study of Simon Community residents. Their report argued that homeless people could settle and maintain a good quality of life in their own accommodation if the proper support structures were put in place for them at the appropriate junctures. While they noted that the guidelines to the *Housing Act, 1988* stipulated that homeless persons should not be at a disadvantage compared to other groups in need of housing, in practice the housing needs of single homeless persons were not being met (Collins and McKeown, 1992, 114).

The limitations of the local authority assessment methodology were also highlighted in a study of the men, women and children who used 12 emergency hostels in Dublin (Kelleher et al, 1992). The data collected during the research showed that, in a three-week period in March and a second three-week period in June/July 1991, the numbers using hostels varied from 545 on 2 July to 595 on 4 March. The vast majority of hostel users were male. Over the six-week Census period, it was estimated that 1,573 people used the hostels. Based on these figures, the number leaving the hostel system, and the length of time in which people stay in hostels, it was estimated that, over a period of a year, between 6,500 and 7,500 separate individuals had used hostels. Thus, the numbers encountered in this study of hostels in the Dublin region suggested a higher prevalence of homelessness than did the official assessments, albeit that much of the variance is explained by the differing methodologies (point-in-time versus period-prevalence).

With total social housing stock falling due to sales to tenants and output low, as discussed later, the numbers officially recorded as in need of social housing grew from 19,376 in 1989 to 28,624 in 1993 and to 39,172 by 1999. Nearly 60 per cent of those on the housing waiting list in 1999 were there because they couldn't afford their existing accommodation, compared to 14.5 per cent a decade earlier. Although *Social Housing – The Way Ahead* (Department of the Environment, 1995), published in 1995, extended the number of housing options available to local authorities, and expenditure on social and affordable housing grew, demand for social housing considerably outstripped supply, as we shall discuss below.

Use of B&Bs as overflow accommodation

Due to the limited supply of social housing and a decrease in the number of beds in emergency hostels relative to demand as a number of shelters had closed or reduced capacity to provide single unit rather than dormitory accommodation; coupled with a lack of appropriate hostel facilities for couples with children and single parent household experiencing homelessness, increased use was made of bed-and-breakfast accommodation in Dublin, particularly for families with children.

In the late 1980s, bed-and-breakfast type accommodation for homeless households was virtually unknown. In 1990, only five homeless households were placed in such accommodation, but by 1999, 1,202 households were placed (Moore, 1994; Houghton and Hickey, 2000). As the number of households placed in bed-and-breakfast accommodation increased, so did the costs, which rose steeply from €660 in 1990 to nearly €6 m in 1999. The increase in the cost was not only a consequence of the increase in the number of households accommodated but also reflected the increase in the average length of stay, from less than a fortnight in the early 1990s to nearly three months in 1999. The 1,202 households placed in bed-and-breakfast accommodation in 1999 comprised 1,518 adults and 1,262 children, and 71 per cent of the adults were female.

Youth Homelessness and the *Child Care Act, 1991*

By the early 1990s, there was extensive evidence of the absence of suitable accommodation for unaccompanied children and young people once they became homeless, particularly, but not exclusively, in Dublin (Daly, 1990). The problem became particularly acute, ironically perhaps, after the implementation of the *Child Care Act, 1991*, which, as outlined in the previous chapter, had been influenced by campaigning work by coalitions of homeless NGOs such as the National Campaign for the Homeless, Focus Point and the Streetwise National Coalition, and gave health boards responsibility for children up to the age of 18.

Prior to the enactment of the *Child Care Act, 1991*, health boards had been responsible for children only until they reached 16 (under the provisions of the *Children Act, 1908*), a situation which created a gap in services for 16- and 17-year-olds. The 1991 Act remedied this situation by defining a child as someone up to the age of 18 and placed, in Section 5, a clear obligation on the health boards to provide accommodation for homeless children (see O'Sullivan, 1995, for further details). Section 5 came into operation in November 1992, but within a short period of time, considerable difficulties emerged in relation to the interpretation and implementation of the section by the health boards, particularly the Eastern Health Board (EHB) (which covered Dublin).

Many of the challenges were related to the alleged inadequacy of provision and the consequent reliance on the part of health boards on B&B accommodation as they attempted to meet the needs of homeless young people. In the EHB region, the number of unaccompanied homeless children placed in B&Bs doubled from 39 in 1991 to 76 in 1993. Critics of Section 5's implementation argued that it excluded homeless children from mainstream child welfare services and effectively positioned them within a secondary child welfare system that provided minimal levels of support and accommodation rather than care and protection (O'Sullivan, 1995, 1998). The debate about the adequacy of the provision of B&B accommodation to homeless children ultimately ended up in the High Court.

Controversy over the use of B&B accommodation, particularly for unaccompanied children under 18, prompted the High Court to explore how the sections related to homelessness children (Section 5) were operated. At the centre of this debate were arguments about how the stipulation that health boards 'take such steps as are reasonable' might be appropriately evaluated, alongside questions about what constituted 'suitable accommodation' for homeless children (see Whyte, 2002 for further details). In a series of High

Court actions, the Courts clearly identified a gap in Irish child welfare legislation in that health boards were adjudged not to have powers of civil detainment. The judgments resulting from these actions led the Department of Health, in conjunction with the health boards, to establish a small number of, euphemistically entitled, High Support and Special Care Units for children.

Despite this, the number of children before the High Court continued to grow and, in July 1998, the High Court issued an order to force the Minister for Health to provide sufficient accommodation for the children appearing before it in order to vindicate the children's constitutional rights (O'Sullivan, 1998). Notwithstanding these challenges, and while concerns persist about the accommodation and care of vulnerable unattached children, the combination of civil society campaigning, concerns expressed by the street level statutory social workers, legislation, litigation and service provision brought an end to the literal homelessness of unaccompanied minors from the mid-1990s.

The residualisation of local authority housing

Although local authority housing output fell by two thirds in the late 1980s, compared with construction levels during the preceding decade, as shown in Figure 5.1, due to high rates of emigration and the 'surrender grants' as discussed in the previous chapter, most of the deliberations in the period up to the passing of the *Housing Act, 1988* had taken place in the context of relatively good availability of social housing. The pessimistic tone of the initial reviews of the impact on homelessness of the *Housing Act, 1988* reflects the deterioration in the availability of local authority housing from the late 1980s into early 1990s, due to the decline in construction and sale of over a third of the stock.

The *Programme for Economic and Social Progress* (PESP), the second national social partnership agreement reached in 1991, has a little more to say about housing and homelessness than its predecessor. Tellingly, it characterised the decline in social housing construction as a positive achievement made possible by reduced waiting list – reductions that had been primarily due to emigration and grants to encourage working tenants to leave the social housing system:

> Significant reductions in the size of the local authority housing programme were possible in the mid and late 1980s as the numbers on local authority waiting lists fell from the peak level of 30,000 households in 1982. In December 1988, there were just under 17,700 approved applicants for local authority housing.

The PESP noted that waiting lists had again started to rise but offered no significant policy changes to speed up the construction of social housing.

Despite a small increase in construction from 1989, the scale of tenant purchase resulted in the stock of local authority housing declining by almost

Figure 5.1: Social housing output, 1923–1996

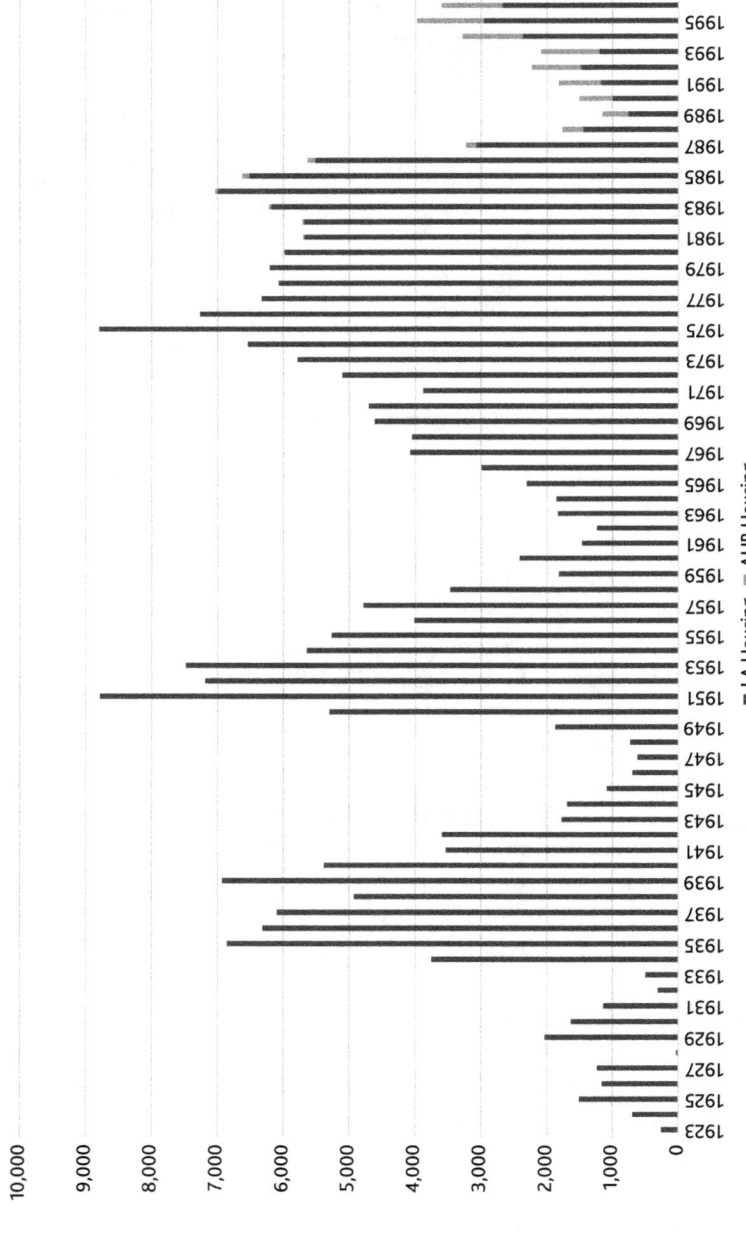

Source: Department of Local Government and Public Health Annual Report (various years) (Dublin: Stationery Office). Department of the Environment (various years): Annual Housing Statistics Bulletin (Dublin: Department of the Environment).

a quarter (22.5 per cent) – from just over 120,000 units in 1987 to just over 93,000 in 1991. All this made it much more difficult for low-income households to secure social housing, with the number of households on the housing waiting list increasing from 17,685 in 1988 to 28,624 in 1993.

As discussed in the previous chapter, from the time it was introduced in 1984 until it was abolished in 1987, the surrender grant supported 7,700 mainly employed households to move out of local authority housing, resulting in an increased concentration of people who were unemployed and had other social problems in the remaining local authority housing estates, particularly in urban areas (Nolan, Whelan and Williams, 1998). As argued by Fahey (1998, 290–291), the impact of the tenant purchase schemes was that

> for the majority of local authority tenants, renting from the local authority has assumed the character of a staging post on the route to heavily subsidised home ownership rather than a life-time alternative tenure. While this is beneficial for those who succeed in making the transition, it is less healthy for those left behind.

Thus, the combined impact of these policies was to create a residual sector of local authority housing dominated by a narrow social mix of marginalised households, predominantly unemployed and unskilled, with high rates of crime and a lack of social amenities. This residualisation of social housing represented a marked shift away from the social housing policies and provision that characterised the first five decades after Independence and was linked to a deepening stigmatisation of local authority estates and the people who lived in them, with long-term consequences (O'Connell and Fahey, 1999).

O'Connell (1998, 25–26) argued at this time that:

> We have now arrived at the point where the local authority has become the tenure of the most disadvantaged groups in Irish society. It has always by legal definition housed such groups but historically also provided a fair level of what could be described as general needs housing. Now it is almost exclusively housing long-term unemployed households, lone parent households, households depending on low-paid insecure work and the elderly poor. Most of the others have departed. Thus, others who traditionally rented from the local authority, such as skilled, semiskilled and other blue-collar workers have availed of tenant purchase schemes and surrender grant schemes and moved into the affordable end of the suburban owner-occupier market.

Despite the fact that local authorities were very large-scale landlords, there was little evidence of a business plan for the maintenance of the homes or investment in the social fabric of the communities (O'Connell, 1999). Now that so many tenants were unemployed, the rental income, which linked through differential rents to the income of tenants, was insufficient to cover the upkeep of the homes let alone provide social supports and amenities.

Local authorities had no system of estate management, and tenant participation was largely non-existent. The social problems which emerged with large-scale new build sites were not anticipated and the organisation and maintenance of local authority housing remained highly centralised. In 1965 Pfretzschner had observed:

> The concept of social service as a basic ingredient in the housing system is almost totally lacking ... Neither the 'professional housing manager' nor the 'professional social welfare worker' is to be found in the country. There are no professional housing managers partly because there are no educational institutions preparing for such a position, and because graduates from other countries have not, as yet, been recruited in Ireland. The management of housing estates is not considered to be such a specialised function that other than routine administrative training is required. Managers are recruited through normal civil service channels, and frequently perform administrative duties other than those pertaining to housing. (1965, 118)

His remarks regarding housing management were broadly applicable a quarter of a century later. It was not until the establishment of a Housing Management Group in 1996 (Housing Management Group, 1996) that this situation started to change appreciably. These challenges led to the suggestion that the role of local authority housing 'is no longer to meet basic housing needs but to segregate what has become a clearly defined housing underclass' (O'Connell, 1993, 258). Based on data from the seminal 1987 ESRI study of poverty in Ireland, Nolan et al showed that approximately '40 percent of those below the income poverty lines, and almost half those below the 60 percent line and experiencing basic deprivation, are in local authority housing, mostly rented rather than tenant purchase' (1994, 217).

Local authorities in the early 1990s, in the years after the implementation of the homeless provisions of the *Housing Act, 1988*, were faced with a declining stock of housing units, a massively reduced social housing budget, largely welfare-dependent tenants, increasingly difficult estates to manage and virtually no form of estate management (except for selling the stock).

The *Plan for Social Housing*, non-profit rental housing and the management of local authority housing

It is in this context that a reduced role for local authorities in the provision of social housing came into active discussion from the early 1990s. *The Plan for Social Housing* (1991b), the *Lord Mayor's Commission on Housing in Dublin* (1993), the *Memorandum on the Preparation of A Statement of Policy on Housing Management* (1993) and the successor document to the *Plan for Social Housing*, *Social Housing – The Way Ahead* (1995) all argued for a new role for housing authorities in Ireland, in a mixed economy of social housing providers.

The cumulative effect of this flurry of policy documents was to encourage non-profit housing agencies, now known as Approved Housing Bodies (AHBs), to play an enhanced role in the provision of non-market rental housing in Ireland. The most radical proposal came from the *Lord Mayor's Commission on Housing* (1993) in Dublin, which argued that local authorities should be providers of housing only as a last resort, and that a range of alternative options should be first explored before the provision of a permanent local authority house. The key concept underpinning the report was that local authorities become *enablers*, rather than *providers* of housing in the first instance as had been the case traditionally.

In the Introduction and Chapter 1, we outline the significant role that non-governmental organisation, such as the Iveagh Trust and the Dublin Artisans Dwellings Company, had played in housing provision before the foundation of the State. While the Iveagh Trust continued to provide housing (and accommodation to people who were homeless or at risk in its Iveagh Hostel), with the growth of Local Government provision, such bodies had ceased to be a significant provider of new homes until the 1960s. From the early 1960s, what were now known as voluntary housing agencies started to play a minor role in the provision of housing for people with 'special needs' (for example the elderly, people with disabilities and people who were homeless), though primarily for the elderly.

The value of the contribution that non-profit/co-operative housing could make in the provision of housing for low-income households gained momentum during the 1980s after the introduction of a new funding mechanism for not-for-profit bodies, the Capital Assistance Scheme (CAS), in 1984.

By 1988, the NESC Report on Housing outlined the rationale for an expanded role for non-profit and co-operative housing associations. The five primary positive attributes of co-operative and non-profit housing as outlined by NESC were:

- co-operative and voluntary housing is often focused around groups with special housing needs and can provide accommodation which is more suitable in terms of location, type of dwelling and ancillary services (such as special sheltered housing for the elderly, or adapted dwellings for the disabled);
- co-operative housing is an effective means of providing housing – both rental and owner-occupied – to lower income groups;

- tenant rental or tenant management co-operatives are structured so that rentals in the public and private sectors actively improve and maintain their own accommodation;
- voluntary and co-operative housing like public rental and owner-occupied housing, requires state financial support – however, expanded voluntary and co-operative sectors will diminish the need for the state to build, allocate, manage and maintain housing;
- voluntary and co-operative housing is particularly suitable in inner urban areas in providing modest owner-occupied housing and low-cost rental accommodation, and co-operative housing can contribute to successful programmes of urban renewal (1988, 57).

In 1988, the homeless NGO Focus Ireland established a linked Approved Housing Body, Focus Housing, and started to explore opportunities to use the CAS funding to provide homes for people who were homeless. The first result of this was the conversion of a former convent in Stanhope Green into 96 self-contained units plus ten newly built family homes.

From 1991, funding was made available under a Rental Subsidy Scheme (RSS) for voluntary agencies to provide housing for households on the 'general needs' waiting lists, that is, not only for those with special needs such as disability, old age or homelessness. The process of increasing the amount of housing provided by such bodies was slow as it took a number of years before such voluntary bodies had developed the expertise and scale to provide significant numbers of housing units.

Nevertheless, as the construction of social housing began to accelerate after the lull of the late 1980s, it was not through a resumption of large-scale local authority housing starts as had been the norm in the past, with non-profit agencies becoming significant players in the provision of rental housing with the provision of 6,700 units of housing between 1981 and 1996.

Part of the rationale underlying this change in direction in the provision of social housing lay in tenant dissatisfaction with local authority housing management, and the social segregation evident in local authority housing estates. In response to this dissatisfaction, the Department of the Environment published a *Memorandum on the Preparation of a Statement of Policy on Housing Management* in March 1993. The core statement in the Memorandum is that:

> The housing stock owned by local authorities constitutes an asset of major value provided by public funds. Each year, considerable resources, in financial and staffing terms, are devoted by local authorities to the management of the stock. There is widespread concern that these resources are not being put to best use and that there is considerable room for improvement in the management of the housing stock. Generally, the role given to tenants in the running of their estates

has been minimal. Clearly, the approach of the past will not suffice for the future and there is an obligation on all local authorities to radically examine their whole approach to housing management. They must identify the deficiencies in their housing management systems, develop objectives and policies for the improvement of these systems and implement them. (1993, 19)

The Memorandum outlined some of the major deficiencies in the local authority housing system and provided a new conceptualisation for the role of the local authorities in the provision and management of housing. It was in many senses a critical document, critical of the manner in which estates had previously been operated and a realisation that in light of the large numbers of households assessed as in need of housing, radical new initiatives were necessary in the provision of local authority housing and management.

However, the key reason for the radical revision of the manner in which local authority estates were operated lay with the cost factor. The total rent that could be collected came under pressure because, as noted earlier, with an increased proportion of local authority tenants relying on social welfare income, the differential rent scheme was not bringing in sufficient rental income to cover maintenance costs.

Between 1982 and 1991 alone, rental income totalled £591 m while total expenditure on maintenance and management was £655m, a deficit of £64 m. In 1991, the total income from the stock of 95,000 dwellings was £72.06 m while the expenditure was £82.18 m, Dublin County Borough alone spent £41.10 m in 1991, yet poor maintenance remained exceedingly high on the list of tenant dissatisfaction. If the proceeds of tenant purchase schemes and miscellaneous receipts are deducted and the rental receipts alone are compared with maintenance and management costs, the gap between them is revealed even more starkly. A consequence of this revenue imbalance was an 'underinvestment in housing maintenance and overuse of refurbishment schemes' (Redmond and Norris, 2014, 153).

While this shift towards a greater role for voluntary housing bodies in the supply of both general and special needs social housing had a long-term impact on the nature of the social housing sector in Ireland, the consequences of this change on homelessness is more difficult to assess. The overarching policy is that the allocation of all social housing is under the control of the local authority whether a particular unit is owned by an AHB or the council itself. But AHBs have some leeway in accepting or rejecting nominations and the probation and eviction policies of AHBs also differ from those of local authorities and can have a significant impact on the profile of their tenants. This has resulted in persistent concerns, albeit without evidence, that the larger AHBs, established to provide homes for 'general needs' tenants rather than 'special needs' tenants, may be reluctant to accept formerly homeless tenants or more likely to terminate their tenancies.

Rent supplements in the private rented sector

Somewhat under the radar, the number of households renting in the private rented sector and receiving a rent subsidy or supplement from the State grew over this period. As discussed in Chapter 3, Rent Supplement had been introduced in 1977 as part of the Supplementary Welfare Allowance scheme, when private rental accommodation accounted for less than 10 per cent of all households. It was funded by the Department of Social Welfare and administered by the regional health authorities.

In 1980, three years after the scheme was established, there were 1,316 recipients of a rent supplement, with the number rising to over 6,500 a decade later (Commission on Social Welfare, 1986, 369). The number of households receiving a rent supplement continued to increase, rising to nearly 37,000 by 1997 at a cost of €96.6 m that year. This was partly due to the rise of unemployment during this period, with the extent of long-term unemployment resulting in many households relying on Rent Supplement not as a short-term measure, but as an on-going contribution to meeting their housing costs. Given the increased importance of rent supplement as a means of meeting the housing costs of low-income households living in the private rental sector, and the increasing cost of the scheme prompted the Department of Social Welfare to establish an interdepartmental group to review the scheme.

In 1995, the review group reported, concluding that rent supplement had 'become a major form of housing support', but that '[t]his development had taken place outside the framework of overall housing policy' (Review Group on the Role of Supplementary Welfare Allowance in Relation to Housing, 1995, 10). In addition, every report on the scheme highlighted the poverty trap created by the scheme, which arose because of the steep clawback for tenants working part-time or on training schemes, and because people working over 30 hours were ineligible for any support (for a summary of this and other criticisms of the rent supplement scheme, see Coates and Norris, 2006). A further *Interdepartmental Committee on the Administration of the Rent Supplement Scheme was established* in 1996. This Committee did not report until 1999, and its recommendations will be discussed in Chapter 6.

Migration

In the first year of this period, 1989, Ireland experienced the highest level of outward migration since the 1950s (Figure 5.2), continuing the trend that was evident in earlier chapters of outward migration reducing the pressure of social

The implications of the Housing Act, 1989–1997

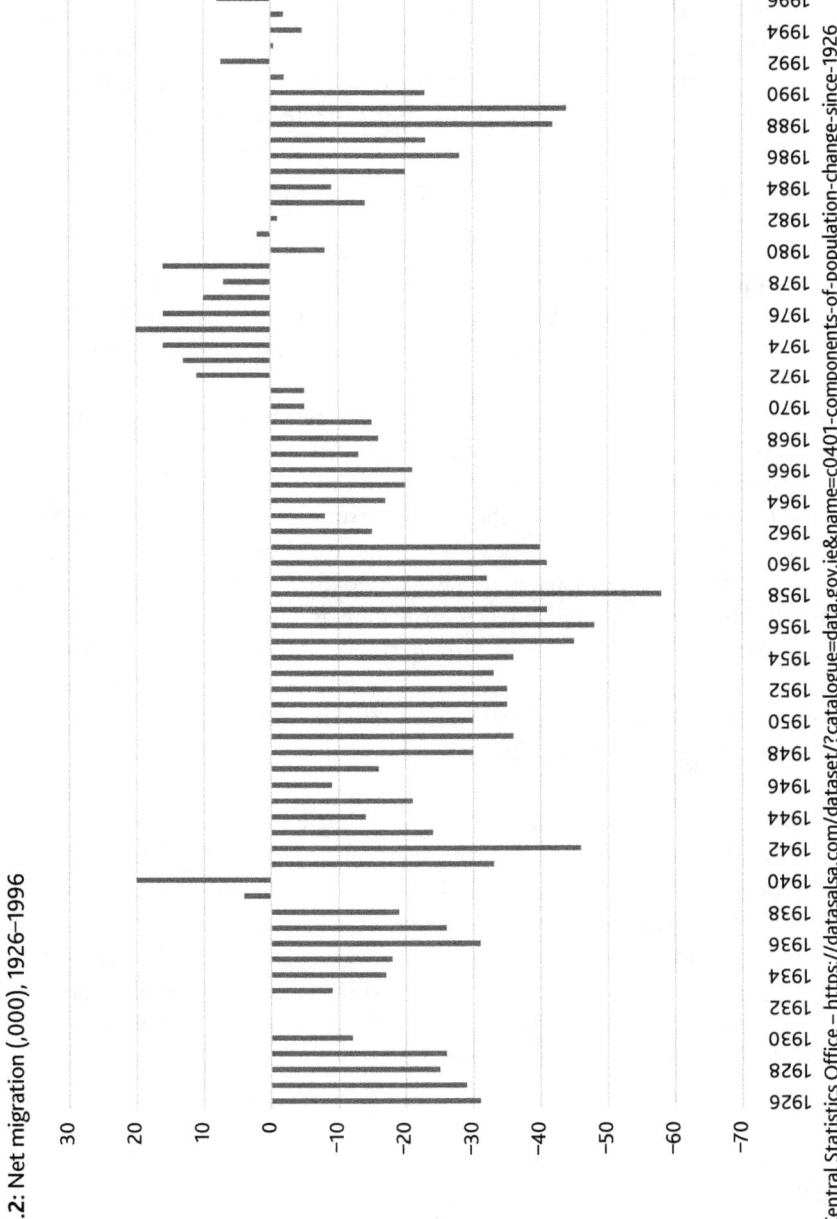

Figure 5.2: Net migration ('000), 1926–1996

Source: Central Statistics Office – https://datasalsa.com/dataset/?catalogue=data.gov.ie&name=c0401-components-of-population-change-since-1926

housing demand, contributing to making social housing more accessible to people moving out of homelessness, despite the low constructions rates and tenant sales. With the improving Irish economy into the 1990s, emigration declined significantly the following year, followed by a number of years of fluctuation with an overall net pattern of small levels of inward migration, mostly Irish people returning from earlier periods of emigration. During this later period, migration is less of a factor in demand for social housing, with other demographic developments playing a greater role.

Social partnership in the homelessness sector

As was noted earlier, the process of social partnership had started to play a significant role not only in relation to wage and taxation policy, but also social policy. However, during the period covered here, housing and homelessness had not emerged as a significant issue across these activities. For example, the second national social partnership agreement, the *Programme on Economic and Social Progress* (1991, 36) simply reiterated the commitment given in the *Plan for Social Housing* to have a more inclusive approach to measuring the extent of homelessness and that 'special steps would be taken by the Department of the Environment to ensure the full implementation both in the letter and in the spirit by local authorities' of the previously issued guidelines issued in 1991 and discussed earlier. It also noted that additional safeguards for households in the private rented sector, such as the provision of rent books and enhanced standards of accommodation, were under review. The third national social partnership agreement – the *Programme for Competitiveness and Work 1994–96* – again had little to say about housing and homelessness, with one paragraph stating that

> [t]he accommodation needs of the homeless will be addressed through further development and funding of integrated services to homeless persons. This will include a continuation of the financial support for local authorities and voluntary housing bodies, through the development of adequate support services in consultation with the statutory and voluntary agencies concerned, and through careful analysis of the extent of homelessness and the factors contributing to it. All local authorities liaise and consult with agencies working with the homeless in assessing the extent of homelessness. (1994, 70)

In 1996, the then Fine Gael/Labour/Democratic Left Government invited eight community and voluntary organisations to join the social partnership discussions (joining the existing Employer, Trade Union and Farmer 'Pillars') (Allen, 1998). While this resulted in a wider range of commitments on social issues, unemployment and poverty, the fourth programme, *Partnership 2000 for Inclusion, Employment and Competitiveness* (1996) again made no mention of homelessness. At this point the Community and Voluntary Pillar did not include any specific housing or homeless voluntary organisations – although the Construction Industry Federation (CIF) was among the employer organisations present (Government of Ireland, Partnership 2000, 5).

While the first decade of social partnership did not generate any significant commitments in relation to homelessness at a national level, the new forms of governance, based on creating a shared understanding of policy issues with a consequent focus on problem solving, were adopted in the majority of policy areas, including at a local governmental level.

The new structures for tackling homelessness emerged in several stages. A *Working Group on Homeless* (Bardas Atha Cliath, 1992), established by the Lord Mayor of Dublin at that time, Gay Mitchell, after the deaths of two men, Danny Lyons (70) and Pat Feery (24), and one women, Pauline Leonard (40), who were sleeping rough in Dublin in December 1992, included a recommendation of greater coordination between the statutory bodies (primarily the Eastern Health Board – the health agency for the greater Dublin region and Dublin Corporation – the local authority agency for Dublin) and various voluntary agencies providing shelter accommodation. The Working Group, comprising the City Manager, the Programme Manager for the Eastern Health Board and the Auxiliary Catholic Bishop of Dublin, noted that the availability of shelter beds was increasingly restricted, in part due to the fact that 60 per cent of the users of shelter beds were occupying those beds for between 5 and 10 years, which in turn resulted from 'the serious reduction in the public house building programme in recent years' (1992, 6).

In February 1993, Minister of State for Housing, Labour's Emmet Stagg, told the Dáil that 'Dublin Corporation has established a Housing Forum which includes representatives of the local authorities in Dublin, the Eastern Health Board and voluntary bodies working on behalf of homeless persons in the area and which meets on a regular basis' (Dáil Éireann debate – Tuesday, 16 Feb 1993 Vol. 426 No. 1). Nevertheless, in 1995, in a review of service provision for households experiencing homelessness in Dublin conducted by Dublin Corporation and the Eastern Health Board, it was noted 'that there are certain deficiencies both in the range of services provided and in the planning and coordination of service delivery' which had led to 'a situation where service provision for the homeless has developed in an unplanned and piecemeal manner often in response to individual initiatives taken by voluntary bodies' (Bardas Atha Cliath/Eastern Health Board, 1995, 1).

Liz McManus of the Democratic Left, who was appointed as Minister for Housing and Urban Renewal in 1994, reported visiting homeless services at this time. She made particular reference to hostels provided by the Legion of Mary, where the poor conditions in the late 1940s had prompted the

Minister for Health at that time to make an immediate allocation of £30,000 to alleviate the situation as noted in Chapter 2. McManus recalled that she:

> visited all the homeless units in Dublin. I even went to the Regina Coeli and The Morning Star hostels that didn't receive any State aid and belonged to another era. Long open dormitories, basic facilities and no security other than a key in the front door. As far as I could fathom these hostels were run by dedicated, but generally frail and elderly, members of the Legion of Mary. My civil servants had never been inside these particular hostels before and wandered around them, wide-eyed, at what they saw. Other hostels were either due for major improvements or had already undergone an upgrade with single or double rooms and proper bathroom facilities. The purpose-built hostels were also visited and it was clear that standards had dramatically improved in recent years. (2011, 13–14)

The report recommended a new administrative structure to deliver homeless services, replacing the Housing Forum. Called the 'Homeless Initiative',[2] it was established in October 1996, with the objective of ensuring that services for homeless people were more effective, particularly by improving their planning, coordination and delivery and by ensuring the development of responses which enabled homeless people to settle and move out of the cycle of homelessness. This was to be achieved through analysis, planning and the development of a strong partnership between all the agencies involved. The Initiative was funded jointly by two Central Government departments (Department of Health, and the Department of Environment), operating under the direction of a management group, comprising two senior officials each from Dublin Corporation and the Eastern Health Board. In addition, a consultative forum consisting of representatives from the Health Board, all local authorities in the greater Dublin region and from voluntary organisations providing services to homeless people (Higgins, 1998). The Initiative also had a full-time director, Mary Higgins, who had been one of the founders of the National Campaign for the Homeless, as well as working for Threshold and other community organisations.

Several years later Higgins (2011, 11) described the vision of the Initiative as:

> bold – and some thought slightly mad and inherently unattainable – but it provided the impetus to drive a complete transformation of the way in which homelessness was understood and responded to. Thus, the approach of prevention, intervention and settlement/housing was devised to replace responses, which were based on meeting emergency needs only and which had served to consign hundreds of people to

living permanently in poor standard accommodation which they had to vacate during the day and where they had no privacy or rights and little by way of comfort. At the centre of this approach was a new model of service delivery which, based on a continuum of care, placed the person who was homeless at the centre of services, so that responses were designed around their aspirations and needs, however complex, and supported people to move out of homelessness and into appropriate housing, and the realisation of their full potential and rights, as quickly as possible.

In an evaluation of the operation of the Initiative over its first five years, it was argued that:

> The Homeless Initiative made a significant contribution to improving the planned co-ordination of services for the homeless in the Dublin region. As an innovative approach to addressing problems of co-operation and co-ordination which apply across many areas of the public sector, the Initiative represented an important new way of working. (Boyle, Butler-Worth and O'Donnell, 2001, 34).

However, others were more critical of the Initiative, with Phelan and Norris (2008, 53) acknowledging the decline of the number of people experiencing homelessness, as it resulted in many service providers being incorporated into 'the sphere of influence of the state' and diluting their 'traditional advocacy role'.

Conclusion

Despite the economic challenges of time and the emerging problems in social housing supply and management, this was a period of optimism in relation to tackling homelessness. While the *Housing Act 1988* had taken time to bed down, it was beginning to result in a clearer picture of the level and nature of homelessness and greater coordination between the health and housing arms of the Government. The problem of homeless children which had been a particular concern from the early 1970s was well on its way to being resolved through the enactment of the *Child Care Act, 1991*. However, it is also clear that successive housing policies promoting homeownership as the tenure of choice in Ireland (and in consequence the relative neglect of other tenures) was reaching its outer limits with serious inequities in the housing system (Drudy and Punch, 2001). The aspirations on homelessness were struggling to make headway as waiting lists for social housing grew due to a number of factors, including low levels of construction, accelerated tenant sales and, ironically, towards the end of the period, reduced emigration due to a strengthening economy.

While social partnership was creating a more stable and successful economic climate, it was also generating new forms of problem solving that deepened the interaction between State agencies as well as between State and voluntary agencies. Emerging from this, the establishment of the Homeless Initiative at the end of this period was a crucial catalyst in devising new ways of responding to homelessness at a local operational level. This local partnership also played an important role in escalating the partnership approach to homelessness back up to a national level. This was to bear fruit when, in August 1998, the new Government set up a *Cross-Departmental Team on Homelessness* under the auspices of the Cabinet Sub-Committee on Social Inclusion (Brownlee, 2008). This was to provide the stimulus for the development of a national strategic and partnership-based approach to tackling homelessness which will be discussed in the next chapter.

6

A decade of strategies, the Celtic Tiger and austerity, 1997-2011

Introduction

In this chapter, we document how the strategic innovation and optimism about homelessness evident during the 1990s continued for several years into the 2000s with the publication of the first national homelessness strategy, *Homelessness – An Integrated Strategy* in 2000 and second strategy *The Way Home: A Strategy to Address Adult Homelessness in Ireland* in 2008. In hindsight, this represented a high point in optimism that homelessness could be eliminated, with a clear commitment to 'ending homelessness' being articulated for the first time with a range of strategy statements to prevent homelessness and to provide coordinated services for the homeless published and implemented, at least in part. Significantly, funding for homeless services also increased with direct funding from the Department of Housing under Section 10 of the *Housing Act, 1988* increasing from €20 m in 2000 to €48 m in 2011.

The chapter also explores shifts in policy in relation to social housing construction over this period, with a number of policy documents continuing the significant shift away from the primacy of local authorities towards Approved Housing Bodies. Social housing output was relatively high over this period until the impact of the global financial crisis (GFC), with local authorities delivering 5,000 units per annum, supplemented by AHBs delivering between 1,500 and 2,000 units per annum. The decline in the number of households privately renting, documented in the previous chapter, was reversed during this period and the policy drivers and implications of this are discussed.

However, the publication of the new homeless strategy in 2008 coincided with a domestic economic crisis in Ireland, following the global financial crisis. This chapter discusses the housing context of these events and of the three-year financial aid programme the Government agreed in 2010, which required drastic cuts to Government spending. The housing market experienced a severe contraction with new output declining and house prices falling by 50 per cent (Byrne and Norris, 2018). This period of austerity saw €20.5 bn in public expenditure cuts and tax increases of €11.5 bn (Roche, O'Connell and Proythero, 2016).

Despite the scale of the economic and social disruption in Ireland, particularly to the housing system, there was no immediate impact on the level of homelessness. Nevertheless, a number of the factors that would contribute to the subsequent rapid increase in homelessness began to take shape, and this chapter will set them out.

Political and economic context

The period covered by this chapter saw three governments, all involving Fianna Fáil as the largest party. While there were short periods of significant cuts in government spending, such as after the 2002 election, most of the period until the 2008 financial crisis was characterised by considerable economic growth and rising incomes, referred to as the Celtic Tiger. The Celtic Tiger was the consequence of three factors identified by Daly: 'public policy, political culture and the accommodation reached with international capital' (2005, 138).

This period starts with the Fine Gael/Labour/Democratic Left 'Rainbow' Coalition calling an election in June 1997 in some of the healthiest economic circumstances the country had seen. The different coalition parties received very different verdicts: Fine Gael gained seats, Democratic Left returned the same number of seats as in 1992, while Labour lost half its seats. Although the Progressive Democrats also lost seats, they had the necessary numbers to form a coalition with a resurgent Fianna Fáil under Bertie Ahern. Although that Government was dogged with allegations of corruption in the planning system dating from earlier periods of rapid house building, the general prosperity saw the first ever re-election of both parties in a coalition with the Fianna Fáil/Progressive Democrats Government returned in the May 2002 election. This election was immediately followed by a period of substantial cutbacks in government spending and a subsequent return to high levels of growth.

However, this later period of growth was characterised by more widespread concerns about economic sustainability and serious vulnerabilities in the economy, particularly related to the indebtedness in the property sector. The 2007 General Election saw the Fianna Fáil and the Progressive Democrats form their third successive government, however due to the seat losses experienced by the Progressive Democrats, the growing Green Party also joined this coalition, their first period in office.

Emergence of a homelessness strategy

Despite the economic turmoil at the end of this period, the most significant policy development in relation to homelessness came at the beginning with the emergence of a strategic approach to tackling homelessness, articulated in a range of different strategic documents and national and Dublin level.

The Housing Need Assessment of 1999 showed that, after remaining around 2,500 for a decade, the number of homeless individuals had more than doubled from 2,501 in 1996 to 5,235 in just three years. While the Government argued that the increase was attributable, at least in part, to a change in methodology (Brownlee, 2008), there was acknowledgement that some urgent intervention was required in response.

As part of the work that resulted in the Dublin Homeless Initiative, the previous government had convened the first ever joint working group between the Department of Environment and the Department of Health. The beginnings of what was to become a new national strategic approach to homelessness can, perhaps, be traced to around a year after the election of the new Government, with the establishment of a Cross-Departmental Team on Homelessness, which was established under the auspices of the Cabinet Sub-Committee on Social Inclusion (Brownlee, 2008). The terms of reference for the cross-departmental team were to 'develop an integrated response to the many issues which affect homeless people including emergency, transitional and long-term responses as well as issues relating to the health, education, employment and home-making' (Department of the Environment and Local Government, 2000, 3). As Higgins (2001) has argued, prior to the development of this strategy and related developments, homelessness was:

> regarded as something apart – much like homeless people themselves – and responses have tended to be 'special' and 'separate', rather than mainstream, with little focus on developing an understanding of the problem or how to prevent it. Within this policy context local authorities have had difficulty in developing responses which will address the needs of homeless people effectively and the implementation of the 1988 Housing Act and subsequent policies have had only limited impact. (Higgins, 2001, 5)

The cross-departmental team produced *Homelessness: An Integrated Strategy* in 2000 which, as well as itself setting out a strategic approach, put in place a process in government which resulted, eight years later, after a number of specialist national and local strategies and reviews, in the publication of *The Way Home: A Strategy to Address Adult Homelessness in Ireland 2008–2013*. This 2008 Strategy statement by the Department of Environment, Heritage and Local Government opens with the declaration that articulates a perspective which had been gaining momentum over the intervening years:

> From 2010, long-term homelessness (i.e. the occupation of emergency accommodation for longer than 6 months) and the need for people to sleep rough will be eliminated throughout Ireland. The risk of a person becoming homeless will be minimised through effective preventative

policies and services. When it does occur homelessness will be short term and people who are homeless will be assisted into appropriate long-term housing. (Department of Environment, Heritage and Local Government, 2008, 7)

This is a very different type of statement than had been made by previous governments in relation to homelessness. Previous government policy statements had been concerned about how homelessness was to be managed, that is with ending one form of provision in favour of another, or with assigning clear responsibilities or with integrating responses. In contrast, the 2008 statement was the first articulation of an intended outcome of policy: that people should no longer 'need' to sleep rough or remain homeless for more than a few months. This new approach had been constructed on the basis of initiatives over the previous decade and Higgins (2011) argues the partnership approach and mission in the 2008 national Strategy had been 'adopted by the Government' from the work of Dublin Homeless Initiative.

The wider housing context

A key development of the strategic focus on homelessness during this period was a new emphasis on providing people who were homeless with housing options which they would be able to sustain as long-term homes, allied to appropriate care planning. Access to housing was therefore crucial in delivering the aspirations of the homeless strategy. Despite this strategic and conceptual shift, the alleged absence of appropriate housing for the homeless became a core criticism levelled at the revised national homeless strategy by a number of voluntary agencies, so before looking in detail at how the homeless strategy evolved, it is helpful to look at the housing context over this period.

Social housing

During the first years of this period, new social housing supply slowed to around 4,000 units per annum but then accelerated to reach a peak of nearly 9,000 units in 2007 – comparable to the highest peaks in new supply in 1950 and 1975, as shown in Figure 6.1. As the impact of the global financial crisis began to play out in slashed government capital budgets and the collapse of the property development sector generally, new social housing supply fell by two-thirds to around 3,000 in 2010 before halving again in 2011.

Most commentators have focused on the *declining share* of social housing during this period as private housing providers recorded unprecedented output (Finnerty, 2002; Redmond and Kernan, 2005). Thus, despite maintaining a steady output, social housing agencies' share of total housing

A decade of strategies, the Celtic Tiger and austerity, 1997–2011

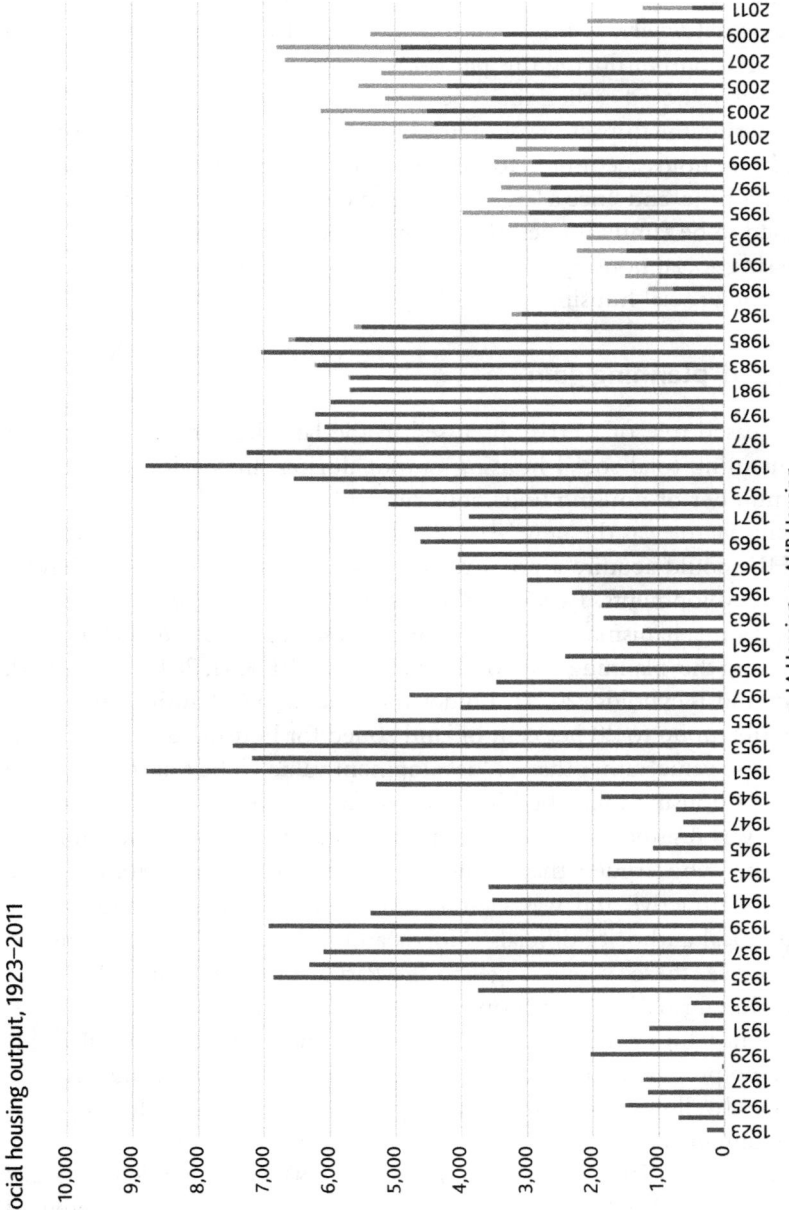

Figure 6.1: Social housing output, 1923–2011

Source: Department of Local Government and Public Health Annual Report (various years) (Dublin: Stationery Office). Department of the Environment (various years); Annual Housing Statistics Bulletin (Dublin: Department of the Environment).

output had fallen to less than 10 per cent of all housing construction over this period. However, it should be noted that the percentage share of social housing has been in steady decline since the 1950s. More significantly, one can argue that the relative share of total output is not the core issue; rather it is the actual *number of new lettings* created. On this measure, there was a high level of output during this period.

However, as noted earlier, the type of social housing supply is also crucial in considering the impact of social housing supply on homelessness. Single-person households accounted for some 80 per cent of homeless households during this time, and since a large proportion of the new social housing stock continued to be family homes, the historic problems faced by single people in accessing social housing re-emerged after the brief interlude of the early 1980s, when social housing lettings had been more available.

Part V and 'planning gain'

The increased role of AHBs, discussed in the last chapter, was one factor in maintaining total social housing output during this period despite the falling number of housing units constructed by local authorities. Another significant factor was the new 'Part V' policy under which local authorities and AHBs could acquire a proportion of new housing units from private housing developments. Part V of the *Planning and Development Acts 2000– 2020* was a mechanism to facilitate delivery of social and affordable housing by capturing the 'planning gain for the community' (DKM, 2012; Redmond, Hegarty and Reynolds, 2021). Under the scheme, local authorities could initially obtain up to 20 per cent of land zoned for housing development at 'existing use value' rather than at 'development value'. The transfer could be in terms of housing units, building land or, on rare occasions, other assets.

Part V was resisted by developers, in particular the Irish Home Builders Association who argued that home purchasers would find mixed tenure estates less attractive and was seen as slowing down the planning process by some local authority officials (Norris and Shiels, 2007). In response to this resistance, there were changes to the Part V of the Planning Acts over time, including halving the proportion of social and affordable homes to 10 per cent.[1] From the introduction of the scheme in 2002 until 2011, the scheme provided a total of 15,114 units – which was just 3.5 per cent of all the dwellings constructed during this period (not including one-off developments).

Of these 15,114 Part V units, 5,721 (38 per cent) were provided for social housing (3,757 to local authority stock and 1,964 to AHBs). This represented 13 per cent of all the social housing units completed during the period. It is notable that the benefits of the scheme peaked in 2009 and 2010, when the market for housing sales had collapsed due to the financial crisis, when a total of 1,846 units were transferred to local authorities (DKM 2012, 31). The majority of Part V dwellings (62 per cent) were 'affordable' units which were sold to low-to-mid income households.

In addition to the housing units themselves, sites for 944 units were transferred and €122.4 m was received as payments in lieu of land transfers, a quarter of this being accounted for by two local authorities (Dun Laoghaire/ Rathdown and Kildare).

A new housing strategy

In 2007, the Government launched a new housing strategy entitled *Delivering Homes, Sustaining Communities*. The Strategy drew heavily on two NESC reports, one on housing policy (2004), the other on the future of the Irish welfare State (2005). In relation to welfare, NESC advocated a life-cycle approach to meeting the needs of citizens and, in housing, advocated the substantial expansion of social housing output. A core element of the 2007 Government Strategy was the provision of a:

> planned and concerted increase in investment in existing social housing over the coming years. This provides an opportunity to tackle some long-standing problems in communities that have experienced multiple disadvantages. The focus will be on ensuring that this investment results in the development of strong communities rather than over-reliance on refurbishment of dwellings. (2007, 11)

Despite the growth in new social housing supply from the middle of the decade until 2009, the number of people on the waiting list for social housing more than tripled from 1996 (27,427) to 2011 (98,318). This increased need for social housing reflected both internal demographic factors arising from Ireland's youthful population, but also the reversal of the previous history of outward migration as a large number of jobs were being created by the booming economy. Inward migration consisted not only of Irish people who had emigrated in previous years but were now able to return but also, for the first time, immigration of non-Irish people, mostly EU citizens, coming to Ireland to work. This increase will be discussed in more detail later in the chapter, after consideration of the various homeless reports and strategies over the decade.

Private rented sector

As noted in the chapter introduction, the private rented sector had been declining both in real terms and as a proportion of the housing stock since the foundation of the State. Due to the introduction of a range of financial incentives for landlords, particularly in the 1990s, the sector started to grow and continued to grow over this period: from a historic low of 81,424 units or 8 per cent of the housing stock in 1991, by 2011, the absolute number of private rented units had increased to 305,377 or 18.5 per cent of the housing stock, a dramatic reversal of half a century of decline (Central Statistics Office, 2012).

In addition to various financial incentives and easy access to buy-to-let mortgages, a further significant factor in creating this larger role for the private rental sector was the enactment of the *Private Residential Tenancies Act, 2004,* following the report of the *Commission on the Private Rented Sector* in 2000. The legislation provided a reasonably comprehensive set of mutual rights and obligations for both landlords and tenants. As this sector of the housing market expanded it became progressively easier for low-income households, particularly single male households, to access accommodation in this sector with the aid of a Rent Supplement from the Department of Social Welfare. Rents also decreased significantly from 2001 onwards but stabilised in 2005. On a longer-term basis, rent levels, while volatile, remained at much the same level over this period. The private rented housing sector became a key provider of low-cost accommodation for households unable to either purchase housing on the open market or unable to access tenancies in the various social and affordable housing programmes.

Growth of the sector during this period was built on the presumption that the market would continue to be dominated by landlords who owned one or two properties more as investments than as a long-term commitment to renting as a livelihood. Consequently, 'buy-to-rent' investors would only come forward if they could readily gain vacant possession of their properties to obtain the best return. There was also a view, albeit contested, that a landlord's right to obtain 'vacant possession' would be upheld by the Constitution (Hogan and Keyes, 2021, 27). Hence, regulation of the sector then proceeded on the basis that it must remain relatively easy for landlords to terminate tenancy agreements when they wished to sell or to use the property family members or for themselves. The extent to which growth of the private rental sector depended on investments made on this basis was to have long-term implications as these landlords decided to sell up and so terminated their tenancies to achieve the best return on their investment.

As noted in the previous chapter, the number of households receiving Rent Supplement in the private rented sector increased significantly in the second half of the 1990s. This trend continued after 2000, as the economy boomed, and continued further as the economy went into recession and unemployment rose: the number of households in receipt of a rent supplement peaked in 2010, at 97,000 at a cost of €516 m that year.

The *Interdepartmental Committee,* whose establishment in 1996 to look at transferring Supplementary Welfare housing payments to local authorities was referred to in the previous chapter, reported in June 1999. The Committee recommended that where tenants had a long-term need, rent assistance should be provided by local authorities, while the existing welfare-based Rent Supplement arrangement should continue to provide rent assistance for people with short-term needs, such as periods of unemployment or illness. It proposed that a further *Planning Group on the Local Authority Rent Assistance* would be established to identify the operational issues regarding the transfer of long-term claims, which represented the large majority, to the local authorities. However, when this *Planning Group on the Local Authority Rent Assistance* reported, it did not, in fact, recommend the transfer of Rent Supplement to the Local Authorities, but, rather, took a different view and proposed the establishment of a new housing subsidy scheme, the *Rental Accommodation Scheme* (RAS).

Rental Accommodation Scheme (RAS)

As originally proposed, this new scheme was to cater for the accommodation needs of persons who had long-term housing needs rather than those going through a temporary crisis. The Planning Group proposed that being in receipt of a rent supplement for over 18 months indicated such a long-term housing need. In contrast to Rent Supplement, in which a subsidy is paid directly to the tenant, the new RAS involved payment to landlords: local authorities entered into contracts directly with private landlords and paid the full market-related rent to them, while tenants paid a differential rent to the local authorities. While some Rent Supplement tenancies were converted into RAS tenancies, local authorities could also allocate tenants to RAS properties in the same way as to their own or AHB properties. Crucially, in terms of avoiding the insecurity in the private rental sector that contains a risk of homelessness, the local authority remained responsible for rehousing the tenant if the agreement with the landlord came to an end. RAS tenants have the same rental arrangements and some of the security of tenure of local authority tenants, while living in privately rented homes. RAS was rolled out in 2004 and by the end of the decade nearly 18,000 RAS tenancies had been set up, but as noted, despite these RAS tenancies, the number of households in receipt of Rent Supplement continued to increase, peaking at just over 97,000 households in 2010.

Local homeless action plans

Under the *Planning and Development Act, 2000*, each local authority was required to prepare a housing strategy. The objective of these housing strategies was to ensure that: sufficient land is zoned to meet the housing requirements in the region; there is a mixture of house types and sizes to meet the needs of various households; that housing is available for people on different income levels and provides for the need for both social and affordable housing.

One of the key proposals in *Homelessness – An Integrated Strategy* (2000) was that each local authority should, in addition, also produce a *Homeless Action Plan*. Unlike the housing strategies, however, local authorities were not under any statutory obligation to produce these plans, and no clear guidance was in place about what the plan should include.

In a review of the homeless plans (Hickey et al, 2002), data deficiencies in relation to the extent of homelessness in local authority functional areas emerged as a fundamental problem in devising the plans. As a consequence, quite diverse methodologies were utilised to estimate the extent of homelessness in local authorities' functional areas. In addition, the authors noted that 'the content, both general and specific, in the analysed action plans varies significantly from county to county' and that in terms of strategically addressing homelessness, 'the outcomes of the Plans are in general disappointing' (2002, 107). A crucial finding of the analysis was that outside of the major urban areas, there was 'little sense from the ... plans on the process for diminishing the incidence of homelessness in source areas outside of major urban areas', and that '(w)ithout appropriate strategies non-metropolitan local authorities will continue to "export" their homeless constituents to large cities' (2002, 91).

Homelessness: a preventative strategy

The second major strategic document which emerged over this period was the *Homeless Preventative Strategy* which was published in early 2002. Its key objective was to ensure that 'no one is released or discharged from State care without the appropriate measures in place to ensure that they have a suitable place to live with the necessary supports, if needed' (Department of Environment and Local Government et al, 2002, 3).

Specific proposals included the establishment by the Probation and Welfare Service of a specialist unit to deal with offenders who are homeless; the provision of transitional housing units by the Prison Service as part of their overall strategy of preparing offenders for release; and ensuring that all psychiatric hospitals have a formal and written discharge policy. Initial progress was made on all these recommendations, but in most cases the proposed approach was abandoned after a few years. For instance, the specialised housing unit was set up in 2002 but was dissolved in 2006 to be later replaced by a completely different approach – a cross-agency team. The Prison Service initially agreed to build transitional housing units, but dropped this objective after an internal review, as it did not consider the housing of former prisoners to be part of its core function (Maher and Allen,

2014). Over time, each of the State agencies which had been charged with providing accommodation for people they discharged decided it was not their remit to do so, without any decision as to who in fact had that remit.

Similarly, there was apparent progress on the vexed question of which statutory agency had responsibility for the homeless which appeared to be, at last, clarified, with the Strategy stating,

> it recognises that both local authorities and health boards have key central roles in meeting the needs of homeless persons. Local authorities have responsibility for the provision of accommodation for homeless adults as part of their overall housing responsibility and health boards are responsible for the health and care needs of homeless adults. (2002, 6)[2]

However, in practice, the lack of clarity about funding for key functions persisted.

The implementation of these strategy documents on homelessness was monitored by the Cross-Departmental Team on Homelessness, which in turn reported to the Cabinet Sub-Committee on Social Inclusion, chaired by the Taoiseach (Prime Minister).

Reviewing the homelessness strategies

In January 2005, the Department of Environment, Heritage and Local Government announced an independent review of the Government's homeless strategy(s). The terms of reference for this review were: i) evaluate the progress made in the implementation of the Integrated and Preventative Homeless Strategies and their associated homeless action plans; ii) make recommendations to promote further progress in addressing the issue of homelessness, taking into account the levels of funding available, and with particular reference to evaluating the continued relevance of the Strategies and Action Plans in addressing the issue of homelessness; iii) identify issues which may be affecting the achievement of the objectives and targets of the Strategies and Plans and evaluate the effectiveness of the overall service provision arrangements and funding mechanisms currently in place in addressing the short-, medium- and long-term needs of homeless persons.

This review, which was published in February 2006 (Fitzpatrick Associates), systematically reviewed the 43 specific policy proposals in the two strategies and put forward 21 recommendations to aid the implementation of the strategies. The substance of the report, in addition to the recommendations, was accepted by the Government and virtually universally by voluntary agencies working with the homeless.

In relation to the Integrated Strategy, the consultants suggested that over 60 per cent of the objectives outlined were either fully or significantly progressed. In relation to the Preventative Strategy, just under 30 per cent were fully or significantly progressed at that point, though as noted before, much of the implementation was subsequently reversed.

In the case of the Integrated Strategy, 21 of the objectives were deemed by the consultants to be still relevant, some adjustment was required in terms of organisational ownership of the objective and in 15 cases, that the objective required some refocus. In the case of the Preventative Strategy, 12 of the objectives were deemed by the consultants to be still relevant, in all cases the correct agency was responsible for the objective, while nine of the objectives required some refocusing.

While these outcomes were broadly positive, the review noted that a dominant feature of homeless services was the inconsistency of approach and organisation throughout the country. This was particularly the case outside of urban areas and this inconsistency resulted in a 'lack of equality in the treatment of homeless persons in different areas' (2006, 28). To deal with these inconsistencies, the review recommended that the production of locally based homeless action plans should be put on a statutory basis.

The report argued that while there was now sufficient provision of emergency accommodation, the key challenge for the future was to refocus attention on the provision of long-term housing options and to 'develop appropriate short- and long-term care mechanisms that prevent institutionalisation in "emergency" accommodation and limit the recycling of homelessness' (2006, 32). The report argued that in moving the homeless strategies forward, all agencies working in this area needed to refocus their energies to make 'itself largely obsolete, which should, after all, be its overarching goal' (2006, 128). To aid achieving this objective, the report recommended that the two existing strategies needed to be revised and amalgamated, a National Homeless Consultative Committee be established and all government policy should be proofed for any impact it might have on homelessness.

In 2006, the Social Partners launched the fifth national agreement, *Towards 2016*, which included more extensive consideration of housing and homelessness than previous agreement, including the commitment that:

> it is proposed to amalgamate and update the Government's Integrated and Preventative Homeless Strategies taking on board the recommendations of the recent independent review of the strategies. The situation of homeless persons who are currently in long-term emergency accommodation is of particular concern. The revised strategies will have as an underlying objective the elimination of such homelessness by 2010 (recognising that this involves addressing the needs of up to 500 households). Particular emphasis will also be

placed on improved coordination of service provision through the extension of joint agency approaches at local level to facilitate the development of a holistic response to the needs of homeless persons. This will be achieved through the further development of a case management approach, based on individual needs assessment with provision for access to multiple services by all the statutory agencies involved. The involvement of the voluntary and cooperative housing sector will be strengthened through the establishment of a National Homeless Consultative Committee including representatives of the social partnership C&V (Community and Voluntary) Pillar under the aegis of the Housing Forum. (2006a, 55)

In 2006, a *National Homeless Consultative Committee* (NHCC) was established to provide input into the development of the revised homeless strategy and ongoing Government policy on addressing homelessness. In addition, a data sub-group of this body was formed to facilitate data collection and management. A Health Impact Assessment and a Poverty Impact Assessment of the revised homeless strategy were commissioned, and consultation events hosted, with relevant parties being invited to view and discuss draft versions of both assessments.

Civic Society

The commitment of statutory agencies to prepare for a revised strategy took place against the backdrop of a new phase of activism from homeless NGOs. The National Campaign for the Homeless, the umbrella organisation for research and public policy advocacy during the mid-1980s and early 1990s had been wound up in 1994, with the Streetwise National Coalition following suit in 1995.

In 2006, the then four largest homeless NGOs (Focus Ireland, the Society of St Vincent DePaul, Threshold, the Simon Communities of Ireland) came together to form a new coalition, named *MakeRoom*, the objective of which was to campaign for an end to homelessness by 2010. MakeRoom's agenda was somewhat more ambitious than that proposed by the statutory sector, as they boldly stated: 'By an end to homelessness we mean nobody sleeping rough, nobody living in emergency accommodation for longer than is an emergency and nobody becoming homeless because of a lack of appropriate services'. Through an extensive e-mail and lobbying campaign, MakeRoom was successful in getting every political party to publicly commit to ending homelessness by the target date of 2010. Thus, by the end of 2006, an unprecedented consensus had emerged between the State, voluntary agencies and political parties that homelessness should and could be ended by 2010.

Brownlee (2008), in reviewing the period leading up to the publication of the independent review of the homeless strategies, observed a near universal consensus on tackling homelessness amongst voluntary and statutory bodies. However, he argued that since 2006 much of the optimism that homelessness could be ended had dissipated in a relatively short period. Some of this he attributed to the gradual downturn in Government finances due to global economic conditions. He also identified the change in key personnel in both voluntary and statutory agencies, and the creation of a new national statutory agency in 2006, the Health Service Executive, that replaced the regional health boards and experienced considerable bureaucratic difficulties in financing homeless services. These are undoubtedly contributory factors, but Brownlee also controversially argued that some voluntary agencies were reluctant to realise the ambition of the Strategy as it may result in the diminution of their services. As Brownlee (2008, 39) argues:

> although there will always be a need for a core level of services to ensure that people are homeless for only as long as it is an emergency, the realisation of this goal will require a major process of reprioritisation and change management. Yet it is immensely difficult for any organisation, be it private, public or voluntary, to seek to make any of its services obsolete, particularly when there still seems to be demand for such provision. There also appears (to be) disagreement on the level of resources required to address homelessness in Ireland, with statutory sources generally appearing to share a belief that funding is adequate if deployed in the correct areas moving forward, while voluntary sector providers push for additional investment.

The Way Home: the revised national homeless strategy

In August 2008, the revised national homeless strategy, entitled *The Way Home: A Strategy to Address Adult Homelessness in Ireland, 2008–2013* was launched, and accepted the broad thrust of the recommendations in the review of the earlier strategies. The Strategy set out six strategic aims: i) prevent homelessness, ii) eliminate the need to sleep rough, iii) eliminate long-term homelessness, iv) meet long-term housing needs, v) ensure effective services for homeless people and vi) better coordinated funding arrangements. The 90-page document set out a range of targets and priorities, but perhaps the crucial section related to funding. Reflecting the continued optimism that has shaped it, the Strategy stated that:

> Funding will be related to meeting known and emerging needs of homeless people. Where services no longer service a need, they will

be reconstituted or funding may be terminated, as appropriate. Of course, if such services are provided by a voluntary body, it may choose to continue providing its services in the absence of funding from a statutory agency being available. (Department of the Environment, Heritage and Local Government, 2008, 60)

After a further campaign by *MakeRoom*, a separate detailed Implementation Plan was published in 2009, which included two further strategic aims: data/information and monitoring/implementation.

The Strategy outlined the projects which would be funded in the future, including:

- Projects/services that address any gaps in the provision of emergency, transitional and long-term accommodation. The need for long-term accommodation for formerly homeless persons will be an ongoing overarching priority in the context of this strategy.
- Projects/services which reduce the numbers of people sleeping rough.
- Projects/services which reduce the length of time homeless people spend in emergency accommodation.
- Projects/services which will enable homeless people to settle successfully in their own long-term accommodation and optimise their independence.
- Projects/services to prevent people from becoming homeless in the first place and/or intervene early in relation to people at risk of homelessness.
- Projects/services to improve the health and well-being of homeless people or people at risk of homelessness.
- Projects/services that link homeless people or people at risk of homelessness with educational/training activities that enhance the skills, qualifications and employment potential (2008, 61).[3]

More significantly, the Strategy did not envisage funding projects that 'do not contribute significantly to achieving these priorities, or do not meet the needs of homeless people or people who are at serious risk of becoming homeless' (2008, 62). In addition, the Strategy stated that funding will not be provided where there is 'unnecessary duplication of services', 'services which are not cost-effective' or where there are 'poor quality services' with no plan to improve these services.

To facilitate achieving these objectives, the Strategy proposed establishing 'Regional Homeless Fora' which would bring together relevant staff from neighbouring local authorities, relevant staff from other agencies, such as the HSE and youth services, along with representatives from homeless NGOs in the region. Each Regional Homeless Forum would be led by one local authority and would be responsible for preparing and implementing a regional homeless strategy.

In addition to these enhanced regional structures, the Strategy envisaged the Cross-Departmental Team on Homelessness taking a 'stronger and more proactive role in leading and monitoring the implementation of [the] strategy, in supporting local authorities and homeless fora in its local implementation' (2008, 68). Thus, while the Strategy saw local authorities and the homeless fora as the means of achieving the objectives of the Strategy, Central Government would play a more active role than hitherto.

As key criticism of earlier attempts by local homeless fora had been the absence of a statutory basis, the Strategy proposed to place them on a statutory basis. It provides that the purpose of the plans would be: 'to ensure that responses to the needs of households who are homeless or at risk of homelessness are comprehensive, coherent and effective'. They were to contain measures that:

- prevent homelessness from occurring or recurring;
- ensure adequate and appropriate emergency responses;
- develop where necessary specialist services to achieve an increase in responsiveness of mainstream services to prevent homelessness;
- provide for the elimination of long-term homelessness;
- provide for long-term housing needs, with support needs as necessary;
- develop high quality, effective and holistic responses to the needs of people who are homeless;
- address the use of bed and breakfast accommodation, where necessary, and ensure that administrative and other systems are efficient, effective and accountable.

Outcomes: the extent of homelessness in Ireland

While the numbers of households eligible for social housing had been rising from the initial assessment of 19,376 households in 1989, there was a particularly sharp increase between 1996 and 2002, in the early part of the 'Celtic Tiger' period. This was followed by a 9.8 per cent decrease recorded between 2002 and 2005 to reach 43,684 households, comprising 87,635 individuals, of whom 41 per cent were child dependents, a slight reduction in the proportion of children from earlier assessments. That decade saw a substantial increase in the Irish population and this needs to be considered when measuring housing needs.

As noted in the previous chapter, from 1991 in addition to the Assessment of Housing Need, local authorities conducted a separate, but parallel, Assessment of Homelessness. A key rationale for this was to ensure that homeless households not registered for local authority housing would be recorded.

This period has started with the doubling of recorded homelessness between 1996 and 1999, although part of the increase could be attributed to changes in methodology in the Housing Needs Assessments (HNA). This increase had contributed to the drafting of the new Strategy, and in 2002, two years after the Strategy was published, the HNA showed that although there had been a further increase of 7 per cent in homelessness (an increase from 5,235 to 5,581 individuals) the speed of growth was much slower.

Eighty-seven per cent of those counted as homeless in 2002 were located in the five main urban areas, with 35 out of a total of 90 local authorities recording no homeless persons in their functional areas. Indeed, 12 local authorities had not recorded a homeless person in the five assessments that had taken place.

Three years later, the 2005 HNA indicated positive results from the new approach with a significant decline to 3,031 individuals – 2,571 adults and 460 child dependents. These individuals comprised 2,399 households, which while down on the 2002 figures was considerably higher than in the 1990s. Of these households, 2,078 were one-person households, with the remaining 321 incorporating more than one person.

It would appear that, for the 2005 and subsequent assessments, all households deemed to be homeless were registered for local authority housing and the separate assessment of homelessness was discontinued. Thus, the figure of 2,399 households just noted is comparable with the assessments of homelessness between 1999 and 2002.

Uniquely, for the 2005 Assessment, Local Authorities were required to provide a more detailed breakdown of the category 'homeless', and to record current accommodation and an assessment of the housing need. A breakdown is provided in Table 6.1. The single largest category were households in sheltered long-term accommodation. A further 397 households were categorised as living in transitional accommodation. Over 80 per cent of those living in long-term sheltered accommodation were recorded in Dublin, with just over 40 per cent of those in transitional accommodation in Dublin. Nearly 500 households were living in various hostel-type accommodation provided either by voluntary or statutory agencies. Of those, just over 80 per cent were recorded in the five main urban areas. Households living in bed and breakfast-type accommodation counted for a further 16.5 per cent of all homeless households, with 85 per cent recorded by Dublin City Council.

As shown in Table 6.2, only 184 households were deemed by the local authorities to require high support accommodation, particularly for households with addiction difficulties and psychiatric/behavioural difficulties. Dublin City Council, which recorded 56 per cent of all homeless households in the State in 2005, recorded only nine households in the category, suggesting that based on the assessments by local authorities, standard affordable social housing was the primary mechanism to end homelessness for the majority of households not already in supported accommodation.

Table 6.1: Breakdown of the category homeless in the Assessment of Housing Need, 2005

Are living in sheltered long-term housing accommodation	566	23.6
Are living, because they have no other accommodation in night time emergency hostel accommodation provided by local authorities and voluntary bodies	496	20.7
Are living in transitional housing accommodation	397	16.5
Are living in bed and breakfast accommodation	396	16.5
Have no accommodation they can reasonably occupy or remain in occupation of	228	9.5
Are living in other accommodation (for example County Home – hospital – and so on)	207	8.6
Are sleeping rough	41	1.7
Are currently serving custodial sentences and have applied for local authority housing	27	1.1
Total	2,399	100

Table 6.2: Accommodation needs of homeless households, 2005

Local authority housing on the basis of being considered capable by the local authority of independent living in the community	1,003	41.8
Already catered for in long-term sheltered housing accommodation and not seeking social rented housing	460	19.2
Suitable to be accommodated in supported transitional accommodation with a view to moving on to independent accommodation	381	15.9
Suitable to be accommodated in private rented accommodation	227	9.5
In need of high support accommodation (for homeless persons with addiction difficulties and psychiatric/behavioural difficulties)	184	7.7
Sheltered voluntary housing because the local authority does not consider to be capable of independent living in the community in a house/flat	144	6
Total	2,399	100

More detailed data on homelessness in Dublin

In addition to the estimates of homelessness from the HNA, from 1999 onwards the Economic and Social Research Institute (ESRI) was commissioned to conduct a periodic assessment of the extent of homelessness in the greater Dublin area on behalf of the Homeless Initiative, using a significantly improved approach to enumeration than was used in local authority assessments, and provided 'a robust minimum figure for the number of people using homeless services during the week of the survey' (O'Connor,

2008, 61). This assessment found a total of 3,890 homeless persons in the Dublin, Kildare and Wicklow area, of whom 2,900 were adults (1,850 male and 1,050 female), with a total of 990 dependent children (Williams and O'Connor, 1999). The assessment also found that there were 275 people sleeping rough in the Dublin, Kildare and Wicklow areas in March 1999.

A second assessment in 2002 (again conducted by the ESRI on behalf of what was now the Homeless Agency) showed virtually no increase in the number of homeless individuals between 1999 and 2002 (when 2,920 homeless individuals were recorded), but a marginal decrease in the number of homeless households was recorded (Williams and Gorby, 2002). Both the 1999 and 2002 assessments found that single-person households were the dominant homeless type in Dublin, with seven out of ten of all households falling into this category.

In 2005, a third assessment was conducted by the Homeless Agency (Wafer, 2006). However, it utilised a somewhat different methodology to that employed by the ESRI in 1999 and 2002. The single most significant change was the removal of a substantial number of households who, in previous assessments, were described as being homeless only on the local authority waiting list, that is, assessed as homeless by the local authority but not recorded as utilising homeless services. In 1999, 1,550 households were recorded in this category, 1,090 in 2002 and only 44 in 2005. In effect, 707 households were de-activated in the 2005 assessment when, as a consequence of validating their homeless status on the housing waiting list, it was determined that these were no longer active cases.

A comparison of the number of people recorded as using homeless services across the three reports shows a marginal decline between 1999 and 2005, from 1,350 to 1,317. Significantly, the numbers recorded as sleeping rough declined from 312 in 2002 to 185 in 2005, to 59 in 2011. This decline can in part be attributable to the opening of a dedicated residential service for rough sleepers (Costello and Howley, 1999; Costello, 2000).

Migration

The pattern of negative net migration seen in the previous chapter was followed by several years of significant inward migration as shown in Figure 6.2. In the early stages of the boom, this was due to the return of people who had been born in Ireland and had emigrated during the various phases of recession and mass unemployment. As the boom continued, an increasing number of non-Irish nationals arrived to take up work, primarily EU citizens. Many of them came to work in the construction industry and associated services. Whatever their citizenship, they required a home if they were to take up employment and the overwhelming majority of them became tenants in the growing private rental sector. However, with the onset of the global financial crisis, outward migration resumed in the final two years of this period.

Understanding Homelessness in Ireland since Independence

Figure 6.2: Net migration ('000), 1926–2011

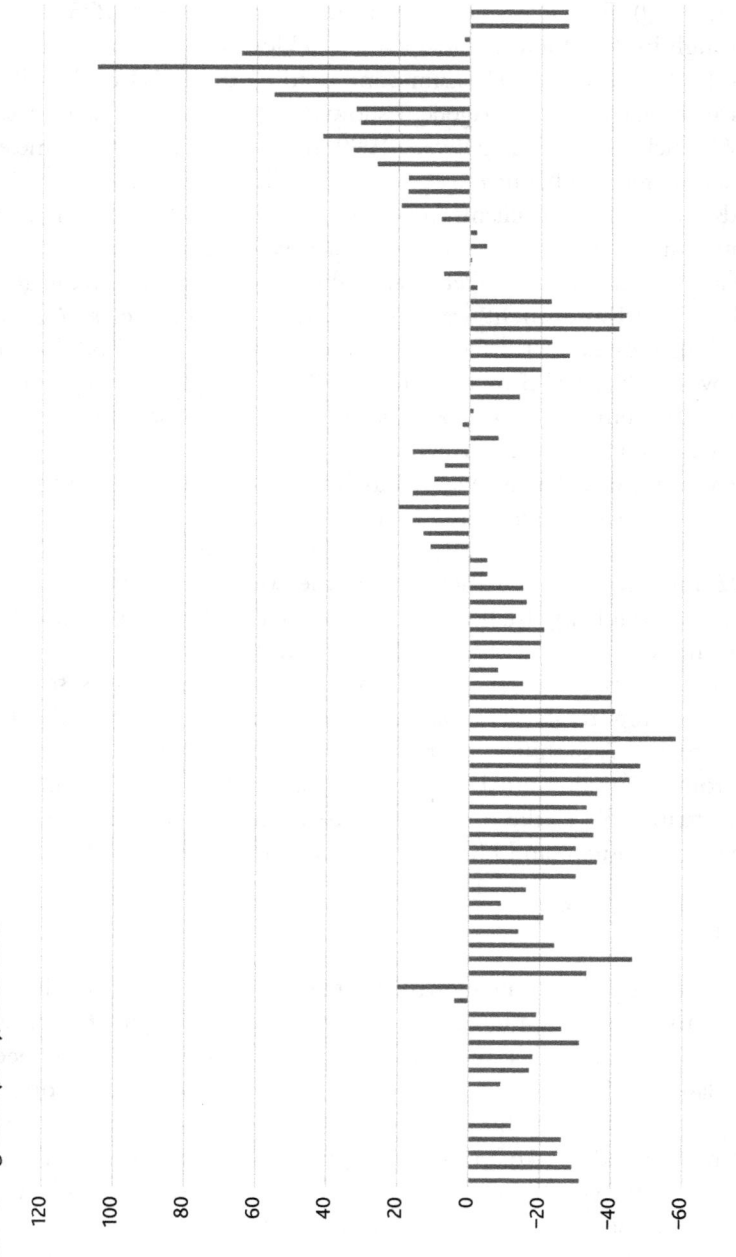

Source: Central Statistics Office – https://datasalsa.com/dataset/?catalogue=data.gov.ie&name=c0401-components-of-population-change-since-1926

The global financial crisis

After more than a decade of economic growth from the mid-1990s, known as the Celtic Tiger, the Irish economy began to experience difficulties from 2008, brought into sharp relief by the collapse of Lehman Brother bank in the US and the start of the global financial crisis. The Celtic Tiger era had been characterised, particularly in the later part, by high levels of housing construction along with rising property prices and high levels of bank debt. The economic difficulties led to a fall in property prices undermining the solvency of the banking system.

In November 2010, the Irish Government applied to enter an agreement with the International Monetary Fund, the European Central Bank and the European Commission (known as the Troika). Under the agreement, the Troika essentially took over Irish fiscal policy. Under the four-year National Recovery Programme (NRP), Ireland received a package of loans amounting to over €60 billion and agreed to implement a programme of €15 billion spending cutbacks and budgetary reforms (Houses of the Oireachtas 2013). During the three years from 2008 to 2010, Irish Gross Domestic Product (GDP) contracted by 7.5 per cent.

In 2010, the Government deficit reached 32.12 per cent and in 2013 the general government debt peaked at 132.2 per cent. Overall unemployment rose from 5 per cent in 2007 to a high of 15.5 per cent in 2012, with youth unemployment up to 30.9 per cent in 2012. Ireland's outward migration rate tripled between 2008 and 2012, before peaking at 89,000 in 2013 (CSOa, various years), while immigration into the country slowed; in 2011, the net migration rate (that is, the difference between number of immigrants and the number of emigrants) dipped to -27.4 per cent (EMN, various years).

It is not within the remit of this book to analyse the causes of 2008 crash (see Donovan and Murphy, 2013; Ó Riain, 2014), but in several countries including Ireland the roots of the global financial crisis can be partly traced to an overheated property market driven by profit, unregulated lending and widespread over-indebtedness, with market-led government policies playing a major role in 'boom and bust' housing market dynamics (Byrne and Norris, 2018). The collapse of this system, based on excessive and rising property prices, resulted in failures in the banking system with consequent impacts on State finances and on the availability of investment capital for, among other things, further house building. If the roots of the crisis lay in the housing market, it also bore the brunt of the impact. In the aftermath of the crash, Ireland's housing market collapsed, bringing down with it private developers and the private construction sector. Along with this, social housing construction ground to a halt. There were perhaps surprisingly little immediate implications from all this on the level of homelessness, and we will trace the longer-term impact in the next chapter.

Conclusion

The doubling of homelessness at the start of this period, shaped a complex and concerted new approach to tackling homelessness which emerged at the same time as the Irish economy was starting into its longest sustained period of growth. The homelessness response was also shaped by the social partnership arrangements that were successfully in place, with the national social partnership confirming the new coordinated Strategy from the national level and the local partnership approach pioneered in Dublin being replicated across the country in Regional Homeless Fora.

'Social housing' now consisted of a range of options from the traditional local authority offer, an increasing number of offers from the Approved Housing Body sector and an enhanced role for the private rented sector (Finnerty and O'Connell, 2014), which was to become even more significant as discussed in the next chapter.

After the demise of the National Campaign on Homelessness and the Streetwise National Coalition, homeless NGOs found a new way of working in coalition for change through MakeRoom. Despite some reservations, a significant number of homeless NGOs shaped the ambition that saw homelessness as a phenomenon that could be ended and convinced the Government to set the date of 2010 as the year in which important milestones – ending rough sleeping and long-term homelessness – would be achieved.

Right at the start of the period, in 1999, the Land Commission, an institution which had shaped Irish housing policy since the foundation of the State was finally, and quietly, dissolved. As we saw in the Introduction and Chapter 1, the issue of land reform from the late 19th century onwards had a profound impact on the scale and spatial distribution of social housing in Ireland. By the time it had completed its work, 'almost 2.5 million acres had been distributed at a cost of €287 m' (Dungan, 2024, 548). Ferriter, in his analysis of the economic crash, noted that

> [p]erhaps what was ironic was that one hundred years after that revolution in land ownership had been largely completed it was replaced by a native class of landowners and speculators who, with external speculators, were to exercise their domination of land and Irish economy in an even more invidious way than some of the most wretched of the nineteenth-century landlords. (2024, 155)

7

From austerity to economic recovery, 2011–2016

Introduction

Chapter 7 sets out how an era of optimism that homelessness could be eliminated through national and local strategies was interrupted by the global financial crisis of 2008 and Ireland's domestic policy responses to it. This chapter will focus on the period 2011 to 2016 where the implications of the crisis, and the decisions taken in response to it, continued to reverberate. The chapter will look at the broad economic context of austerity budgeting, the impact of budgetary cutbacks on poverty and deprivation and the impact on the housing sector and supply. We also argue that a number of strategic decisions made in the 20th century came home to roost during this second decade of the 21st century, both driving up homelessness and constraining the capacity of Government to respond to the increase. By the end of the period, all these factors had fed into significant increases in the number of homeless households and increasing public identification of the problem as a 'crisis'.

This chapter will first provide an overview of the levels of homelessness over this period, with the first detailed point-in-time figures becoming available on a monthly basis from 2014, which coincided with a rapid increase in homelessness. We look at changes in the provision of rental housing, capital funding and increased reliance on the private sector to provide what were termed as 'social housing solutions' and trace their impact. We then consider the way in which, against the background of a deteriorating housing system in terms of affordability and supply, policy on homelessness shifted towards a 'housing-led' approach and the first references to Housing First. Finally, we examine the new data collection and reporting systems which were introduced from 2014, and which underpin our analysis from that date.

Political and economic context

As a result of public reaction to the financial crisis, the General Election on 25 February 2011 inflicted the largest ever defeat on an incumbent government (Fianna Fáil/Green Party) and elected a Fine Gael-led Coalition with Labour, with Enda Kenny as Taoiseach. The Programme for Government published by the incoming Government included an explicit commitment to ending long-term homelessness and rough sleeping (Government of Ireland, 2011). This 'statement of common purpose', published by the new coalition, also referenced a commitment to introducing a Housing First approach to accommodating homeless people, the need to focus on youth homelessness and an overall commitment to homelessness prevention. This Government remained in office for the entire period covered by this chapter, although there were multiple changes in Ministers responsible for housing.

From 2011 until 2014, Fine Gael's Phil Hogan was the Senior Cabinet Minister for Environment, Community and Local Government, but the increased political challenge faced in the housing sector was reflected by the Minister of State, Labour's Willie Penrose, being given lead on the housing and homelessness portfolio and appointed as a 'Super Junior', that is a Junior Minister who attended Cabinet meetings, albeit without a vote.

Just eight months later, Penrose resigned as Minister, in protest against the closure of an army barracks in his own constituency (Gilmore, 2015) and was replaced by Labour's Jan O'Sullivan who occupied the role until July 2014. When Joan Burton took over as Labour Leader and Tánaiste, after the ousting of Eamon Gilmore, Alan Kelly of the Labour Party was appointed to the full Cabinet role of Minister for the Environment, Community and Local Government. Partly in response to the growing public concern about the issue, the portfolio for housing (and homelessness) was linked to the senior ministerial position and the first time that the Minister responsible for housing and homelessness was a full Cabinet Minister.

Homelessness overview

Despite the scale of the economic crisis facing Ireland over this period, the first few years are characterised by a paradoxical optimism about homelessness. The number of people who were homeless over this initial phase was relatively small and stable. The number of adults in emergency accommodation in Dublin in September 2013 was 1,431, marginally lower than it had been a year earlier. The 2013 Housing Need Assessment reported that there were 2,499 homeless households, up 6 per cent from 2,348 in 2011 but only 100 higher than it had been in 2005 at the height of the Celtic Tiger. While the austerity measures introduced in response to the global financial crisis were having a negative impact on virtually every other measurement of poverty and social exclusion, the 'overhang' of empty housing and unfinished housing estates from the boom years (Kitchin, O'Callaghan and Gleeson, 2014), colloquially known as 'ghost estates', appeared to be able to insulate homelessness from these negative impacts. Higher vacancy rates in the private rental market and lower rent levels also helped to reduce the impact on homelessness during this early period of the crisis. Finally, the social welfare system also helped to cushion many people from the immediate impact of job losses, so that – along with reliance on private resources – risks of homelessness tended to come sometime after job loss or wage cuts, and accessing of homeless services even longer after that

During the second half of the period, however, homelessness began to rise, first slowly and then with increasing acceleration. The increase occurred not only among single adults but, for the first time in over a decade, there was an increase in families becoming homeless. In 2013, there were an average of 76 families becoming homeless in Dublin each month, in 2014 this had risen to 79 per month and by 2016 it was 94 per month.

This period is also characterised by the transition in 2014 from estimating the level of homelessness on the basis of a range of survey and partial administrative data sources to the publication of robust and comprehensive administrative data on the number of people who are accommodated in emergency homeless accommodation on a monthly basis. Ironically, the trend of increasing homelessness coincided almost exactly with the new monthly publication of the official homeless figures. These newly available homelessness statistics, the increase in families entering emergency accommodation and the high-profile death of a rough sleeper near Government buildings promptly ignited public anxiety and alarm, making homelessness a focal point in both political and media discourse during this period.

Economic context of the austerity years

In the years following the global financial crisis, Ireland went through a period of significant structural, economic and demographic change and adjustment. The changes had long-term consequences for the housing system and consequently for the nature and extent of homelessness. The incoming Fine Gael/Labour Government attempted to renegotiate the terms of the agreement with the Troika but, as Ajai Chopra of the IMF noted, 'the subsequent Government modified a few elements of it, but the fundamental structure remained' (Houses of the Oireachtas, 2013, 351).

The last budget from the Fianna Fáil/Green Coalition – the National Recovery Plan, Budget 2011 – included €6 billion in cuts. The first budget of the new coalition, Budget 2012, included a further €3.8 billion in cuts. This continued an intense period of restricted government spending and budgetary reforms in Ireland, particularly between 2009 and 2014 (Dukelow and Considine, 2019). These economic conditions led to a significant rise in consistent poverty, along with a sharp rise in the enforced deprivation rate. In 2013, there were 698,000 people living in poverty in Ireland (which is nearly one in seven of the population), and over 211,000 were children;

1.4 million people were experiencing deprivation, an increase of 128 per cent since 2008.

While the sudden and substantial contraction in the economy resulted in real hardship for many individuals, it is important to note that in contrast to many countries hit by the GFC, inequality in Ireland fell during this period, after transfers are taken into account (FitzGerald, 2014; Cousins, 2016). This was a result of a number of factors, including the fact that the 'bursting of the property bubble' inevitably hit those at the top of the income distribution hardest (FitzGerald, 2014). While many thousands lost their jobs, the decisions by successive governments to, broadly speaking and with some important exceptions, maintain the welfare floor was significant in mitigating the impact (FitzGerald, 2014, 4).

The FG/Lab Government decision not to cut 'core' welfare payments, despite the huge increase in the number of people requiring support, resulted in very substantial social welfare expenditure. Social welfare expenditures, which accounted for 13 per cent of GNP in 2007 had risen to 20 per cent by 2011 (FitzGerald, 2014, 5), reflecting both the contraction in GNP and the higher number of individuals depending on welfare over that period. The decision to protect welfare expenditure during a period of overall reductions in expenditure, of course, had consequences in terms of cuts in other areas of public expenditure.

There were two exceptions to this broad protection of core welfare rates: young adults and lone parents (majority of which are lone mothers), with subsequent consequences for housing precarity for some people in these groups. During the recession there were particularly severe cuts to 18- to 24-year-olds (rates cut by 51 per cent to €100 and for 25-year-olds rates were cut by 30 per cent to €144). Lone parents faced cuts to child welfare payments and increased conditionality in accessing payments. Entitlement to One Parent Family Payment (OFP) – which was previously available to claimants whose youngest child was 18 (or 22 if in full-time education) – was removed for parents whose youngest child reached age seven. Child benefit rates were not considered 'core' welfare payments and were cut initially (though increased again after the 2015 budget). Analysis of EU-SILC data clearly showed that consistent poverty and deprivation rates were particularly high for lone parents (Watson et al, 2018). The consequences of this in terms of homelessness are discussed later in the chapter.

The community and voluntary sector were significantly eroded during this period due to widespread cutbacks (with drug initiatives particularly hit) while further cutbacks also hit the already chronically underfunded mental health services (Harvey, 2012). This resulted in a reduced capacity of civil society to support communities and advocate for the rights and entitlements of service users. The crash also has a significant impact on middle-income households, where aside from the level of job losses which impacted on all income groups, a significant part of the population between 35 and 50 years were left with a high-level debt due to the collapse in property prices (Maître, Russell and Whelan, 2014).

These challenges had very considerable impacts on poverty rates and social exclusion from 2009 onward, and some negative impacts in the housing system (for example a significant increase in the number of mortgages in arrears). While they were no doubt responsible for a number of individual households entering homelessness during this period, significantly they did not have an immediate impact on the total number of people in homeless services which, as already noted, did not start to rise for a number of years after the first wave of austerity measures when the overall economy had started to recover.

Despite the scale and impact of austerity measures in Ireland, there was very limited civil society protest against the measures for the first few years of the crisis. Homeless NGOs helped lead an NGO and Trade Union campaign called 'The Poor Can't Pay' which opposed cuts in basic welfare payments with limited success. However, with the establishment of a new semi-state company to be responsible for water infrastructure in 2013, public frustrations began to coalesce around proposals which were included in the Troika agreement to introduce charges for domestic water consumption. As the Department of Environment was responsible for water policies, as well as housing and homelessness, the large-scale public protests against water charges and the series of policy about-turns took up considerable political attention in the department during this period. Ultimately the Government dropped the proposals for water charges and reimbursed those who had already paid.

After this, many of the activist groups and trade unions who had been active in the water charges protests began to turn their attention to the question of housing and homelessness, with the hope that they could make a similar impact on policy. The consequences of this will be discussed later.

The impact on the housing system

As noted in the previous chapter, the collapse of the banking system – driven by inflated property prices – led to a breakdown in State finances and a shortage of investment capital, including for further house construction (Byrne and Norris, 2018). In the aftermath of the crash, Ireland's housing market collapsed, bringing down with it private developers and the private construction sector. Along with this, social housing construction ground to a halt. Private sector house building plummeted from 93,019 units completed in 2006 to 8,301 in 2013 (DHLGH, various years). Some of the homes completed during this later period were 'ghost estates' now being finished off, while others were 'one-off developments', usually houses constructed by individuals and not offered for sale on the market.

As a result of the large number of people who lost their jobs or experienced wage cuts, along with the high cost of housing prior to the crash, mortgage arrears hit an all-time high during the second half of 2013 when just over 18 per cent of homeowner or principal dwelling house mortgages were in arrears (Central Bank of Ireland, 2013). A large number were also in negative equity. A considerable amount of policy attention was paid to the difficulties faced by owner-occupiers who were in mortgage arrears, and following the *Report of the Inter-Departmental Working Group on Mortgage Arrears* in 2011 and *Central Bank Code of Conduct on Mortgage Arrears* in 2013, the primary policy objective was to prevent households from losing their homes rather than to deal with the level of debt, and hence repossessions of dwellings in arrears were relatively modest with, for example, 766 repossessions in 2013. It is not clear whether such measures prevented households becoming homeless or whether this group would have never entered homelessness anyway (very few former owner-occupiers entered homeless services over the coming years). Less attention was paid to the 27 per cent of buy-to-let (BTL) mortgages which were in arrears in 2013, with 8 per cent in arrears of more than 720 days at the end of 2013 (Central Bank of Ireland, 2013), but as was the case with principal dwelling house mortgage arrears, repossessions were few with only 282 repossessions in 2013, with a total of 2,739 BTL properties repossessed between 2013 and 2016.

Concerns around the stagnant supply of social and affordable housing were also coming to the fore during this period. For example, in 2014, National Economic and Social Council (NESC) published a report reviewing the social and affordable housing sector which highlighted various long-term challenges based on their analysis. As well as their concerns around flagging supply due to borrowing constraints, the report also brought into question the long-term suitability of differential rent across the social housing sector and noted the policy resistance to social segregation which may be limiting housing output and further noted that the parallel residualisation of social housing 'may lack policy coherence' (NESC, 2014, 14). The report also drew specific attention to the needs of low-income tenants in the private rented sector in the context of a 'dualist profit-rental' (NESC, 2014, 44) system which had enhanced tenants' exposure to rising private rents, thereby undermining the sector as a long-term sustainable solution for tenants.

At the time of the crash, as noted earlier, there were widespread unfinished housing estates or developments – the 'ghost estates'. This was a legacy issue on account of the surplus construction during the economic boom before the sudden global financial crisis which grounded the construction industry.

While many of these were in areas where there was local housing need, a significant proportion had been built in smaller towns or isolated areas, where it was assumed, people would be willing to commute long distances in order to purchase an affordable home. Even as the economy recovered from 2011 and housing demand increased, it was clear that many of these developments would never be viable.

For many years, these estates and developments blighted parts of the country, particularly in rural areas, and had a significant impact on families and individuals who were living within unfinished developments. Annual surveys and progress reports on 'Unfinished Housing Developments' were published between 2010 to 2017. In 2010, for example, 9,976 dwellings were 'near complete' while 9,854 dwellings were 'at various early stages of construction activity' (DEHLG, 2010, 1). The shift from having an excess of housing to experiencing significant unmet housing need is also captured in these reports over this period. In 2010, the Government stated that 23,250 dwellings were 'complete and vacant' which fell to 1,084 in 2017, signalling the increase in housing need across these years. By 2017, the number of 'unfinished' developments nationwide had been reduced by 91 per cent (DHPLG, 2017).

The sudden and enormous reduction in building construction outlined above did not just impact on immediate housing completions, it had a destructive impact on the building industry, with long-term implications. While some construction work continued in finishing out the ghost estates and one-off housing, many construction firms went bankrupt, leading to further long-term decline in house building. During the boom period a large number of construction workers had come to live and work in Ireland, largely from Eastern Europe. Many of these returned to their countries of origin, while many Irish-born construction workers also emigrated in search of employment. There were 63,800 qualified skilled craft-persons with construction-related skills in the whole economy in 2015 compared with 121,000 in 2007, while registration to apprenticeship programmes declined significantly over this period. The skills shortage was particularly difficult when the economy began to recover, and building was scaling up again.

It is worth noting that in some cases there was no alternative to the policies adopted during this period due to the scale of the crisis and the level of public debt. However, a comparison with Finland and Denmark during this period indicates that there was some room for different choices: despite experiencing longer, albeit less severe recessions, both countries continued to build social housing and did not effectively close down their construction sectors (Allen et al, 2020, 161). Irish policy choices, together with Troika influence, appear to be strongly influenced by a sense that the Irish problem was an enormous surplus of housing that would remain a burden for decades, with no need to build again in the foreseeable future.

The mixed economy of social housing

The global financial crisis (GFC) had different effects in different countries, depending upon, among other factors, the extent to which their banking system was exposed to risks in the property market. The impact of the GFC on the social housing sector in Ireland played a significant role in the subsequent rise in homelessness (and the housing crisis in general). To understand the particular vulnerability of the Irish social housing sector to the conditions created by the GFC, it is necessary to take a more detailed look at some of the aspects of social housing policy which have been referred to in earlier chapters and how their implications played out in the extreme circumstances which arose from 2008 onwards.

From the first decade of the century, we see the consequences of a range of policies from the previous century play out in largely unforeseen and entirely unintended ways, significantly constraining the capacity of the State to respond to the challenges following the GFC. The range of policies which now became deeply problematic included centralised capital funding of social housing, the setting of rents based on tenant income rather than housing costs, reliance on the private sector (both through Part V and the use of subsidised private rentals for social housing tenants) and the depletion of housing stock by sale to its tenants.

As a result of changes in the financing of social housing in the late 1980s discussed in Chapter 5, investment in future housing supply became largely dependent on Central Government capital allocations. During periods of recession and expenditure restrictions, cuts in capital funding are more attractive to the Government than cuts in revenue expenditure, so that during every recessionary period since this change, we see reductions in social housing supply. Expenditure on social housing was 'transformed from countercyclical measure which counterbalances the market into a procyclical measure which fuelled Ireland's housing boom' (Byrne and Norris, 2018, 50).

Following this pattern, during austerity years, capital funding was increasingly restricted for social housing, with less than 20 per cent of expenditure for social housing in 2014 on capital expenditure, with an attendant decline in construction output as shown in Figure 7.1 (Byrne and Norris, 2018).

We have seen in earlier chapters that AHB and Part V acquisitions had come to play a greater role in social housing construction. Government financing for construction by AHBs followed the same structure as funding for local authority acquisition and so collapsed in parallel with the collapse of local authority construction. The availability of Part V acquisitions was, of course, entirely dependent on the health of the private construction sector. So, with the collapse of housing markets and private construction, the Part V strand of social housing supply also came to an end – with a slightly delayed

From austerity to economic recovery, 2011–2016

Figure 7.1: Social housing output, 1923–2016

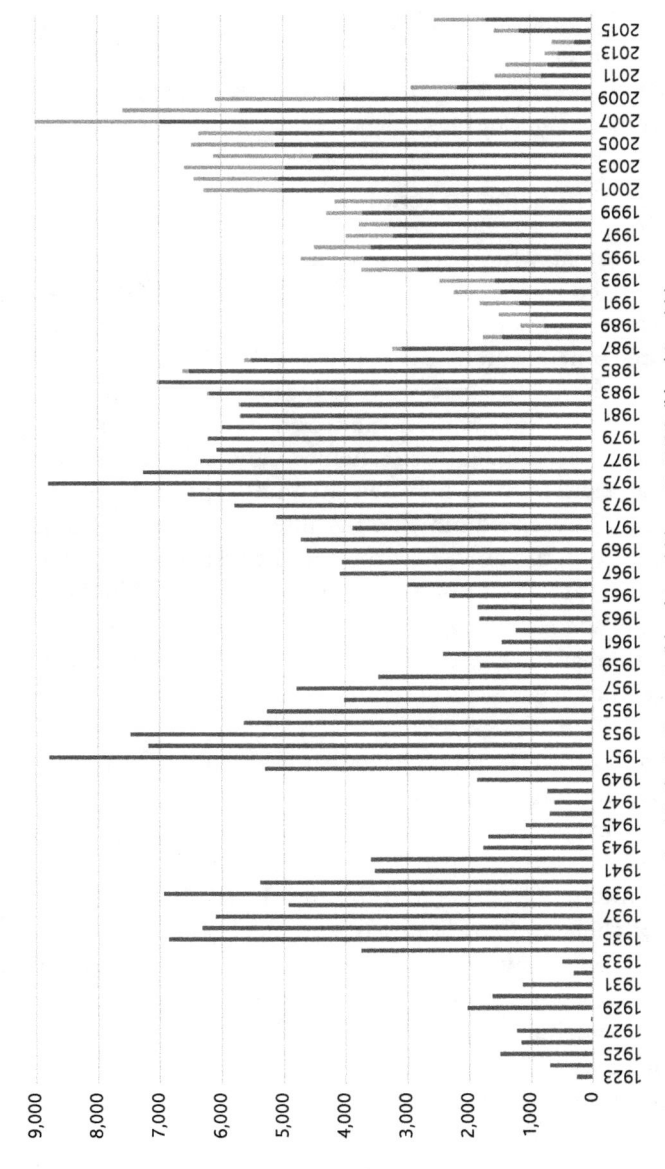

Source: Department of Local Government and Public Health Annual Report (various years) (Dublin: Stationery Office). Department of the Environment (various years); Annual Housing Statistics Bulletin (Dublin: Department of the Environment) – https://www.gov.ie/en/department-of-housing-local-government-and-heritage/organisation-information/housing-statistics/

impact. Indeed, as noted in the last chapter, the Part V scheme only started to gain momentum as the crash approached, with a peak in 2009 and 2010 with 1,846 units transferred to local authorities (DKM, 2012, 31). A review by the Auditor and Comptroller General found that in 2009 there was a stock of 3,700 unsold affordable dwellings held by local authorities (NESC, 2014, 12). Many of these were then used for social housing tenants on leasing arrangements, reducing the immediate impact of the austerity policies on social housing tenants and homelessness.

Sale of social housing to tenants

A further element which decisively shaped the supply of social housing as the State tried to respond to the challenges of the GFC was the legacy of the various programmes to sell social housing units to their tenants. The multiple tenant purchase schemes that had been rolled out across the country since the 1970s significantly reduced the size of the council housing sector and changed the composition of the tenants over this period. As noted in Chapters 4 and 5, these schemes allowed tenants to purchase their dwellings at a discount of between 40 and 60 per cent of market value, depending on household income. Because the State was selling dwellings at such a discount, the proceeds from the sale were not sufficient to finance a replacement unit. As a result, these schemes contributed to the decline of the overall social housing stock. The sale of social housing to tenants slowed further after the recession, but notwithstanding this reduction, 3,533 dwellings were sold between 2011 and 2020 (O'Sullivan, Palcic and Reeves, 2025).

Tenant purchasing as a policy measure is a point of particular heated debate. On the one hand, some consider the sale of social housing to support the diversification of neighbourhoods while relieving the local authority of mounting repair bills on an ageing housing stock. Many people, including Ministers and Teachta Dála (TDs), see their family's purchase of their council home as a particularly symbolic step in their family's progress. However, to sell off social housing stock – particularly in areas of high housing need or in areas where housing is particularly attractive – contributes to the further decline of the sector and reduces the role of the social housing in bringing balance to the overall housing market (Byrne and Norris, 2018). Furthermore, the cost of these sales to the exchequer is considerable, particularly when stock is sold for a discount of up to 60 per cent. This loss becomes even more apparent when, under recent social housing acquisition programmes, a local authority purchases a second-hand dwelling – originally built by the authority as social housing and sold at a discounted price – only to buy it back at an inflated market rate (Norris and Hayden, 2018).

One final component of the new 'mixed economy of social housing', which is the context for the emerging homeless crisis in the second decade of the century, is the number of tenants living in privately rented accommodation but receiving 'social housing supports' (that is, various rent subsidies). The introduction of these schemes is discussed in Chapters 5 and 6. As noted earlier in Chapter 6, the boom period was characterised by a significant increase in the number of households living in the private rental sector, rising from 10 per cent in 2006 to 19 per cent in 2011. Partly as a result of these factors, the proportion of low-income households residing in local authority housing declined. In the 1990s, local authority housing accommodated approximately three-quarters of low-income households in receipt of State housing supports, but by 2016, local authority housing accommodated just half of this cohort (Norris and Hayden, 2018).

These factors came together with the rapid increase in unemployment following the economic crash – with large numbers of laid-off workers seeking the support of these subsidies to help pay their rent. In parallel, the use of the private sector as a source of socially supported housing rose from 28 per cent in the boom years, to 42 per cent during the recession, before dropping back to 33 per cent by 2016 (Watson and Corrigan, 2019, 213). By 2014 nearly 30,000 households were transferred from Rent Supplement to the Rental Accommodation Scheme (RAS), and although it had fallen from its all-time high of nearly 100,000 in 2010, there were still over 66,000 recipients of Rent Supplement, costing €338m per annum.

Introduction of Housing Assistance Payment (HAP)

In the same year, a third new social housing support, the *Housing Assistance Payment* (HAP) was introduced, and it was intended that long-term recipients of rent supplement would now transfer to HAP rather than RAS, and RAS was to be gradually reduced, with HAP becoming the primary social housing support. This policy was underpinned by legislation under the *Housing (Miscellaneous Provisions) Act, 2014*.

Where tenants qualify for support, HAP, like RAS, is paid directly to landlords by local authorities on behalf of the tenants, subject to prescribed rent limits. In return, a recipient household pays a differential rent to the relevant local authority. An important feature of HAP, like RAS but unlike Rent Supplement, is that the payment is not withdrawn when/if the recipient finds work, so that it does not act as a barrier to taking up employment. However, in contrast to RAS tenancy, in HAP the local authority does not enter in a leasing agreement with the landlord and does not commit to finding the tenant an alternative housing solution if the tenancy ends through no fault of the tenant. As a result, HAP tenancies do not guarantee security of tenure, unlike the security associated with social housing tenancies, or even RAS tenancies.

In addition, the 2014 Act included a provision that HAP tenants are considered to have their housing need resolved and so are removed from the social housing waiting list (and therefore do not feature in the Social Housing Needs Assessment data). HAP tenants can be placed on a separate list of people who are looking for a transfer to mainstream social housing (the 'transfer list'). This was in stark contrast to RS where recipients *were required* to be on the housing list, whether they wanted to move to social housing or not. As a result of this change, the number of people assessed as needing social housing (referred to as the social housing waiting list) fell considerably – moving quickly from being an overestimate (as it included RS recipients who did not want a social house) to being an underestimate (as it excluded HAP recipients who did want to move to social housing).

The number of households entering HAP tenancies rose sharply from 420 in 2014 to 11,250 in 2016 (and rising further thereafter). The main household type entering a HAP tenancy were single parents with their children – accounting for 39 per cent of all HAP households between 2015 and 2016 (Kilkenny, 2019). Dublin local authorities were not significantly involved in the early years of the HAP scheme, as the programme was expanded on a phased basis. The level of exchequer funding increased from less than €0.5 m in 2015 to €57.7 m in 2016 and trebled the following year to €152.7 m (Kilkenny, 2019). Therefore, the scheme operates at a significant cost to the exchequer, as the local authority pays market-related rents to the landlord but collects income-related rents from the tenants. This point on HAP expenditure will be returned to in the next chapter.

As rents increased across the country during this period, together with an overall scarcity of available rental properties, local authorities were given discretion to increase the HAP caps by up to 20 per cent in certain circumstances. This was later increased to 35 per cent. Even with this substantial increase in the 'HAP cap' for some, in most cases HAP no longer covers the full cost of the rent meaning that households must pay a 'top up' to their landlord. In theory, local authorities only sanction such arrangements where the total rent paid by the tenants is less than 30 per cent of their income, but there is evidence that in practice many tenants pay more than this. Under the RS scheme, such 'top-ups' to landlords were prohibited as they resulted in the tenant having insufficient income to live on (Focus Ireland, 2012), and indeed 'top-ups' in the RS scheme were a source of controversy. By contrast, under the HAP scheme – as will be discussed in greater detail in the following chapter – top-ups became a typical characteristic of HAP tenancies.

In December 2014, the Dublin Region Homeless Executive (DRHE) began operating a specific Homeless HAP (HHAP) scheme in the Dublin region for those who are homeless and, subsequently, included those deemed at risk of homelessness. This was expanded to Cork city in 2015 and rolled out nationally in January 2018. Budget 2016 provided that a Homeless HAP tenant could, on a case-by-case basis, be permitted to rent a property with a rent of up to 50 per cent above the basic rate. To be eligible for Homeless HAP, a household must be assessed by the relevant local authority as homeless under Section 2 of the *Housing Act, 1988*. In addition to the subsidised rent, HHAP provides additional supports including the payment of a deposit and up to two months' rent in advance. Since 2015, the DRHE has also operated a 'Place Finder' service (a similar service began in Cork city in 2017 and in January 2018 it was rolled out nationally). This sets out to provide supports to homeless applicants or those in vulnerable situations, in accessing HAP properties; though inconsistencies have been identified across local authorities in terms of staffing and operations (Office of the Ombudsman, 2025).

This Government investment in expanding the HAP scheme for households eligible for social housing came at a time of increased dysfunction in the housing market – particularly the private rented sector. From 2014, the NESC published a series of important studies on the Irish housing system, looking at social housing, private rental and homeownership. The third of these, *Ireland's Private Rental Sector: Pathways to Secure Occupancy and Affordable Supply* (2015) examined many of these challenges in the private rental sector. It noted the high level of tenant's dependent on different forms of rent supplement schemes, the dominance of small-scale investors and level of encumbered buy-to-let mortgages. Their analysis found that:

> [w]ith growing housing demand and very little new supply in recent years, there are some severe pressures in the rental sector in Dublin and other cities. This is evident in increasing rents, pressures on government to increase rent supplement rates and, for a small proportion of low-income households who cannot meet rising rents, economic evictions leading to homelessness. The limited supply and high cost of rental housing is now a threat to Ireland's competitiveness and job creation. (NESC, 2015, iii–iv)

Consequence of the mixed economy for social housing

According to Byrne and Norris (2018), had there been continued investment and acquisition of social housing during these austerity years, it could have provided a counterbalance within the housing market to buffer against 'boom and bust' cycles of the market. In other words, in the absence of sufficient social housing stock, housing policy becomes a 'pro-cyclical' system, adding 'fuel to the property furnace' (Byrne and Norris, 2018, 60). As investment in social housing declined and housing need grew, the State began to shift from 'object' to 'subject' subsidies to deliver social housing – leading to a rapid increase of sourcing social housing *via* private sector leasing. This also marked a shift from funding social housing through *capital funding*, which had characterised social housing provision in previous decades, towards funding social housing through *revenue finding*. As a consequence, the boundaries between social housing, private renting and home ownership in Ireland have 'grown increasingly nebulous' (Norris and Fahey, 2011, 495).

The range of policy decisions made in earlier decades created a 'mixed economy of social housing' highly reliant on the private sector, limiting the existing and forthcoming supply of social housing, but this was not the proximate cause of rising homelessness. Tenants in local authority or AHB social housing rarely have their tenancy terminated and few of the households who entered homelessness had previously been tenants of local authorities or AHBs. And as noted earlier, few of them were former owner-occupiers. So, while the deeper causes of the rising number of homeless households lie elsewhere, the *immediate crisis*, at least as far as families are concerned, fell most heavily on households who had been renting in the private rental sector.

Immediately after the crash, rent levels fell, but as the economy began to recover from around 2011, rent levels began to recover. With low-income households trying to access private rental accommodation with HAP along with middle-income household's dependent on the sector at market rates, there was acute pressure on the private rented market, which in turn, drove average prices up. Between Q1 2012 and Q4 2016, new rents increased nationally by 36 per cent, from €756 to €983, and in Dublin by 47 per cent, from €982 to €1,449 (Residential Tenancies Board (RTB), 2017). This eventually prompted the Government to introduce measures to alleviate the rental inflation, with the publication of *Stabilising Rents, Boosting Supply: A Package to Deliver Rent Certainty and Housing Supply* in November 2015 (DECLG, 2015).

This guaranteed rents to remain the same for a two-year period before they could be increased again, together with longer notice periods for tenancy terminations and incentives for landlords to take on tenants in receipt of rent supplement or HAP. Further, the RTB (formerly the PRTB) was also given new powers to ensure landlords inform tenants of their rights, evidence of landlords' justification for any rent increase, such as the market rent for similar dwellings in their area.

Homeless policy shift: a shift to 'housing-led'

As these underlying pressures were building up, paradoxically, the political priority was to address the surplus of housing in the wake of the property market collapse, particularly in light of the scale of unfinished housing and dereliction across the housing stock. Along with this concern and the economic constraints of the Troika, State-sponsored social housing construction was completely off the agenda for the first few years of the new Coalition.

In this context, in February 2013, the Minister for Housing and Planning, Jan O'Sullivan, launched a *Homeless Policy Statement* (Department of Environment, Community and Local Government, 2013). The policy was grounded in the findings of a paper commissioned by the Department (O'Sullivan, 2012), as well as consultations with other departments, agencies, and the voluntary sector. It was both concise and ambitious in its aims – explicitly recognising that 'long-term secure housing is the best outcome for people affected by homelessness' and signalled a clear need for the State to be 'moving away from expensive emergency or shelter type accommodation' (DECLG, 2013, 2). It clearly stated the Government's aim to end long-term homelessness with a target of the end of 2016 (noting *The Way Home* had previously aimed to end long-term homelessness by 2010), and it aimed to achieve this through increased supply of secure, affordable, and adequate housing for long-term homeless populations, as well as greater emphasis on prevention and the provision of appropriate supports (with an emphasis on floating supports in housing). The policy also flags youth homelessness and the importance of measuring progress using robust data.

The Statement reflected the thinking that was developing at European level which had been set out at a *European Consensus Conference on Homelessness* in 2010 organised by FEANTSA and Belgian Presidency of the European Union. This conference first advanced the term 'housing-led' in order to describe all policy approaches that identify the provision of stable housing to prevent or resolve homelessness and marked 'a shift from using shelters and transitional accommodation as the predominant solution to homelessness' (European Consensus Conference, 2010, 14). This call for 'housing-led' approach was also echoed in a European Parliament Resolution published in 2011 when it called on all Member States to adopt 'a specific focus on "housing-led" approaches under the social innovation strand of the European Platform against Poverty and Social Exclusion' (European Parliament, 2011, No. 6). There was, therefore, European consensus emerging – bolstered by the positive results from 'Housing First' first seen in the United States (Tsemberis, 2010) and Canada (Goering et al, 2014) and then increasingly in Europe (Busch-Geertsema, 2014) – that permanent, standard housing for long-term homeless individuals is more likely to provide a positive setting for addressing any additional health or personal problems.

There was also a growing recognition that a more traditional shelter-style approach to homeless service provision is more expensive to the exchequer (the question of cost-effectiveness was also noted in the European Consensus Conference). In rolling out Housing First in Ireland, as will be discussed in a subsequent section, the model developed was heavily influenced by the Pathways to Housing First model from New York in terms of fidelity to the principles of the programme and focusing on high and complex needs rough sleepers (Greenwood, 2015). However, in policy approaches, the influence of the European 'housing-led' is evident. For O'Sullivan and Tsemberis (2024, 13) Housing First can be conceptualised 'as a dedicated programme for a specific cohort experiencing homelessness, that is those experiencing chronic/long-term entrenched homelessness and experiencing psychiatric distress and or substance misuse, and housing-led as an overarching policy that understands homelessness primarily as an outcome of housing precarity'.

To assist the Minister in monitoring and measuring progress towards ending homelessness in 2016, a three-person *Homelessness Oversight Group* was established – and included a senior social policy academic, a retired former senior civil servant and a senior financial services professional from the private sector. The group published its report in December 2013 (ten months after establishment) (Homelessness Oversight Group, 2013). The report acknowledged the lack of robust data to determine effective implementation, but regarded that notwithstanding this vacuum of evidence, progress was too slow if the goal of ending long-term homelessness was to be achieved by 2016 using current approaches.

However, in an important policy recommendation, the Group argued that resolving long-term homelessness was achievable if the Department provided funding to bring existing, currently vacant, social housing back into use and all such units were allocated to the long-term homeless. The Oversight Group estimated that there were between 1,500 and 2,000 such long-term void social housing units, which was broadly what was required to end long-term homelessness within a three-year period. It recommended that a *Homelessness Policy Implementation Team* be set up with responsibility for achieving the 2016 objectives to enhance coordination across the sector and to publish a structured plan 'to make the transition from shelter-led to a sustainable housing-led response to homelessness' (Homelessness Oversight Group, 2013, 5).

In response, the Government approved the establishment of a Homelessness Policy Implementation Team and a Central Implementation Unit in February 2014, who were tasked to implement the Homelessness Oversight Group's First Report. There were some confusion around whether the 2013 Statement replaced the 2008 strategy, and further it was not clear the nature of the relationship between the new Homelessness Policy Implementation Team and Homelessness Oversight Group with the National Homeless Consultative Committee (NHCC) or Cross-Departmental Team on Homelessness.

In May 2014, the *Implementation Plan on the State's Response to Homelessness* was published (Department of Environment, Community and Local

Government, 2014a). This contained *80* specific actions to achieve the 2016 target set in the *Homelessness Policy Statement*. The policy of bringing vacant social housing back into use, which was at the heart of the Oversight Group's strategy, featured strongly in the Implementation Plan, but the proposed allocation had fallen from 100 per cent allocation to long-term homeless households to 50 per cent allocation to this group, with the remainder going to the existing waiting list.

As noted above, in July 2014, the Minister responsible for housing and homelessness, Jan O'Sullivan of the Labour Party, was replaced by her party colleague, Alan Kelly, who was also the incoming Deputy Leader of Labour. Furthermore, in the Cabinet reshuffle arising from internal changes in the Labour Party, Kelly was now a full Cabinet Minister while O'Sullivan has been a Minister of State, albeit with a right to attend Cabinet meetings as a non-voting member. While both Ministers were members of the same political party within the same Government, this ministerial change marked a significant shift in policy stance. Two weeks after Kelly was appointed, a leak of the progress report from the Homeless Oversight Group stated that 'significant progress has not been made towards the 2016 goals' (Irish Times 23.07.2014) and repeated its call for 'ring-fencing' of housing brought back into use specifically for people moving out of long-term homelessness.

While Kelly did not formally announce a change in approach to homelessness, the Oversight Group was never reconvened and was effectively disbanded. The 80 specific actions set out in the 2014 *Implementation Plan* were given reduced prominence. As homelessness began to increase towards the end of the year, without formal announcement, the *Implementation Plan* was replaced by a series of Action Plans produced by the new Minister.

Homelessness begins to rise

In April 2014, three months before Kelly's appointment, the Department of Environment had started to publish figures setting out the number of people in emergency accommodation each month. Details of this data series are discussed later, but their publication had largely unforeseen consequences: from the first month of their publication these statistics showed a steady increase in the number of individuals and families that were in homeless emergency accommodation.

As the number of people continued to rise during the second half of 2014, on 1 December, Jonathan Corrie, who had been sleeping rough, was found dead on the street facing Leinster House, the Irish Parliament. Corrie's death, so close to the set of Parliament, provoked a public outcry. Vigils were held and civic and religious figures condemned the situation that had led to this death. Sensing an imminent political crisis, within a few days Minister Alan Kelly rapidly convened a 'Summit on Homelessness' in the

Custom House, the headquarters of the Department of the Environment, Community and Local Government. A very wide range of organisations and individuals were invited to the Summit, including not only the large homeless service charities but also smaller volunteer organisations and soup runs. Arising from the Summit, the Department published an *Action Plan to Address Homelessness*, which identified 20 actions that would be taken (Department of Environment, Community and Local Government, 2014b).

Along with the existing 80 actions from the earlier plan, the combined 100 actions broadly ranged from establishing Housing First in Dublin for rough sleepers; identifying vacant units for permanent accommodation (including 'voids' across local authorities); prioritising homeless households for social housing allocations; preventing homelessness for those discharged from institutional settings; and securing rent for homeless households (through the pilot Homeless Housing Assistance Payment). There were also, in what was to become a recurring theme, immediate actions to address rough sleeping in Dublin, including 260 additional emergency beds, a *Nite Café*, transport with support services, and a review of the Homeless Freephone service. Reviews of progress in achieving the now 100 action points were published each quarter until Kelly left office in 2016.

With progress in tackling the 'ghost estates', growing lists for social housing and increased pressure in the private rental market, the very low output of housing began to be an increasing cause of public policy concern. Increasing the construction of new social housing had been one of the objectives set by Kelly on becoming Minister. In November 2014, he published the *Social Housing Strategy 2020* (Department of Housing, Local Government and Heritage, 2014) which set out a six-year strategy to restore the State as providing 'a central role in the direct provision of social housing through a resumption of building on a significant scale' (DHLGH, 2014, iii), setting out to provide 35,000 new social housing units over a six-year period. As this would clearly not be enough new housing to tackle the growing housing lists, the plan also committed to support 75,000 households through 'an enhanced private rental sector' in the form of rental supplements (DHLGH, 2014, vii). Concerns were raised by advocacy groups around the capacity of the private rented sector to deliver on this level of social housing provision. Further concerns were expressed about the precarious nature of some of these tenancies as it was claimed that landlords were beginning to sell up and evict their tenants.

Introduction of Housing First in Ireland

Against the backdrop of these economic, political and policy changes, the Housing First approach to homelessness was slowly establishing a practical and policy foothold in Ireland. Between 2011 and 2013, Dublin was one of ten

EU cities participating in an EU PROGRESS-funded three-year exchange and evaluation programme entitled 'Housing First Europe' on how to develop and implement Housing First. The aim of this European initiative was to understand the potential and limits of the Housing First approach which had been pioneered in New York City. The Dublin Housing First Demonstration Project (DHFDP) was set up in April 2011. The project sought to maintain a high 'fidelity' – or similarities – to the original Pathways to Housing First model developed in the United States (including targeting those who had endured long-term rough sleeping and facilitated direct access to housing and wrap-around supports). To access these service users, the DRHE used the Pathway Accommodation and Support System (PASS) online accommodation and support system to target individuals engaging in rough sleeping, and who have mental health, addiction and related support needs.

The DHFDP operated under a partnership model between statutory and voluntary sector – and drew in other supports where relevant including a range of health services such as psychiatry, speciality nursing in substance use and general practitioner care. The human resources which drove the administration of the demonstration project were volunteered from within existing homeless services, under a limited budget. The initial aim was for the team to support 30 adults with significant rough sleeping history into permanent housing ('significant' defined as rough sleeping over a number of years).

A substantial reconfiguration of the team and its management took place after an interim evaluation, and a new 'comparison group' who received 'treatment as usual' was established to inform the final evaluation (Greenwood, 2015). The final report, published in 2015, determined an 'impressive' level of fidelity to the Pathways' Housing First model in spite of a 'shoestring budget and staffing' (Greenwood, 2015, 37). The evaluation found that DHFDP participants were much more likely to sustain their tenancies than the comparison group, who had continued to cycle through emergency accommodation, institutions and rough sleeping. Further, the DHFDP participants experienced a range of positive outcomes pertaining to their health, mental health, well-being, and greater participation in everyday activities. Additional insights were gleaned from focus group data on how Housing First participants benefited from the service compared to the comparison group:

> Housing First participants focused on autonomy, choice and mutual trust, whereas the Comparison Group participants focused on rules, regulations, mistrust, coercion and concerns about victimisation by other users. Their lives were preoccupied with activities relating to getting and keeping housing, staying safe and dealing with physical illness. They reported fewer goals and focused on safety and security

whereas Housing First participants described a wide array of intimacy, esteem and actualisation goals. (Greenwood, 2015, 37)

Notwithstanding these funding shortfalls in the early pilot of Housing First in Dublin, the Dublin Housing First pilot was considered a success, the DRHE moved to immediately commission a fully tendered service that maintained fidelity to the original NYC model. In 2014, Dublin City Council published *Pathway to Home: The Homeless Action Plan Framework for Dublin, 2014–2016* (Dublin City Council, 2014) which explicitly stated as a key strategic aim to '[b]uild on the success of the Dublin Housing First Demonstration Project and invest in developing a more comprehensive service with greater capacity to address all aspects of habitual and long-standing rough sleeping and homelessness'.

The first Housing First service formally began in October of that year and was delivered via a partnership between two NGOs, Focus Ireland and the Peter McVerry Trust. The initial target at that time was to achieve 100 successful tenancies for individuals who were formerly sleeping rough. The progress and developments of the expansion of Housing First in Ireland will be returned to in a later section.

Homelessness 2011–2016: developments in measuring homelessness

As noted earlier, the main method of counting homelessness since 1989 had been through the Housing Needs Assessment and since 1999, in Dublin, the tri-annual 'Counted in' survey. There was a growing consensus across the sector and across policy outputs on the need to address the absence of adequate and regular homelessness data (Downey, 2011; O'Sullivan, 2012).

When the Dublin Region Homeless Executive decided to discontinue the 'Counted In' survey in 2012, this absence of reliable regular data became an issue of concern at the NHCC, resulting in the NHCC establishing a sub-group to make recommendations about how homelessness would be most effectively measured. The sub-committee, chaired by one of the authors of this book, Eoin O'Sullivan, and involving representatives of local authorities, the Department of Housing and homeless service providers, including another author of this book, Mike Allen from Focus Ireland, recommended that a new system, based on data collected for the PASS system (Pathway Accommodation & Support System) should be adopted. PASS had initially been established in Dublin as a bed management and client support system in 2011 and was rolled out nationally in 2013. This development allowed for data to be reported on the number of adult individuals (and accompanying child dependents) experiencing homelessness and residing in designated emergency accommodation. The sub-committee recommended that this data be published quarterly, and the recommendation was accepted by the

Department with the subsequent amendment that, since the data was readily accessible, it should be published monthly.

The publication of these 'Monthly Reports' commenced in April 2014 on a trial basis, and from June 2014, with some modifications, has been produced on a continuous monthly basis providing stock data on the number of adults, child dependents and households in homeless emergency accommodation in a given week each month. In comparative terms, using the *European Typology of Homelessness and Housing Exclusion* (ETHOS) as a framework, this monthly data provides data in ETHOS category 2, people staying in a night shelter; and category 3, people in accommodation for the homeless, and in 2014 only, category 4, people in a women's shelter.

As was recognised in the sub-committee report, the Monthly Reports do not capture those using emergency or temporary shelters not funded by the local authorities, nor do they include all those rough sleeping, domestic violence refuge accommodation, those in Section 10 funded long-term supported accommodation, those in direct provision nor households in insecure or inadequate accommodation. Only a small number of services with less than 200 beds nationally do not, for various reasons, receive (nor do they necessarily seek) Section 10 funding, and therefore are not included in the PASS data. These limitations and significant changes in the methodology of the reports are discussed in further detail in Appendix 1.

In addition, from 2014 onwards, at the end of each quarter, local authorities were required by the Department of Housing to produce *Performance Reports* providing data on a range of indicators, including the number of new and repeat adult presentations to homelessness services per quarter; the number of adults in emergency accommodation for more than six months; the number of adult individuals exiting homeless services; and the number of rough sleepers. *Quarterly Financial Reports* are also published outlining expenditure across a number of categories including expenditure on emergency accommodation.

The production of the Monthly Reports and the Quarterly Performance and Financial Reports followed on from the publication in 2013 of a *Homelessness Policy Statement* by the Department of Housing. A number of indicators were identified to measure progress in ending homelessness in Ireland, which was the overarching ambition of the Policy Statement, and the purpose of these indicators was to 'give a clearer picture of homelessness in Ireland: the rate of entry, duration and exits, together with the type and nature of accommodation' (Department of Environment, Community and Local Government, 2013, 4).

Trends in homelessness

Pre-2014 scale of homelessness

As already outlined, prior to the published monthly figures, the extent of homelessness was not regularly and consistently reported. For the first time in 2011, the National Census captured all persons in homeless accommodation and sleeping rough on Census night, culminating in a *Special Report on Homeless Persons in Ireland* (CSO, 2012). This provided an insight into the profile of the homeless population, including location, age profile, marital status, number of children, nationality, ethnicity and religion, economic status, education, general health, and disability. This exercise was repeated in the subsequent Census in 2016 and 2022, with some technical adjustments. The 2011 report found a total of 3,808 people residing in homeless accommodation services across the country in April 2011 (64 of whom were sleeping rough). The rough sleeper count was performed by the Dublin Region Homeless Executive formerly the Homeless Agency) on behalf of the Central Statistics Office on Census night (while for other areas, persons sleeping rough were identified by 'local field staff').

One-third of those experiencing homelessness across Ireland in 2011 were women (n=1,263), which broadly reflected Counted In 2008 data (32 per cent women). Of these 3,808 persons, 992 (or 26 per cent) were in long-term accommodation – a category which was later removed from the homeless Census in 2016 (in line with recommendations from stakeholder consultations). There were 249 family units in 2011 (with child dependents), the majority of whom (n=185, 74 per cent) were lone parents with children. Therefore, the figures for those experiencing homelessness were relatively low at that point, particularly the numbers of those who were roofless. This was about to change.

Post-2014: major increases in family homelessness

In June 2014, according to the first monthly homeless count based on PASS, there were 344 families in emergency accommodation across Ireland (79 per cent, or 271 families, were residing in the Dublin region). Over the next 18 months alone, this number was set to increase by 156 per cent to 884 families across the country (87 per cent of whom were in the Dublin region) (Mayock, Sheridan and Parker, 2015). While homeless organisations had been commenting for some time on the 'pressure on their services', there was nothing in the *Homeless Policy Statement* of 2013, or the general discussion about homelessness at this time which anticipated this unprecedented scale of increase.

However, already at the time the Implementation Plan was published in Spring 2014 – when there were 184 families in homeless accommodation in the Dublin region – it references the growth of families presenting as homeless in the region and flags that 'the number of families presenting as homeless has grown to unsustainable levels' (DECLG, 2014, 7). This indicates the degree to which the subsequent 156 per cent growth between July

2014 and January 2016 was not at all predicted. The number of adult-only households also began to increase at this time also, particularly in Dublin, as did the number of available beds for 'singles' (see O'Sullivan, Reidy and Allen, 2021a).

In the next Census of 2016, there were 896 families among the homeless population (up 260 per cent from previous 2011 Census), representing 2,968 persons, and accounting for 43 per cent of all those in homeless accommodation. Of these, 896 families, 597 (or 67 per cent) were one-parent families, and female parents accounted for 96 per cent of all one-parent families (CSO, 2017).

Due to the substantial increase in family homelessness, a growing number of families were placed into hotel rooms or into private emergency accommodation as there were not enough existing emergency facilities to accommodate this growth. In the DECLG homeless figures that same month, almost half (45 per cent) of homeless persons were residing in hotels, B&Bs and other residential facilities used on an emergency basis. The staff working in the facilities did not have the appropriate skills or training for working with persons experiencing homelessness. Accommodating all these families, sometimes for long periods of time, was not only very harmful with unknown long-term consequences for parents and their children (Walsh and Harvey, 2017), but it also extremely expensive to the State (discussed in next section in greater detail). Due to the perceived negative impact of hotels and B&Bs, and the expenditure question, there were policy shifts after 2017 to build and renovate congregate homeless facilities known as 'family hubs', which will be discussed in the next chapter.

Social housing allocations to homeless households

As noted above, the *Homeless Oversight Group* recommendation that all renovated social housing units should be allocated to households exiting long-term homelessness had been watered down to 50 per cent. From 2015, Minister Kelly took a different approach to ensure that a proportion of all new social housing tenancies went to homeless households. After first encouraging local councils to do this, in January 2015, he put in place a legally binding directive to the larger urban local authorities, requiring them to increase the proportion of new social housing tenancies allocated for homeless households, and households including people with a disability. In order to discourage people from becoming homeless so as to increase their chance of being allocated social housing, the directive stipulated that households had to already be homeless before the policy was announced, though this condition was not widely reported in the media. The measure was to run for six months until July 2015. The Dublin local authorities were instructed to allocate 50 per cent of social housing allocations to eligible homeless households (and to those with disabilities), and later in Cork and other urban areas where the allocation was set at 30 per cent.

According to the Department, this measure would substantially increase the proportion of social housing allocations which had been going to homeless households. *The Irish Times* reported that prior to the directive

> 10 percent of social housing was allocated to homeless individuals or families in Dublin city and 4–6 per cent in the other three Dublin local authority areas. However outside Dublin those figures were considerably lower, ranging from zero to 7.5 per cent. In 2013, 8,820 housing allocations were made by housing authorities across the State and just 359 or 4.1 percent of these allocations went to homeless households. (Alan Kelly pledges 1,000 houses to homeless, *The Irish Times*, 31 January 2015)

This measure contributed to 'about 2,000 households' exiting homelessness in 2015, but nevertheless, this measure faced very significant resistance from a wide range of interests – including the then Chairperson of the Housing Agency, the CEOs of the four Dublin local authorities and local councillors from across the political spectrum (O'Sullivan, 2020). The critics of the measure argued that it resulted in families deliberately making themselves homeless so that they could 'jump the social housing queue'. While individual stories were cited to promote this view, no evidence was put forward to support it. On the contrary, comparing the number of families becoming homeless before the measure, during the measure and after it lapsed, we can see a steady increase in the numbers entering homelessness each month which is entirely unaffected by the changes in housing allocation policy. On the other hand, the figures for exits from homelessness reflect the advantages of having a priority in allocations.

In July 2015, Kelly extended the directive to April 2016 and changed the eligibility criteria to include people who had become homeless since the first directive but before the extension, which allowed critics to claim that families who had become homeless after the directive first emerged were eligible for priority treatment. By 2016, a general election had taken place, and Kelly was no longer Minister. As we shall see in the next chapter his successor chose not to renew the directive and, in a continued backlash against the measure, Dublin City Council then moved to remove the moderate priority measure that it had itself put in place.

Homeless services expenditure

In 2015, the Department of Environment, Community and Local Government commissioned private auditors to carry out an analysis of homeless services, services outputs, staffing costs and overall expenditure

(Mazars, 2015). The report was primarily desk-based and did not formally engage with homeless service providers or service users (as had been originally intended in the terms of reference) and so the recommendations that are yielded from the report are, as the authors themselves repeatedly state, 'limited in nature' and that it was 'not possible to provide any real substantive recommendations' (Mazars, 2015, 26).

Notwithstanding the substantial limitations of the review, the report did query how, in the context of a 'housing-led' policy framework, the substantial Government expenditure on short-term emergency accommodation and short-term accommodation 'does not appear to reconcile that [housing-led policy] objective' (Mazars, 2015, 26). Further, in the years that followed the publication of this report, expenditure on emergency and short-term services was set to sharply increase. The aforementioned Quarterly Financial Reports shows funding and expenditure for services under Section 10 the *Housing Act 1988*. They showed the striking increase in expenditure on homeless services from €54.4 m in 2013 to €116.3 m in 2016, representing a 312 per cent increase over a very short period of time. Over this four-year period (2013–2016), the Department of Housing and Local Authorities spent just over €321 m, with €201 m on emergency accommodation.

Migration

During this period, the net inward migration seen during the Celtic Tiger years reversed strongly as shown in Figure 7.2. While a significant number of the EU-citizens who had come to work in the construction and services sector remained in Ireland, many of them having settled with their children here, large numbers also left. Similarly, Irish-born construction workers, and others who had lost their jobs in the recession, emigrated – or re-emigrated. This renewed outward migration further reduced the overall pressure on housing supply. However, unlike in previous periods of high outward migration, because of the nature of migration pressures and changes in the housing system, the impact was felt less in the social housing sector and more in the private rental sector – with private sector rents falling significantly, albeit briefly, during this period. NESC's analysis also identified the high concentration of non-Irish nationals in the private rental sector while Census 2011 had identified that almost half of the households in the private sector were headed by a non-Irish national (CSO, 2011; NESC, 2015).

Conclusion

The period between 2011 and 2016 in Ireland – spanning only a five-year electoral cycle – was one of significant economic and structural change. It was a period of two distinct halves with respect to housing and homelessness.

Figure 7.2: Net migration ('000), 1926–2016

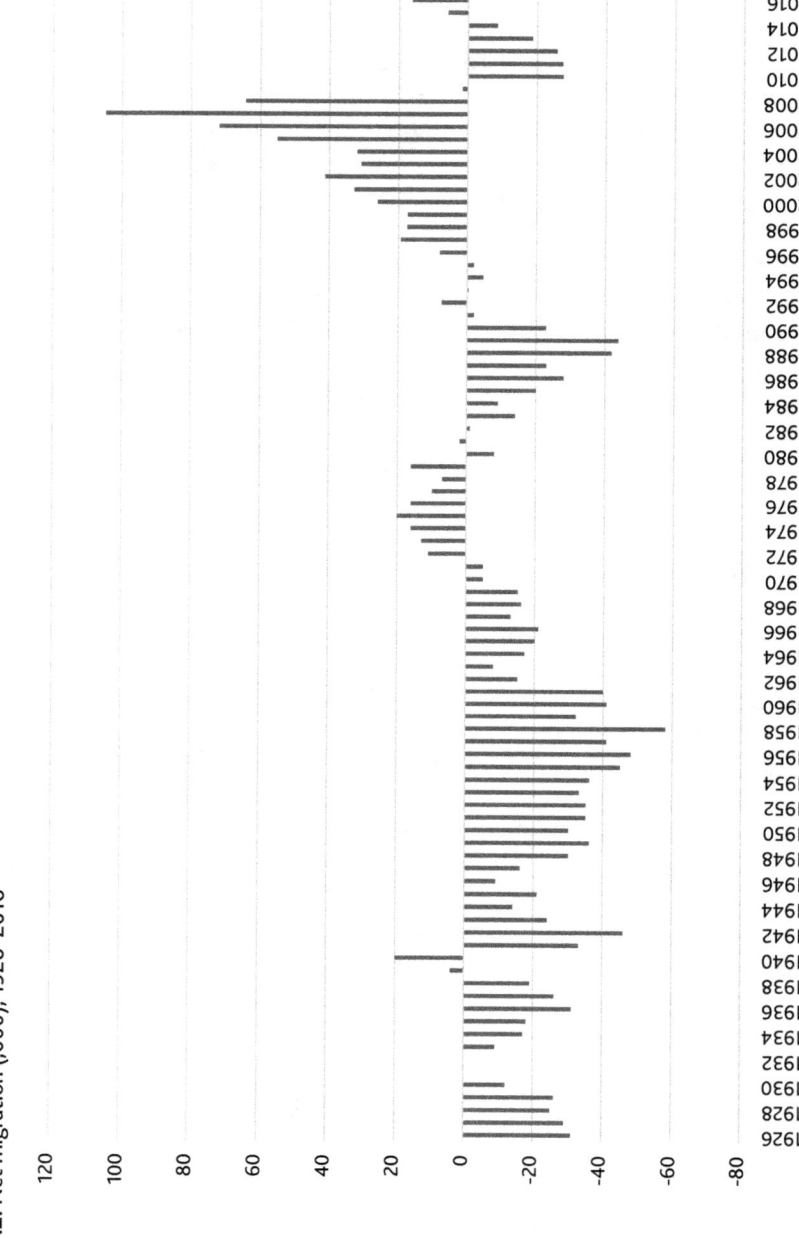

Source: Central Statistics Office – https://datasalsa.com/dataset/?catalogue=data.gov.ie&name=c0401-components-of-population-change-since-1926

Under a new Fine Gael-Labour Coalition, the first half saw widespread austerity measures and budget cuts under the shadow of the Troika stipulations, which particularly impacted those who became unemployed or those in receipt of social transfers. It was a time in which there was a perceived oversupply of housing as a result of the dramatic impact of the economic crisis and associated collapse of the housing market, which brought the construction industry to its knees. Against this background, homeless figures were relatively stable and, buoyed by progress in new ways to tackle homelessness at a European and North American level, there was an optimism among policy-makers that long-term homelessness could be ended using a housing-led approach.

The *Homelessness Policy Statement* (2013) marks the high point of this optimism. The Government appointed *Homelessness Oversight Group* went further in appraising progress and identifying areas of potential weakness which policy-makers could focus on in the subsequent years.

Paradoxically, the emergence of this housing-led approach coincided with the emergence of a severe shortage of housing. Not only were few houses being completed either for social rental or the private market, but the capacity also to construct housing at any scale in both the private and public sectors had been almost completely destroyed by the years of austerity. In the case of the social housing sector, this decommissioning of capacity had its roots in decisions made decades earlier.

From 2014, timely and accurate homeless data was published, ironically making publicly visible the sudden and rapid increase in homelessness. The stark story told by the monthly data was suddenly given a human face with the death of a man who had been sleeping rough near the gates of Leinster House, Jonathan Corrie. The rising figures and public outcry, along with a change of Minister, set aside the optimism contained in the targeted, methodical 80-point action plan published by the Government and replaced it with 'summits', catering to pressure from the public for more emergency shelters.

The dominant area of civic activism and protest during this period was the introduction of water charges as part of a strategy to create a national water authority and redress many years of underinvestment in water infrastructure. This resulted in large-scale public protests and political mobilisation. The water charges dispute was resolved by a number of Government policy about-turns, such as the abolition of planned charges and the reimbursement of those who had already paid. Many of the activist groups and trade unions who had been active in the water charges protests began to turn their attention to the question of housing and homelessness, with the hope that they could make a similar impact on policy. As the election came along in February 2016, homelessness had reached a then record 5,811 individuals – including 1,881 children – and housing and homelessness was for the first time one of the major concerns of voters.

8

Homelessness becomes a 'national crisis', 2016–2020

Introduction

In Chapter 7, we examined the early recovery period following Ireland's deep economic recession and the impact these dynamics had on homelessness, housing and related policy responses. The housing crisis in Ireland continued to deepen between 2016 and 2020. Around this time, house prices and rents began to increase sharply, as demand for privately rented properties rose while supply retracted – all of which rendered those in the lower end of the private rented sector at greater risk of housing precarity and homelessness. By 2016, the number of households experiencing homelessness was increasing at an exceptional rate, particularly among families who had never experienced homelessness before. While many households transitioned in and out of homelessness relatively quickly, a sizeable number were getting 'stuck' in emergency accommodation for lengthy periods, unable to secure an affordable rental property. During this period, housing and homelessness continued to receive political attention in response to an increasingly frustrated electorate. In this post-austerity period, we see a remarkable recovery and economic boom, a growth in employment and decline in unemployment, net inward migration and a decline in poverty. However, despite this ostensible recovery from the GFC, Daly warned that '[o]verall, the crisis leaves Ireland's service infrastructure underdeveloped and arguably weaker than before the crisis (with housing and health especially underdeveloped), while it leaves the welfare state in its highly targeted income maintenance mode rather than as an instrument that transforms economy and society' (2019a, 131).

The chapter will first explore the primary drivers of homelessness during this period, and consider the policy outputs in response, including the cross-party report published by the *Oireachtas Committee on Housing and Homelessness* and the subsequent report published by the Government – *Rebuilding Ireland*. The mainstreaming and rapid expansion of the Housing Assistance Payment (HAP) is then discussed in some detail, as well as the costs associated with this expansion. This leads the discussion to the overall rising Government expenditure on homelessness – specifically on emergency accommodation which included payments to private providers such as hotels and B&Bs and the establishment of new 'family hubs'. Finally, the rise of housing activism and street-based services is addressed, in the context of the wider dissatisfaction and public exasperation towards the homelessness problem. This chapter interrogates these key developments during what could have been a pivotal opportunity for Government action in combating homelessness. The chapter ends by setting the scene at the beginning of the COVID-19 pandemic, which coincided with a General Election in early 2020.

Indecisive General Election and cross-party initiative

The outcome of the February 2016 General Election gave no clear mandate to any party or group of parties. Both of the previous Government parties' lost seats. Fine Gael lost 26 seats, but for Labour, which had held the Cabinet role of Minister of Housing, the result was devastating: the party lost all but seven of its previous 37 seats. Despite its own losses, Fine Gael remained the largest party in the Dáil but did not have sufficient numbers to form a majority government, even with the support of willing independents. Negotiations to form a minority government with a 'confidence and supply' arrangement with Fianna Fáil continued over a three-month period.[1]

During these negotiations, in April 2016, Dáil Éireann agreed to establish a *Special Committee on Housing and Homelessness* to advance a series of recommendations for Cabinet on forthcoming housing policy. The Committee contained 14 TDs (three Fine Gael, three Fianna Fáil, two Sinn Féin, one Labour and five independents) and was chaired by Fianna Fáil TD, John Curran. Within two months, it published a wide-ranging, unanimous report, representing a cross-party consensus on the multiple challenges and possible policy solutions to housing and homelessness. The report foregrounded the overall dysfunction of the housing market with specific reference to the 'chronic undersupply of social housing' which, the Committee concluded, has 'exacerbated the homelessness crisis' (Committee on Housing and Homelessness, 2016, 107).

The cross-party report recognised the dysfunction of the housing market at that time, characterised by rising homelessness, increased housing precariousness, depleted stock of social housing, difficulties for households to access finance and an over-reliance on the private rented sector to house low-income households. The report also highlighted the many structural constraints facing the construction sector which was inhibiting the rate of construction of new builds – referencing the cost structure for development, difficulties of financing the cost of construction, availability of land for construction and infrastructural issues. One of the innovations of this Committee's work was a consultation in which the Committee met with around 60 people who were living in homeless accommodation, with a record of the consultation included as an appendix to the report.

The cross-party Committee made a number of priority recommendations, which included the following actions:

- *Increase social housing stock* by at least 50,000 units over five years through a programme of acquisition, refurbishment and new build.
- *Institutional reform*: establish of a Housing Procurement Agency to assist local authorities and AHBs to deliver their social housing programme through funding and procurement.
- To mobilise *funding for social and affordable housing* and for the Government to establish an off-balance sheet funding mechanism to provide additional investment in social and affordable housing; for NAMA to use cash reserves to tackle housing and homeless crisis; to mobilise all possible sources of funding.
- *Help for renters*: to increase security of tenure, for example establishing legal safeguard to allow tenants to remain in situ during and after sale of property (unless severe financial hardship could be proven by landlord); for rent supplements to reflect market rates and be subject to rent reviews to Consumer Price Index; for appropriate legislative safeguards to ensure rent certainty.
- *Help for homeowners*: to implement strategies to deal with those in mortgage distress such as legislation for a moratorium on home repossessions and long-term solutions for those in mortgage arrears.
- Actions to *counter homelessness*: to reinstate the policy of ring-fencing 50 per cent of local authority allocations for households with priority in Dublin and areas with high rates of homelessness (to be reviewed every six months); to significantly expand and prioritise Housing First; to ensure alternative accommodation is found for those residing in shelters earmarked for closure.
- *Greater coordination and resourcing of services*: to improve coordination between mental health and homeless services.

Further to these recommendations, the Oireachtas Committee's report also questioned the State's reliance on, and subsidising of, the private market to accommodate households eligible for social housing. The Committee flagged the scale of this expenditure could be excessive in the long-term, particularly in the context of rising rents.

However, according to Mary Daly of the European Social Policy Network, there were some "fundamental issues" the Committee's report did not tackle, for example, specific measures to tackle rising house prices, characterising the market as "too vibrant" (Daly, 2019b, 2). Daly also argued that the Irish housing market was overly dominated by private actors and developers, and a greater public policy influence was required to address the crisis.

Notwithstanding these points, the Oireachtas Committee's report outlined ambitious and largely progressive recommendations across multiple dimensions of the Irish housing market. Moreover, the report represented a cross-party consensus, proposing far-reaching reforms and legislative change focusing on improving housing supply through mobilising funding and construction as well as enhancing tenant rights. The Government's subsequent *Rebuilding Ireland* policy did not, however, mirror the ambition of the reforms proposed in the Oireachtas Committee's report nor did it capitalise on the political consensus achieved in this initial report.

Rebuilding Ireland: the new Government's response

Prior to the launch of the Oireachtas Committee's report, in May 2020, an agreement was reached by Fine Gael and a number of Independent TDs to form a minority government underpinned by the aforementioned 'confidence and supply' arrangement with Fianna Fáil, with Enda Kenny continuing as Taoiseach. This arrangement, which continued until the subsequent 2020 election (with a change of Taoiseach in 2017), meant that Fianna Fáil agreed to support the minority government in return for a published set of policy commitments. One of the commitments was to publish a new housing and homelessness policy within 60 days of taking office. Fine Gael's Simon Coveney was appointed as Minister for Housing, Planning and Local Government (May 2016–June 2017).

Fulfilling the 60 days commitment, in July 2016, Minister Coveney launched *Rebuilding Ireland: Action Plan for Housing and Homelessness*. This was the first government strategy to address both homelessness *and* housing supply in the same document. It referenced the need for the State to address the 'dysfunctional and under-performing housing sector' and firmly rooted homelessness as a housing issue for the first time (Government of Ireland, 2016, 9). The Strategy was organised into five 'pillars' of which the first was the *Homeless Pillar* which contained 38 actions. Most of these could be described as short-term actions (that is, to be delivered within the same political cycle) which were aimed to provide 'an urgent response to the crisis' (Government of Ireland, 2016).

These actions included the planned introduction of 'Rapid Build Housing'[2] (target of 1,500 units); to triple the Housing First target in Dublin (to 300); and the provision of additional support to assist those with complex needs, including mental health and addiction, access and maintain housing. On prevention, the policy committed to greater access to housing for young people leaving care; providing for specific vulnerable groups such as those experiencing domestic violence; and those being released from prison. It also committed to increasing rental subsidies and an 'accelerated roll-out' of the HAP scheme, as well as the expansion of the Dublin Region's Tenancy Protection Service to other geographic locations.

While previous homeless strategies had contained specific targets, such as eliminating long-term homelessness or the need to sleep rough, for example, *Rebuilding Ireland* contained no such targets. Nor did it attempt, as previous strategies had done, to conceptualise homelessness as a problem that could eventually be ended. The only specific numerical target for homelessness was to ensure that by mid-2017, commercial hotels would only be used in 'limited circumstances' for emergency accommodation. Given the subsequent reliance on (and expansion of) privately-run facilities to accommodate homeless persons across the State, this failed target perhaps signalled the Minister and Government's own underestimation of the dynamics underpinning the continued flow of households into emergency accommodation.

Rebuilding Ireland did however include a renewed commitment to Housing First. Building on actions taken by the previous Government, there was a policy commitment to increase resources for Housing First, publish an implementation plan, and expand the programme outside Dublin for the first time. The *Housing First Implementation Plan* was subsequently published in 2018 (Government of Ireland, 2018) and will be expanded upon later in the chapter.

Pillar 4 of *Rebuilding Ireland* also outlined a range of measures to improve the rental sector and committed to the development of a private rental housing strategy. In December 2016, following a public consultation via a stakeholder event, the Government published a *Strategy for the Rental Sector* which introduced a series of reforms. These included: the introduction of Rent Pressure Zones (RPZ) to particular urban areas with a limit of 4 per cent increase in rent per year; the extension from four- to six-year tenancy cycles; extension of eviction notice periods; and additional actions to professionalise the private rented sector. Many of these reforms enhanced regulation across the private rented sector but it can be argued that the reforms failed to address the fundamental problem of insecurity of tenure for tenants, which was leading to homelessness in the first place. Landlords were still able to serve valid termination of notice to tenants under the provisions of the *Residential Tenancies Acts 2004–2019* if they wished to sell the property, refurbish the dwelling or give it to a family member. As will be described in the next section, landlords evicting tenants in order to sell was a key driver of rising homelessness during this period.

Rebuilding Ireland put in place an infrastructure to monitor implementation of the policy to allow for appraisal of progress.[3] As can be seen in Figure 8.1, the policy did herald the resumption of social housing delivery, with nearly 14,500 units built and nearly 11,000 acquired, a total of just under 25,500 units over the period 2016–2020 compared to just under 6,000 units in the period 2011–2015.[4] AHBs provided just over 40 per cent of the social housing new

Figure 8.1: Social housing output, 1923–2020

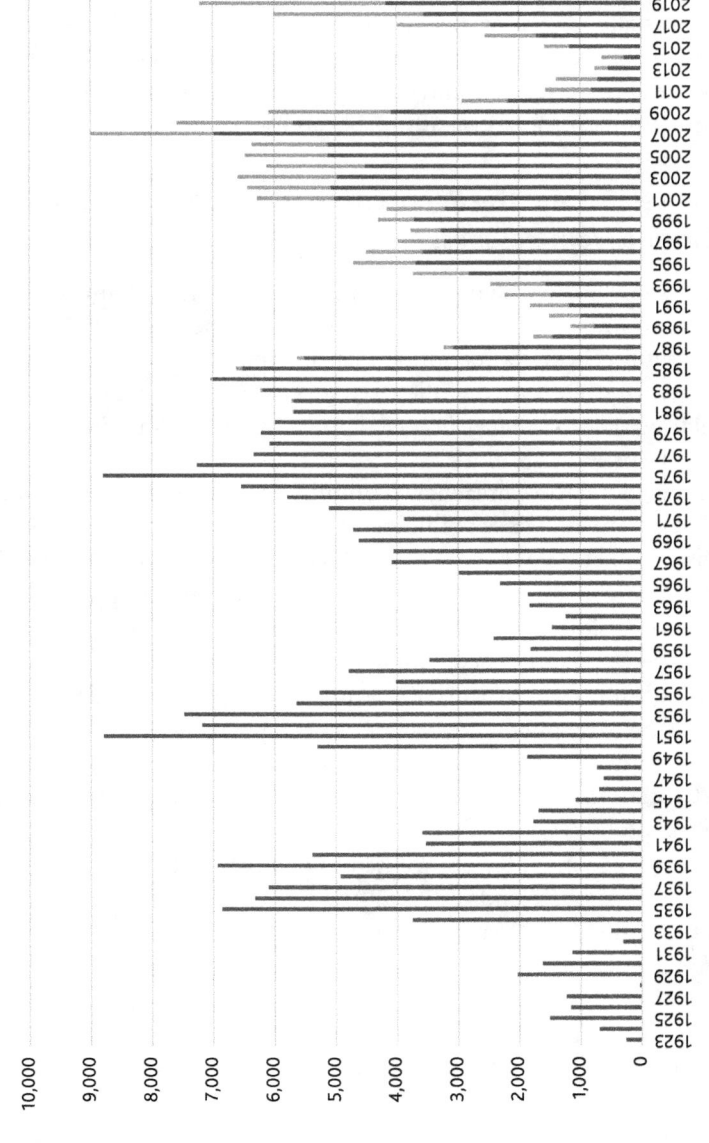

Source: Department of Local Government and Public Health Annual Report (various years) (Dublin: Stationery Office). Department of the Environment (various years); Annual Housing Statistics Bulletin (Dublin: Department of the Environment) – https://www.gov.ie/en/department-of-housing-local-government-and-heritage/organisation-information/housing-statistics/

builds and acquisitions, with the latter accounting for 43 per cent of the output. This enhanced programme of new build and acquisitions, and specifically in the case of Local Authority output, coupled with a significant curtailment of the local authority purchase scheme over this period (O'Sullivan et al, 2024), resulted in the highest ever stock of Local Authority housing with 141,128 units at the end of 2020 (NOAC, 2021, 61). Separately, the Land Development Agency was established in 2018. This State-owned commercial body is a government land management initiative to develop public land for housing delivery, with a primary focus on affordable and social homes.

Rebuilding Ireland and the *Report of the Oireachtas Committee on Housing and Homelessness*

Rebuilding Ireland noted that it was informed by the Report of the Oireachtas Committee on Housing and Homelessness and included an appendix outlining how its recommendations reflected and incorporated the recommendations from the all-party group (Government of Ireland, 2016, 9).[5] However, *Rebuilding Ireland*'s approach was distinct in a number of important respects.

For example, while the Oireachtas Committee report recommended that local authorities return to direct building of social housing at scale, *Rebuilding Ireland* envisaged that 63 per cent of the 138,000 'units of social housing' to be delivered between 2016 and 2021 would come from the private rental sector *via* rental subsidies, only a minority would be new build social housing units. This represents a difference both in terms of what should be considered 'social housing' and in the nature of the role of the State in addressing the housing shortage. The policy document itself characterises this direction or 'transition' towards the private sector, as providing: 'a better mix between private and social housing, rather than the reliance on large mono-tenure public housing projects which characterised housing investment in the 1960s and 1970s, many of which have since had to be regenerated in more recent years' (Government of Ireland, 2016, 20).

One of the differences between *Rebuilding Ireland* and the Oireachtas Committee's report was that the latter was largely drafted by politicians, while *Rebuilding Ireland* was drafted by civil servants, with significant input from staff at the National Economic and Social Council (NESC) who themselves were carrying out policy analysis and advancing recommendations through their publications during this period (NESC, 2014, 2015). The politicians' document actually achieved a cross-party consensus on a number of contentious issues, while *Rebuilding Ireland* quickly became exclusively a Government document, regularly criticised by all opposition spokespersons both for what it set out to achieve and what it failed to deliver. By February 2018, John Curran, Chair of the cross-party Committee, was denouncing

Rebuilding Ireland as an 'epic failure for 9,104 homeless people', despite his party being in a 'confidence and supply' agreement with the Government.[6]

Failure to incorporate some of the key findings from the cross-party Committee report can be regarded as a lost opportunity, both in terms of its proposed greater role for direct State action and for the failure to sustain a cross-party consensus on solutions to a still-growing crisis. Indeed, the lost potential of cross-party consensus is hard to assess, but an interesting comparison exists in the case of the health system where consensus on the *Sláintecare* strategy emerged from a cross-party committee over a similar period. The political consensus behind *Sláintecare* has largely been maintained, even though the outcomes fall far short of expectations (Thomas et al, 2021).

Another area where inaction resulted in an important policy direction being discontinued was the decision by Minister Coveney not to continue any of the priority allocation policies of the previous FG/Labour Government. As noted in the previous chapter, a recommendation from the Homeless Oversight Group to bring local authority voids back into use and to preferentially allocate them to people who were long-term homeless was replaced by Minister Kelly with a directive that a percentage of all social housing allocations should go to households that were homeless (or disabled). Although there was no evidence to support their claim, the criticism from the CEOs from the four Dublin local authorities and elsewhere that this policy resulted in families voluntarily becoming homeless resulted in Kelly not renewing this directive before he left office. Coveney's decision not to extend the directive brought to an end this policy.

This directive was reviewed by the Housing Agency at the request of the Department of Environment, Community and Local Government in 2016, but the review was never published. Although the brief review (22 pages) concluded that the Ministerial directive should lapse at the end of April 2016, based on 'the analysis contained in the review', it was largely absent of any evidence. Assertions such as 'there is emerging evidence' that the directive 'contributed to the expectation that a household presenting as homeless will receive secure tenure housing from the State after a very short period of time' (2016, 15) or 'evidence on the effectiveness of specific categories of specific needs on the waiting lists is mixed' (2016, 13) were made but such claims were not supported by any empirical evidence.

Rise of housing and homelessness activism: Part 1

In the week before Christmas 2016, a group of housing activists gained entry to and occupied a derelict office block in the centre of Dublin called Apollo House. They did so in protest of the housing and homelessness crisis. Apollo House was NAMA[7]-controlled and due for demolition to be replaced by a new office block. The occupation was led by a campaign group called 'Home Sweet Home' and consisted of housing activists, artists and trade unionists.

The protesters claimed there was insufficient emergency accommodation for homeless people over Christmas, a claim which the Government denied. The protesters provided shelter for rough sleepers to draw attention to the homelessness crisis and their wider demands. The occupation gained widespread attention and public support and drew in substantial funds from the public via a GoFundMe account, as well as substantial donations of food, clothes and general supplies. While there were other examples during this period where buildings were occupied by activists, the Apollo House occupation was the most high-profile, partly due to the involvement of artists such as the musician Glen Hansard and film director Jim Sheridan, who produced a film about the event. Marches and open-air concerts, which included other well-known musicians, helped to keep the story high on the news agenda over the Christmas and New Year period.

The receivers of the building took High Court action to evict the protesters and an order demanding that the building be vacated by noon on 11 January was issued. The protesters declared they would not leave until certain demands were met. Minister Coveney and officials from the Housing Department met the protesters in talks that lasted for several hours, ending dramatically without agreement near midnight. Discussions which had included Sheridan and Hansard, as well as the trade unionist, Brendan Ogle, who had been involved in earlier protests against water charges, were reportedly related to the future of the homeless individuals residing in the building being accommodated and on broader political themes such as the role of NAMA, rough sleeping and rent control.

Despite the lack of formal agreement, Minister Coveney made a number of conciliatory announcements, specifically a commitment to 210 extra emergency beds in Dublin and 'arrangements for the transition of people currently in Apollo House to alternative suitable accommodation with appropriate supports' (Brennan, 2017). The protesters left on 12 January, 27 days after the initial occupation. The departure was accompanied by criticisms that Coveney had misled them about the quality of alternative emergency accommodation available and declarations that the protests would continue in other forms.

In parallel with the increase in housing activism in Ireland, there was a substantial increase in 'on-street' services for those perceived to be in need. These services typically provided food, provisions, clothes or toiletries and operated separately to mainstream services which are funded or part-funded through Section 10 funding. These street-based services were dependent on volunteers and were rooted in activism or other grass-roots movements, while a number were faith-led. The most significant of these new volunteer-led organisations was *Inner City Helping Homeless* (which will be returned to in the next chapter), which was formed in 2013 but came to greater prominence during this period. As well as providing support for people on the street, the organisation was extremely active on social media and mainstream media, frequently critical of Government and larger, long-standing homeless organisations.

This growth in volunteer-led street-based assistance to people who were homeless occurred in a number of countries over this period and was the subject of critical analysis about its limitations and impact on public policy (Parsells and Watts, 2017; Parsell, 2018, 2023; O'Sullivan, 2020). While many of these activist and volunteer-led groups included the need for more affordable and social housing in their demands, the overall impact tended to re-focus attention on the issue of rough sleeping and rooflessness, with the only tangible outcome from the Apollo House occupation being the provision of over 200 new emergency beds.

A change of Minister, but not direction

In Spring 2017, the retirement of the Taoiseach Enda Kenny resulted in a Cabinet reshuffle, with the newly-elected Taoiseach, Leo Varadkar TD, appointing Eoghan Murphy as Minister for Housing, Planning, Community and Local Government – the 6th Minister to hold responsibility for homelessness in just seven years.

On 14 June 2017, with a new record of 4,571 households in emergency accommodation, the Taoiseach announced in the Dáil that he had requested the new Minister for Housing to review *Rebuilding Ireland* within three months 'and to consider what additional measures may be required' (Dáil Éireann Debate, Vol. 953, No. 4, Wednesday, 14 June 2017). Addressing the Irish Council for Social Housing AGM on 3 July, Mr Murphy stated that what was being undertaken was not 'a wholesale review' and added: 'we're not starting from scratch again. The plan is good and is delivering important results' (quoted in Burns et al, 2017). In the event, no revised strategy was published although some targets were amended, making it increasingly difficult to assess whether targets and objectives (as opposed to 'actions') had been reached.

During this period, the *National Consultative Committee on Homelessness* was not convened by the Department of Housing and was effectively stood down without any formal announcement. In September 2017, Minister Murphy established a *Homelessness Inter-Agency Group*, under the chairmanship of John Murphy, a former senior civil servant. This Committee produced one report in June 2018, which contained a number of cross-departmental recommendations but became controversial due a recommendation that people lose their position on the housing list and their right to emergency homeless accommodation if they turn down a housing offer. In the familiar pattern, there is no record of the *Inter-Agency Group* meeting again after this initial report.

Primary causes of homelessness and private rented sector trends

By the end of Q1 2019, the Government was reporting that 31 of the 38 actions from the Homelessness Pillar of *Rebuilding Ireland* had been 'completed'. Despite this, the number of households in emergency accommodation continued to rise rapidly over this period. While the Government claimed that the actions would take time to have effect, others saw the continued rises as suggesting that the plan failed 'to fundamentally disrupt the structural failings of the system' (O'Sullivan, 2020, 76).

More broadly, despite the commitment to greatly accelerate the construction of local authority units, in the first three years of *Rebuilding Ireland*, just over 3,300 units of social housing were built by local authorities (which accounted for 30 per cent of the total 'build' output) (O'Sullivan, 2020). Therefore, despite the Oireachtas Committee recommendations, there was a continued dependency on the subsidisation of the private rental sector to fulfil social housing demand through the rent supplements system.

As we have argued in Chapter 7, the underlying causes of Ireland's current homeless problem since 2010 are to be found in decisions taken much earlier in relation to social housing supply, which resulted in an insufficient supply of social housing and an over-reliance on the private rental sector. While this is the root of the problem, the consequences of these policies played out most dramatically in the private rental sector.

A notable feature of the Irish housing market is that was, at this time, dominated by 'small landlords'; landlords who own one to two properties made up about 85 per cent of all landlords and supplied an estimated 53 per cent of the private tenancies in the rental market, while more than half (55 per cent) of these properties had been lived in previously by the landlord. Furthermore, all but 4 per cent of small landlords viewed their position as a part-time landlord or 'not my primary occupation' (RTB, 2021a). This renders the private rental sector particularly exposed to flux and changes associated with the previously discussed boom and bust cycles of the Irish housing market.

During this period, one in four rental properties had been acquired with a 'buy-to-let' mortgage and, according to Central Bank statistics, 25.2 per cent of buy-to-let properties were in mortgage arrears at the end of 2014 (Central Bank of Ireland, 2014). Therefore, many landlords sought to sell their properties or leave the rental market when house prices began to rise.

As already noted, while the Government had introduced more protections for tenants in private rental properties since the enacting of the *Residential Tenancies Act, 2014* provisions for landlords to end tenancies where they, or a family member, want to move into the property or where they decide to sell the property. These provisions were considered essential in encouraging landlords to enter the private rental market as investors. Where few landlords were leaving the market and there was a ready supply of alternative accommodation, such a provision is not necessarily problematic. However, with more landlords selling up, and a falling supply of private rental tenancies, households increasingly found it impossible to find alternative accommodation before their notice of termination expired.

Following an amendment in 2016 to the *Residential Tenancies, Act 2004*, Approved Housing Bodies ('AHBs') – and subsequently in 2019 student-specific accommodation – were included under the regulatory remit of the Residential Tenancies Board (RTB)[8] (renamed from the Private Residential Tenancies Board). RTB data between 2016 and 2020 showed that the number of private rented tenancies declined by almost 7 per cent from 319,822 tenancies in 2016 to 297,837 in 2020. This was deemed by the RTB Annual Report 2020 as a 'significant reduction' year-on-year (RTB, 2021b, 67), and following additional survey data analysis with landlords carried out by the RTB in 2020, they concluded that this reduction was a result of a planned departure of small landlords from the sector, who expressed a clear intention to sell their property (RTB, 2021b, 15).

There is robust evidence linking the dramatic rise in homelessness from 2014 to these broader dynamics in the rental market – specifically with regards to landlords leaving the market, the retracting supply of private rental sector units coupled with the broader policy dependence on the private rental sector for social housing (Walsh and Harvey, 2015; Long et al, 2019; Gambi and Sheridan, 2020). This also marked a shift in the causes of homelessness and profile of those entering emergency accommodation. Research that tracked the housing trajectories of 237 families who entered homelessness in 2019 found that 68 per cent became homeless through loss of accommodation in the private rental sector, with 58 per cent of families (n=137) reporting that they had to leave due to the private rented property being removed from the market via a 'no-fault eviction' (including landlord selling, moving back in or giving to family member, or bank repossession). Even though 60 per cent of the families reported highly stable housing histories – characterised by lengthy tenancies in the private rental market – they entered homelessness when they were unable to find alternative rental accommodation, often after staying with friends or family before presenting as homeless to their local authority (Long et al, 2019; Gambi and Sheridan, 2020). In this way, during this period households were increasingly becoming homeless almost entirely due to the decisions of their landlord and the difficulties of finding alternative accommodation. A historically higher proportion of these were families with children and most of those entering homelessness had never experienced homelessness previously.

Affordability in the private market was another key issue which impacted on homeless rates, and in particular, impeded low-income households to exit homelessness. These rising rents were acutely linked to increased demand. National average rents rose each quarter between 2016 and 2020 (RTB, various years). In Q1 2016, the average rent nationally for new tenants stood at €955 and had increased by 33 per cent to €1,269 by Q4 2020. In the Dublin region, rents for new renters increased by 27 per cent from €1,336 in Q1 2016 to €1,733 in Q4 2020.

In response to the rising homeless figures, the Government responded by increasing the termination notice periods and the introduction of 'preventative Homeless HAP' for households nearing the end of their notice period. Despite these measures ensuring that 5,700 households in Dublin alone avoided homelessness, the number of available properties continued to decline; a longer period to search for alternative accommodation was not enough to reduce the number of families entering emergency homeless accommodation.

Many studies that emerged during and after this period identified a range of population groups that faced additional barriers in accessing private rented housing such as affordability problems and discrimination. Lone mothers, migrants, ethnic minority groups, young people, as well as people with complex support needs were all found to be disproportionately represented in homelessness data and research (Long et al, 2019; Russell et al, 2021). Discrimination against HAP tenants has been prohibited since 2015 under *Equal Status Acts 2000–2018* – which 'prohibits discrimination in the provision of accommodation services against people who are in receipt of rent supplement, housing assistance or social welfare payments'. However, discrimination is not always easy to prove and so incidents of discrimination that make it to the Workplace Relations Commission are likely to underestimate the scale of discrimination. Moreover, many do not seek redress or challenge this discrimination in the courts due to the vulnerable position tenants are in the housing market (Threshold, 2021).

Mainstreaming of HAP

While the previous chapter addresses the origins and legislative underpinnings of the HAP and HHAP schemes, the following section focuses on the scaling up of HAP as the primary 'social housing solution' in Ireland at this time. While it was rolled out in phases in 2014, it was scaled up nationally from 2017 and operated in all local authority areas from January 2018 (Office of the Ombudsman, 2025). The scheme was foregrounded in multiple policy documents and strategies around this expansion period. *Rebuilding Ireland* had committed to an 'accelerated roll-out' of the HAP scheme, aiming to support just under 84,000 households over the lifetime of the plan (Government of Ireland, 2016, 48). *Rebuilding Ireland* also stated that the private rental market would provide the primary source of social housing, an equivalent of 85 per cent of new social housing tenancies or 84,000 households in that period (Government of Ireland, 2016; Kilkenny, 2019).

This reliance on the private rental market was a continuation of the strategy of the previous Government, *Social Housing Strategy 2020* (2014) which projected that by 2020 up to 75,000 would move into HAP (or RAS) (Kilkenny, 2019). Ministers defended this shift as an essential bridging measure while new built social housing was accelerated after the crash, but as already referenced earlier in this chapter, it was also seen to reflect a deeper policy resistance to mono-tenurial social housing estates that dominated housing provision in the 20th century (O'Sullivan, 2020).

Each year between 2016 and 2020, the provision of HAP tenancies via the private sector greatly exceeded direct build by both local authorities and Approved Housing Body units combined. The HAP scheme continued to replace long-term use of Rent Supplement (RS) which, although it remained an option for households, was used for those in more short-term housing need, such as a change in circumstances that renders a person unable to meet rent payments on a temporary basis (Threshold and SVP, 2019). The Homeless HAP (HHAP) Place Finder service also became embedded and provided intensive support to those at risk of homelessness across all local authorities.

The maximum amount of HAP that can be paid (or 'HAP cap') varies depending on size of household and local authority – as set out in secondary legislation at this time. As rents increased over these years, local authorities had discretion to increase the HAP caps by up to 35 per cent in certain circumstances. Due to rent increases, in most cases HAP does not cover the full cost of rent, even with this discretionary increase meaning that most HAP tenants must pay a 'top up' – that is, the difference between the HAP cap and the actual cost of rent for their property to their landlord. In this way, HAP tenants pay their differential rent to the local authority as well as rent to their landlord – unlike social housing tenants.

Expansion of HAP and changing profile of tenants

As rents rose and more households became dependent on HAP, the scheme extended to households who would not necessarily have sought social housing tenancies but, due to major shifts in the housing market, were being drawn into housing precariousness and risk of homelessness. Thus, the reliance on rental subsidy schemes within the private rental sector has broadened, and the profile of individuals and families accessing social housing supports changed. Crucial to this was the fact that the HAP scheme *permits* recipients to be in employment.

Data published by the Central Statistics Office (CSO, 2023) showed that, for example, in 2015 the median annual earned income for households newly entering HAP was €8,982 but by 2020 this had risen to €15,230 (CSO, 2023). Similarly, in 2015, 35.5 per cent of households newly entering HAP were in some form of paid employment and by 2020 this had risen to 59.4 per cent (CSO, 2020). Employment rates among HAP recipients in 2020 was particularly high in the four Dublin local authorities, Kildare and Cork city – the highest rates were 72.8 per cent in Dun Laoghaire-Rathdown followed by 65.5 per cent in South Dublin (CSO, 2023).

More than four in ten (44 per cent) HAP tenants spent less than a year on a local authority waiting list while just one in ten (12 per cent) waited seven years or more (CSO, 2020). The proportion of new HAP households who were referred from homeless services rose steadily from 3.1 per cent in 2014 to 21.1 per cent by 2019 (CSO, 2020). Again, this changing profile reflected the significant shortfall of affordable housing.

Criticisms of HAP

Notwithstanding the significant investment and commitment to scaling HAP scheme households across the country, multiple criticisms have emerged in relation to its limitations. These critiques are outlined in a succinct and targeted investigation into the HAP scheme conducted by the Office of the Ombudsman in 2025 which identified issues including administrative inefficiencies, emerging inequities and particular vulnerabilities for homeless applicants (Office of the Ombudsman, 2025).

Administrative inefficiencies identified in the scheme include both difficulties and delays of application process or payments for some – which can have serious implications for the applicant in particular but also prove problematic for landlords, perhaps reducing the likelihood for engagement of prospective landlords (Office of the Ombudsman, 2025). Further, delays in the validation of HAP applications can, in some cases, mean a tenant may pay a number of months' rent before the application is formally approved. This is identified as being 'unfair' given that the tenant has already been deemed eligible for social housing supports (Office of the Ombudsman, 2025, 10). The Ombudsman report detailed a range of other administrative inefficiencies and provided a clear set of recommendations in resolving them (Office of the Ombudsman, 2025).

Crucially, rent subsidy schemes set a maximum threshold of rent that can be paid, meaning that only a small proportion of the lower priced properties are accessible to potential HAP/RAS/RAS tenants. The political 'confidence and supply' agreement in 2016 included a commitment to 'Increase rent supplement and Housing Assistance Payment (HAP) limits by up to 15 per cent taking account of geographic variations in market rents, and extend the roll out by local authorities of HAP, including the capacity to make discretionary enhanced payments' (Fine Gael, 2016, 4).

In July 2016, HAP rates were increased by a weighted average, including 30 per cent increase in the Dublin area. There was a short-term reduction in the numbers of families becoming homeless in the months after the rates increased (Stanley and Allen, 2018), but this effect declined as rents continued to rise. No further increase was made during the lifetime of that Government, despite rents increasing by 33 per cent and between Q1 2016 and Q4 2020 (RTB, various years). The Simon Communities' snapshot surveys of availability of HAP properties provide reliable and regular evidence on the dearth of properties available to HAP recipients (Simon Communities, various years). For example, the March 2019 survey showed that 92 per cent of the 517 properties available to rent were above rent supplement or HAP limits, and therefore out of reach for those in pursuit of a HAP property.

As the programme expanded, and as referenced in the previous chapter, local authorities were permitted to authorise a 20 per cent and later 35 per cent discretionary payment or 'uplift' for HAP tenants, so that they would be able to meet the rental costs. The Homeless HAP allowed for a 50 per cent discretion (if necessary to secure suitable accommodation). By 2019, almost 28.3 per cent of all HAP tenancies required the 20 per cent discretionary uplift payments by local authorities. Furthermore, a growing number of households had to pay their landlord 'top ups' – that is, the difference between the HAP cap and the actual cost for rent. According to data provided to the Office of the Ombudsman, in May 2023, about two-thirds of households in the scheme are known to have paid these 'top ups' (Office of the Ombudsman, 2025, 5). Where the 20 per cent discretionary uplift is not given (or is insufficient to match market rents), some tenants may miss out on rental opportunities or may be forced to pay even higher 'top ups' (Threshold and SVP, 2019).

As a result, tenants can end up paying considerably higher rents than households with identical incomes in local authority or AHB properties. Of note, HAP tenants do not have access to the same benefits as social housing tenants, including various hardship clauses and arrear repayment plans should the tenant face times of financial hardship (Office of the Ombudsman, 2025). While the Department of Housing, Local Government and Heritage introduced a 'landlord guarantee' which ensured continuity of payment of HAP, 'this does not address the aspects of the HAP scheme that contribute to a household's financial difficulties in the first place', such as 'top ups' (Office for the Ombudsman, 2025, 15).

Even aside from potential prejudice from landlords, potential HAP tenants have to compete for available tenancies with households who may be better able to provide deposits or pay rent in advance and who do not require the level of paperwork required to access HAP payments. The Ombudsman's investigation found that vulnerable groups such as Travellers, people with disabilities and people leaving international protection accommodation can face additional difficulties sourcing HAP accommodation (Office of the Ombudsman, 2025).

In terms of security, HAP tenants can, like other private renters but unlike those renting from local authorities or AHBs, face no-fault eviction due to the landlord selling or taking the property for his/her own use. Where this occurs, unlike with RAS, a HAP tenant must find a new rental property on their own; this can be extremely challenging in a competitive and inflated market, leading to housing precarity, and in some cases, homelessness. Further, HAP tenants may be reluctant to report poor standards and conditions of a property to local authorities out of fear they will lose their property or payments would be stopped. This overlaps with overall need for inspections of standard in private rental properties, particularly in light of the 'significant State funding' involved in the HAP scheme (Office of the Ombudsman, 2025, 17).

Expenditure on HAP

Between 2015 and 2020, expenditure on HAP increased by 495 per cent, from €15.6 m to €464.6 m, reflecting both the rapid expansion of the programme, but also the broader increase in rents and use of 'uplift' payments. The average lease cost per month for units in 2016 was €920 rising to €1,085 in 2020 (Griffin, 2021). Despite the fact that the State does not have to maintain properties as it does with local authority units – which can be costly – the long-term ability or capacity of the State to continue to scale and maintain HAP payments has been flagged, particularly in the context of an inflated rental market and rising rents (Kilkenny, 2019). Most HAP scheme payments went to individual landlords (there were 32,019 individual HAP landlords registered in 2019), but increasingly, it also includes the transfer of funds to private corporate landlords – usually international investors. The number of institutional landlords increased from 52 in 2014 to 2,297 in 2019, who received over €261 m from the State between 2014 and 2019.

Homelessness trends: 2014–2019

As outlined in the previous chapter, detailed monthly homelessness data were available during this period. The number of adults, both adult-only households and adults with child dependents in emergency accommodation rose rapidly and consistently from 2014 to 2019, as seen in Figure 8.2 (which include 2014 and 2015 data to illustrate overall trend), with a 426

Figure 8.2: Adults in families and adult-only households in Local Government emergency and temporary accommodation, June 2014–December 2019

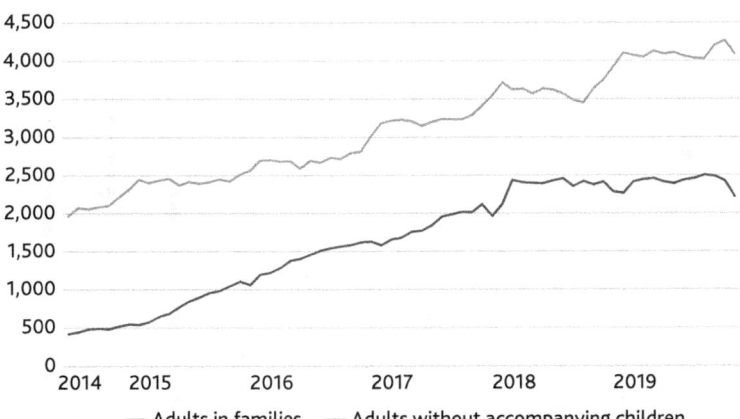

Source: https://www.gov.ie/en/department-of-housing-local-government-and-heritage/collections/homelessness-data/#homelessness-data

per cent increase in the number of adults in families and a 108 per cent increase in adult-only households. Eoghan Murphy, the Minister with responsibility for housing and homelessness between 2017 and 2020, noted in his account of serving as Minister, that he and his officials 'dreaded the monthly homeless numbers' and that '[e]very month we would try new phrases and tactics in an attempt to explain ourselves out of the growing mess' (Murphy, 2024, 119). During this period, both Murphy and the Taoiseach, Leo Varadkar had publicly expressed the view that Ireland had a low rate of homelessness by international standards. Measuring homelessness comparatively is beset with definitional and measurement issues, but Appendix 2 provides a comparison of Ireland with Denmark and Finland, countries with similar sized populations and have comparable data. Based on this robust data, Ireland has a comparatively high rate of homelessness at a point-in-time compared to Denmark and Finland (see Allen et al, 2020 for further details).

Over the period, the number of people counted as sleeping rough or unsheltered in the bi-annual Dublin one night point-in-time count fluctuated between 100 and 180 as shown in Figure 8.3. There were 142 people sleeping rough in Dublin on the night of the official *Winter Rough Sleeping Count* carried out in November 2016, representing an increase of 50 per cent since the 2015 winter count (Dublin Region Homeless Executive, 2016). This increased to a high point of 184 in the Q4 2017, but then dropped to less than 100 in winter 2019. Data on rough sleeping during the period was not routinely, systematically or consistently collected outside Dublin.

Figure 8.3: Unsheltered point-in-time count Dublin, 2014–2019

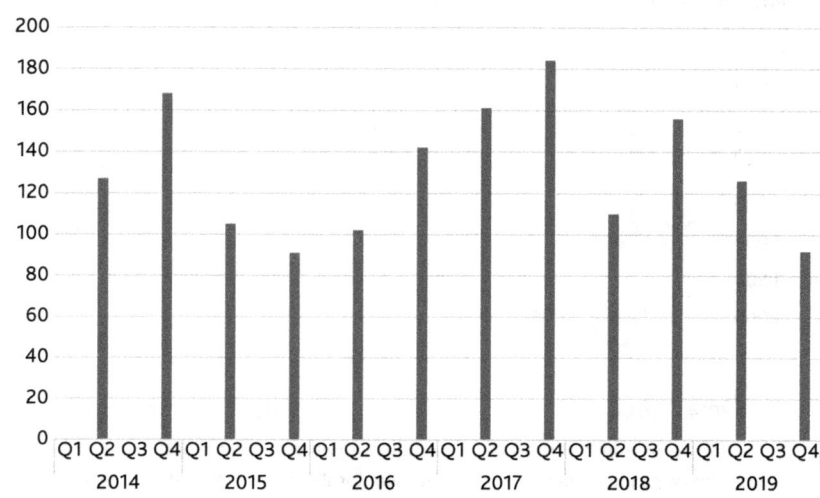

Source: https://www.homelessdublin.ie/info/publications

Point-in-time rough sleeper data (and the term 'rough sleeper') can give the misleading impression that there is a fixed group of people, often envisaged as having similar characteristics, who comprise the 'rough sleeping population'. From 2016, a large number of individuals sleeping rough typically alternate between rough sleeping and accessing emergency accommodation, according to street outreach teams (O'Sullivan et al, 2021b).

Notwithstanding the daily hardship and suffering for those experiencing rooflessness, the number of rough sleepers in Ireland has evidently remained relatively stable in Dublin, particularly in comparison to the very substantial increases in the number of people in emergency homeless accommodation. Between 2016 and 2020, there were three deaths of rough sleepers (two female and one male) and, while any untimely death on the streets is a tragedy for those involved, the mortality rate of rough sleepers overall was described as 'consistently low' during this period (O'Carroll, 2021, 34). As will be discussed later, these cold statistics on rough sleeping were in striking contrast to the public debate and media coverage of homelessness during the period which focused extensively on the plight of rough sleepers.

As already referenced, while the administrative PASS data system was not originally designed for research purposes, it has capacity to derive insights into the dynamics of homelessness that has provided an unprecedented sophisticated understanding of homelessness, particularly in Dublin (see, for example, Morrin, 2019; Waldron, O'Donoghue-Hynes and Redmond, 2019; Bairead and Norris, 2020; Matthews, 2022; Maphosa,

Figure 8.4: Number of new adults entering Section 10 funded emergency and temporary accommodation, 2014–2019

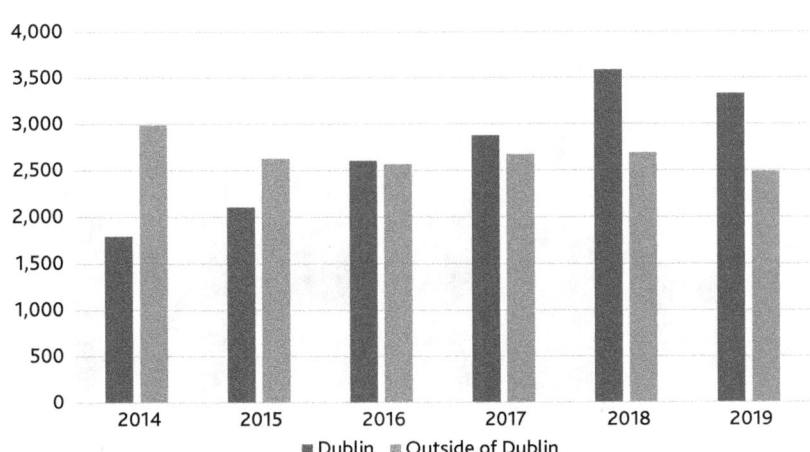

Source: https://www.gov.ie/en/department-of-housing-local-government-and-heritage/collections/homelessness-data/#homelessness-data

2024; Waldron, Redmond and O'Donoghue-Hynes, 2024; Maphosa and Mayock, 2025).

Since the beginning of 2014, the Department of Housing has published *Performance Quarterly Reports* on the number of entries to homelessness services, the number of exits from homelessness, the duration of stays in emergency accommodation, contacts with rough sleepers and the number of adults with support services during that quarter.

Over the period 2014–2019, 33,200 unique adults entered emergency accommodation – equally divided between Dublin and outside Dublin as shown in Figure 8.4. The numbers of new entries peaked in 2018 with nearly 6,300 new entries nationally, before dropping slightly to 5,800 in 2019.

Over the same timeframe, 16,900 adults exited to housing, either a social housing tenancy or a private rented tenancy with income support via HAP or Rent supplement. As with entries, the number of exits to housing was equally divided between Dublin and outside Dublin as shown in Figure 8.5. The duration of stay in emergency accommodation increased over this period with 793 adults in emergency accommodation for more than six months (cumulatively or consecutively) in Q1 2014 compared to 3,782 in Q4 2019 – an increase of 377 per cent.

The popular perception of those experiencing homelessness is that they have complex needs due to their high levels of disabilities and/or substance misuse and hence face significant difficulties in exiting emergency accommodation and securing independent accommodation. However, drawing on a typology of shelter pattern use developed by Kuhn and

Figure 8.5: Adults' exits from emergency accommodation to housing, 2014–2019

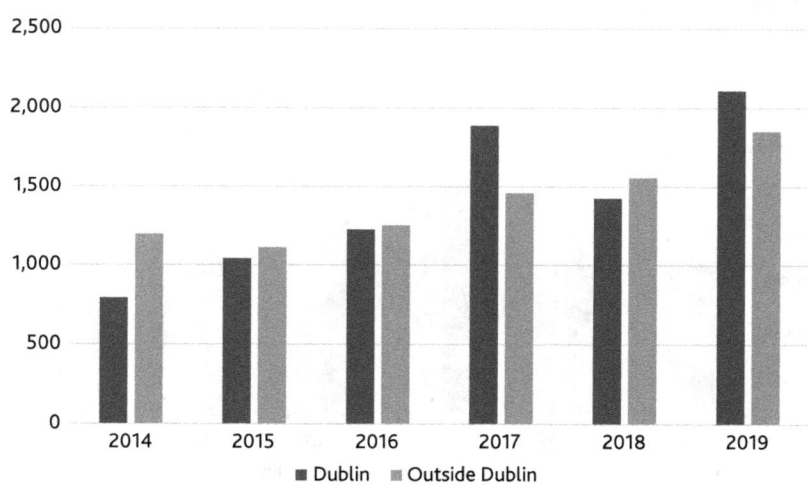

Source: https://www.gov.ie/en/department-of-housing-local-government-and-heritage/collections/homelessness-data/#homelessness-data

Culhane (1998), Waldron, O'Donoghue-Hynes and Redmond (2019) in their exploration of patterns of shelter use in Dublin between 2012 and 2016 utilising the PASS data identified that long-stay shelter users, who comprised 12 per cent of all users, occupied 50 per cent of all bed nights. A further group of episodic users who used shelters intermittently accounted for 10 per cent of shelter users, using 15 per cent of bed nights. Thus, 22 per cent of shelter users – the chronic and episodic – accounted for 65 per cent of all bed nights between 2012 and 2016 (Waldron, O'Donoghue-Hynes and Redmond, 2019). This demonstrates that the vast majority of those who used shelter beds in Dublin, the transitional shelter users, during this period exited their emergency accommodation relatively quickly and did not return, which implies that they did not have any significant psychosocial difficulties; rather, they had a temporary loss of secure accommodation, but this residential instability was resolved relatively quickly.

Analysis of the PASS data in relation to families showed that families experience distinct patterns of shelter utilisation compared to the general population of homeless adults (Parker, 2021; Waldron, Redmond and O'Donoghue-Hynes, 2024). Analysing families' shelter usage in the Dublin region between 2011 and 2016, Parker (2021) found that families were much more likely to experience long-term homelessness, representing a far greater proportional share of those in the chronic cluster than has than has been reported elsewhere internationally. More specifically, 33 per cent of families accessing State-funded emergency accommodation experienced long-term patterns of shelter use, while just 57 per cent and 10 per cent utilised services on a transitional and episodic basis, respectively, suggesting that families in Ireland face considerable barriers to exiting homelessness that result in prolonged shelter stays (Parker, 2021).

Publication of the *Housing First Implementation Plan 2018*

The *Housing First Implementation Plan 2018–2021* sought to build on the Dublin Housing First scheme which was operational since 2014. Housing First in Ireland, by that time, was considered a success by policy-makers. By August 2018, 250 tenancies had been created across the four Dublin local authorities, with a tenancy sustainment rate of 85 per cent (Government of Ireland, 2018, 10). The 2018 *Implementation Plan* sought to expand the programme out to other parts of the country, with a target of 663 tenancies. The target groups for Housing First continued as individuals rough sleeping or long-term homeless with complex support needs. Notwithstanding the positive tenancy sustainment outcomes among those who were housed through the programme, given that there were 6,024 single adults nationally in July 2018, the degree to which Housing First was impacting overall trends in homelessness was arguably limited. Moreover, the continued inflow of adult-only households into homeless accommodation and struggling to exit meant that the overall numbers in emergency accommodation kept rising.

Expansion of homeless emergency infrastructure

The previous chapter highlighted the sense of optimism in resolving homelessness during the economic recovery phase, during which homeless rates were comparatively low and there was surplus housing stock around the country. As already described, this translated into housing-led policy design and a reconfiguration of homeless services in the Dublin region. However, as the numbers in emergency accommodation began to rise significantly after 2014, the State reacted by finding short-term solutions to the steady flow of people requiring emergency accommodation, with particular focus on temporarily accommodating families. As a result of this ongoing flow of families presenting as homeless and requiring emergency accommodation, local authorities sought to source private emergency accommodation in the form of hotels and B&Bs. As discussed in the previous chapter, the harmful impact of this was clear and it was considered a last-resort provision, which was why Minister Coveney committed to ending the use of hotels to accommodate families one year after the publication of *Rebuilding Ireland*. However, by mid-2017, the number of families in commercial hotels had gone in the opposite direction and significantly increased.

Family hubs

In response to this growing level of family homelessness and the increased public criticism of the use of hotel accommodation, in 2017 the Government introduced a new policy of establishing emergency homeless accommodation for families, which they referred to as 'family hubs'. Although family hubs were not referenced in *Rebuilding Ireland*, and no policy rationale was published setting out their objectives apart from being preferable to hotels and B&Bs, they became a central part of the response to family homelessness during the *Rebuilding Ireland* period (O'Sullivan, 2017).

Family hubs were a controversial policy innovation because they seemed to accept that large-scale family homelessness was to become a permanent phenomenon and because standards varied considerably between different hubs. Furthermore, given the high proportion of homeless single-parent, female-headed families (Mayock, Sheridan and Parker, 2015; Mayock and Sheridan, 2020), they contained echoes of previous institutional responses to impoverished females. The first family hub, operated by the Respond, a leading Approved Housing Body, was opened in a building which had formerly been used as a Magdalene Laundry; the fact that this was a site of punitive institutionalisation of women in the past did not go unnoticed by commentators (O'Donnell and O'Sullivan, 2020; Sheridan and Parker, 2023).

By the beginning of 2020, there were 32 family hubs in operation, with almost 720 units of accommodation for homeless families. Twenty-five of these were located in Dublin, two in Kildare, and one each in Clare, Cork, Galway, Limerick, and Louth. Some of these were operated by NGOs, while a growing percentage were operated by private for-profit companies, with NGOs providing the social care support for the families.

Shift towards for-profit providers

Overall Central Government expenditure on homeless services grew from nearly €116m in 2016 to €212.2m in 2020. By 2020, emergency accommodation accounted for 80 per cent of all Central Government expenditure on services for those experiencing homelessness (O'Sullivan et al, 2023). Until this time, homeless emergency accommodation has been primarily delivered by NGOs, funded under service level agreements with the local authorities. Dublin City Council continued to directly run some hostels until 2015, when they tendered them out to be run by an NGO. Despite the intention of *Rebuilding Ireland* to reduce the use of commercial hotels, over this period the substantial growth in emergency homeless infrastructure is accompanied by a parallel increase temporary accommodation operated by private individuals and for-profit companies, referred to as Private Emergency Accommodation (PEA) (Nowicki, Brickell and Harris, 2019).

Central Government expenditure on PEAs rose substantially over this period from €54.6 m in 2016 to €106 m in 2020, whereas expenditure on NGO-provided emergency accommodation increased from €29.1 m to €65 m.

Rise of housing and homelessness activism: Part 2

Homelessness was evidently a symptom of widespread housing precariousness and broader residential instability across Ireland. The housing crisis was debated almost on a daily basis within public and media discourse, as many critiqued the growing proliferation of hotels, high-end student accommodation and apartment units being built in urban areas, often to the detriment of affordable housing and community spaces. Equally, there was a growing public concern for the well-being of children and their parents living in emergency accommodation, often for lengthy periods, as well as a sense of outrage in response to often high-profile deaths of individuals sleeping rough, as already referenced.

Although the Apollo House occupation had ended with defiant assertions that the campaign would continue, there were no protests of similar prominence in subsequent years. However, public debate continued. While artists continued to occasionally speak out about the issue, there was no similar coming together of high-profile voices. Though, a number of attempts were made to reform the coalition between trade unions and civic society organisations to express public frustration about the scale of the housing and homelessness crisis. October 2017 saw the launch of the *Campaign for Public Housing* involving a range of radical left political parties and civil society organisations; the *National Homeless and Housing Coalition* – a wider group involving different radical left parties, civil society organisations and homeless charities – organised a number of marches and protests which drew thousands of supporters.

In September 2018, *Raise the Roof*, a broad coalition convened by the Irish Congress of Trades Unions (ICTU), was established, setting out a broad set of policy demands and organising national and local protests, sometimes attracting over 12,000 supporters. While these movements and occasional occupations of buildings gained some public attention, and housing and homelessness remained one of the most important issues for voters throughout this period, none of the initiatives gained the level of media coverage and public debate as achieved by Apollo House.

Separately, 'sleep outs' and similar fundraising events were becoming increasingly popular, often in the form of annual fundraising events for many homelessness charities. While these initiatives reflect the concern among the general public, their focus on rooflessness or 'literal homelessness', can also distort the wider understanding of the causes and nature of homelessness (O'Sullivan, 2020).

In a review of the operation of 'on-street' services in Dublin, there were an estimated 16 to 20 groups operating in the Dublin area providing mobile soup runs, stalls and tables that distributed food, drink and other items in city centre locations in 2021 (Higgins, 2021). These groups were established between 2015 and 2020, and they used social media to harness goods and volunteers, while some also using their platform to critique the Government in their response to homelessness. Higgins' review found significant risks associated with these services, as they were entirely unregulated and did not explicitly comply with customary standards normally applied to charities, food safety or other services providing for people experiencing homelessness.

Most on-street services are not registered as charities but appeal for goods, and services – and sometimes financial support – from the general public, while volunteers are not subject to necessary skills or background checks. The services are not subject to the Dublin Region Homeless Executive (DRHE) National Quality Standards or Environmental Health Services, and there have been incidents of disruption and flouting of rules, regulations and accepted practices going about their work. Further, the review found that people who are homeless are not necessarily the main users of the services, though it is not fully known who uses the services and why (Higgins, 2021).

In a separate review of homeless day services in Dublin which focused on mainstream services operating within a strategic and funding statutory framework led by the Dublin Region Homeless Executive, the researchers found that the 'on-street' services were 'unintentionally undermining the effectiveness of mainstream day services, by reducing the necessity for homeless people to use day services' hot food provision' which serves as 'a vital "hook"' enabling service contact, support and appropriate referral systems to function (Kelleher and Norris, 2020, 53).

Migration

During this period, net inward migration grew strongly adding further pressure, in particular on the private rented sector housing market as shown in Figure 8.6. This was due to higher levels of immigration, slowing emigration and, of note, substantial numbers of returning emigrants. Of the 85,400 people who immigrated to Ireland between April 2019 and April 2020, 28,900 (33.8 per cent) were estimated to be Irish nationals, an increase of 2,000 (7.4 per cent) compared to the previous year (CSO, 2020). By April 2020, there were an estimated 644,400 non-Irish nationals' resident in Ireland, accounting for 12.9 per cent of the population (CSO, 2020). Net migration, combined with natural increases vis-a-vis birth and death rate, amounted to a growing population.

Given the high numbers of non-Irish nationals in the private rented market as noted by NESC (2015) and others (McGinnity et al, 2022), as

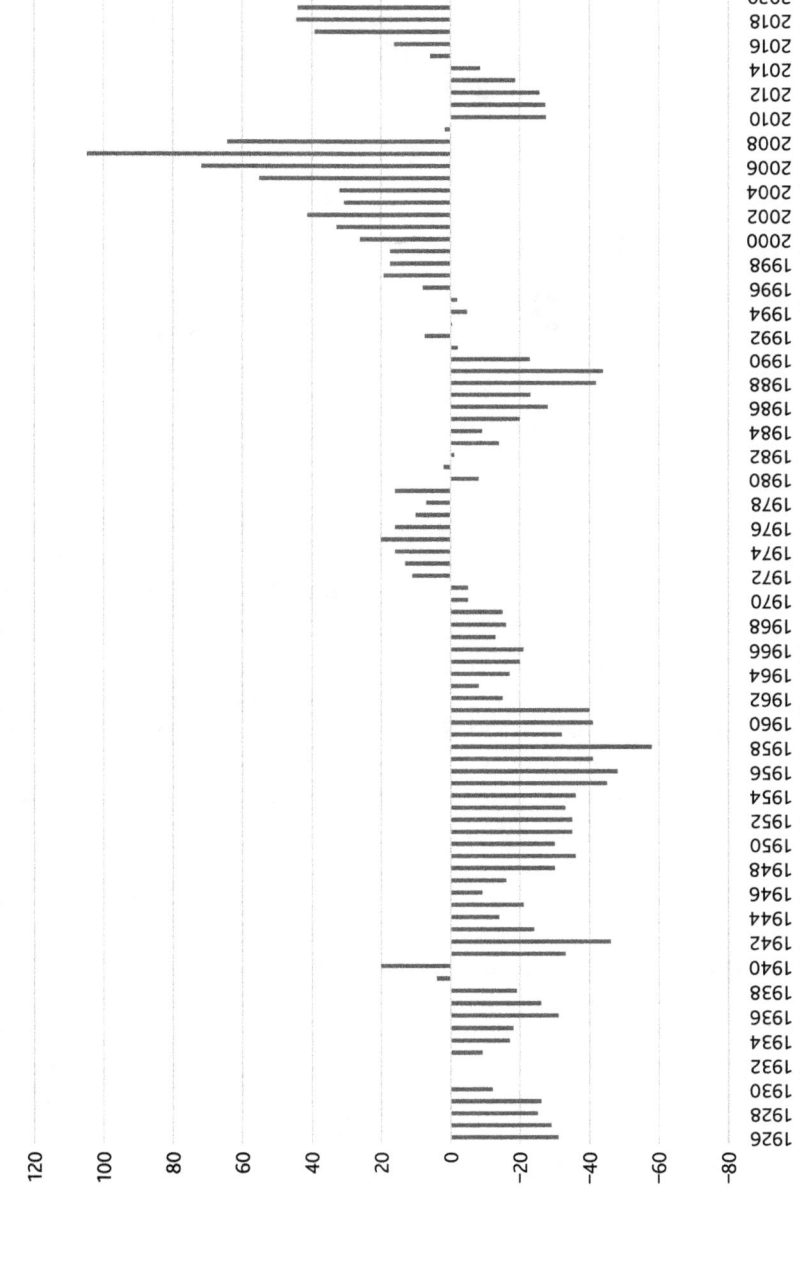

Figure 8.6: Net migration (,000), 1926–2020

well as other vulnerabilities that contribute to housing precarity (see Lima, 2025), the proportion of migrants entering homelessness increased during this period. For example, Dublin Region Homeless Executive data from 2019, Matthews (2022) reported that the proportion of EU citizens newly presenting as homeless doubled from 10 per cent in 2016 to 22 per cent in 2019, while 44.2 per cent of families in emergency accommodation 2019 were headed by non-Irish national (EU and Non-EU citizens combined) (Lima, 2025, 7).

Conclusion

The eve of the COVID-19 pandemic

This chapter details a short but significant period in the story of homelessness in Ireland, and a time of social, political and economic change. With growing numbers of landlords leaving the market in response to rising house prices bringing many of those who took out mortgages on buy-to-let properties out of negative equity, people at the lower end of the private rented sector increasingly found themselves with nowhere to go, as supply declined and rents relentlessly increased. The number of adults and families in emergency accommodation increased also, sparking significant and sustained public debate. The fact that there were so many families – most notably single mothers and their children – presenting to their local authority as homeless each month provoked an emergency response by the Department and local authorities – via the rapid expansion of emergency facilities and PEAs, at considerable public expense. Single, adult-only households were also flowing into homelessness and getting stuck for longer periods of time, and emergency shelter beds were opened and expanded in response. This meant homelessness policy was decidedly moving away from the housing-led direction committed by the previous government and back towards traditional shelter-led responses.

Under Pillar No. 1 of *Rebuilding Ireland*, focusing exclusively on homelessness, the stated actions – most of whom were considered completed within the lifetime of the plan – evidently failed on multiple fronts. Under the plan, the private rented sector – which was already crowded and competitive – became the key source of social housing 'solutions' for those eligible, driven by the expansion of HAP. This served to mount more pressure on an already over-pressured and increasingly expensive rental sector. As the number of households in emergency accommodation rose, so too did the political pressure on yet another Minister for Housing. Department alterations of definitions and measurement of homeless figures – which did not keep figures down but rather only served to undermine their reliability – perhaps reflected this mounting pressure. High-profile takeovers of derelict buildings, increase in street-based and volunteer-led services serving food became visual symbols of perceived government inaction.

This particular electoral cycle could have heralded ambitious and transformative policy measures and legislative reform to protect lower income households from homelessness and facilitate routes for homeless households into social housing. Given the buoyant economic recovery, there was an opportunity for even greater State investment in social housing delivery and protection of security of tenure in the rental sector, particularly given the fact that the electorate was evidently highly sympathetic towards the plight of homeless people. Yet, as was seen in previous governments, incremental and cautious policy tweaking of tenancy laws continued and the enhanced reliance on the private sector to deliver social housing. This lost opportunity is most clearly exemplified by the lack of policy uptake of the many ambitious and progressive cross-party recommendations articulated in the *Oireachtas Committee's Housing and Homelessness* report.

On 14 January 2020 the Government called a General Election in which housing and homelessness was widely expected to play a key role. That afternoon, Elias Adane, who had come to Ireland from Eritrea as an unaccompanied child refugee, was asleep in his tent on banks on the Grand Canal near Leeson Street Bridge, ironically in the constituency of the Minister for Housing at that time, Eoghan Murphy. The DRHE and Waterways Ireland were operating a digger in the area to remove tents from public areas due to 'health and safety' concerns. Mr Adane either did not hear or respond to the shouted warnings. His presence in the tent was only realised when the digger lifted up the tent, and Adane suffered life-changing injuries to his spine as a result.

9

Pandemic, migration and a housing crisis, 2020–2024

Introduction

In this chapter, we set out how homeless services and policy responded during the period of the COVID-19 pandemic and the immediate post-pandemic period. Like many other European countries during the pandemic, temporary protections were afforded to tenants in Ireland *via* emergency legislation to protect them against rent arrears and eviction which, as will be discussed in this chapter, appeared to have a positive impact in curbing the flows into emergency accommodation, particularly for families. Furthermore, Dublin was considered as a positive case study in Europe in meeting the needs of people experiencing homelessness during the lockdown period.

However, following this emergency period from 2020 to 2021, and the lifting of these proactive and progressive measures, the number of households in emergency accommodation began to climb once again. The pandemic was also a time of significant social and economic upheaval and knock-on challenges in construction, housing output and supply chains – all of which directly impacted the provision of housing and a consequent effect on the trends in homelessness.

The post-pandemic period also saw the first impact of the Russian invasion of Ukraine which, as well as having global repercussions on energy prices and inflation, resulted in an influx of Ukrainian refugees requiring accommodation. At the same time, there was an increase in the number of International Protection Applicants from other countries. In parallel, a small, yet disruptive, far-right contingent became more active; carrying out arson and threats of violence at sites of new emergency facilities earmarked to accommodate migrants. Cross-cutting these separate and related issues, there was a growing public disquiet towards the Government handling of the housing crisis.

This chapter breaks down the impact of these consequential global events which occurred over a short period of time on homelessness in Ireland, as well as the Government policy responses – both emergency measures and long-term policy mechanisms. The chapter concludes by considering how these macro-level changes have culminated in complex and ever-changing political, demographic and economic tensions which are all intimately connected to the housing and homelessness crisis.

New coalition government

Just weeks after the Irish general election on 8 February 2020, the country went into lockdown triggered by the World Health Organization (WHO) declaration that COVID-19 was a global pandemic. A caretaker government stayed in office, with Minister Eoghan Murphy of Fine Gael, remaining as Minister for Housing, Local Government and Heritage. Five months of protracted negotiations followed the election and, finally, on 27 June 2020, Fianna Fáil, Fine Gael and the Green Party formed a majority coalition government. This marked the first time in the history of the State that Fine Gael and Fianna Fáil – previously long-standing political rivals – entered into a coalition together.

As part of this coalition agreement, Fianna Fáil's leader Micheál Martin served as Taoiseach for the first half of the Government's term (June 2020 to December 2022), after which Fine Gael's leader Leo Varadkar became leader (December 2022 until April 2024 when he resigned as party leader), before the new Fine Gael leader Simon Harris took over as Taoiseach from April 2024 onwards. After the new Government was formed, Fianna Fáil's Darragh O'Brien was appointed as Minister for Housing for the duration of the Government. In April 2020, former Minister Murphy resigned his seat and withdrew from politics (Murphy, 2024).

Even though the dominant political parties remained in power, with the support of the Green Party, it is worth noting the significant decline in their overall vote share, reflecting a growing dissatisfaction among the electorate towards the status quo. For the 2020 election, housing and homelessness were regarded as priority issues for voters and a key talking point both in the media and election canvassing. According to an IPSOS MRBI exit poll of the 2020 election, housing and homelessness was the second most cited concern among the electorate at that time (health was considered as the primary issue) (McGee, 2020). The election also signalled a generational split – with younger voters experiencing housing and socioeconomic adversities more likely to vote in support of more radical parties such as Sinn Féin.

In the *Programme for Government: Our Shared Future* published in June 2020, progress in addressing the housing crisis was pitched as a key mission for the incoming Government (Government of Ireland, 2020). The document signalled an apparent commitment to local authorities, Approved Housing Bodies and State agencies as being central to delivering housing, however it also lacked specific detail or proportions on targets for numbers to be built, bought or leased. It also committed to developing cost-rental housing as a new model for affordable housing provision. The programme committed to producing a new housing and homeless strategy, Housing for All, which will be discussed later.

While the incoming Government committed to further increased funding to tackle homelessness, emphasising a commitment to 'move away from dormitory-style accommodation on a long-term basis' and towards 'long-term sustainable' accommodation and further expansion of Housing First (Government of Ireland, 2020, 55–56). The Government committed to a *National Youth Homelessness Strategy*, which was subsequently published in autumn 2022 (Government of Ireland, 2022a). The Government also pledged to hold a referendum on housing and to establish a housing commission 'to examine issues such as tenure, standards, sustainability, and quality-of-life issues in the provision of housing' (2020, 58).

COVID-19 pandemic and emergency measures

On 27 March 2020, Ireland was placed into full national lockdown, which was extended several times until June 2020, after which point localised restrictions continued until August. Further lockdowns were introduced in October until December 2020, but following a surge in COVID-19 infection rates, a full lockdown was reimposed in late December 2020 that lasted until May 2021. After the widespread vaccination rollout among the adult population, there was a substantial easing of restrictions (by September 2021, over 90 per cent of all adults in Ireland were fully vaccinated).

During this time, in parallel with the 'stay-at-home' orders imposed by the Government, temporary emergency legislation was introduced which included a range of policy measures related to homelessness and housing. The details of these measures, and their significance, will now be examined in greater detail.

Prohibition on the termination of tenancies

In March 2020, the transitional or 'caretaker' Government passed the *Emergency Measures in the Public Interest (COVID-19) Act, 2020* which contained legislative enactments specifically designed to protect tenants from eviction and rent increases for those who entered rent arrears due to COVID-19. Similar provisions to protect rental tenancies were introduced across Europe during these rolling periods of restrictions and lockdowns (Pleace et al, 2021).

In Ireland, legislation applied to all landlords including private for-profit providers, Approved Housing Bodies (not-for-profit) and all local authorities. but the protections were particularly important for those living in the private rented market due to its inherent precariousness, limited security of tenure and strong rent inflation and this measure protected them from losing their homes (Waldron, 2022a, b; Byrne and McArdle, 2022; Byrne and Sassi, 2023).

The legislation initially placed moratoriums on both terminating tenancies and rent increases between 27 March and 1 August 2020 but the level of protection afforded to tenants was reduced over time. For example, the initial three-month period provided comprehensive legislative protection from termination of a tenancy for all tenants, but by August 2020, protection from termination of tenancies was restricted only in cases where rent arrears were associated with COVID-19, namely due to loss of employment and income.

Over the next 12 months, five pieces of legislation extended and modified the existing provisions of the *Residential Tenancies Acts 2004–2016* with respect to termination of tenancies but over time the criteria of entitlement to these protections were reduced before being phased out altogether (O'Sullivan et al, 2024).

Interagency collaboration to support those in emergency accommodation

Dublin was identified as a positive case study in the efficiency and effectiveness in service changes and adaptations in responding to the needs of homeless people (Owens and Matthiessen, 2021; Pleace et al, 2021). Early in the pandemic, a *Guidance for Homeless and Vulnerable Groups* was swiftly issued by the statutory Health Services Executive (HSE) to homeless services and later updated (HSE, 2021). While this guidance focused primarily on Dublin homeless settings, it contained general measures on how to prevent, test and facilitate the quarantining of service users who tested positive. The HSE also appointed a Clinical Lead for the Homeless Response to implement and coordinate operational changes. Recognising the need for accommodation, and the closure of congregate shelters, Dublin Region Homeless Executive rapidly set about acquiring additional accommodation for emergency use – much of which was self-contained tourist accommodation that was not being used – to allow for suspected cases to be isolated and to 'shield' medically vulnerable people due to age or medical condition (O'Carroll, Duffin and Collins, 2020; Sheridan, 2022).

Moreover, all emergency accommodation services were extended to 24-hour provision, meaning that residents did not have to vacate the accommodation during the day. The system of 'one-night-only' bookings for certain categories of adults experiencing homelessness (for example those without a local connection or residence status) was replaced with long-term bookings (Cahill, 2020). Dedicated shower facilities were also opened for rough sleepers who were unable to avail of day services which had temporarily closed. Many of the people who were long-term homeless and those with complex support needs were transferred to single-occupancy units with service supports including visits from public health and drug support professionals and delivery of prescription medication to their accommodation. This enhanced access to services and promoted more consistent service engagement (O'Carroll et al, 2020; Finnerty and Buckley, 2021; Sheridan, 2022). The supervision of opiate substitution therapy (OST) was rapidly amended to allow a number of NGOs to collect OST on behalf of clients, while there was more flexibility in Benzodiazepine (BZD) provision and availability of Naloxone to relevant service users (O'Carroll, Duffin and Collins, 2020).

These concerted efforts and interagency collaboration certainly curtailed the incidence of disease and death caused by COVID-19 (O'Carroll, Duffin and Collins, 2020). Between 1 December 2020 and 16 March 2021, there were 222 confirmed COVID-19 cases in homeless services with four COVID-related deaths (Lima, 2021), compared to the 19 deaths predicted if homeless services had not rapidly adapted (O'Carroll, Duffin and Collins, 2020).

As well as reducing pandemic deaths, there is also evidence that the changes enhanced the general quality of service provision, particularly for those who had long-term homeless histories. Single-unit accommodation provided the long-term homeless cohort with privacy and safety for many individuals who were more accustomed to shared sleeping facilities and some transitioned to long-term housing after the pandemic, with the superior accommodation and service supporting offering them a period of stabilisation, though there was also evidence of service users initially experiencing isolation when transferred to single-occupancy units during lockdown (Altena, 2020).

Enhanced rate of social housing allocations during pandemic emergency period

Due to an enhanced exit rate out of homelessness during this period and in the year prior to the pandemic, 2,600 homeless adults were provided with tenancy in Dublin between 2019 and 2020. In addition, there were just over 2,000 adult exits to social housing supports between 2019 and 2020. A verbal report at the September 2020 meeting of the Housing Strategic Policy Committee in Dublin City Council noted that in order to protect vulnerable and older people who are homeless during the pandemic, DCC had 'front-loaded our homeless lettings for the year' and that lettings would have to be 'rebalanced' during the rest of the year – in other words, all the 2020 housing allocations to homeless households were made in the first half of the year. Additionally, there were also 2,762 exits via HAP during 2020, accommodating a total of 3,161 individuals.

Trends in homelessness, 2020–2024

In the third week of February 2020, immediately before the COVID-19 pandemic and lockdowns were introduced, there were 5,902 households in

Figure 9.1: Number of new adults entering Section 10 funded emergency and temporary accommodation, 2014–2024

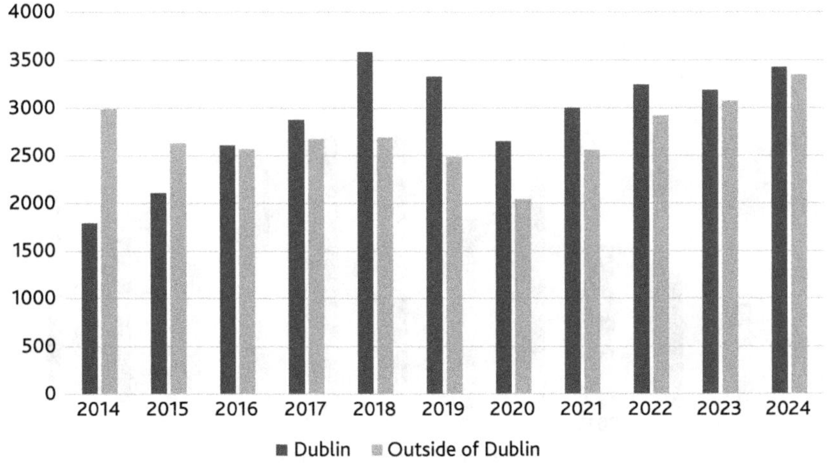

[Bar chart showing numbers of new adults entering emergency and temporary accommodation from 2014 to 2024, with bars for Dublin and Outside of Dublin. Y-axis ranges from 0 to 4000.]

■ Dublin ■ Outside of Dublin

Source: https://www.gov.ie/en/department-of-housing-local-government-and-heritage/collections/homelessness-data/#homelessness-data

emergency accommodation nationally according to PASS data. As outlined in the previous chapter, between July 2014 and February 2020, the number of households in homeless accommodation at a point-in-time had increased almost every month leading up to this period.

During the pandemic period, the number of households in emergency accommodation declined for the first time since 2014 from just over 6,000 in January to 5,417 in December 2020, a drop of nearly 10 per cent. This overall decline reflected substantial differences between families and adult-only households which will be discussed later. This decline in the overall homeless rates levelled out during 2021, before it increased again at a substantial rate in mid-2021 and continued to climb over the period 2022–2024. After the pandemic, between January 2021 and December 2024, the total number of adults in emergency accommodation rose by 73 per cent (from 5,987 to 10,354 adults).

The reasons for these fluctuations are related to the increase and then decrease in exits from emergency accommodation and a similar pattern in new adult entries (see Figures 9.1 and 9.2). It is this interaction between rates of entry and exit that determine the numbers in emergency accommodation at a point-in-time.

Homeless trends were distinct between families and adult-only households, as can be seen in Figure 9.3. At the beginning of the pandemic, there were 1,488 families in emergency accommodation, which decreased to a low of 932 families by June 2021. As 'eviction to sell' had been a known driver of

Figure 9.2: Adults' exits to housing from emergency accommodation to housing, 2014–2024

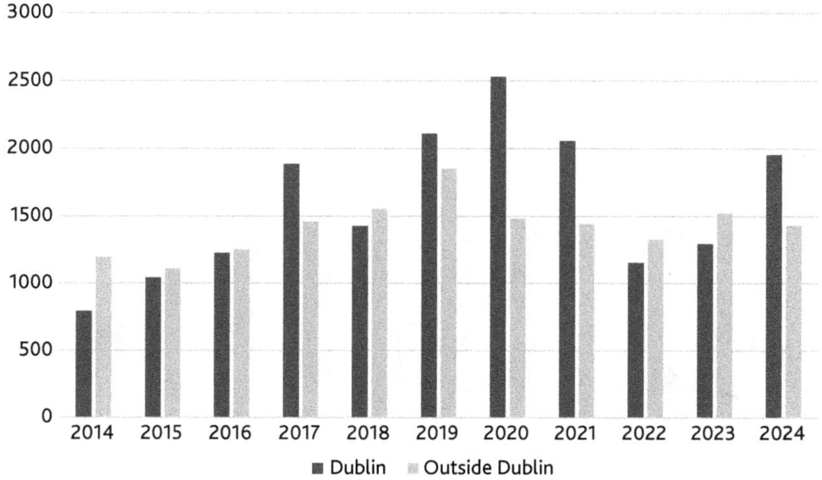

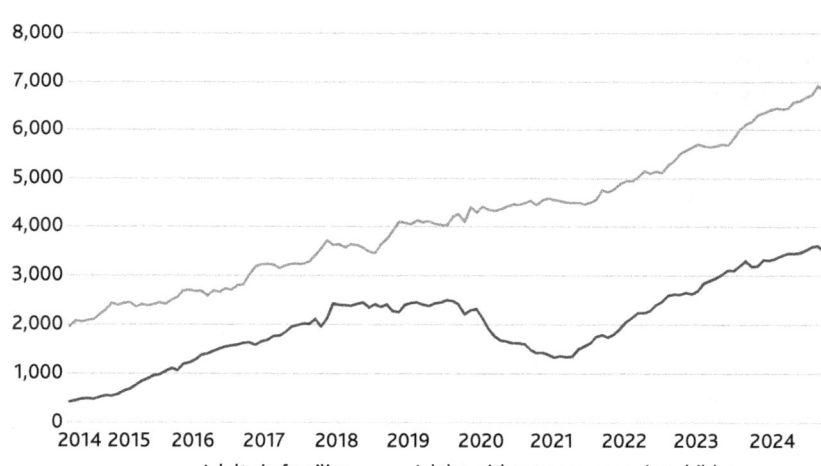

Source: https://www.gov.ie/en/department-of-housing-local-government-and-heritage/collections/homelessness-data/#homelessness-data

Figure 9.3: Adults in families and adult-only households in Local Government emergency and temporary accommodation, June 2014–December 2024

Source: https://www.gov.ie/en/department-of-housing-local-government-and-heritage/collections/homelessness-data/#homelessness-data family homelessness for several years (Long et al, 2019) this reduction in families in emergency accommodation was most likely attributable to policy initiatives, such as eviction bans, along with enhanced allocation to social housing as discussed above.

By contrast, the number of adult-only households in emergency accommodation continued to increase steadily, unaffected by the eviction ban. At the beginning of the pandemic there were 4,414 adult-only households which had increased to 4,957 by March 2022, two years later. These increases seen after the pandemic emergency period resulted from the inability of households to exit homelessness in the context of a chronic shortage of affordable housing rather than any change in the numbers becoming homeless, which remained broadly steady.

In late 2022, the period subsequent to the periodic lockdowns, in response to increases in the cost of living and homelessness, the Government introduced a further temporary ban on evictions, effective between October 2022 until March 2023. The ban similarly covered 'no fault evictions' from private rented tenancies, AHB housing, cost-rental tenancies and student accommodation. While the eviction bans linked to 'stay-at-home' regulations had been broadly accepted as one of the necessary public health measures, the further ban provoked widespread public debate and media commentary. Until the October 2022 ban was introduced, the Government had indicated there would be no further bans. As the date for the ban to be lifted approached in March 2023, there was considerable anxiety among private rented tenants who were worried that landlords would quickly move to sell properties after the ban.

In response to this political pressure, the Government announced the extension of the *Tenant in Situ Scheme* which gave local authorities an opportunity to buy properties from selling landlords who had rental supplement tenants in their properties. A similar Cost Rental Tenant In Situ (CRTiS) Scheme was also introduced in April 2023 which allowed for the statutory Housing Agency to purchase properties where the tenants were not in receipt of rent supplements but who were below an income threshold of €53,000. Private tenants were also given the right of first refusal if their landlord was selling. These focused initiatives – while targeted and innovative in design – were not sufficient in scale to fully address the scale of the numbers entering emergency accommodation, reached record-breaking numbers, as will be discussed later in the chapter.

The discontinuation of the ban on evictions and the 'eviction to sell' in 2022 exacerbated homeless rises, in parallel with a surge of landlords seeking to sell following the pandemic as house prices increased significantly during the post-pandemic period. The national Residential Property Price Index (RPPI) increased by 2.2 per cent in the 12 months to December 2020, by 14.2 per cent at December 2021, 7.7 per cent at end 2022, 4.1 per cent at end 2023 and 8.8 per cent at end 2024 (Central Statistics Office, 2025).

Rising prices were seen to be related to strong demand, increased savings during the pandemic, and weakening housing supply.

Unsheltered homelessness, 2020–2024

The number of people recorded as sleeping rough in the *point-in-time* count wavered between lows of 90 and highs of 139. The one-night street count in Dublin did not take place in March 2020 as scheduled due to the COVID-19 pandemic, and in late November 2020, the one-night count was replaced with a week-long count, which is now repeated in spring and winter each year. As seen in Figure 9.4, in November 2020, 139 unique individuals were identified as rough sleeping in Dublin; 125 in April 2021; 95 in November 2021; 91 in March/April 2022; and 91 again in November 2022. It decreased again to 83 by the spring count in 2023, before increasing to 118 by Winter 2023 and to 134 in Winter 2024.

The number of *unique individuals* who were recorded as sleeping rough and who were also in contact with the designated Outreach Team ranged from between 600 to 750 individuals in the Dublin region per quarter during this period. Of these, between 70 and 80 per cent were also accessing emergency accommodation during this period, highlighting again the fluidity between street-based settings and emergency accommodation amongst the majority of rough sleepers. This suggests that a significant number who are recorded in rough sleeper counts are also likely to be recorded in the monthly PASS stock data. What is striking is that despite the substantial increase in the number of adults in emergency accommodation over this period, the number of unsheltered adults remained low and steady, demonstrating the increase in the provision of emergency accommodation in Dublin prevented a surge in rough sleeping amongst those eligible for such accommodation.

On 4 December 2023, the Government announced that they ceased offering beds to all male International Protection Applicants due to lack of capacity, which, according to Government data, led to over 600 asylum seekers awaiting an offer of accommodation by mid-January 2024. By December 2024 this had increased to just over 3,000 (Department of Children, Equality, Disability, Integration and Youth, 2024). Some of these men may have found shelter with their communities of origin, or in mosques while others were living in tents in various parts of Dublin, particularly near the International Protection Accommodation Services (IPAS) offices in the city centre. Asylum seekers who are forced to sleep rough are not included in the Rough Sleeping Count, as it is an estimation of the number of people eligible for homeless services who are sleeping rough.

While waiting for a determination on their application, applicants (with the exception of some single men as noted above) are provided with accommodation by IPAS. At the end of 2024, there were nearly 33,000

Figure 9.4: Unsheltered point-in-time count in Dublin, 2014–2024

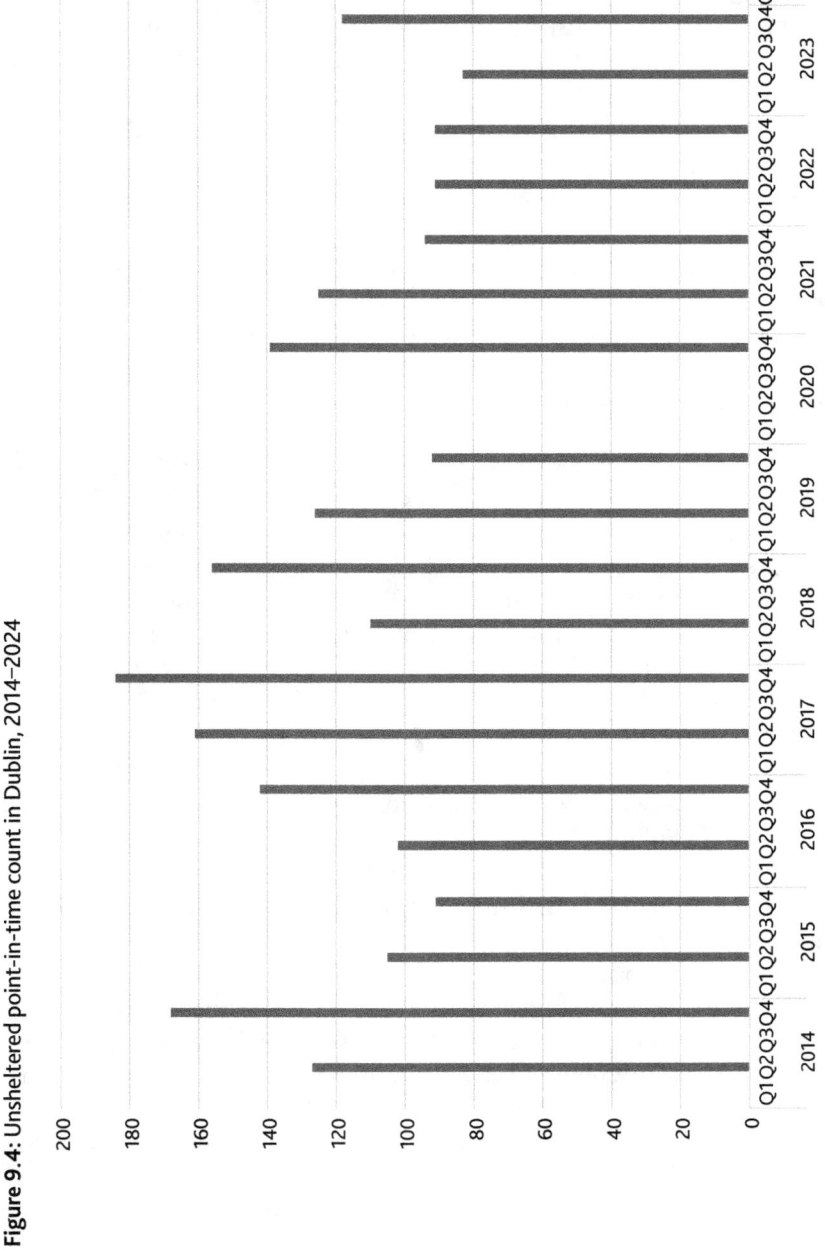

Source: https://www.hometessdublin.ie/info/publications

adults and children in IPAS accommodation. Most of these were awaiting their applications to be heard but just over 5,000 had been granted status to remain but were unable to locate alternative accommodation. IPAS have intensified their efforts in recent years to discharge those with status to remain from IPAS accommodation, but some are unable to locate alternative accommodation and require emergency accommodation.

As discussed below, Ireland underwent significant demographic change in the post-pandemic period, particularly in relation to inward migration, and this was increasingly reflected in the composition of those accessing homelessness services. Between 2022 and 2024, the number of EEA/UK and Non-EEA citizens in emergency accommodation at a point-in-time increased from 26 per cent to 48 per cent. This was particularly concentrated in Dublin where 55 per cent of those in emergency accommodation at the end of 2024 were EEA/UK and Non-EEA citizens. Twenty-six per cent of single adults who entered emergency accommodation in Dublin in 2024 came from IPAS accommodation as IPAS providers sought to discharge those with status to remain.

Expenditure on homeless services

Expenditure on homeless services continued to surge with the expansion of emergency accommodation during this period. The budget available from the Department of Housing, Local Government and Heritage to fund local authorities deliver homelessness services in 2020 was initially €166 m but this was revised twice due to the COVID-19 measures giving a total budget of €270.9 m which increased to €316 m in 2023. Budget 2024 committed to funding of €242 m from the Department of Housing but required a supplementary allocation of €143 m in November, giving a total budget of €385 m for 2024. In addition to the funding from the Department of Housing, funding is also provided by the Department of Health for homeless health-related services which has averaged nearly €38 m per annum between 2013–2024 (O'Sullivan, Byrne and Allen, 2023).

However, the most inclusive measure of expenditure on services for those experiencing homelessness is the expenditure by local authorities which includes both the funding received from the Department of Housing and the contribution from the local authority's own resources (a minimum of 10 per cent of the expenditure). Figure 9.5 shows the total expenditure on services for households experiencing homelessness by local authorities from all sources between 2009 and 2024. From 2009 to 2014, average annual expenditure was €73.5 m, but increased significantly from 2015 onwards, with an expenditure of €484 m by local authorities in 2024 to provide services for those experiencing homelessness. Expenditure on emergency accommodation between 2020 and 2024 continued to account for the majority of this expenditure.

Pandemic, migration and a housing crisis, 2020–2024

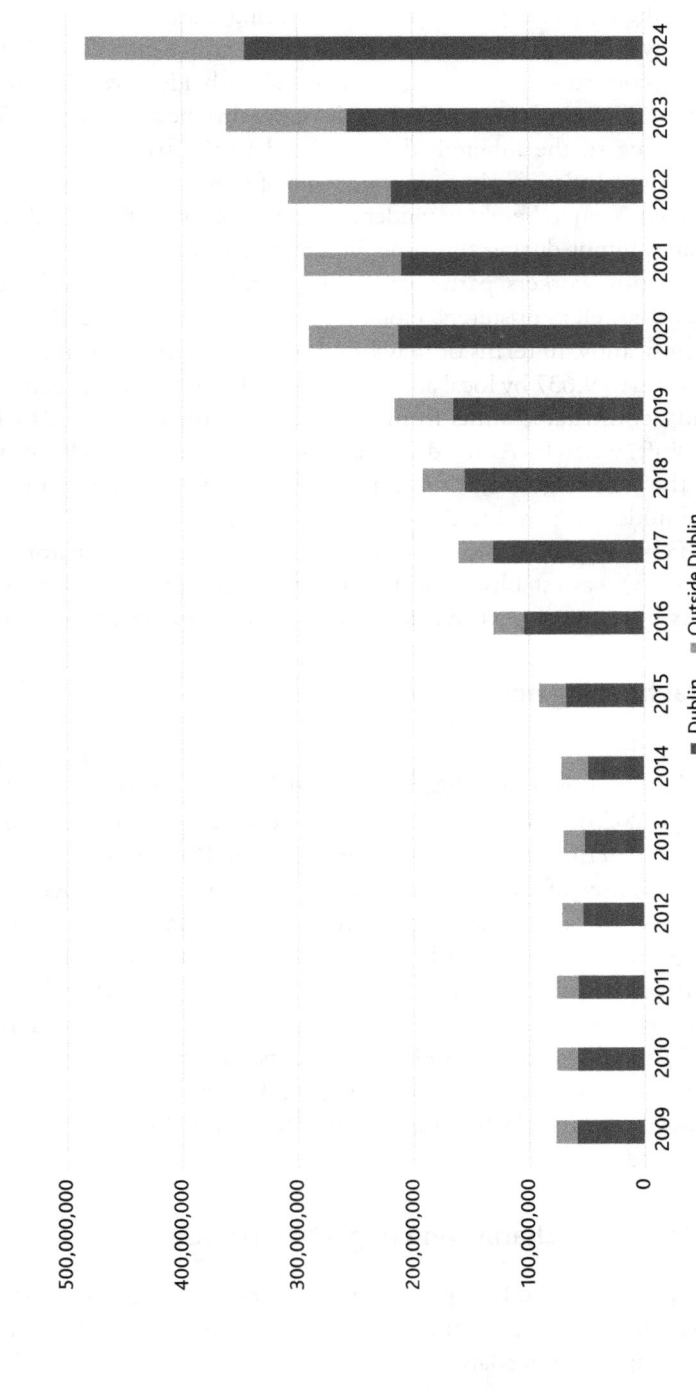

Figure 9.5: Expenditure on services for households experiencing homelessness by local authorities Dublin/outside Dublin, 2009–2024

Source: https://www.gov.ie/en/department-of-housing-local-government-and-heritage/collections/homelessness-data/#homelessness-data

Social housing output

As highlighted in Figure 9.6, social housing output (including both local authority build and AHBs) has overall increased since the near collapse of social housing construction following the financial crash. However, despite exceeding 6,000 in 2019, in 2020 and 2021 this figure dropped to just over 5,000 units a year, due to the inherent delays related to the pandemic and lockdown restrictions. Inflation also impacted cost of materials and construction costs which was seen to heighten tender costs and delivery and generally complicate housing output during this time. There was also a documented shortage of construction workers, particularly those working in mechanical and electrical services as well as plasterers, block layers and tilers (SCSI, 2023).

Significantly, in terms of new build output, AHBs delivered 11,240 units compared to 9,637 by local authorities, with local authorities acquiring 3,662 already constructed units from the market compared to 1,214 by AHBs. This shift, whereby AHBs delivered more new builds than local authorities, is all the more significant with nine AHBs delivering the majority of these new builds compared to 31 local authorities.

In February 2021, the Approved Housing Bodies Regulatory Authority (ABHRA) was established to regulate voluntary and co-operative housing bodies in terms of governance, financial management and performance.

Social housing needs assessments

The number of households assessed as having a social housing need declined slightly over this period from 61,880 in 2020 to 59,941 in 2024 (Housing Agency, 2025), but as discussed earlier, recipients of the HAP rent subsidy are excluded from this figure. In July 2024, the Parliamentary Budget Office of the Houses of the Oireachtas published a report on ongoing need for social housing and argued that HAP recipients should be included in what they term 'Ongoing Need' for social housing due to '(1) the potentially precarious nature of private rental agreements; (2) the difficulty in securing private rental accommodation which meets the criteria for HAP support; and (3) the fact that many HAP recipients continue to meet the eligibility criteria to avail of social housing' (2024, 3). The figure for 'ongoing need' for social housing declined by 6.5 per cent over this period from 121,701 households in 2020 to 113,683 in 2024.

Demographic change and migration trends

As seen elsewhere in Europe, Ireland has undergone significant demographic change in this post-pandemic period due to global conflict, climate change and multiple and overlapping economic and social crises around the world.

Figure 9.6: Social housing output, 1923–2024

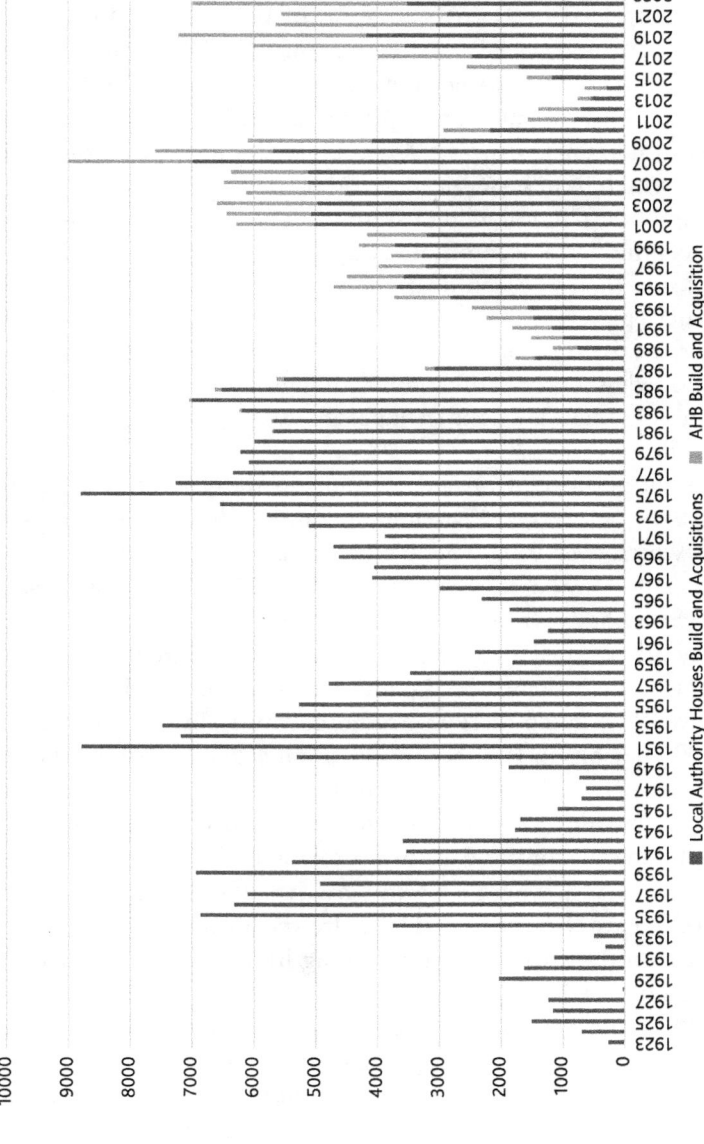

Source: Department of Local Government and Public Health Annual Report (various years) (Dublin: Stationery Office). Department of the Environment (various years): Annual Housing Statistics Bulletin (Dublin: Department of the Environment) – https://www.gov.ie/en/department-of-housing-local-government-and-heritage/organisation-information/housing-statistics/

In Ireland, the continued growth in the economy created a requirement for additional workers. According to official Census statistics, the population of Ireland was estimated as 5,380,300 by the end of April 2024 (CSO, 2024a).

In March 2022, the European Commission activated a *Temporary Protection Directive* (2011/55 EC) to provide immediate protection in EU Countries for people displaced by Russia's invasion of Ukraine. By October 2024, 109,566 Ukrainians had been issued Personal Public Service numbers in Ireland under the Directive since the outbreak of the war (CSO, 2023b) and according to Government sources, a total of 101,200 arrivals had come to Ireland from Ukraine, with 74,500 people living in State accommodation (57,000 of which in fully-serviced accommodation).

In December 2023, following extensive public debate, the Government decided to limit State accommodation for a maximum of 90 days. After refugees leave their accommodation, they will be entitled to apply for standard social protection assistance subject to meeting the standard eligibility conditions. At the time of writing, it is not yet known the impact this will have on homelessness or roofless rates, though given the lack of affordable housing options, there is a significant possibility that some Ukrainian refugees may enter homelessness.

The overall number of inward migrants in the year to April 2024 was estimated to be 149,200 – a 17-year high – and the third successive 12-month period in which over 100,00 people immigrated to Ireland.

Net migration stood at 79,300 in April 2024, which, combined with natural increase between births and deaths, led to a population increase of 350,000 between April 2020 and April 2024 (see Figure 9.7).

Over this period, there was also an increase in International Protection Applicants (IPAs) living in IPAS accommodation, in increasing from just under 7,000 persons in IPAs accommodation at the end of 2020 to nearly 33,000 at the end of 2024. Under international law, governments have an obligation to provide accommodation for International Protection Applicants and, where that accommodation is provided, they are not considered homeless. However, where a person has had their claim for protection upheld, they have a right to reside in Ireland (leave to remain), can put their names on the local authority housing list and so become part of the overall housing need.

Since 2021, the State has granted temporary protection to more than 100,000 Ukrainian nationals and more than 26,000 people in international protection (IPAS, 2024). This resulted in significant pressure on the broader emergency accommodation system which was exacerbated by the affordable housing crisis and lack of move-on options for those trying to exit emergency accommodation. As of 31 August 2023, there were 5,650 people with leave to remain status (1,580 of whom were children) residing in IPAS (Parliamentary Question 42538/23, 2023). These individuals can access Job

Pandemic, migration and a housing crisis, 2020–2024

Figure 9.7: Net migration (,000), 1926–2024

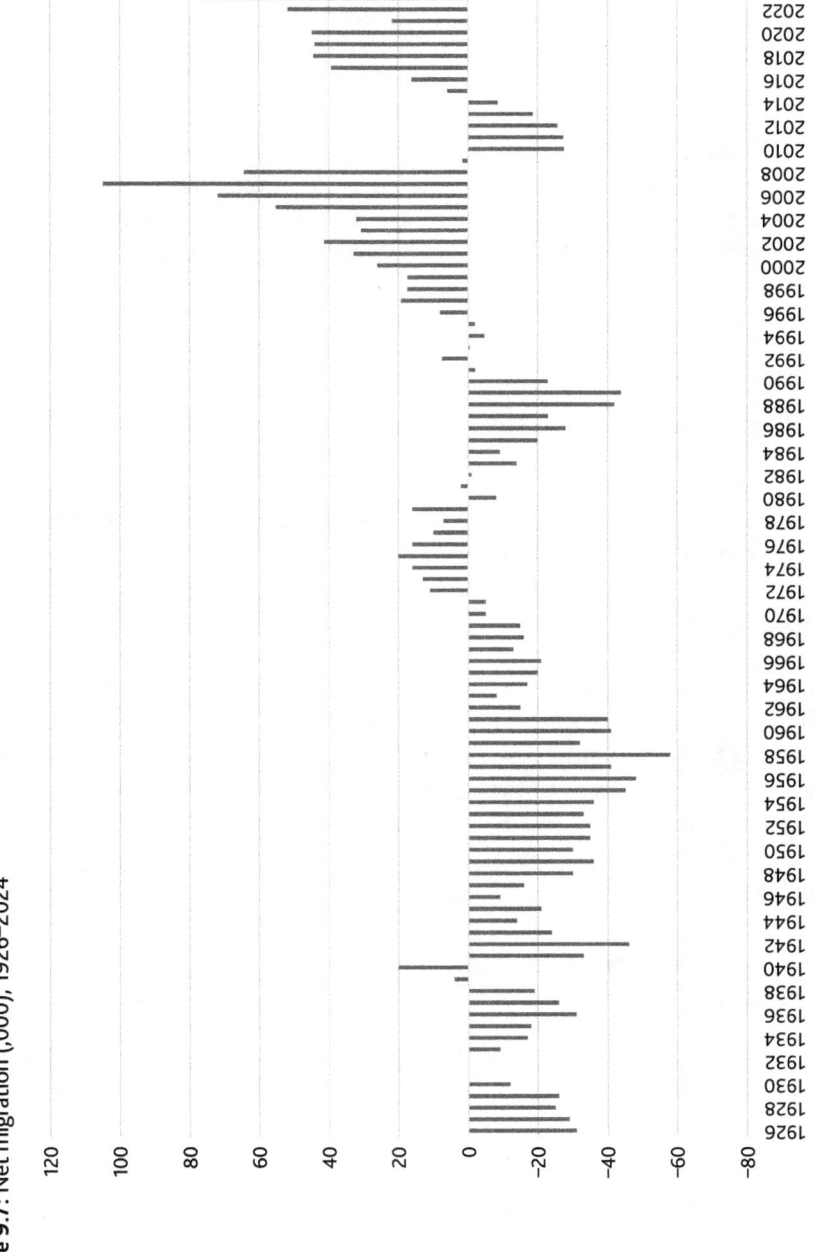

Source: Central Statistics Office – https://datasalsa.com/dataset/?catalogue=data.gov.ie&name=c0401-components-of-population-change-since-1926

Seekers Allowance (JSA) and are eligible to be on the social housing list and have access to Homeless Housing Assistance Payment.

This highly pressurised situation and the need to rapidly scale up emergency accommodation facilities raises serious concerns around the capacity and sustainability of the emergency accommodation system more broadly, and its relationship with the broader homeless crisis. It has also led to further 'pinch points' in the housing crisis. For example, Ukrainian refugees who were being accommodated in student accommodation facilities were transferred out to other forms of temporary accommodation to make way for the incoming students starting their academic year. The contracting of entire hotels to provide emergency accommodation also sparked public debate on the impact it had on tourist revenue and public services, placing pressure on the Government to source alternative accommodation options (Burns, 2023). Scenes of anti-immigration sentiment, far-right factions leading protests outside accommodation hosting migrants and, in extreme cases, attacks on roofless migrants or encampments also began to emerge in 2023 (Naughtie, 2023). There were also alarming scenes of Dublin city on a November night in 2024 which resulted in shops being looted and buses and trams set on fire. All of this fed into an intense and sometimes divisive public debate on immigration, but also on housing and discussions of entitlement and access to housing.

Policy developments

There were a number of homelessness policy developments during this period, both at a national and European level. The housing crisis in Ireland continued to worsen and a new plan was required to replace *Rebuilding Ireland* to make it more relevant to the current challenges facing the Government. This led to the publication of *Housing for All* in 2021. Some months previous to this, an ambitious European-level plan was signed by all Member States which provided a target to end homelessness by 2030.

Lisbon Declaration on the European Platform on Combatting Homelessness

On 21 June 2021, the Minister for Housing, Local Government and Heritage, along with all other European Member States, signed the *Lisbon Declaration on the European Platform on Combatting Homelessness*. The Declaration represents a joint commitment to work towards ending homelessness across European Member States by 2030 and was developed under the Portuguese Presidency of the Council of the European Union in collaboration with the European Commission and FEANTSA (the European Federation of Homeless Service Providers). The Declaration committed Member States to working towards ending homelessness by 2030 and to promote a person-centred, housing-led and integrated approach.

The Lisbon Declaration contains five fundamental principles:

1) No one sleeps rough for lack of accessible, safe and appropriate emergency accommodation;
2) No one lives in emergency or transitional accommodation longer than is required for successful move-on to a permanent housing solution;
3) No one is discharged from any institution (e.g. prison, hospital, care facility) without an offer of appropriate housing;
4) Evictions should be prevented whenever possible and no one is evicted without assistance for an appropriate housing solution when needed;
5) No one is discriminated against due to their homelessness status.
(Lisbon Declaration on the European Platform on Combatting Homelessness, 2021, 4)

In parallel to the Declaration, the European Platform for Combatting Homelessness (EPOCH) was also launched to support Member States, cities and service providers in sharing best practice and promoting mutual learning, supporting the harnessing of EU Funding possibilities, strengthening data and monitoring on homelessness and reviewing progress on working towards ending homelessness by 2030. The main financing instruments for both the Declaration and the Platform initiatives are through the European Social Fund (ESF+), which receives contributions from all Member States. This initiative marked progress in terms of European ambition and desire for greater coordination in tackling homelessness, but it remains to be seen whether momentum will be maintained over the coming years and that a high-level goal such as ending homelessness can be realised.

The Declaration was foregrounded in the Government's subsequent *Housing for All* strategy published a few months later, which will be discussed in detail in the following section. However, in relation to the Declaration, the Irish Government is explicit in its commitment to the Declaration:

In signing the Declaration, Ireland has agreed to promote the prevention of homelessness, access to permanent housing and the provision of enabling support services to those who are homeless. We have confirmed that we will welcome the involvement of all relevant stakeholders in the design and implementation of policy measures. We are committed to supporting our policy measures with adequate funding and to sharing our good practices in combating homelessness. (Government of Ireland, 2021)

Housing for All: A New Housing Plan for Ireland

In September 2021, the Government published a new, long-term housing strategy *Housing for All* (Government of Ireland, 2021). This Plan set out the proposed housing policy set to run until 2030 with an overall goal to increase the supply of housing to an average of 33,000 per year over the next decade across social, affordable and private housing. The second pillar of this Plan aimed to 'eradicate homelessness' and also contains details on increasing the supply and delivering reform to the social housing system.

On homelessness, the Plan directly references the Lisbon Declaration in working towards ending homelessness by 2030, though it does not specifically reiterate a target outside of the context of the Lisbon Declaration. Other priorities contained in the Plan included a commitment to expanding Housing First to 1,200 tenancies over five years and expansion of street outreach services, to support the health of people experiencing homelessness and a commitment to prevent and address family, child and youth homelessness. Underpinned by *Housing for All*, the *Housing First National Implementation Plan 2022–2026* was published by the Government in 2022 which provided for the creation of 1,319 additional tenancies over the period, or an average of 264 tenancies per annum with specific targets for each region (Government of Ireland, 2022b). Between 2022 and 2024, 766 tenancies were established under the Plan (Department of Housing, Local Government and Heritage, various years).

Housing for All also established a National Homeless Action Committee (NHAC) which provides a cross-governmental and interagency oversight group to implement the interagency elements of the strategy and 'to ensure better coherence and coordination of homeless-related services in delivering policy measures and actions' (p 50). The NHAC is chaired by the Minister for Housing, Local Government and Heritage and contains members from key departments, agencies and stakeholders. The committee also has a role in addressing emerging homeless-related issues and in developing further responses. Since the recorded increase in homelessness from 2014 onwards, the *NHAC* is the fourth such oversight/governance structure established. As noted earlier, the *National Homeless Consultative Committee*, the *Homelessness Oversight Group* and the *Homelessness Inter-Agency Group* were in turn all quietly disbanded without explanation.

While *Housing for All* seeks to address the persistent imbalances in the Irish housing market, there are a number of critiques that have emerged from advocacy groups and experts in the field. Primarily, there is the continued policy reliance on the private residential sector using subsidies such as the Housing Assistance Payment (HAP) and Rental Accommodation Scheme (RAS), which as has already been outlined, fails to deliver a secure and sustainable housing solution as it does not protect against landlords leaving the market.

Despite the commitment to eradicating homelessness, and the Lisbon Declaration foregrounded in the Plan, it commits to further developing emergency accommodation through Local Authority- and AHB-owned facilities or land to develop purpose-built facilities, signalling the resignation towards the expansion of emergency facilities.

Furthermore, the Plan commits to reforming the Tenant Purchase Scheme, meaning that those who are eligible can purchase their home with a discount of 25 per cent (maximum discount). While the Plan states that 'we strike a balance between enabling tenants to purchase their homes and replenishment of the social housing stock to make homes available for those on the waiting list', it also states that the Plan will allow 'older tenants' to buy their homes if they have the means (Government of Ireland, 2021, 62). This equates to a continuation of previous tenant purchase policies in which, as we have documented, has resulted in the erosion of the stock of social housing available to let.

The sixth pillar of the *Housing for All* plan was to establish a *Commission on Housing*, which was also promised in the *Programme for Government* 2020. The Commission was tasked to take a long-term strategic view of housing on issues such as tenure, standards, sustainability and quality-of-life. Central to this would be that a sub-committee on the new Housing Commission would bring forward Government proposals on the referendum on housing on the complex constitutional questions arising from such an amendment.

Above all, the Housing Commission signified a growing recognition in Government and across departments that a long-term approach to housing was required, transcending electoral cycles to create a sustainable housing system. The Housing Commission comprised 12 members, including two international experts selected through ministerial appointments, and nine other members who were selected following a publicly advertised process. The group first met in January 2022, and a range of sub-committees were established which drew in other key stakeholders and relevant experts and published their report in the summer of 2024.

The outcome of the Housing Commission report largely falls outside the scope of this book, but it is relevant to note that the Commission concluded due to the shortfall in housing construction since the economic crisis, 'there was a housing deficit of between 212,500 and 256,000 homes' (The Housing Commission, 2024, 28). The Commission recommended that '[u]rgent consideration must be given to addressing the current housing deficit (pent-up demand) to bring down the accumulated housing supply deficit' (The Housing Commission, 2024, 28). Although consideration of homelessness was not included in the Commission's terms of reference, their report includes a section on homelessness which echoed the objectives of the Lisbon Declaration and highlighted the importance of social housing allocations on bringing down the level of homelessness.

As noted, after significant campaigning by civic society organisations and some political parties during the election, the Government had committed to a referendum on housing in its Programme for Government. It had referred the question of the wording for the referendum to the Housing Commission. In its 2024 report, the Commission recommended a wording for the referendum, but this was opposed by a minority report from within the Commission. In March 2024 two referendums on matters unrelated to housing and homelessness were put forward by the Government and dramatically defeated. This outcome essentially put an end to any expectation of a referendum on housing in the near future.

Housing for All and the Programme for Government 2020 – as already referenced – promised to deliver a *Youth Homelessness Strategy 2023–2025* which was duly published in November 2022. The three-year strategy sought to work towards ending homelessness for young people aged 18–24 through prevention and exits and improving the experience of young people accessing emergency accommodation (Government of Ireland, 2022a). The strategy contained 27 actions and called for a whole of Government response. It marked the first strategy published by the Government in over 20 years and is monitored by a steering group established in 2023 (under the auspices of the NHAC) to provide a progress report of actions to NHAC.

Housing activism and street-based activities during and after COVID-19

In mid-2021, allegations emerged that Anthony Flynn, a well-known Dublin City councillor, who was also a homelessness advocate, and founder/CEO of the Inner City Helping Homeless NGO, had sexually assaulted vulnerable service users. The allegations against him led to his initial suspension from Inner City Helping Homeless, but Flynn died by suicide in August 2021 before any criminal charges were filed. The scandal and his subsequent death caused shock among housing and homeless activists, particularly as his charity had amassed significant donations, volunteers and operational capacity across Dublin city and had been a key player in the Apollo House occupation discussed previously.

While street-based services continued, the scandal perhaps temporarily quelled activities in this space during this period (though there was also a natural reduction of volunteering activities during this COVID-19 pandemic period due to various restrictions on movement). Moreover, the scandal supported the claim by many State agencies and NGOs on the need for regulation of services that operated outside of the remit of publicly funding services, while the incident sparked a review of Garda vetting procedures for the homelessness sector.

However, it was not just volunteer-led organisations that came under scrutiny during this period. In 2023, one of the largest NGO homeless services providers in the State, the Peter McVerry Trust, entered a deep financial crisis resulting in the Government approving exceptional funding for the Trust of up to €15 m in November 2023. Investigations were conducted by the office of the Comptroller and Auditor General (2024), the Charities Regulator (2024) and the Approved Housing Bodies Regulatory Authority (2024). In the wake of the controversy, Dublin Region Homeless Executive also announced that it was planning to commission an independent audit of all charities it funds to run homeless services.

More broadly, housing activism began to evolve and develop in 2022 in the context of the chronic shortfall of affordable housing and the rising cost of living in the post-pandemic period. For example, *Raise the Roof*, the coalition led by the Irish Congress of Trades Unions, involving student unions, homeless organisations and other civil society groups as well as opposition political parties and politicians, helped to drive home this messaging in political opposition to the coalition partners. In April 2022, the *Community Action Tenants Union* which has been criticised as being largely comprised of 'white-settled, young, politically engaged, private rented tenants' (Sassi et al, 2025, 96), but also council tenants, launched its national campaign which consists of organising public housing tenants in campaigning for more public housing and to oppose profit-led developments such as luxury apartments, co-living schemes and hotels. The Revolutionary Housing League represents a smaller initiative but has been increasingly occupying buildings and sites, though the number of active members remains very small. Other social media groups established a large following in which platforms and influencers discuss the prices of property in Ireland. It is of note that contemporary housing activism focuses largely on the private rented sector, whereas in the 1960s and 1970s, it was primarily on the situation of local authority tents, reflecting the very significant growth on private rented housing over the past two decades.

Conclusion

In conclusion, this last, pandemic and post-pandemic, period in our review of the century since Independence cannot be compared with any previous period, with wider global events resulting in demographic change, economic upheaval, fluctuation of homelessness trends and rapidly shifting policy and service delivery responses. While the same Government remained in power over this period of change, significant elements of the electorate had signalled a shift away from mainstream political status quo with the rise of support for Sinn Féin, strongly driven by their distinct approach to housing delivery (though opinion polls also fluctuating and the future is not certain). At the same time there was growing support for a variety of independents and small parties. While support for the far right was not reflected in the ballot box, far-right and anti-immigration groups used disruptive and sometimes violent protests to resist accommodation provision for asylum seekers, occasionally spilling over into attacks on homeless accommodation.

Across both sides of the political divide, housing and homelessness remain central issues as growing swathes of the population – notably those aged under 40, one-parent households, migrants, low wage workers, ageing renters and those dependent on welfare payments – remain either stuck in rental accommodation or facing severe housing precariousness and instability.

The sweeping and rapid measures introduced during the COVID-19 pandemic recalibrated service delivery and supports, although the longer-term duration of these changes remains unclear. Service systems and stakeholders across health, drug and homelessness services came together and formed close collaborations to deliver own-door emergency accommodation and tailored service supports, delivered directly to individuals where they were residing. Further, local authorities often responded efficiently and effectively in sourcing appropriate facilities to allow for vulnerable service users greater protection from the virus. All of these activities provided an enhanced service offering to those experiencing homelessness, particularly the long-term homeless, who had previously typically experienced congregate shelters and periodic rooflessness.

A range of measures, which had been advocated for several years with little effect, such as tenancy protections, prioritised housing allocations and greater collaboration between health and housing services, were rapidly introduced during 2020 and the first half of 2021. But as normal life resumed, so too did the more conventional responses to homelessness and many of these changes were reversed or simply faded away.

After several decades of low inflation, cost-of-living increases again became a significant pressure on low incomes households. While rent regulation succeeded in moderating rent increases, rising rents continue to be a significant problem, particularly for low-income households, with 60 per cent of HAP tenants making recorded 'top-up' payments to their landlords.

Regulation of rent levels in the private rented sector had moved from being considered 'unconstitutional' to being on the verge of being adopted as a long-term nation-wide policy. Meanwhile the momentum to put 'The Right to Housing' into the Constitution by way of referendum has reached a peak on being included in the 2020 Programme for Government. The defeat of two unrelated referendums in 2024 had severely dented the prospects of the housing rights referendums progressing, but whatever prospect existed was further undermined by the minority report from the Housing Commission which argued that the Oireachtas already had sufficient powers to 'regulate private property rights'.

Joe Lee's *Ireland 1912–1985*, a critically acclaimed and widely read analysis of the performance of the Irish State published in 1989, identified the dominance of the 'possessor principle' over the 'performance principle'. In Lee's view, this hindered the economic and social development for all in independent Ireland by privileging those who possessed land, capital and other resources. Reflecting on this analysis, fellow historian Gearoid Ó Tuathaigh noted that in the 30-year period since the publication of Lee's work much had changed for the better in Ireland. Nonetheless, Ó Tuathaigh observed that: 'Irish society has been gripped by a housing crisis … [b]ut property rights endured, and political leaders still need to tread carefully in disturbing them. In this sense, the possessor principle remains a presiding concern of political leadership and of decision-making in contemporary independent Ireland' (Ó Tuathaigh, 2024, 120).

Conclusion: Reflections on Homelessness in Ireland

Continuity and change

As we set out the story of 'homelessness' over the hundred years since the foundation of the Irish State, we were conscious of the unsettling question of whether we are, in fact, talking about the same thing from start to finish. Is the modern Supported Temporary Accommodation facility the modern equivalent of the Casual Ward in the County Home? Has it been meaningful to talk about the overcrowded tenements at the foundation of the State as part of the same story as the hotel rooms used for homeless families as it celebrated its centenary? While it is clear that the social context in which homelessness occurs changes over time, and also that there has been progress in terms of the quality of services, at the end of writing the book we are more firmly convinced of the value of understanding the experience of 'vagrants', 'sturdy beggars', 'the homeless' and, now, 'people experiencing homelessness' as some form of continuity. In doing so, we can see how a range of social, economic and personal factors repeatedly combine, over the century, to leave a number of individuals without a secure place to call home.

The precise nature of these forces, and the nature of their interaction, change over time but they retain recognisable common features: poverty, ill-health, poor housing, migration and bad luck. And while the people impacted change, shifting across age, gender and ethnicity, they too have recognisable common features: while we are occasionally told of eye-catching cases where formerly prosperous people 'end up on the street', these cases are exceedingly rare and exceptional and in no way representative of those who experience homelessness. People from certain disadvantaged localities, and with certain experiences and characteristics which make them vulnerable, have been consistently those who occupy the Casual Ward, the charitable dormitory bed, the Supported Temporary Accommodation or the Homeless Hub.

On a few occasions, the buildings used to accommodate people who are homeless reveal a thread of continuity: the Supported Temporary Accommodation being provided by De Paul Ireland today on Dublin's Back Lane has been renovated several times but remains recognisably the same building constructed by the Society of St Vincent De Paul in 1915 to provide low-cost accommodation to working men. The Family Hub operated by the AHB Respond in High Park, Dublin, had an earlier life as a Magdalene Laundry run by the Sisters of Our Lady of Charity of Refuge.

Throughout the century, homelessness needs to be understood in the context of *home* and the deprivation of it. Over the last hundred years, our idea of 'home' has evolved, and we now have much higher expectations of privacy, cleanliness and comfort than the majority of people did a century ago, but the human consequences of being *without* whatever constitutes a home remain remarkably constant. We have seen that the term 'homelessness' is a relatively recent usage but, by defining the condition as a lack of something, an absence of home, it highlights the continuity of the condition as a human experience. While the things that may accompany that absence can change over time (better sleeping arrangements, support from care workers, access to cooking facilities and so on) what remains constant in any experience of homelessness is that absence of something that all humans require to be fully human.

But there is a real sense in which the nature of the story does change as we come into the 21st century. This is partly because we have so much more data on homelessness from this point and so can understand in detail the transitions of large numbers of people into and out of homelessness. Perhaps coincidentally, this increase in the amount of data available occurs at a time when homelessness begins to be more commonly seen as a consequence arising from how we run our society, which can be fixed with the right mix of policy and resources, and less as a reflection of the perceived moral failure of the people who experience homelessness. Other insights emerge from the data, such as the extent of flows into and out of homelessness or the way that people who sleep rough frequently rotate in and out of services rather than conforming to a 'service resistant, entrenched' stereotype. Given the consistency in the 11 years of data now available it is highly likely that these have always been features of homelessness, but were previously unrecognised. The paradox of the final quarter of a century is that the increased data on homelessness deepens our understanding of how homelessness comes about and reinforces our certainty that it can be solved, even as the data records homelessness rising to unprecedented levels.

In the first part of the conclusion, we look at the questions that recur repeatedly over the century, then turn our attention to some of the insights which can be drawn from the wealth of data available of the last decade, before finally turning our attention to lessons which can be drawn from the underlying policies or approaches that made a difference over the entire period.

Recurring questions

It is comparatively unusual to look at the story of homelessness over a long period, from a historic perspective, as we have done in this book. It is more common to break the story into discrete periods, most commonly characterised as periods of 'crisis', or to explore it from the perspective of particular policies or particular groups of people. These more familiar approaches tend to leave us looking at a series of apparently unrelated episodes with no discernible underlying patterns. This results in homelessness constantly being 'rediscovered' or being described as 'having a new face' or being the 'new homelessness'.

Looking from the longer-term perspective we can see deeper patterns: a number of questions emerge, being apparently resolved only to re-emerge in a different context at a later point. One of the largest sets of questions which emerges from this perspective is: who is responsible for responding to homelessness? Is it the role of the State itself or of its citizens or the religious or charitable institutions? If the State has a role, which part of the State is required to act? Is homelessness a question of health, of social disorder or of housing? These questions play out repeatedly over the century and still have resonance today in some of the political discussions and public attitudes to homelessness.

Whose job is homelessness: the State or charitable associations?

Prior to Independence, responsibility for providing accommodation to people who had no home was shared between the State, in the form of the workhouses, and a number of largely faith-based charitable organisations, primarily in Dublin. On the foundation of the State, the workhouses were renamed 'County Homes' and a policy was established of removing these 'casuals' from them. While this was a stated policy goal from an early stage, there were no proposals for any new State services which would provide appropriate services and accommodation for the displaced 'able-bodied' men and women who had no home. This absence of an alternative response partially explains why the policy took such a remarkably long time to implement, with the final Casual Wards only closing in the late 1980s.

That no proposal for alternative State services for people without a home emerged in the first 30 years of Independence, reflected a view within the State administration that it had little role to play in responding to homelessness. This view was also echoed in the voluntary providers of services of the time. As we have seen, the leader of one of the major voluntary providers of services for homeless people, Frank Duff of the Legion of Mary, took a strong view that accommodation for people who were homeless should be 'under the management of some voluntary body, animated by religious ideals'. In this view, the State did not even have a role in funding the services, and the Legion of Mary continues to run services in Dublin on this basis today.

Duff's resistance to a role for the State in accommodating those who are homeless was, at least in part, driven by a recognition that several States had a very poor record of providing such support in a humane way. He advised the 1925 Commission on the Relief of the Poor that it should 'not think that the State does better in other countries' arguing the more Poor Laws develops without religious guidance the 'more severe become its methods towards this particular type of man.' These fears should be seen in the context of the establishment of labour colonies for vagrants in Holland, Belgium, Germany and elsewhere, along with the generally punitive tone of public policy towards people who were homeless in States with very different political complexions. The Commission echoed similar concerns to those expressed in Duff's proposal where it argued that any proposed services that had 'even [a] distant relationship to the Poor Law would probably mean their destruction' (1927, 87) – that is the 'destruction' of the homeless people who used the service.

One remarkable feature of this debate in the early years of the State is that a number of the leading figures in the non-State delivery of services who provided a robust ideological argument that the State should not be involved in this area were themselves senior figures in the Civil Service. For example, Frank Duff was a civil servant, and joined the Land Commission in 1908, while his brother went on to be the Secretary in the Department of Justice before his death in 1949. Bob Cashman, vice-Chair of the Dublin Simon Community in the early 1970s, and President of the Society of St Vincent De Paul during the same period was a Civil Servant in the Department of Local Government.

It was not until 1953, in the Health Act of that year, that a legal basis for the State providing 'institutional assistance' to people who were homeless was established. The *Housing Act, 1988* provided a legal basis under which local authorities became responsible for providing support to people who were homeless, linking the response to homelessness to the housing authorities for the first time. But even this did not oblige the local authority to itself provide such accommodation. Most continued to leave the responsibility to voluntary organisations, gradually introducing a range of mechanisms to fund, or partially fund, these services over time.

This debate is frequently discussed in the context of Ireland's distinct history of entrusting a range of social, medical and educational services to faith-based organisations (Dukelow and Considine, 2017). The largely non-State provision of homeless services is frequently seen as just another example of this Irish model; however, the case of homelessness is a bit more complex, and the non-State nature of Irish homeless services is less of an outlier than other social and health services. In the first half of the 20th century, faith-based organisations were frequently the primary providers of services to homeless people in countries with very different patterns of welfare state development. Even well-developed welfare states had a relatively small population of single people, predominantly men, who had 'fallen through the cracks' of what was envisaged as a universalistic welfare state and whose welfare was attended to by a range of faith-based organisations (Pleace et al,

2018; Allen et al, 2020). Similarly, from the 1970s, many countries saw a shift to a mixture of faith-based and secular non-profit organisations.

As other European States moved beyond 'Poor Law' approaches to homelessness into the development of a welfare state approach, Irish social policy continued to be shaped by a deep-rooted ethos of laissez-faire, paternalism and subsidiarity, influenced by personally held beliefs about the role of the State, beliefs often themselves influenced by catholic social teaching (with a small c). This complex amalgam of ideological views nurtured an enlarged role for voluntary organisations in service provisions, which we argue fosters a view that recipients of social services should be the subject of compassion rather than agents of political change.

The approach of favouring voluntary, non-State, responses to homelessness long outlived any value as an opposition to the punitive approach of the workhouse. It was not until the late 1970s that a new form of non-government homeless organisation emerged which asserted that the State has responsibilities for the homeless and, if it did not itself fulfil those obligations, it should provide funding to those who did. A patchwork of individual 'grants' provided to NGOs emerged, often announced by a Minister in relation to a particular charity but without any clear rationale or consistent level of funding.

From around 2000, the patchwork of funding to voluntary services was gradually, but only partially, replaced by formal 'Service Level Agreements' (SLAs). Some services, particularly where a new service was being introduced, were put out to tender by the local authority, with the various homeless charities competing, largely on the basis of price, to provide the service. The relatively few homeless services that had been run directly by local authorities, primarily in Dublin, were gradually closed or transferred to be run by the charitable sector. In 2015, Dublin City Council transferred the running of its last remaining emergency accommodation services to Dublin Simon. The role of local authorities then became one of commissioning, funding and regulating services, which were provided by charitable organisations.

The State, in the form of local authorities, continued to control the gateways into and out of homelessness. They hold the statutory role of assessing whether a person is deemed to be homeless under the *Housing Act, 1988* and so whether they are entitled to be accommodated by a homeless charity funded by them. They are also currently responsible for all allocations to social housing tenancies, including AHB tenancies, as well as determining whether a person is eligible for rental subsidies for a private rental tenancy.

In the last 20 years, an increasing number of private 'for-profit' entities have emerged to provide accommodation for people who are homeless. Initially this largely involved private companies or individuals renting buildings to local authorities to be operated as hostels by voluntary organisations. In more recent years, particularly in relation to emergency accommodation for families, sometimes referred to as Family Hubs, the private company also provides facilities management. To date, for-profit entities have not completed to provide 'case management' or social care work, and all such work continues to be undertaken by registered charities.

Despite moving to this role of providing services which have been commissioned and funded by the State, many of the homeless NGOs which emerged from the 1970s onwards continue to assert that they have a role in 'providing a voice for' people who are homeless, which was part of their founding mission. Since 2014, the official 'homeless' figures, effectively those accessing State funded emergency accommodation, have been published by the Department of Housing each month. When these show a rise, all the main homeless charities issue press statements which include some degree of criticism of government policy. Some public authorities struggle with the idea that an organisation they regard as a subcontractor can also make public criticisms of public policy.

A further lack of clarity about these relationships arises because, reflecting the history in which many of these services were initially provided without any State support, many of the SLAs do not provide sufficient funds to deliver the service, and the charity must raise funds to cover the full cost.[1] This model, in which most homeless charities must raise a substantial proportion of their funds, means that they have a sufficient degree of independence from government to allow a critical perspective. It also requires that they remain visible to potential donors, and this can also create an incentive to maintain a high profile in the media but also can result in promoting events to generate non-State funding, such as sleepouts, that have the potential to distort an accurate understanding of the nature of homelessness. The Legion of Mary and a few other small traditional organisations continue with their services entirely unfunded by public money, and now largely stay out of the public debate on homelessness.

Of course, responses to homelessness in civic society were not confined to providing shelter and service, and from the 1970s different forms of public protest also emerged, through *Dublin Housing Action Committee*, *The National Campaign for the Homeless* to *Make Room*, *Apollo House* and *Raise the Roof*, all of which organised around a demand that the State should take a more active role in responding to homelessness.

One remarkable feature of the civic society response to homelessness in the recent past has been the growth of volunteer-based organisations providing humanitarian support, including sleeping bags and tents but primarily food, to people who are homeless. In contrast to an earlier wave of voluntary organisations which provided food (such as Focus Ireland's Coffee Shop, Merchant's Quay or the Capuchin Day Centre), the more recent volunteers provide food on the street, sometimes explicitly adopting the famine-era term of 'soup kitchen'. These groups maintain a detached and critical relationship with both the professional NGOs and the State services. Of these groups, only the Inner-City Homeless Help attempted to follow the well-worn pathway from volunteer group to professional service, albeit unsuccessfully. The remaining services appear to be content to remain as volunteer organisations serving immediate humanitarian needs. While these groups are critical of the failure of the State to provide for people who are homeless, they do not seek additional State resources for their work. In some senses, their approach would have been familiar a century ago, with their emphasis on alleviating human suffering and their willingness to give time and energy to help others indefinitely.

Whose job is homelessness: health or housing?

While wider society was working out whether the State had any role in responding to homelessness, there was a parallel debate inside Government about which part of Government would take on that responsibility: specifically, whether it should be seen as a health matter or a housing matter.

As noted before, the first legislative response to this was Section 54 of the *Health Act, 1953*, which provided that the health service should provide 'institutional assistance' to those who were homeless. It wasn't until a decade later, in the 1966 White Paper on *The Health Services and their Further Development*, that it was first argued that local authorities had a role – specifically that they should build homes for the estimated 5,000 people who were still accommodated in County Homes but 'who do not require medical and nursing care at hospital level'. The *Housing Act, 1966* then made provision, for the first time, for local authorities to provide homes for those unable to do so from their own resources.

Although the 1966 Act saw the first shift towards seeing homelessness as a housing – rather than a health – issue, responsibility was still unclear. People found themselves directed back and forth between the local authorities and the health boards, and different approaches were taken in different parts of the country. This was one of the motivating issues for Senator Brendan Ryan's campaigning work in the early 1980s. At the end of the debates of that decade, the *Housing Act, 1988* gave clearer legislative responsibility to local authorities in responding to homelessness, as well as setting out specific powers available to them.

This legislative change did not definitively resolve the issue at an operational level, with the health boards continuing to provide funding for a number of social care services within the homeless sector. The issue again surfaced during the 'era of strategies', where the two roles appear to be finally stated clearly: 'Local authorities have responsibility for the provision of accommodation for homeless adults as part of their overall housing responsibility and health boards are responsible for the health and care needs of homeless adults'.

Conclusion

The approach to the 'health or housing' question is particularly interesting during the period from around 1995 to 2010 where forms of local social partnership emerged, most strongly in Dublin. As has been noted, homelessness had been treated as, to adapt Higgins' phrase, a 'thing apart' in social partnership at a national level with no reference at all in the early agreements. However, analogous partnership arrangements developed 'apart' at a local level. The period of social partnership is frequently characterised as being primarily about negotiated arrangements between Government on one hand and employers, trade unions and, latterly, civic society on the other. However, one important role that social partnership structures provided was the coordination between different arms of Government (O'Donnell, 2000). This was of particular importance in the case of homelessness, because of the need to bring together a range of different resources and expertise which reside in different agencies. So, during this period, plans and protocols that closely integrated the housing and health roles of the State were agreed within the homeless partnership and implemented through it.

For this short partnership period, the answer to the question 'health or housing?' question was settled as 'both together'. Otherwise, it is a question which seems to need to be re-answered with every change of Minister or senior officials. Even as late as 2020, the former Minister for Housing, Eoghan Murphy, writing about his term in office, stated:

> [t]here was the more traditional face of homelessness: mostly men, with complex health needs, whether related to mental health or addiction or other issues, some sleeping rough, but the vast majority in the emergency accommodations system. The Custom House [the building where the Department of Housing is situated] felt that the response should be health-led. It was hard to disagree. (2024, 202)

Murphy goes on to note, apparently oblivious to the decades-long governance debate, that 'some of my officials blamed the previous Minister, Alan Kelly, for [the Department] taking on the responsibility'.

The challenge of integrating the housing and health functions of Government has its most recent reprise in the delivery of the Housing First programme, where the partnership between the two departments is given a high profile in formal documents and launches, but is less evident on the ground (Allen and Byrne, 2024).

At one level the debate about which department is responsible comes down to the question of who funds what. While the funding for homeless services provided by the Department of Housing under Section 10 of the Housing Act, 1988 is relatively clearly set out in the budget, the provision by the Department of Health under Section 39 of the Health Act, 2004 is harder to estimate as it is amalgamated into the overall Social Inclusion

Budget. In 2024, the Commission on Housing noted this absence of a dedicated funding line and recommended 'a dedicated budget line in the HSE Service Plans for support services for homeless people' (2024, 205).

From another perspective this concentration on departmental funding responsibilities masks a deeper question about how we understand and respond to homelessness, its causes and the most effective responses. In practical terms, this question involves finding ways to deliver health, addiction and mental health service to people who are marginalised and often leading chaotic lives, while ensuring that medical services do not interpret homelessness itself as an illness to be cured or 'the homeless' as a distinct section of society permanently characterised by debilitating mental health or addiction problems. This tendency of the health system to perceive homelessness as a medical problem is perpetuated by the research methodologies which still predominate when medical researchers turn their attention to homelessness. The predominance of static studies in medical research consistently leads to distorted results which depict people who are homeless as almost entirely suffering from mental health and/or addiction issues (O'Sullivan et al, 2020).

It is also worth noting that although difficulties continue to exist over responsibility for homelessness between the Departments of Housing and Health, responses to homelessness in Ireland remain firmly framed within a social inclusion paradigm. In part due to massive expenditure on various forms of emergency accommodation, the numbers unsheltered have remained relatively low over the past decade, and punitive responses, or policies of social exclusion, which demand criminal justice or policing responses to homelessness are noticeably absent in Ireland, in comparison with some Member States in the European Union, where punitive responses are evident (Jones, 2013).

How do we pay for housing?

The second major set of questions which emerge throughout the century has been the relationship between housing and homelessness – or more particularly how housing is provided for households whose income is too low for them to afford market rents. Access to affordable housing is critical for all forms of homeless households, but different strands of the housing system are important for families and for single people.

For families, for most of the century, social housing has been the primary protection from homelessness or route out of homelessness. It is only in the last quarter of a century where State-subsidised private rental housing has increasingly been used as a 'social housing solution' that the dynamics of the private rental market have been important for low-income families. For single homeless people, due to the persistent shortage of single occupancy social housing, the most relevant part of the housing system has been, and remains, the lower-rent or subsidised part of the private rental market. Social housing policy needs to take into account a wide range of issues from finance to community development, from the needs of low wage workers to the need for social integration. While social housing policy can have profound implications for the level and duration of homelessness, it is rarely the primary consideration and, despite the repeated political assertion that homelessness is a 'priority', the implications of housing policy for homelessness are often given lower priority than other considerations.

One of the decisions with the most significant long-term consequences was the introduction of social housing rents that were calculated on the tenants' ability to pay rather than the cost of the housing or market conditions. Such 'differential rents' were introduced from the 1930s onwards to solve two related problems. First, the problem of how housing was to be provided for the 'slum-dwelling' households whose income was insufficient to cover the actual cost of providing their housing. The 'slum-dwelling' households could just about afford the private rents in the slums because rents were kept low by minimal levels of maintenance and endless subdivision. Until the 1930s, social housing rents were related to the costs incurred by the local authority in providing the housing unit, but even after discounts due to investment of public funds, the resultant rents were too high for many families moving from the slums that were being cleared. The second, related problem was the social stratification caused by all social housing being taken up by the higher income households who were the only ones who could afford it. Differential rents provided a useful solution to both these significant challenges and also, in the absence of any income-related subsidy for tenants in social housing, played a significant role in keeping down income-related poverty. From the mid-1960s onward all social housing rents have been differential rents. The State's failure to consistently provide housing authorities with the difference between the cost of providing and maintaining the homes and the rent that they could collect from tenants has contributed to a number of detrimental outcomes. As social housing became residualised, this gap has grown. As the average income of tenants declined, so too has the level of rents collected. Norris and Hayden (2018) conclude that: 'The very low level of rent charged to council housing tenants and the complete disconnect between the rents charged and the costs of the housing service means that local authorities have no incentive to maintain dwellings efficiently or to ensure they are swiftly re-let when they become vacant'.

As discussed in Chapter 7, in 2013 the *Homeless Oversight Group* estimated that the scale of social housing voids meant that they could accommodate 1,500 to 2,000 long-term homeless households if they were renovated. Since 2014 this level of unused housing has been addressed annually by the Minister of the day providing special funds to local authorities to 'bring voids back into use'. This scheme provides a good news story for both local authorities and Ministers for many years, with little or no serious discussion of why the problem of derelict voids re-occurs each year and whether a better system could be devised. Norris and Hayden concluded that, because Central Government only stepped in to provide renovation funding only when homes had been vacant for a long period, this scheme 'reinforces the incentive' for local authorities to leave housing units unmaintained or even void, as well as adding additional motivation for sales to tenants. *The Housing Commission* (2024) recommended that all social rents should be on a cost rental basis, with the inability of some tenants to afford the rent being met by a new income-related rent subsidy programme.

A second set of decisions with long-term consequences were taken from the 1980s onwards, in relation to the financing of social housing construction, and only revealed their full consequences in the aftermath of the financial crisis. As we discussed in Chapter 5, from the 1980s it was decided to fund the provision of social housing largely through Central Government grants and, later, to shift away from local authority construction of social housing to providing it through Section 5 of the *Planning Act, 2000*, essentially as a by-product of private housing construction. While these decisions did not impact on the output of social housing for many years, when the financial crisis hit in 2008, the State discovered it had entirely eroded its autonomous capacity to construct the social housing it needed.

Only 75 units were constructed by local authorities in 2015, and despite the resumption of higher levels of local authority housing constructions since that date, social housing supply is disproportionately dependent on AHBs and councils purchasing homes from the private construction sector. While the proximate reason for this lost decade in social housing construction was the financial crisis, the vulnerability of the sector to such events was the result of decisions made about the role of the State many years earlier. This lost decade of social housing construction forms a significant proportion of the 212,500 to 256,000 'housing deficit' identified by the Housing Commission in 2024. While it would be too simple to say that this was the cause of the quadrupling of homelessness since 2014, the social housing deficit certainly limited the State's capacity to respond to the challenges it faced over that period.

Lessons emerging from the last decade: the fluidity of homelessness

Homelessness is a dynamic process and capturing the experience of homelessness at a point-in-time does not reveal the fluidity of the experience of homelessness. Comparatively rare longitudinal data shows that most households who experience a spell in an emergency shelter, for example, will exit to secure housing and not return to emergency accommodation (O'Donnell, 2020). Time frames are thus critically important when measuring homelessness, as the numbers who experience homelessness, and their characteristics, will differ significantly depending on the time frame used (Shinn and Khadduri, 2020, 26–27).

Shorter timeframes largely capture those experiencing long-term homelessness with longer timeframes capturing the significantly larger number of people who enter and exit homelessness each year, using shelters for very short periods of time or a single episode without returning to homelessness (Scutella and Woods, 2024). Definitions of homelessness also shape how we understand homelessness and hence the policies and services we deploy to respond to it. Studies using broad definitions find strong evidence for structural causes of homelessness driven primarily by poverty, while studies with more narrow definitions highlight the challenges faced by individuals – in particular the minority experiencing long-term or repeated homelessness, which is associated with high and complex treatment and support needs (Pleace and Hermans, 2020).

As a consequence of the nationwide roll-out of the PASS system in 2014, a decade of administrative data on those accessing emergency accommodation for those experiencing homelessness has provided a deeper understanding of the dynamics of homelessness. The most commonly quoted data about homelessness in Ireland comes from a point-in-time (PIT) measure, that is the number of adult users of emergency accommodation over one week each month, which is published by the Department of Housing on the last Friday of every month. Comparatively, most countries only have a point-in-time measurement of homelessness, and as set out in Appendix 2, based on this measure Ireland has experienced the greatest increase in homelessness across the Member States of the European Union over the past decade where similar data exists.

These monthly point-in-time reports show an increase from 2,385 to 10,354 adults in emergency accommodation, an increase of 334 per cent, between June 2014 and December 2024, and consistently, approximately 70 per cent of adults in emergency accommodation at a point-in-time are in Dublin. A less common way of understanding trends in homelessness is understanding the flow of adults (this data is contained in the less user-friendly quarterly performance reports) into emergency accommodation per quarter. On this measure, nearly 62,000 unique adults entered emergency accommodation for the first time between 2014 and 2024, an average of just over 1,400 adults per quarter, an annual figure that increased from 4,780 in 2014 to 6,276 in 2018 and with the exception of the COVID-19 period, then remained largely stable, with almost equal numbers entered in Dublin and outside Dublin, in contrast to the point-in-time data which shows 70 per cent of adults in emergency accommodation in Dublin.

Over the same period over 33,000 adults exited emergency accommodation to housing (included in the housing exits are 900 adults in a Housing First Tenancy), an average of just over 750 adults per quarter. The number of adult exits peaked in 2019 and 2020, but despite increases in adult exits over the period 2022–2024, the number of exits is substantially lower than 2019–2020 and, more significantly, exits have not kept pace with entries. Fifty-seven per cent exited to social housing or to secure housing provided by a municipal or a not-for-profit provider. The remainder exited to private rented housing with income supports or quasi-secure housing, and in Dublin only, a further 7,300 adults exited emergency accommodation by entering medical or correction facilities or returning to their families (accurate data is not available outside Dublin, but it can be reasonably assumed a roughly similar number experienced such exits outside of Dublin), or what can be term insecure exits.

Data on prevention is only available on a national basis from 2022, and just over 6,100 adults were prevented from entering emergency accommodation in Dublin and 5,500 outside of Dublin. These adults were assessed as meeting the criteria to be regarded as homeless under the legislation and accessed new tenancies rather than entered emergency accommodation. Just over half of the adults prevented from entering emergency accommodation were provided with housing in the private rented sector with the Homeless Housing Assistance Payment (HHAP).

Thus, rather than seeing the point-in-time figure as an accumulation of adults in emergency accommodation, with each month adding more adults to the existing pool of adults, a dynamic picture is evident, where each quarter 970 adults are prevented from entering emergency accommodation, nearly 1,400 new adults do enter emergency accommodation and 750 exit to housing and 300 to other exits. The accumulated gap between these two flow figures, entries and exits, generates the point-in-time figure.

Those entering emergency accommodation in Dublin are more likely to get 'stuck' for longer periods of time, hence the 70 per cent of all adults in Dublin who were in emergency accommodation for more than six months at a point-in-time, compared to the almost equal flow figure between Dublin and outside Dublin. By the end of 2024, in Dublin, 19.3 per cent of single adults and 25 per cent of families were in emergency accommodation for more than two years, compared to 9.6 and 9.5 per cent outside Dublin. One key reason why households in Dublin, rather than outside Dublin, are getting stuck in emergency accommodation is that at the end of 2024 nearly 32 per cent of households in Dublin were non-EEA compared to 14 per cent outside Dublin. Non-EEA households generally are required to be resident for five years before qualifying for social housing and social housing supports, and face other barriers such a discrimination by private landlords and household size as well as tending to be further down waiting lists due to to the time they have been living in Ireland.

Understanding homelessness as a fluid process where large numbers of adults enter and exit emergency accommodation demonstrates that much of contemporary homelessness in Ireland results from residential instability and insecurity rather than a form of individual disability or deliberately attempting to 'game the system'. That the majority of those in emergency accommodation in June 2014 were not there in, for example, June 2020 highlights that the provision of secure stable housing both prevents entries to emergency accommodation and provides a sustainable exit from emergency accommodation. The growth in the numbers of emergency accommodation at a point-in-time is not the gradual increase of a cohort of helpless and hopeless households, but rather the inability of the housing system to prevent and exit households at the same rate as households enter emergency accommodation.

One of the most important developments in the last 15 years or so has been a deeper understanding of the gendered nature of homelessness, how women's experience of homelessness differs from the more researched experience of men, and how their pathways into and out of homelessness are often distinct (Mayock and Sheridan, 2020; Bretherton and Mayock, 2024). The association between homelessness and domestic abuse is also increasingly recognised (Mayock and Neary, 2021). This enhanced understanding of women's experiences of homelessness, however, has not yet been fully reflected in either policy or service provision. This better understanding of women's experiences of homeless, however, has not yet been fully reflected in either policy or service provision.

Migration

At the time of writing, migration – in the form of inward migration into Ireland – features strongly as one of the challenges driving up homelessness and placing strains on the wider housing system. From the longer-term perspective, we can see that patterns of migration out of Ireland have played a crucial role reducing housing pressure, in particular on social housing, over most of the century. This book looks at homelessness within the Republic of Ireland, but a wider lens would have documented the extensive experience of homelessness of Irish emigrants in most of the major immigration destinations over the century.

At the start of the book, the official term to describe the experience we now know as homelessness was 'vagrancy', indicating the extent to which the problem of not having a home has always been linked to the experience of moving or of having to move, from one place to another. The Poor Laws which, as we have shown, established the blue-print for the homeless systems we see today, emerged as a response to the displacement of people due to industrialisation and land enclosures. The person who has had to migrate from a place in which they were secure to a place where they are unknown and insecure has always been a central feature of homelessness and the response of homelessness services. The difference in the current period is that, for the first time, Ireland has become a destination for migrants from other places, rather than a departure point or a place of return.

It is equally true that the official responses to vagrancy are being dusted down to control global migration and can be seen in the reassertion of requirements that recipients of homeless services must be able to prove 'local connection' or 'habitual residence'. Local connection rules were developed in relation to entitlement to relief, and this legacy of local connection rules remains prevalent across Europe for those seeking to access homelessness services (Baptista et al, 2015). It remains to be seen whether the punitive responses, which we have noted as not being evident in Irish policy responses, may yet emerge.

In this sense, the current phase of large-scale global migration, while it raises real challenges in communication and in scale, is nothing radically new for the homelessness sector. There is, however, a much more fundamental challenge to the now established 'housing-led' responses to homelessness in cases where the person who is homeless has no legal entitlement to housing in Ireland. People in these circumstances fall outside even the strongest optimism that 'homelessness can be ended', potentially resulting in a return to responses which can at best only be palliative in nature.

What makes a difference?

Homelessness and the allocation of social housing

We have made the link between housing and homelessness a central theme of this book, but it is important to be clear that this link is not always a straightforward one: if we want to end homelessness, having sufficient, affordable housing is an essential condition – but it is not, on its own, a sufficient condition. The availability of appropriate social care supports to those who need them is one of the further conditions needed, but even if we look at housing alone the question of how we distribute or allocate available social housing is also central.

Since the foundation of the State the general principle has been that social housing is allocated on the basis of need, but how need is assessed and responded to has important implications for homelessness. In the first place, to be eligible for social housing your household income must be below certain levels set out by Central Government. In general, there are more eligible households than there are social houses, so in practice, homes are allocated on the basis of other assessments of need. For most of the period, need was assessed through a points-based system, with particular forms of need recognised by applying additional points. From 2011 local authorities were allowed to take into account the length of time that a household had been on the waiting list (Norris and Hayden, 2018) and this has since become the primary means by which local authorities allocate social housing to eligible households.

While a point-based system gave some scope to prioritise households that were homeless, such 'homeless points' were also balanced against points (such as for overcrowding, disability, and so on) which would be applied to other households. A 'time on list' system inevitably gives lower priority to people who are more geographically mobile, have chaotic lifestyles, are young, or do not think of applying to be on the housing list because they mistakenly consider themselves to be securely housed.

Although access to social housing is one of the primary tools available to the State in tackling homelessness, the idea of giving preferential access to households on the basis of their homelessness always met with resistance. In 1984, the Ad Hoc Committee on Homelessness set out its view that prioritising the homeless 'could discriminate against many people already on housing authority waiting lists and would cause confusion and inequity in providing alternative routes to housing by housing authorities'. This view that giving priority to homeless households was unfair and may also result in families deliberately becoming homeless to 'jump the queue' has dominated policy on this issue.

As we discuss in Chapter 7, in 2013 the Homeless Oversight Group proposed that long-term homelessness could be ended, even in the absence of new housing supply, through a programme of renovating an estimated 1,500–2,000 social housing units which were derelict and void, and ring-fencing them for the households that were experiencing long-term homelessness. In the event, the properties were brought back into use but the proportion to go to the long-term homeless was quickly reduced to half, before the 'ring-fencing' was abandoned entirely by the subsequent Minister, Alan Kelly. Kelly, instead, applied the idea of ring-fencing in a new way, issuing a directive stipulating that up to 40 per cent of all social housing allocations should go to people who were homeless (or had a disability). While this measure was successful in slowing down the rapid increase in homelessness over that period, it met with strong resistance from local elected members of all political parties and from the senior management of local authorities based on the unsubstantiated claim that acted as a 'pull factor' in families becoming homeless. The policy was then abandoned by the subsequent Minister, Simon Coveney, who argued that, because there would be an increased supply of social housing, prioritisation would no longer be necessary. Coveney's assessment that social housing supply would increase proved correct, albeit more slowly than he had envisaged, but the assumption that this would lead to more homes for long-term homeless households did not materialise. Indeed, the backlash against using housing allocation as a tool to tackle long-term homelessness resulted in a number of councils deleting from their Scheme of Lettings their pre-existing scheme for giving priority to a modest number of homeless households.

Rebalancing the allocations policy in favour of homeless households was again applied during the COVID-19 epidemic, where councils, in particular Dublin City Council, front-loaded allocation of social housing to homeless families and individuals who were particularly vulnerable. Again, the policy worked and, in this case, it contributed, along with other factors, to a rapid decline in family homelessness during this period. The policy was never formalised and, while not abandoned, was used less intensively after the pandemic, contributing to a new escalation in family homelessness.

The 1980s experience of increased allocations to homeless households shows that the policy is not without its risks – the process in which disadvantaged families were concentrated into already disadvantaged areas is clearly to be avoided but is also avoidable. Equally, the perceptions of unfairness associated with Kelly's initiative will make any similar programme unsustainable. But the evidence strongly suggests that, without some allocations programme that ensures that the long-term homeless can access available social housing, simply increasing housing supply will not result in an early or rapid decline in homelessness. Designing such an allocations programme which is effective but also is recognised as fair and not creating any perverse incentives would appear to be a crucial part of any successful programme to tackle homelessness.

Homeless policy and the ideology of Government

While we structured the book to pay attention to the succession of political parties through Government, this attention did not reveal any great ideological shifts in the approaches which are taken by administrations which claimed different political perspectives. This is not to say that different ideological positions are not expressed along the way: for instance, the question of the balance between the rights of property and other social and economic rights – such as the right to a home – is a feature of debate at the time the State was founded, again during the drafting of the 1937 Constitution, again around the Kenny Report in 1973 and yet again in proposals in 2024 for a referendum on the right to housing. What is striking is that the re-iteration of this debate does not result in ideological shifts in policy. Although, the case for the rights of property to yield some ground to the right to a home wins battles, in for instance the Kenny Report, the view that private property rights are paramount wins the war, often via a minority report, and the status quo prevails.

Where shifts in policy do occur, they do not necessarily reflect what might be assumed to be the ideology of the parties concerned: in the UK, the practice of selling public housing to tenants at a discount rate is identified with the right-ward shift of Margaret Thatcher, however, it existed in Ireland from before the foundation of the State and took on its modern momentum partly due to Labour Party pressure in 1950s. Equally, while it might be in line with a right/left expectation of attitudes to homelessness that, in the 1980s, Labour Party Ministers proposed to bring in an obligation on local authorities to house people who were homeless, they also intended to introduce the distinctly right-of-centre provision that no such obligation existed if the person was deemed to have made themselves 'intentionally homelessness'. It was the subsequent Fianna Fáil Government who decided to set the balance in a different way: no obligation to provide housing, so therefore no need for provisions to catch the supposed chancers. In the Irish context, these different positions do not seem to represent different ideologies in conflict, but different ways of balancing different objectives and prejudices.

But this is not to say that different ideological positions were not available. At the foundation of the State, Tom Johnston, then Leader of the Labour Party, argued that the constitution of the Free State should include the view that property was held in trust for the public welfare. In the 1980s, Senator Brendan Ryan articulated the view of not-for-profit homeless organisations that the State had a moral obligation to house the homeless and that any risk of abuse of this right was so negligible as to not require any defensive gatekeeping. It is just that these alternative ideological perspectives never prevailed.

To some extent this consistency in the ideological framing of legislation and policy reflects the broader consensus at a political level in Ireland but, as the internal civil servant discussions which ultimately led to the *Housing Act, 1988* suggest, it also reflects the dominance and continuity of the public service and its senior officials.

In more recent years, a significant part of the growing electoral strength of Sinn Féin can be attributed to a more radical approach to housing policy, if not to homelessness. Despite the high priority which the electorate places on housing, this has not translated into a role in Government, so it is not possible to judge how the public service would respond to housing policies which break with tradition, or the impact of these on homelessness.

Homeless policy and the role of 'crisis'

We have discussed the effect of 'crisis thinking' in fragmenting a long-term understanding of Ireland's homeless problem and the responses to it, but the role of 'crisis' deserves further exploration. Ireland's housing and homeless story is punctuated by crisis events – particularly deaths – that become symbolic and, in some way, shape or colour the tone of public policy for years to come. A collapsing tenement, causing the death of citizens, was needed to precipitate a shift in policy not once but twice: first the collapse of Church Street in 1913 and then 50 years later on Bolton Street and Fenian

Street in 1963. The death of John Broderick in a Causal Ward in Thurles in 1988 finally led to the closure of such facilities after over 50 years of ineffectual policy decision. The deaths of three people sleeping rough in Dublin in December 1992 (Michael O'Mera, Pauline Leonard and Patsy Feery) during the negotiations that would result in the first Fianna Fáil/Labour Coalition contributed to the establishment of the Homeless Initiative, which later became the Homeless Agency. The death of Jonathan Corry in the street outside Leinster House in December 2014 shaped public and policy responses to homelessness in the following years.

One way of looking at these shifts would be to see them as dramatic correctives to neglectful policy-makers. In this view, Irish policy making is so sclerotic that it requires this sort of dramatic and symbolic event to deliver change: collapsing tenements (and men and, very occasionally, women dying on your streets) are nature's way of telling you that you are doing something wrong. Another way of looking at these crisis responses is that they lead to a lot of immediate activity, little of it deeply purposeful and some of it perverse.

The role of crises in the story of homelessness is paradoxical: without the regularly recurring homelessness crises, there would be little public policy attention to homelessness at all but when the crises do come along, enormous energy goes into responding only to the immediate issues, often in a way that has long-term negative effects: more emergency beds are promised. Homelessness does not get the close and persistent attention which is required to tackle its underlying causes because public policy is either in a panic over a crisis or indifferent because there is no crisis.

One striking example of this occurred at the end of the 1980s when the decline in housing waiting lists was not seen as an opportunity to move out of crisis mode and start some longer-term thinking about planning and housing delivery but rather as an opportunity to slow down housing construction. The social partnership agreement at the start of the 1990s gives the impression that it was an aspiration of Government to reduce social housing delivery, and the fact that it was possible to do so was to be welcomed: 'Significant reductions in the size of the local authority housing programme were possible in the mid and late 1980s as the numbers on local authority waiting lists fell from the peak level of 30,000 households in 1982' (PESP, 1991, 35). More recently, in 2019, this 'panic or ignore' dichotomy problem was dramatised by the then Chair of the Housing Agency who, while delivering a strong critique of homelessness being treated as a crisis, created controversy by insisting that it should instead be understood as 'normal'.

The impact of this crisis response is most clearly seen in the response to the death of people who are sleeping rough. Minister Emmet Stagg set the pattern in response to the aforementioned deaths in Dublin in 1992 by promising that no-one who was homeless would be left without a bed for the night and this has been repeated by virtually every housing Minister since. As the nights get longer and colder each year, Ministers repeatedly assure the Dáil that additional hostel beds will be put in place to ensure that no-one needs sleep on the street. The positive outcome of this recurring approach is that for most of the intervening time, a smaller proportion of people who are homeless sleep rough in Dublin and other Irish cities than in other comparable European cities (OECD, 2024). The negative outcome has been to make the provision of emergency beds, rather than homes, appear as the most appropriate response to homelessness. This is not just a governmental pre-occupation. A key demand of the radical protestors who took over Apollo House in late 2016, was more emergency beds and part of their response was to establish a new hostel. There is a strong case that policies driven by recurrent crises and deaths on the street resulted in an enlarged provision of emergency beds and a larger homeless sector rather than a deeper exploration of lasting solutions.

The role of partnership

As noted earlier, although the weakness in the data makes it difficult to be definitive, one of the most prolonged periods in which homelessness declined was the period characterised by local partnership from around 1993 until 2011. Ultimately, the objectives of ending long-term homelessness and the need to sleep rough by 2010 were derailed by the global economic crisis. But considerable progress was achieved before Government responses to the crash brought both progress and the partnership structures which had delivered it to an end. During the partnership period, The Homeless Agency uniquely had a direct reporting relationship to the Cabinet Sub-Committee on Social Inclusion, an important factor in terms of bringing the issues to Government Ministers and getting them to understand what the issues were and the need for joined-up responses. None of the various governmental arrangements since has demonstrated this strength of local collaboration and capacity to engage the Central Government.

Higgins (2001b) argues that the partnership approach found in the national strategies of 2000 and 2008 was adopted upwards from the successful approach of Dublin's Housing Initiative rather than seeing them as a sideways extension of the national social partnership approach. This might explain why the local partnership arrangement continued to operate for a time even after all the national structures of social partnership were put to the sword during the global economic crisis. But the endorsement from the national Government that had sustained them was gone. This partnership phase formally came to a close with the enactment of the *Housing Act (2009)* and the subsequent restructuring of the Homeless Agency into the Dublin Region Homeless Executive. The legislation, while further clarifying different roles of the State actors, brought them together under the auspices of the local authority rather than as partners in a shared structure.

One of the goals of this rebalancing of roles was to more closely link the provision of homelessness services with provision of housing. The change coincided with the full impact of the global crisis on housing, so it is impossible to know whether this policy goal would have been achieved in better circumstances. However, the diminished engagement with the health agencies was clear. While the 2009 legislation created a legal requirement for each region to convene a 'consultative forum' which was to include both the relevant statutory authorities and representatives from the NGO sector, the fora did not retain the 'partnership' ethos of the previous period and operated more as local authority meetings to which others were invited. Outside of Dublin, where some of the earlier ethos persisted, these bodies are rarely convened any more frequently than required to approve the three- or five-year regional strategy.

From what we can tell from the available data, this partnership period coincides with one of the lowest periods of homelessness as efforts were made to end long-term homelessness and the need to sleep rough by 2010, and the partnership collapse coincides with the start of the long decades-long rise in homelessness. However, a strong case can be made that it was the same economic crisis that swept away the social partnership which, via a range of economic and social decisions, was responsible for the rise in homelessness, and even retaining that ethos would not have prevented the deterioration that occurred. It is also true that the local partnership arrangements related to homelessness also involved some of the mutually self-interested fuzziness for which social partnership has been criticised – for instance while ending long-term homelessness was one of the core objectives of the period, it seemed to suit everyone that, in the data available at the time, there was no agreed way of measuring whether progress was being made or not. However, given the more robust data now available, and the stronger evidence on the causes and flow-patterns of homelessness, the value of this form of collaborative problem-solving might be one of the strongest lessons of the century.

Conclusion

The most recent decade of rapid and persistent rise in homelessness, in the context of a generalised housing crisis, can leave the impression that this is a century-long story of failure. Taking the longer view, it is important to recognise that there has been considerable progress in many respects – the accommodation provided to people who are homeless, despite continued shortcomings, are an improvement on the County Homes and hostels which dominated for most of the period; in most cases the staff working in homeless services are qualified in social care and the services are well regulated; we have a State-wide case management system, PASS, which allows the needs of each homeless person to be recorded, along with the responses to those needs; societies' understanding of homelessness is now less likely to focus on the perceived moral failure of the homeless person and to have a better grasp of the complex, structural factors that trigger and perpetuate homelessness. There have also been a number of more transformative successes: the Casual Wards in the County Homes were eventually closed; there are no more unaccompanied children on our streets; Housing First has cross-party support; and over 1,000 men and women who were formerly long-term homeless now have secure homes, with on-going support, as a result.

Nevertheless, the final chapters of this book leave Ireland with a level of homelessness and housing precarity which would have been unimaginable at any time in the past. The central thesis of this book has been that, while you may have to look at individual human frailties to understand *who* is homeless, you need to look at the housing system, and particularly the social housing system, to understand why *so many* people are homeless. We have also made a case that the question is not just the amount of social housing that is available, but how it is allocated. At present, every local authority allocates social housing on the basis of the length of time on the housing list, and none has a system to take into account the length of time a person is homeless. One of the conclusions that can be drawn from our analysis is that it would be possible to significantly reduce the level of long-term homelessness by better deployment of our existing housing stock, rather than leaving homelessness to be a problem only solved when we finally solve our much wider housing problems.

Finally, we make a strong case that the best outcomes were achieved during periods of genuine collaboration and partnership. As we have seen, a large proportion of people who become homeless only require an affordable place to live and will find their way out of homelessness with minimal or no help. For a significant minority, the range of different challenges they face, or have come to face while homeless, require an integration of different social services which do not normally work together. In tackling homelessness for this group with more complex support needs, partnership is not just a governance framework but is an essential part of everyday practice. At this point of unprecedented and almost overwhelming levels of homelessness, it is hard to see how we can return to an era of optimism that homelessness can be ended, but the evidence is strong that policies and priorities that informed that optimism were well-founded. Drawing out the lessons from the successes and failures of our first hundred years could put us back on a path to eradicate homelessness in the first decade after the centenary.

APPENDIX 1

Measuring homelessness in Ireland

Monthly reports

The PASS (Pathway Accommodation & Support System), established in Dublin as a bed management and client support system in 2011, was rolled out nationally in 2013, and this development allowed for data on the number of adult individuals with accompanying child dependents experiencing homelessness and residing in designated emergency accommodation funded by Section 10 of the *Housing Act, 1988* and local authority contributions during the third week of every month in each county to be generated on a monthly basis. The publication of these monthly reports commenced in April 2014 on a trial basis, and from June 2014, with some modifications, has been produced on a continuous monthly basis. Data is generated from PASS on the profile of households in the designated services by household composition, the gender, age and nature of accommodation provided for adults and the number of accompanying child dependents. In comparison with the quarterly performance reports, the monthly reports provide stock data on the number of adults, child dependents and households in a given week each month.

In comparative terms, using the European Typology of Homelessness and Housing Exclusion (ETHOS) as a framework, this monthly data provide provides information on category 2, people staying in a night shelter; and category 3, people in accommodation for the homeless and in 2014 only (see below), category 4, people in a women's shelter.

The monthly reports do not capture those using emergency or temporary shelters not funded by the local authorities, do not include all those rough sleeping, those in Section 10 funded long-term supported accommodation, or those in direct provision or households in insecure or inadequate accommodation. Only a small number of services with less than 200 beds nationally do not, for various reasons, receive, nor indeed seek Section 10 funding, and therefore are not included in the PASS data.

Data on the numbers sleeping rough or literally homeless is collected via a point-in-time or originally a one-night street count, and from the second half of 2020 a week-long street count, twice a year in Dublin (in March and November). Outside of Dublin, data is published in the quarterly performance reports (see later) on the number of rough sleepers at one-night point-in-time. Data from Dublin shows that the majority of those rough sleeping also use emergency shelters, so that a significant number are likely to be captured in the monthly reports.

On households in insecure or inadequate accommodation, data is collected via the Housing Needs Assessment, which was carried out by the local authorities on a bi-annual basis, and now annual basis. Among the categories of need for social housing support are 'unsuitable accommodation due to particular housing circumstances', 'reasonable requirement for separate accommodation', unsuitable accommodation due to exceptional medical or compassionate grounds, 'over-crowded accommodation' and 'unfit accommodation'. In the annual assessments conducted between 2016 and 2024, on average 35,600 households were assessed as being in these categories.

The monthly reports do not include persons in long-term supported accommodation but funded via Section 10. Census data in 2011 identified 992 individuals in such long-term supported accommodation, with the 2016 Census identifying 1,772 individuals. The 2022 Census did not collect data on those in long-term supported accommodation by agreement with the Census Homeless Methodology Liaison Group.

The monthly reports also do not include persons who are in Direct Provision Centres (DPCs) provided by the International Protection Accommodation Service who have been granted refugee status or leave to remain in Ireland, but are unable to exit direct provision due to their inability to secure rental accommodation. At the end of June 2024, there were 5,500 such persons in Direct Provision Centres, or 18 per cent of the overall number in DPCs (Dáil Éireann Debate, Wednesday – 10 July 2024).

Modifications to the monthly reports
Removal of refuges in January 2015

From 1 January 2015, accommodation or refuges for those escaping from gender-based violence (ETHOS category 4) was funded via Section 10: a total of 21 residential services with a bed capacity of approximately 250, with annual funding of just over €2.1m was transferred to the statutory Child and Family Agency (TUSLA), and those accessing these residential services have not been enumerated in the monthly data since that date. This was the result of a recommendation from the Homelessness Oversight Group (2013, 23):

> such refuges are not homeless emergency accommodation and would prefer to see both a discrete funding stream and separate reporting for the provision of State support to the accommodation needs of persons experiencing domestic violence. This would seem to appropriately reside within the scope of the recently established Child and Family Agency. We recommend therefore that existing funding arrangements

for the provision of refuge accommodation and services would be transferred to the Child and Family Agency.

The Policy and Procedural Guidance for Housing Authorities in Relation to Assisting Victims of Domestic Violence with Emergency and Long-term Accommodation Needs states that

> It is a matter for Tusla to monitor women's refuges in terms of capacity, usage, through flow, etc. The official monthly homeless data published by this Department and produced by housing authorities via the Pathway Accommodation & Support System (PASS) relates to the State-funded emergency accommodation arrangements that are overseen by housing authorities only. PASS is not operational in the refuge sector. (2017, 3)

To date, the Child and Family Agency has not published data on a monthly basis on the number and characteristics of those accessing such residential services. The Census of 2022 recorded 325 adults and children in such accommodation. The absence of this data results in an underestimate of the number of women experiencing homelessness and the consequences of domestic violence in women's journeys into homelessness (Mayock and Neary, 2021; Mayock et al, 2012).

Re-categorisation of households March, April and July 2018

In March 2018, 253 adults accommodated 'in houses and apartments' who had hitherto been included in the monthly data were excluded, and in April a further 121 adults were excluded on the same basis that they were not in emergency accommodation, giving a total of 374 adults. Following further investigations by the Department of Housing, 'further cases of houses and apartments being recorded as emergency accommodation' were identified, containing a further 251 adults, giving an overall total of 625 adults (with 981 accompanying child dependents) excluded for the monthly reports. On 27 September 2018, a note was prepared by the Homelessness and Housing Supports Unit in the Department of Housing summarising the re-categorisations.

Introduction of PASS 2

PASS was upgraded in June 2021 and monthly reports based on the upgraded system commenced in July 2021. From July onwards, dependents in families aged over 18 are classified as adults rather than child dependents as was previously the case. Thus, the increase in the number of adults aged 18–25 from July 2021 is largely attributable to this change.

Quarterly performance reports

From January 2014 onwards, at the end of each quarter, local authorities were required by the Department of Housing to produce performance reports providing flow data on a range of indicators: this included the number of new and repeat adult presentations to homelessness services per quarter; the number of adults in emergency accommodation for more than six months; the number of adult individuals exiting temporary and emergency accommodation to tenancies in the local authority sector, Approved Housing Bodies or private rented sector (including those in receipt of the Housing Assistance Payment) with, or without support; and in cases, as discussed above, the number of rough sleepers.

Quarterly financial reports

Local authorities are required to produce detailed quarterly financial reports outlining the distribution of Central Government and local authority funding on preventative actions, emergency and long-term supported accommodation, and other services for those experiencing homelessness. The reports also provide data on the distribution of this expenditure to NGO and private sector providers of the range of services listed above. These reporting requirements arose from the issuing of a Protocol Governing Delegation of Section 10 Funding for Homeless Services to Local Authorities.

Local authorities must make a contribution of a minimum of 10 per cent of the cost of providing services for those experiencing homelessness. Expenditure by local authorities drawing on Department of Housing funding and their own funding streams is captured under the heading 'A05 Administration of Homeless Service' in the Local Authority Revenue Budgets.

APPENDIX 2

Recent trends in homelessness in Ireland in comparative perspective

Although estimates have been published on the approximation of the extent of homelessness in Europe, it is also recognised that such approximations need to be treated with caution given the variations in definitions and methodologies in enumerating homelessness in Member States (for example Horvat and Coupechoux, 2024, 18). At a basic level, we know that, for example, a one-year *period-prevalence* measure of homelessness will be several times as large as a one-night *point-prevalence* estimate. Thus, for example, the number of people who enter and exit emergency accommodation over a one-year period will be far higher than those counted over a one-night or one-week timepoint and the profile of those monitored over a one-year period will be different from those monitored at a particular point-in-time.

Figure A.1 shows trends in the number of households experiencing homelessness based largely on point-in-time or point prevalence (and flow data or period-prevalence in the case of Austria) in several European countries where relatively consistent time-series data exists. Given the diverse definitions used in measuring homelessness across these countries (that span the dimensions of ETHOS Light), their diverse data sources (from administrative sources to survey data), varying temporal dimensions and differing units of analysis (from individual adults, adults and child dependents or households) (see Baptista and Marlier, 2019; Develtere, 2022; Dubois and Nivakoski, 2023; OECD, 2024), the time-series data below are presented as an index designed to identify comparative trends rather than absolute numbers.

It shows four clusters: i) countries that have seen substantial increases in the last decade (Ireland, England and Scotland); ii) countries that have seen relative stability (Austria and Denmark); iii) two countries that experienced increases between 2008 and 2018 but have seen a recent decrease (the Netherlands and Sweden); and iv) countries that have achieved significant long-term reductions (Norway and Finland).

There are a small number of countries where it is possible to identify more long-term trends using comparable, consistent time-series data, namely Denmark, Finland and Ireland (Allen et al, 2020). Figure A.2 shows trends in the number of households in temporary and emergency accommodation over the period 2008–2024 (excluding households staying with family and friends), while Figure A.3 provides trends on the number of households in

Appendix 2

Figure A.1: Index of homelessness at a point-in-time in selected countries, 2008–2024

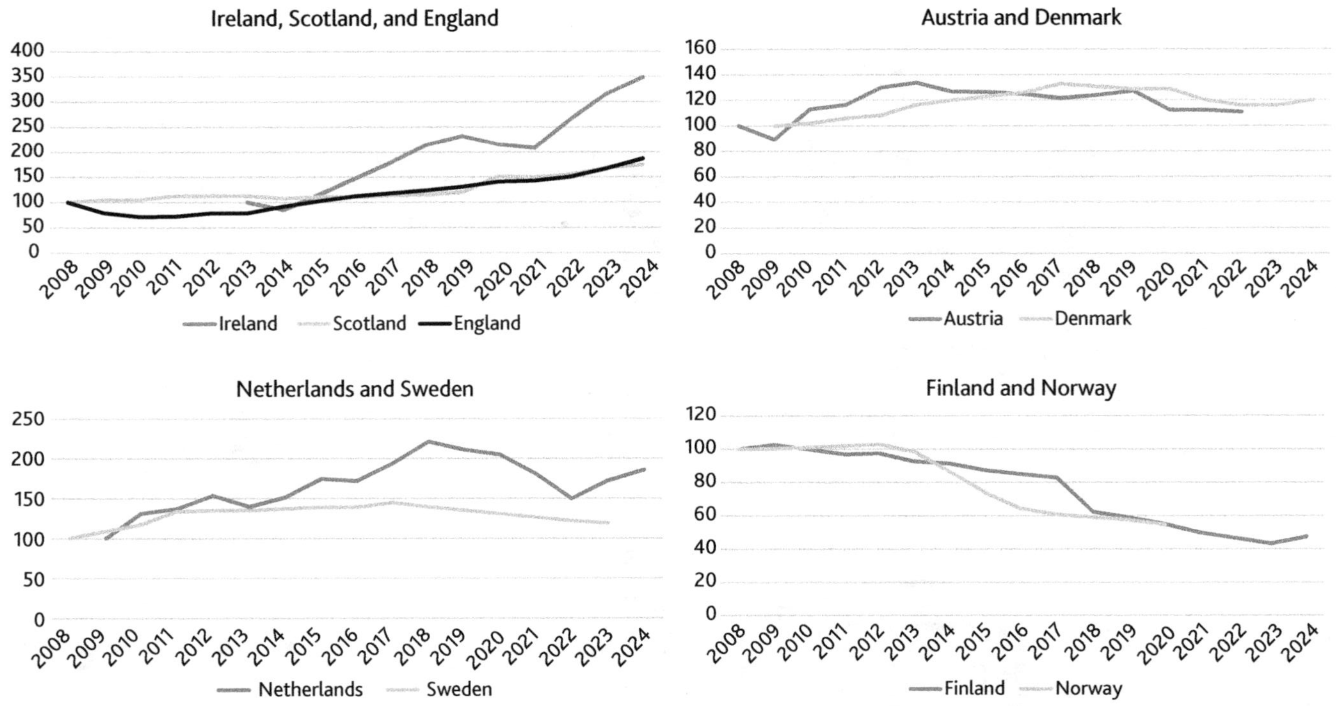

Figure A.2: Households experiencing homelessness and staying in temporary and emergency accommodation in Denmark, Finland and Ireland, 2008–2024

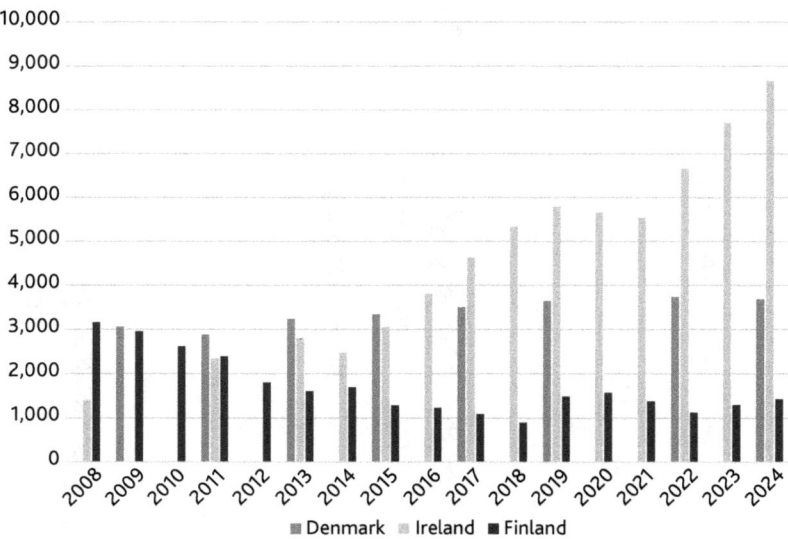

Figure A.3: Households experiencing homelessness and staying in temporary and emergency accommodation in Denmark, Finland and Ireland per 1,000 households, 2008–2024

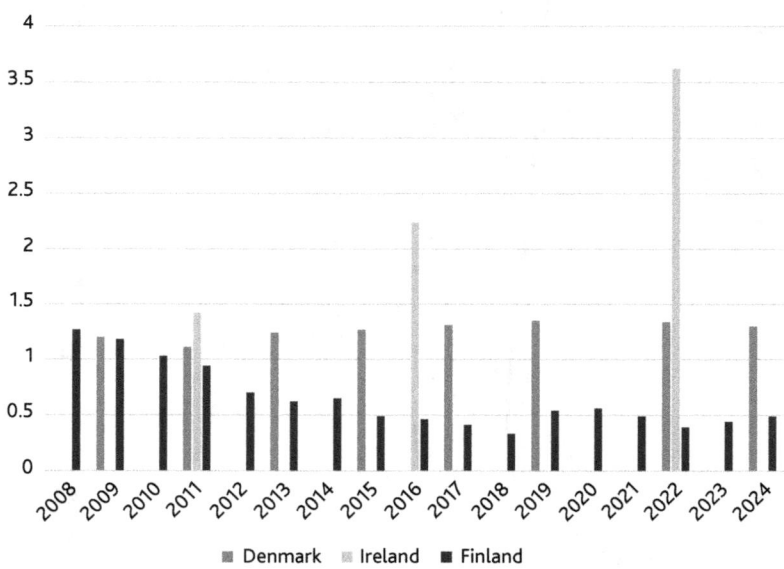

emergency accommodation per 1,000 households. These data show that both the absolute number of households in emergency accommodation and the number relative to the overall number of households in the population consistently declined in Finland, remained broadly stable in Denmark and grew rapidly in Ireland. Several explanations for these divergent trends are explored in Allen et al (2020), but their central conclusion was the importance of an adequate supply of secure, affordable housing, that is, secure occupancy (encompassing both security of tenure and rent certainty) in both, preventing entries to homelessness in the first instance and ensuring rapid exits for those that entered homelessness.

Notes

Chapter 1

1. This helps explain the difficulty encountered by comparative scholars on welfare regimes in classifying Ireland. Indeed, in the one of the most recent analyses of the comparative performances of welfare regimes, Headey, Muffels and Quiggin (2023) deal with Ireland in a separate appendix to the main book because in their view Ireland 'more or less defies classification' with attempts to-date differing 'almost comically' (2023, 183).
2. By 1950, there were 57,549 persons in receipt of home assistance, with 23,077 in country homes, county hospitals and other public institutions, including approved external institutions (with 8,585 in the County Homes only), compared with 21,650 recipients of home assistance in 1924–1925 and 18,113 in Poor Law institutions.
3. Duff was also largely responsible for drafting the aforementioned Land Act, 1923 when he worked in the Department of Lands, Agriculture and Fisheries between 1922 and 1924 (Kennedy, 2011, 71–73).
4. Commission on the Relief of the Poor – Statement of Evidence of Mr. F. Duff – the Problem of the 'Down and Out'. Oireachtas Library, Dublin.
5. The members of the Board were Michael P. Colivet, Senator Thomas Johnson and Michael J. Buckley. Buckley was a senior engineer in Dublin City Council; Johnson was a former leader of the Irish Labour Party and Colivet was a former Sinn Féin politician and civil servant.

Chapter 2

1. Department of An Taoiseach S14474 N/2. A similar account was also provided by the Chief Medical Officer that that time, Dr James Deeney, who in his autobiography describes the inmates as including 'old unmarried uncles who had become a nuisance, grocer's "curates" who had become alcoholics, unmarried old women without support, a vast hoard of old people, many crippled with arthritis, often demented through malnutrition and hardship, lonely miserable and hungry ... [t]o see a poor old man just admitted and given a bowl of milk and rice and to see him lift it to his face and devour it like a dog, shook you, because you suddenly realised he was starving' (1989, 148).

Chapter 3

1. NAI, Department of the Taoiseach 96/6/515 County Homes Reconstruction and Replacement.
2. The Dennehys squatted in 20 Mountjoy Square in late 1968, a property owned by a well-known property owner, Ivor Underwood, and when Dennis Dennehy refused to comply with a court order to vacate the property he was imprisoned in early January 1969 in nearby Mountjoy prison, where he went on hunger strike until he was released in late January.
3. To add to the motley crew described by Keenan-Thomson, the author of the first article in the 2nd edition of *Crisis*, in a piece entitled *Housing 1969*, was Staf Van Velthoven, an architect and later prominent member of Sinn Féin the Workers Party (SFWP). However, Van Velthoven had arrived in Ireland in October 1948 under the name of Michael van Houle, as he was evading a death sentence which was imposed on him in absentia in Belgium for collaboration with the Nazi's in his role as an *Oostfronter* – a member 'of the Waffen-SS and its fight against communism on the Eastern Front' (Leach, 2009, 157).
4. Of the 14 shelters identified in 1971 in Dublin, eight were still operating in 2024.

Notes

5   Established in the early 1970s, the functions of the National Economic and Social Council are to analyse and report to the Taoiseach (Prime Minister) on strategic issues relating to the efficient development of the economy, the achievement of social justice and the development of a strategic framework for the conduct of relations and the negotiation of agreements between the government and the social partners.
6   Other Simon Communities were established in Waterford and Limerick but only operated for a short period of time.
7   The Rent Tribunal was dissolved in 2016, and its functions were transferred to the Residential Tenancies Board.

Chapter 4

1   The material contained in this section are based on the file – reference number, Department of the Taoiseach 2023/1/194 – *Housing (Miscellaneous Provisions) Bill, 1985 and Housing Act, 1988* held in the National Archives of Ireland.
2   However, the offence of begging remaining on the Statute book until the relevant sections of the *Vagrancy (Ireland) Act 1847* were deemed inconsistent with the Constitution in a successful case taken to the High Court in 2007 (Whyte, 2020). In response to this High Court ruling, the *Criminal Justice (Public Order) Act, 2011* re-criminalised begging in certain circumstances, and in recent years approximately 300–400 incidents of begging are recorded per annum by the Garda Siochana.
3   The only exceptions are the two shelters managed by the Legion of Mary in Dublin, which are located in part of what was the North Dublin Union workhouse complex.

Chapter 5

1   As part of the statutory Assessment of Housing Needs in 1989, 987 households, the majority one-person households, were assessed as homeless, but this figure only included those local authority waiting lists. This decision to include those homeless persons who were not on the local authority waiting list was a commitment given in the Programme for Economic and Social Progress (1991, 36).
2   The Homeless Initiative was replaced by the Homeless Agency in 2000 which in turn was replaced by the Dublin Region Homeless Executive in 2011. The Homeless Initiative was largely focused on coordination, with the Homeless Agency more focused on addressing homelessness. One important facet of the Homeless Agency in the context of social partnership was that the Agency reported directly into the Cabinet Sub-Committee on Social Inclusion, an important factor in terms of bringing the issues directly to Government Ministers.

Chapter 6

1   The 20 per cent figure was reinstated in 2021 under the *Affordable Housing Act 2021*.
2   In addition, although not discussed in this chapter, a *Youth Homelessness Strategy* was published in 2001.
3   This funding criteria was originally devised by the Homeless Initiative (2000) and applied in the greater Dublin region.

Chapter 8

1   A 'confidence and supply' arrangement is when a party or independent members of a parliament agree to support the government in motions of confidence and appropriation votes.
2   Rapid build housing utilises modular house building technology to expand council house building at faster rates and lower costs than traditional bricks and mortar building yet can provide long-term housing.

3   A special Cabinet Committee on Housing, chaired by the Taoiseach was also established to oversee both the development and the implementation of this Action Plan. Monthly updates on housing activity were also set to be published and overall progress reports on the plan have been published on a quarterly basis.
4   Further units were provided via leasing or Part 5.
5   For a full comparison between the Oireachtas Committee recommendations and Rebuilding Ireland policy, see Appendix 2 of Rebuilding Ireland, pp 107–111.
6   https://www.facebook.com/john.curranFF/videos/governments-housing-plan-rebuilding-ireland-epic-failure-for-9104-homeless-peopl/802252346642129/
7   NAMA (National Assets Management Agency) appointed receivers in March 2014 due to outstanding loans of around €370 m. The building had been vacant for some time due to its poor condition. During a High Court hearing in December 2016, barristers for the receivers said there were serious health and safety concerns as the building was not suitable for residential use and had no fire insurance cover.
8   The RTB's main functions are to regulate the rental sector; provide information and research to inform policy; maintain a national register of tenancies; resolve disputes between tenants and landlords; initiate investigations into conduct by a landlord; and provide information to the public to ensure tenancies run smoothly and no issues arise.

Conclusion

1   For example, it was reported that a competitive tender to provide the Dublin region Housing First service was won by the Peter McVerry Trust at what later emerged to be a lower price than required to deliver the service (Hubert 2024), contributing to financial problems in the Trust several years later as a noted in Chapter 9.

References

Aalen, F. H. A. (1990) *The Iveagh Trust: The First Hundred Years, 1890–1990*. Iveagh Trust.

Aalen, F. H. A. (1992) Ireland. In Pooley, C. G. (Ed) *Housing Strategies in Europe, 1880–1930*. Leicester University Press.

Acheson, N., Harvey, B., Kearney, J. and Williamson, A. (2004) *Two Paths, One Purpose: Voluntary Action in Ireland, North and South*. Institute of Public Administration.

Allen, M. (1998) *The Bitter Word: Ireland's Job Famine and its Aftermath*. Poolbeg Press.

Allen, M., Benjaminsen, L., O'Sullivan, E. and Pleace, N. (2020) *Ending Homelessness? The Contrasting Experiences of Denmark, Finland and Ireland*, Policy Press and University of Chicago Press.

Allen, M. and Byrne, E. (2023) Housing First and Structural Change in Ireland. *European Journal of Homelessness* 17(2): 125–136.

Altena, M. (2020) *National Covid-19 Homeless Service User Experience Survey*. Health Service Executive National Social Inclusion Office.

Althammer, B. (2014) Transnational Expert Discourse on Vagrancy around 1900. In Althammer, B., Gestrich, A. and Grundler, J. (Eds) *The Welfare State and the 'Deviant Poor' in Europe, 1870–1933*. Palgrave Macmillan.

Anonymous (1940) I Live in a Slum. *The Bell* 1(2): 46–48.

Approved Housing Bodies Regulatory Authority (2024) *Section 47 Inspectors' Report – Peter McVerry Trust Company Limited by Guarantee*. Approved Housing Bodies Regulatory Authority.

Arensberg, C. (1937) *The Irish Countryman: An Anthropological Study*. Macmillan and Co.

Bairead, C. and Norris, M. (2020) *Youth Homelessness in the Dublin Region: A Profile of Young, Single Emergency Accommodation Users in 2016, 2017, and 2018*. Focus Ireland.

Baker, T. (1984) Housing – Market or Social Service. *Economic and Social Research Institute Public Expenditure – Value for Money*, Papers presented at a conference 20 November 1984, pp 85–98.

Baker, T. J. and O'Brien, L. M. (1979) *The Irish Housing System: A Critical Overview*. Economic and Social Research Institute.

Baptista, I. and Marlier, E. (2019) *Fighting Homelessness and Housing Exclusion in Europe: A Study of National Policies*. European Commission.

Baptista, I., Benjaminsen, L. and Pleace, N. (2015) *Local Connection Rules and Access to Homelessness Services in Europe*. European Observatory on Homelessness.

Barbieri, B. and Bewley, G. (2022) *An Experimental Historical Spending Dataset for Ireland. Irish Fiscal Advisory Council – Analytical Note No. 15.* Irish Fiscal Advisory Council.

Bardas Atha Cliath (1992) *Report of the Working Group on Homeless*, Report No. 360/1992.

Bardas Atha Cliath/Eastern Health Board (1995) *Review of Service Provision for the Homeless in the Dublin Region.* Report to the Department of the Environment and the Department of Health.

Barnes, J. (1989) *Irish Industrial Schools 1868–1908.* Irish Academic Press.

Barrett, R. M. (1884) *Guide to Dublin Charities.* Hodges Figgis.

Barry, F. (2024) A Reappraisal of Cumann na nGaedheal's Economic Policy. *Irish Political Studies* 19(2): 139–191.

Bartlett, T. (2002) Church and State in Modern Ireland, 1923–1970: An appraisal reappraised. In Bradshaw, B. and Keogh, D. (Eds) *Christianity in Ireland: Revisiting the Story.* Columba Press.

Bell, J. (1989) *Women and Children First, A Report by the National Campaign for the Homeless on Homeless Women and Their Children in Dublin.* National Campaign for the Homeless.

Bermingham, W. and O'Cuanaigh, L. (1978) *ALONE – An Account of Some Old People Discovered in Dublin in 1978.* ALONE.

Bhreatnach, A. (2006) *Becoming Conspicuous: Irish Travellers, Society and the State 1922–70.* UCD Press.

Binchy, H. (1967) The Role of Voluntary Agencies. Christus Rex – *Journal of Sociology* 21(3): 253–260.

Blackwell, J. (1987) *Housing Policy as Related to Marginal Groups.* Research and Environmental Policy Centre, UCD, Working Paper No. 39.

Blackwell, J. (1990) Housing Finance and Subsidies in Ireland. In Maclennan, D. and R. Williams (Eds) *Affordable Housing in Europe* (York: Joseph Rowntree Foundation).

Boyle, R., Butler-Worth, M. and O'Donnell, O. (2001) *Homeless Initiative – Final Evaluation Report.* Institute of Public Administration.

Brady, J. (2016) *Dublin, 1950–1970: Houses, Flats and High Rises.* Four Courts Press.

Braga, M., Corno, L. and Monti, P. (2024) *Homelessness: Data, Prevalence and Features.* Bocconi University Press.

Breathnach, C. (2005) *The Congested Districts Board of Ireland, 1891–1923: Poverty and Development in the West of Ireland.* Four Courts Press.

Brennan, C. (2017) Not One Person Left Behind. *The Journal*, 11 January 2017. Available at: https://jrnl.ie/3181178

Brennan, D. (2014) *Irish Insanity: 1800–2000.* Routledge.

Bretherton, J. and Mayock, P. (2024) Women and Homelessness. In Johnson, G., Culhane, D., Fitzpatrick, S., Metraux, S. and O'Sullivan, E. (Eds) *Research Handbook on Homelessness.* Edward Elgar.

References

Browne, N. (1986) *Against the Tide*. Gill and Macmillan.

Brownlee, A. (2008) The Changing Homeless Policy Landscape: Paradise Lost and Found. In Downey, D. (Ed) *Perspectives on Irish Homelessness: Past, Present and Future*. Homeless Agency.

Brundage, A. (2002) *The English Poor Laws, 1700–1930*. Palgrave.

Burke, H. (1987) *The People and the Poor Law in 19th Century Ireland*. Women's Educational Bureau.

Burns, M., Drudy, P. J., Hearne, R. and McVerry, P. (2017) Rebuilding Ireland: A Flawed Philosophy. *Working Notes – Housing*. Jesuit Centre for Faith and Justice. [Online]. Available at: https://www.jcfj.ie/article/rebuilding-ireland-a-flawed-philosophy-analysis-of-the-action-plan-for-housing-and-homelessness/

Burns, S. (2023, 16 January) Many Hotels Are Accommodating Ukrainian Refugees Set to Return to Tourism from March. *The Irish Times*. Available at: https://www.irishtimes.com/ireland/2023/01/16/quite-a-number-of-hotels-accommodating-ukrainian-refugees-plan-to-return-to-tourism-in-march/

Busch-Geertsema, V. (2014) Housing First Europe – Results of a European Social Experimentation Project. *European Journal of Homelessness* 8: 13–28.

Butler, S. (1991) Drug Problems and Drug Policies in Ireland: A Quarter of a Century Reviewed. *Administration* 39(3): 2010–2233.

Byrne, M. and McArdle, R. (2022) Secure Occupancy, Power and the Landlord-Tenant Relation: A Qualitative Exploration of the Irish Private Rental Sector. *Housing Studies* 37(1): 124–142.

Byrne, M. and Norris, M. (2018) Procyclical Social Housing and the Crisis of Irish Housing Policy: Marketization, Social Housing, and the Property Boom and Bust. *Housing Policy Debate* 28(1): 50–63.

Byrne, M. and Norris, M. (2022) Housing Market Financialization, Neoliberalism and Everyday Retrenchment of Social Housing. *Economy and Space* 54(1): 182–198.

Byrne, M. and Sassi, J. (2023) Making and Unmaking Home in the COVID-19 Pandemic: A Qualitative Research Study of the Experience of Private Rental Tenants in Ireland. *International Journal of Housing Policy* 23(3): 523–542.

Cahill, N. (2020) *The Implications of COVID-19 for Housing in Ireland – NEXC Secretariat Covid-19 Working Paper Series*. National Economic and Social Council.

Capital Investment Advisory Committee (1957) *Second Report*. Stationery Office.

Carey, S. (2005) Land, Labour and Politics: Social Insurance in Post-War Ireland. *Social Policy and Society* 4(3): 303–311.

Carey, S. (2007) *Social Security in Ireland 1939–1953: The Limits to Solidarity*. Irish Academic Press.

Carlson, H. (1990) Women and Homelessness in Ireland. *The Irish Journal of Psychology* 11(1): 68–76.

Carroll, L. (2011) *In the Fever King's Preserves: Sir Charles Cameron and the Dublin Slums*. A&A Farmar.

Central Bank of Ireland (2013) *Residential Mortgage Arrears and Repossessions Statistics – Q3 & Q4, 2013*. Central Bank of Ireland.

Central Bank of Ireland (2014) *Residential Mortgage Arrears and Repossessions Statistics – Q3 & Q4, 2014*. Central Bank of Ireland.

Central Statistics Office (2012) *Census 2011 Profile 4 The Roof Over Our Heads – Housing in Ireland*. Central Statistics Office.

Central Statistics Office (2017) *Census 2016 Results Profile 5 – Homeless Persons in Ireland*. Central Statistics Office.

Central Statistics Office (2020) *Social Housing in Ireland 2019 – Analysis of Housing Assistance Payment (HAP) Scheme*. CSO. [Online].

Central Statistics Office (2023a) Population and Migration Estimates, April 2023. [Online]. Available at: https://www.cso.ie/en/releasesandpublications/ep/p-pme/populationandmigrationestimatesapril2023/keyfindings/

Central Statistics Office (2023b) *Arrivals from Ukraine in Ireland Series 11*. [Online]. Available at: https://www.cso.ie/en/releasesandpublications/fp/p-aui/arrivalsfromukraineinirelandseries11/

Central Statistics Office (2024) *Population and Migration Estimates, April 2024*. Central Statistics Office.

Central Statistics Office (2025) *Residential Property price Index December 2024*. Central Statistics Office.

Charities Regulatory Authority (2024) *Peter McVerry Trust CLG – Investigation Report*. Charities Regulatory Authority.

Citizens Housing Council (1938) *Report on Slum Clearance in Dublin*. Cahill and Co.

Clear, C. (1997) Homelessness, Crime, Punishment and Poor Relief in Galway 1850–1914: An Introduction. *Galway Archaeological and Historical Society Journal* 50: 118–134.

Clear, C. (2007) *Social Change and Everyday Life in Ireland*. Manchester University Press.

Coates, D. and Norris, M. (1996) Local Authority Housing Rents: Equity, Affordability and Effectiveness. *Administration* 54(2): 3–26.

Coates, D. and Norris, M. (2006) *Supplementary Welfare Allowance, Rent Supplement: Implications for the Implementation of the Rental Accommodation Scheme*. Centre for Housing Research.

Colemen, U. (1990) *It's Simon: The Story of the Dublin Simon Community*. Glendale Press.

Colivet, M. P. (1954/55) The Housing Board. *Administration* 2(3): 83–86.

Collins, B. and McKeown, K. (1992) *Referral and Resettlement in the Simon Community*. Dublin Simon Community (National Office).

Collins, J. (1942–1943) Public Assistance, in Irish Social Services: A Symposium. *Journal of the Statistical and Social Inquiry Society of Ireland* 27: 110–115.

Collis, R. (1943) *Marrowbone Lane*. Runa Press.

Commission on Emigration and other Population Problems (1954) *Report*. Stationery Office.

Committee on Housing and Homelessness (2016) *Report of the Committee on Housing and Homelessness*. Houses of the Oireachtas.

Conden, C. (1963) *Local Inquiry at City Hall, Dublin 24th June 1963 to 5th July 1963*. National Archives of Ireland. Department of an Taoiseach S17486/63.

Connell, P. (2023) A Partition …: Making of it a Kitchen and a Bedroom': Working Class Housing in Irish provincial Towns in the Late Nineteenth Century. In Laird, H. and Roszman, J. R. (Eds) *Dwelling(s) in Nineteenth-Century Ireland*. Liverpool University Press.

Connolly, T. (2004) The Commission on Emigration, 1948–1954. In Keogh, D., O'Shea, F. and Quinlan, C. (Eds) *The Lost Decade: Ireland in the 1950s*. Mercier Press.

Corlett, C. (2008) *Darkest Dublin: The Story of the Church Street Disaster and a Pictorial Account of the Slums of Dublin in 1913*. Wordwell in association with the Royal Society of Antiquaries of Ireland.

Costello, L. (2000) *A Feasibility Study on the Provision of Accommodation for Homeless Street Drinkers*. Homeless Agency.

Costello, L. and Howley, D. (1999) *Under Dublin's Neon: A Report on Street Drinkers in Dublin*. CentreCare.

Coughlan, J. R. (1950) *The Law of Rent Restriction in Ireland*, 2nd edition. Dollard.

Coughlan, J. R. (1979) *The Law of Rent Restriction in Ireland*, 3rd edition. Dollard.

Cousins, M. (1999) The Introduction of Children's Allowances in Ireland 1939–1944. *Irish Economic and Social History* 24: 35–53.

Cousins, M. (2003) *The Birth of Social Welfare in Ireland 1922–1952*. Four Courts Press.

Cousins, M. (2005) *Explaining the Irish Welfare State: An Historical, Comparative, and Political Analysis*. Edwin Mellon Press.

Cousins, M. (2011) *Poor Relief in Ireland, 1851–1914*. Peter Lang.

Cousins, M. (2015) Philanthropy and Poor Relief Before the Poor Law, 1801–30. In Geary, L. M. and Walsh, O. (Eds) *Philanthropy in Nineteenth-Century Ireland*. Four Courts Press.

Cousins, M. (2016) The Irish Social Protection System: Change in Comparative Context. In Murphy, M. P. and Dukelow, F. (Eds) *The Irish Welfare State in the Twenty-First Century*. Palgrave Macmillan, pp 37–65.

Crossman, V. (2006a) *The Poor Law in Ireland 1838–1948*. Dundalgan Press.

Crossman, V. (2006b) *Politics, Pauperism and Power in Late Nineteenth-Century Ireland*. Manchester University Press.

Crossman, V. (2013) *Poverty and the Poor Law in Ireland, 1850–1914*. Liverpool University Press.

Crossman, V. (2018a) Attitudes and Responses to Vagrancy in Ireland in the Long Nineteenth Century. In Hughes, K. and MacRaid, D. (Eds) *Crime, Violence and the Irish in the Nineteenth Century*. Liverpool University Press, pp 264–279.

Crossman, V. (2018b) The Growth of the State in the Nineteenth Century. In Kelly, J. (Ed) *The Cambridge History of Ireland, Part IV – Shaping Society*. Cambridge University Press.

Crowson, N. J. (2013) Revisiting the 1977 Housing (Homeless Persons) Act: Westminster, Whitehall, and the Homelessness Lobby. *Twentieth Century British History* 24(3): 424–447.

Crowther, M. A. (1992) The Tramp. In Porter, R. (Ed) *Myths of the English*. Polity Press, pp 91–113.

Cullen, F. (2011) The Provision of Working-and Lower-middle-class Housing in Late Nineteenth-century Urban Ireland. *Proceedings of the Royal Irish Academy: Archaeology, Culture, History, Literature* 111c: 217–251.

Curtis, C. (2024) The Irish Agricultural labourer, the State and the Legacy of Peasant Proprietorship, 1922–76. In Dooley, T., McCarthy, T. and Tindley, A. (Eds) *Land Reform and Legislation in Ireland, 1800–2024*. Four Courts Press.

Curtis, M. (2008) *The Splendid Cause: The Catholic Action Movement in the Twentieth Century*. Original Writings.

Dáil Eireann (1986) *Ninth Report of the Select Committee on Crime, Lawlessness and Vandalism: Report on Certain Offences Under the Vagrancy Acts*. Stationery Office.

Dáil Eireann (1920) *Commission of Enquiry into Local Government*. Department of Local Government.

Dalton, R. J. (1945) The Slum Problem in Cork. In McCarthy, B. G. (Ed) *Some Problems of Child Welfare*. Cork University Press.

Daly, A., Lovett, H. and E. Lynn (2025) *Activities of Irish Psychiatric Units and Hospitals 2024*. Health Research Board.

Daly, M. (1990) New Perspectives on Homelessness. In Blackwell, J., Harvey, B., Higgins, M. and Walsh, J. (Eds) *Housing, Moving into Crisis*. National Campaign for The Homeless/Combat Poverty Agency.

Daly, M. (2005) Recasting the Story of Ireland's Miracle: Policy, Politics or Profit. In Becker, U. and Schwartz, H. (Eds) *Employment Miracles: A Critical Comparison of the Dutch, Scandinavian, Swiss, Australian and Irish Cases versus Germany and the US*. Amsterdam University Press.

Daly, M. (2019a) Ireland: The Welfare State and the Crisis. In Ólafsson, S., Daly, M., Kangas, O. and J. Palme (Eds) *Welfare and the Great Recession: A Comparative Study*. Oxford University Press.

References

Daly, M. (2019b) *National Strategies to Fight Homelessness and Housing Exclusion– Ireland*. European Social Policy Network and European Commission.

Daly, M. E. (1984) *Dublin: The Deposed Capital. A Social and Economic History 1860–1914*. Cork University Press.

Daly, M. E. (1992) *Industrial Development and Irish National Identity, 1922– 1939*. Syracuse University Press.

Daly, M. E. (1997) *The Buffer State: The Historical Roots of the Department of the Environment*. Institute of Public Administration.

Daly, M. E. (2006) *The Slow Failure: Population Decline and Independent Ireland, 1920–1973*. University of Wisconsin Press.

Daly, M. E. (2016) *Sixties Ireland: Reshaping the Economy, State and Society, 1957–1973*. Cambridge University Press.

Dawson, C. (1906) Suggested Substitutes for the Present Poor Law System. *Journal of the Statistical and Social Inquiry Society of Ireland* 11(86): 428–438.

De Blacam, M. (1984) *The Control of Private Rented Dwellings*. Round Hall Press.

De Bromhead, A. and Lyons, R. C. (2023) Social Housing and the Spread of Population: Evidence from twentieth century Ireland. *Journal of Urban Economics* 138: 1–18.

Deeny, J. (1989) *To Cure and to Care: Memoirs of a Chief Medical Officer*. Glendale Press.

Delaney, E. (2005) Emigration, Political Cultures and the Evolution of Post-war Irish Society. In Girvin, B. and Murphy, G. (Eds) *The Lemass Era: Politics and Society in the Ireland of Sean Lemass*. University College Dublin Press, pp 49–65.

Delany, A. P. (1930) The Improvement of the County Home. In *Report of the Conference between the Department of Local Government and Public Health and Representatives of Local Public Health and Public Assistance Authorities held at the Mansion House, Dublin on the 8th and 9th July*, 1930. Department of Local Government.

Department of Children, Equality, Disability, Integration and Youth (2024) *Statistics on International Protection Applicants Not Offered Accommodation*. Department of Children, Equality, Disability, Integration and Youth.

Department of the Environment (1989) Report 1988. Stationery Office.

Department of Environment, Community and Local Government (2010) *National Survey of Ongoing Housing Developments*. DECLG.

Department of Environment, Community and Local Government (2013) *Homelessness Policy Statement*. DECLG.

Department of Environment, Community and Local Government (2014) *Social Housing Strategy 2020*. Available at: https://assets.gov.ie/static/documents/social-housing-strategy-2020-9a5940ae-1de8-4453-839f-fb81bd2244b3.pdf

Department of Environment, Community and Local Government (2014a) *Implementation Plan on the State's Response to Homelessness*. Department of the Environment, Community and Local Government.
Department of Environment, Community and Local Government (2014b) *Action Plan to Address Homelessness*. Department of the Environment, Community and Local Government.
Department of Environment, Community and Local Government (2015) *Stabilising Rents, Boosting Supply*. DECLG.
Department of Environment, Heritage and Local Government (2007) *Delivering Homes, Sustaining Communities*. Department of Environment, Heritage and Local Government.
Department of Environment and Local Government, Department of Health and Children, Department of Education and Science (2002) *Homeless Preventative Strategy: A Strategy to Prevent Homelessness: Patients Leaving Hospital and Mental Health Care, Adult Prisoners and Young Offenders Leaving Custody and Young People Leaving Care*. Stationery Office.
Department of Finance (1958a) *Economic Development*. Stationery Office.
Department of Finance (1958b) *Programme for Economic Expansion*. Stationery Office.
Department of Health (1951) *Reconstruction and Improvement of County Homes*. Stationery Office).
Department of Health (1953) *Health Progress, 1947–1953*. Stationery Office.
Department of Housing, Local Government and Heritage (2014) *Social Housing Strategy 2020: Support, Supply and Reform*. Department of Housing, Local Government and Heritage.
Department of Housing, Planning and Local Government (2017) *Resolving Unfinished Housing Developments: 2017 Annual Progress Report on Actions to Address Unfinished Housing Developments*. DHPLG and Housing Agency.
Department of Housing, Planning, Community and Local Government (2017) *Policy and Procedural Guidance for Housing Authorities in Relation to Assisting Victims of Domestic Violence with Emergency and Long-term Accommodation Needs*. Department of Housing, Planning, Community and Local Government.
Department of Local Government (1948) *Housing: A Review of Past Operations and Immediate Requirements*. The Stationery Office.
Department of Local Government (1964) *Housing – Progress and Prospects*. The Stationery Office.
Department of Local Government (1969) *Housing in the Seventies*. The Stationery Office.
Department of Local Government and Public Health (1927) *First Report 1922–1925*. Department of Local Government and Public Health.
Department of Social Protection (2025) *Statistical Information on Social Welfare Services Annual Report 2024*. Department of Social Protection.

Department of the Environment (1979) *The Management of Local Authority Housing, Renting Subsidy and Sales, Policy and Practice*. Department of the Environment.

Department of the Environment (1991a) *Housing Act 1988 – Guidelines for Housing Authorities in Regard to the Accommodation Needs of Homeless Persons – Circular 9/91*. Department of the Environment.

Department of the Environment (1991b) *A Plan for Social Housing*. Department of the Environment.

Department of the Environment (1993) *Memorandum on the Preparation of A Statement of Policy on Housing Management*. Department of the Environment.

Department of the Environment (1995) *Social Housing – The Way Ahead*. Department of the Environment.

Department of the Environment and Local Government (2000) *Homelessness – An Integrated Strategy*. Department of the Environment and Local Government.

Department of the Environment, Heritage and Local Government (2007) *Delivering Homes, Sustaining Communities – Statement on Housing Policy*. Department of the Environment, Heritage and Local Government.

Department of the Environment, Heritage and Local Government (2008) *The Way Home: A Strategy to Address Adult Homelessness in Ireland, 2008–2013*. Department of the Environment, Heritage and Local Government.

Department of the Environment, Heritage and Local Government (2005) *Building Sustainable Communities*. Department of the Environment, Heritage and Local Government.

Department of Health (1951) Reconstruction and Improvement of County Homes, Stationery Office.

Department of Health (1953) Health Progress, 1947–1953, Stationery Office.

Department of Health (1984) *Report of the Ad-hoc Committee on the Homeless*. Department of Health.

Department of the Environment (1995) *Social Housing – The Way Ahead*. Stationery Office.

Develtere, P. (2022) Data Collection Systems and Homelessness in the EU – An Overview. *European Journal of Homelessness* 16: 207–228.

Dickson, D. (2014) *Dublin: The Making of a Capital City*. Profile Books.

Dignan, J. (1945) *Social Security: Outlines of a Scheme of National Health Insurance*. Sligo Champion Publications.

Dillon, B., Murphy-Lawless, J. and Redmond, D. (1990) *Homelessness in County Louth*. SUS Research.

Dillon, T. W. T. (1945) Slum Clearance: Past and Future. *Studies* 34(133): 13–20.

DKM Economic Consultants and Brady Shipman and Martin (2012) *Review of Part V of the Planning and Development Act 2000*. Housing Agency.

Doherty, V. (1982) *Closing Down the County Homes*. Simon Community – National Office.

Dolan, A. (2018) Politics, Economy and Society in the Irish Free State. In Bartlett, T. (Ed) *The Cambridge History of Ireland: Volume IV 1800 to the Present*. Cambridge University Press.

Donnelly Jr, J. S. (2023) A New Ranch War? Cattle Driving and Civil War Agrarian Disorder, 1922–23. *Eire-Ireland* 58(3&4): 174–223.

Donohue, F. (1988) The Role of the Eastern Health Board in providing Services for the Homeless. In Blackwell, J. and Kennedy, S. (Eds) *Focus on Homelessness: A New Look at Housing Policy*. Columba Press, pp 95–111.

Donovan, D. and Murphy, A. E. (2013) *The Fall of the Celtic Tiger: Ireland & the Euro Debt Crisis*. Oxford University Press.

Dooley, T. (2004a) *'The Land for the People': The Land Question in Independent Ireland*. UCD Press.

Dooley, T. (2004b) Land and Politics in Independent Ireland, 1923–48: The Case for Reappraisal. *Irish Historical Studies* 134: 175–197.

Dooley, T. and McCarthy, T. (2015) The 1923 Land Act: Some New Perspectives. In Farrell, M., Knirck, J. and Meehan, C. (Eds) *A Formative Decade: Ireland in the 1920s*. Irish Academic Press, pp 132–156.

Downey, D. (2011) Evidence into Action: How the Dublin Homeless Agency's Data and Information Strategy Have Shaped Homeless Policy Development and Implementation in Ireland. *European Journal of Homelessness* 5(2): 9–110.

Drudy, P. J. and Punch, M. (2001) Housing Inequalities in Ireland. In Cantillon, S., Corrigan, C., Kirby, P. and O'Flynn, J. (Eds) *Rich and Poor: Perspectives on Tackling Inequality in Ireland*. Oaktree Press.

Dublin City Council (2014) *Pathway to Home: The Homeless Action Plan Framework for Dublin, 2014–2016*. Dublin City Council.

Dublin Diocesan Welfare Committee (1974) *Vagrancy – A Report of the Dublin Diocesan Welfare Committee. Presented to His Grace Most Reverend Dr. Dermot Ryan*, May 1974.

Dublin Flatdwellers Association (1973) *Flat Broke: The Plight of the 100,000 in Privately Rented Accommodation*. Dublin Flatdwellers Association.

Dublin Housing Action Committee (1969) *Squatter*. No. 1, June.

Dublin Housing Action Committee (1969) *Squatter*. No. 2.

Dublin Region Homeless Executive (2016) Dublin Region Spring Count on Rough Sleeping on the Night of 24 April 2016. Available at: https://www.homelessdublin.ie/content/files/DRHE_RSCount_Spring16.pdf?v=1507922174

Dublin Region Homeless Executive (various years) *Rough Sleepers Counts*. DRHE. [Online]. Available at: https://www.homelessdublin.ie/info/figures?type=rough-sleeper-count

Dubois, H. and Nivakoski, S. 2023. *Unaffordable and Inadequate Housing in Europe*. Publications Office of the European Union.

Duff, F. (22 March 1950) Memo to the Department of Health (not published).

References

Dukelow, F. and Considine, M. (2019) *Irish Social Policy: A Critical Introduction*, 2nd edition. Policy Press.

Dungan, M. (2024) *Land Is All that Matters: The Struggle that Shaped Irish History*. Head of Zeus.

Dunphy, R. (1995) *The Making of Fianna Fáil Power in Ireland 1923–1948*. Oxford University Press.

Dwyer, M. (2013) Abandoned by God and the Corporation: Housing and the Health of the Working Class in Cork, 1912–1924. *Saothor* 38: 105–118.

Earner-Byrne, L. (2004) 'Moral Repatriation': The Response to Irish Unmarried Mothers in Britain, 1920s–1960s. In P. J. Duffy (Ed) *To and From Ireland: Planned Migration Schemes c.1600–2000*. Geography Publications.

Earner-Byrne, L. (2017) *Letters of the Catholic Poor: Poverty in Independent Ireland, 1920 and 1940*. Cambridge University Press.

Earner-Byrne, L. (2023) The Irish Family: Blame, Agency and the 'Unmarried Mother Problem', 1980s–2021. *Contemporary European History* 32(2): 270–286.

Eason, C. (1928) Report of the Irish Poor Law Commission. *Journal of the Statistical and Social Inquiry Society of Ireland* 14(5): 17–43.

Edwards, G., Hawker, A., Williamson, V. and Hensman, C. (1966) London's Skid Row. *The Lancet* 29(1): 249–252.

European Commission (2021) *Lisbon Declaration on the European Platform on Combatting Homelessness*. European Commission.

European Consensus Conference on Homelessness (2010) Policy Recommendations of the Jury. Available at: http://www.feantsa.org/files/freshstart/Consensus_Conference/Outcomes/2011_02_16_FINAL_Consensus_Conference_Jury_R ecommendations_EN.pdf

European Parliament (2011) Resolution of 14 September 2011 on an EU Homelessness Strategy. Available at: https://www.europarl.europa.eu/doceo/document/TA-7-2011-0383_EN.html?redirect

European Social Policy Network (2019) *National Strategies to Fight Homelessness and Housing Exclusion – Ireland*. European Commission.

Fagan, T. (2014) *Dublin Tenements: Memories of Life in Dublin's Notorious Tenements*. North Inner City Folklore Project.

Fahey, T. (1998) Housing and Social Exclusion. In Healy, S. and Reynolds, B. (Eds) *Social Policy in Ireland: Principles, Practice and Problems*. Oaktree Press.

Fahey, T. and Watson, D. (1995) *An Analysis of Social Housing Need*. Economic and Social Research Institute.

Fallon, D. (2021) *Henrietta Street: From Tenement to Suburbia, 1922–1979*. Dublin City Council.

Fanning, R. (1978) *The Irish Department of Finance 1922–58*. Institute of Public Administration.

Farley, D. (1964) *Social Insurance and Social Assistance in Ireland*. Institute of Public Administration.

Farrell, N. (1988) *Homelessness in Galway*. Galway Social Service Council.

Feeney, J., Ruddy, D. and Browne, V. (1969) Vagrancy in Ireland 1969. *Nusight*, November 1969.

Fennelly, K. (2020) The Institution and the City: The Impact of Hospitals and Workhouses on the Development of Dublin's North Inner City, c.1773–1911, *Urban History* 47: 671–688.

Fernandez, J. (1995) On Planning a Service for the Homeless Mentally Ill in Dublin. *International Journal of Family Psychiatry* 6: 149–163.

Ferriter, D. (2021) *Between Two Hells: The Irish Civil War*. Profile Books.

Ferriter, D. (2024) *The Revelation of Ireland, 1995–2020*. Profile Books.

Fine Gael (1965) *Towards a Just Society*. Fine Gael.

Fine Gael (2016) *A Confidence and Supply Arrangement for a Fine Gael-Led Government*. Fine Gael.

Finn, T. (2012) *Tuairim, Intellectual Debate and Policy Formation: Rethinking Ireland, 1954–1975*. Manchester University Press.

Finnerty, J. (2002) Homes for the Working Classes: Local Authority Housing in the Irish Republic 1947–2002. *Saothar* 27: 65–72.

Finnerty, J. and Buckley, M. (2021) *Systems Accelerant: The Response of the Simon Communities to the 'First Wave' of COVID-19*. Simon Communities of Ireland.

Finnerty, J. and O'Connell, C. (2014) Fifty Years of the Social Housing 'offer' in Ireland: The Casualisation Thesis Examined. In Sirr, L. (Ed) *Renting in Ireland: The Social, Voluntary and Private Sectors*. Institute of Public Administration.

FitzGerald, J. (2014) The Distribution of Income and the Public Finances. *QEC research notes* 2014/2/4. ESRI.

FitzGerald, J. and Honohan, P. (2023) *Europe and the Transformation of the Irish Economy*. Cambridge University Press.

Fitzpatrick Associates (2006) *Review of Implementation of Homeless Strategies*. Department of the Environment, Heritage and Local Government.

Fitzpatrick, S. and Pawson, H. (2016) Fifty Years Since Cathy Come Home: Critical Reflections on the UK Homelessness Safety Net. *International Journal of Housing Policy* 16(4): 543–555.

Focus Ireland (2011) *A Place to Call Home: Twenty-five Years of Focus Ireland*. A&A Farmar/Focus Ireland.

Focus Ireland (2012) *Out of Reach: The Impact of Changes in Rent Supplement*. Focus Ireland.

Fraser, M. (1996) *John Bull's Other Homes. State Housing and British Policy in Ireland, 1883–1922*. Liverpool University Press.

Gahan, D. (2024) The Land Annuities Agitation and the Origins, Implementation and Consequences of the 1933 land Act. In Dooley, T., McCarthy, T. and Tindley, A. (Eds) *Land Reform and Legislation in Ireland, 1800–2024*. Four Courts Press.

Gahan, R. (1942–43) Old Alm Houses, Co. Dublin. *Dublin Historical Record* V: 15–40.

Galway Simon Community (1980) *Galway's Homeless: A Report on Single Homelessness in Galway City*. Galway Simon Community.

Gambi, L. and Sheridan, S. (2020) Family Homelessness in Ireland: The Importance of Research Design in Evidence-based Policy-making. *European Journal of Homelessness* 14(1): 93–106.

Garvin, J. (1944) Public Assistance. In F. C. King (Ed) *Public Administration in Ireland*. Parkside Press, pp 163–172.

Garvin, T. (1974) Political Cleavages, Party Politics and Urbanisation in Ireland: The Case of the Periphery-dominated Centre. *European Journal of Political Research* 2(4): 307–327.

Garvin, T. (1987) *Nationalist Revolutionaries in Ireland, 1858–1928*. Clarendon Press.

Gaughan, J. A. (1980) *Thomas Johnson 1872–1963, First Leader of the Labour Party in Dáil Eireann*. Kingdom Press.

Gilmore, E. (2015) *The Inside Room: The Untold Story of Ireland's Crisis Government*. Irish Academic Press.

Gmelch, G. and Gmelch, S. B. (1978) Begging in Dublin: The Strategies of a Marginal Urban Occupation. *Journal of Contemporary Ethnography* 6(4): 439–454.

Goering, P., Veldhuizen, S., Watson, A., Adair, C., Kopp, B., Latimer, E., Nelson, G., MacNaughton, E., Streiner, D. and Aubry, T. (2014) *National at Home/Chez Soi Final Report*. Mental Health Commission of Canada.

Government of Ireland (1927) *Report of the Commission on the Relief of the Sick and Destitute Poor, including the Insane Poor*. Stationery Office.

Government of Ireland (1943) *Report of the Inquiry into the Housing of the Working Classes of the City of Dublin 1939/43*. Stationery Office.

Government of Ireland (1954) *Commission on Emigration and Other Population Problems*. Stationery Office.

Government of Ireland (1963) *Report of the Commission on Itinerancy*. Stationery Office.

Government of Ireland (1964) *White Paper, Housing – Progress and Prospects*. Stationery Office.

Government of Ireland (1966) *The Health Services and their Future Development*. Government Publications.

Government of Ireland (1969) *Housing in the Seventies*. Stationery Office.

Government of Ireland (1973) *Committee on the Price of Building Land*. Stationery Office.

Government of Ireland (1985) *In Partnership with Youth – The National Youth Strategy*. Stationery Office.

Government of Ireland (1986) *Report of the Commission on Social Welfare*. Stationery Office.

Government of Ireland (1991) *Programme for Economic and Social Progress*. Stationery Office.

Government of Ireland (1996) *Partnership 2000 for Inclusion, Employment and Competitiveness*. Stationery Office.

Government of Ireland (2011) *Statement of Common Purpose: Government for National Recovery 2011–2016*. Government of Ireland.

Government of Ireland (2011) *Report of the Inter-Departmental Working Group on Mortgage Arrears* (Dublin: Stationery Office) with Stationery Office.

Government of Ireland (2016) *Rebuilding Ireland: Action Plan for Housing and Homelessness*. Government of Ireland.

Government of Ireland (2006) *Towards 2016: Ten Year Framework Social Partnership Agreement 2006–2015*. Stationery Office.

Government of Ireland (2018) *Housing First National Implementation Plan 2018*, Stationery Office.

Government of Ireland (2020) Programme for Government: Our Shared Future. Available at: https://assets.gov.ie/static/documents/programme-for-government-our-shared-future-c0e5f2fe-ebb0-4430-9a42-68b34be57a16.pdf

Government of Ireland (2021) *Housing for All: A New Housing Plan for Ireland*. Government of Ireland.

Government of Ireland (2022a) *Youth Homelessness Strategy 2023–2025*. The Department of Housing, Local Government and Heritage.

Government of Ireland (2022b) *Housing First National Implementation Plan 2022–2026*. Government of Ireland.

Gray, P. (2009) *The Making of the Irish Poor Law, 1815–43*. Manchester University Press.

Gray, P. (2012) Conceiving and Constructing the Irish Workhouse, 1836–45. *Irish Historical Studies* 38(149): 22–35.

Greenwood, R. (2015) *Evaluation of Dublin Housing First Demonstration Project: Summary of Findings*. Dublin Region Homeless Executive.

Griffin, B. (2024) *Crime and Criminal Classes in Ireland, 1870–1920*. Cork University Press.

Griffin, H. (2021) *Analysis of Social Housing Current Expenditure Programme*. Department of Public Expenditure and Reform.

Grimes, L. (2023) 'We Did What Needed to Be Done': Cherish, the First Support Group for Unmarried Mothers in Ireland. *Women's History Review* 32(1): 21–35.

Hanley, B. and Millar, S. (2009) *The Lost Revolution: The Story of the Official IRA and the Workers' Party*. Penguin.

Hanna, E. (2013) *Modern Dublin: Urban Change and the Irish Past, 1957–1973*. Oxford University Press.

Hannan, D. F. (1979) *Displacement and Development: Class, Kinship and Social Change in Irish Rural Communities*. The Economic and Social Research Institute, Paper No. 96.

Hannan, D. F. and Commins, P. (1992) The Significance of Small-scale Landholders in Ireland's Socio-economic Transformation. In Goldthorpe, J. H. and Whelan, C. T. (Eds) *The Development of Industrial Society in Ireland*. Oxford University Press, pp 79–104.

Hannan, D. F. and Breen, R. (1987) Family Farming in Ireland. In Galeski, B. and Wilkening, E. (Eds) *Family Farming in Europe and America*. Westview Press.

Hart, I. (1978) *Dublin Simon Community 1971–1976: An Exploration*. Economic and Social Research Institute.

Hart, P. (1998) *The I.R.A. and its Enemies: Violence and Community in Cork, 1916–1923*. Clarendon Press.

Harvey, B. (1984) A Policy for the Homeless. *Irish Social Worker* 3(3): 10–12.

Harvey, B. (1985) Administrative Responses to the Homeless. *Administration* 33(1): 131–140.

Harvey, B. (2008) Homelessness, the 1988 Housing Act and the Relationship between Irish State Policy and Civil Society. In Downey, D. (Ed) *Perspectives on Irish Homelessness: Past, Present and Future*. Homeless Agency.

Harvey, B. (2012) *Downsizing the Community Sector: Changes in Employment and Services in the Voluntary and Community Sector in Ireland, 2008–2012*. Irish Congress of Trade Unions Community Sector Committee.

Harvey, B. and Higgins, M. (1988) The Links between Housing and Homelessness. *Administration* 36(4): 33–40.

Harvey, B. and Menton, M. (1989) Ireland's Young Homeless. *Children and Youth Services Review* 11(1): 31–43.

Hayden, A. (2014) Local Authority Rented Housing: The Path to Decline, 1966–1988. In Sirr, L. (Ed) *Renting in Ireland: The Social, Voluntary and Private Sectors*. Institute of Public Administration.

Hayden, A. (2025) *A Pathway to Homeownership: The Role of Tenant Purchase in Ireland*. Institute of Public Administration.

Headey, B., Muffels, R. and Quiggin, J. (2023) *Western Welfare Capitalisms in Good Times and Bad*. Edward Elgar Publishing.

Hickey, C., Bergin, E., Punch, M. and Buchanan, L. (2002) *Housing Access for All? An Analysis of Housing Strategies and Homeless Action Plans*. Focus Ireland/Simon Communities of Ireland/Society of St. Vincent de Paul/Threshold.

Higgins, M. (1988) Housing Policy as it Affects Single Parents and their Children. In Blackwell, J. and Kennedy, S. (Eds) *Focus on Homelessness: A New Look at Housing Policy*. Columba Press, pp 31–36.

Higgins, M. (1998) Housing, Homelessness and Local Development. In Community Workers Co-operative (Eds) *Local Development in Ireland: Policy Implications for the Future*. Community Workers Co-operative.

Higgins, M. (2001) *Shaping the Future: An Action Plan on Homelessness in Dublin, 2001–2003*. Homeless Agency.

Higgins, M. (2011) Keeping the Vision in Sight. *Cornerstone* 44: 11–12.

Higgins, M. (2021) *On Street Food Services in Dublin: A Review*. Dublin Region Homeless Executive.

Hogan, H. and Keyes, F. (2021) The Housing Crisis and the Constitution. *Irish Jurist* 65: 87–118.

Holohan, C. (2016) Conceptualizing and Responding to Poverty in the Republic of Ireland in the 1960s: A Case Study of Dublin. *Social History* 41(1): 34–53.

Holohan, C. (2020) The Second Vatican Council, Poverty and Irish Mentalities. *History of European Ideas* 46(7): 1009–1026.

Holohan, C., O'Connell, S. and Savage, R. J. (2021) Rediscovering Poverty: Moneylending in the Republic of Ireland in the 1960s. *Irish Historical Studies* 45(168): 282–302.

Homelessness Oversight Group (2013) *First Report*. Homelessness Oversight Group.

Honohan, P. and O'Grada, C. (1998) The Irish Macroeconomic Crisis of 1955–56: How Much was Due to Monetary Policy? *Irish Economic and Social History* 15: 52–80.

Horvat, N. and Coupechoux, S. (2024) *Ninth Overview of Housing Exclusion in Europe*. Fondation Abbé Pierre – FEANTSA.

Houghton, F. T. and Hickey, C. (2000) *Focusing on B&B's: The Unacceptable Growth of Emergency B&B Placement in Dublin*. Focus Ireland.

Housing Agency (2025) *Summary of Social Housing Assessments 2024*. Housing Agency.

Housing Centre (1986) *National Directory of Hostels, Night Shelters, Temporary Accommodation and Other Services for Homeless People*. The Housing Centre.

Housing Commission (2024) *Report of The Housing Commission*. The Housing Commission.

Housing Management Group (1996) First Report Dublin, Department of the Environment and Local Government.

Houses of the Oireachtas (2013) *Report of the Joint Committee of Inquiry into the Banking Crisis*. Houses of the Oireachtas.

HSE (2021) Coronavirus (COVID-19) Guidance for Homeless and Other Vulnerable Group Settings. Available at: https://www.homelessdublin.ie/content/files/COVID-19-Guidance-for-vulnerable-groups-settings.pdf?v=1587041552

Hubert, T. (2024) Skimping on homeless services doesn't work The Currency 2/1/2024 https://thecurrency.news/articles/137581/skimping-on-homeless-services-doesnt-work-the-state-is-about-to-pay-more-for-them/

Inglis, T. (1979) Decline in the Number of Priests and Religious in Ireland. *Doctrine and Life* 30(2): 79–98.

Inter-Departmental Committee Appointed to Examine the Question of the Reconstruction and Replacement of County Homes (1949) (unpublished).

Inter-Departmental Committee on the Care of the Aged (1968) *Report*. Stationery Office.

Irish Communist Organisation (1970) *The Housing Crisis and the Working Class*. Irish Communist Organisation.

Irish Times (23 July 2014) Fears That Target to End Homelessness by 2016 Will Not Be. Available at: https://www.irishtimes.com/news/social-affairs/fears-that-target-to-end-homelessness-by-2016-will-not-be-reached-1.1875002

Johnson, D. (1985) *The Interwar Economy in Ireland. Studies in Irish Economic and Social History*. Dundalgan Press, p 4.

Johnson, T. (1944) Housing. In King, F. C. (Ed) *Public Administration in Ireland*. Parkside Press, pp 175–204.

Jones, D. S. (1997) Land Reform Legislation and Security of Tenure in Ireland after Independence. *Eire-Ireland* 32&33(4): 116–143.

Jones, D. S. (2001) Divisions within the Irish Government Over Land-Distribution Policy, 1940–70. *Eire-Ireland* 36(3&4): 83–110.

Jones, S. (Ed) (2003) *Mean Streets: A Report on the Criminalisation of Homelessness in Europe*. FEANTSA.

Kaim-Caudle, P. (1965) *Housing in Ireland: Some Economic Aspects*. The Economic Institute.

Kaim-Caudle, P. (1967) *Social Policy in the Irish Republic*. Routledge and Kegan Paul.

Kearns, K. C. (1977) Irish Tinkers: An Itinerant Population in Transition. *Annals of the Association of American Geographers* 67(4): 538–548.

Kearns, K. C. (1984) Homelessness in Dublin: An Irish Urban Disorder. *American Journal of Economics and Sociology* 43(2): 217–233.

Kearns, K. C. (1994) *Dublin Tenement Life: An Oral History*. Gill and Macmillan.

Keenan-Thomson, T. (2006) *Women, Republicanism, Radicalism, and Street Politics in Ireland: 1956–1973*. Dissertation submitted for the degree of PhD, Trinity College Dublin.

Kelleher, C., Kelleher, P. and McCarthy, P. (1992) *Patterns of Hostel Use in Dublin*. Focus Point.

Kelleher, J. and Norris M. (2020) *Day Services for People Who are Homeless in Dublin: A Review*. Dublin Region Homeless Executive.

Kelleher, P. (1990) *Caught in the Act: Housing and Settling Homeless People in Dublin City – the Implementation of the Housing Act, 1988*. Focus Point.

Kelly, B. (2016) *Hearing Voices: The History of Psychiatry in Ireland*. Irish Academic Press.

Kelly, B. (2022) Anthropological Perspectives on the Trajectory from Institutionalisation to Community Care in Irish Psychiatry. *Irish Journal of Psychological Medicine* 39(2): 121–130.

Kelly, O. (2015) Alan Kelly Pledges 1,000 Houses to Homeless. *The Irish Times*, 31 January 2015.

Kennedy, F. (1972) Public Expenditure in Ireland on Housing in the Post-War Period. *Economic and Social Review* 3(3): 373–401.

Kennedy, F. (2011) *Frank Duff: A Life*. Burns and Oates.

Kennedy, K. (1993) *The Unemployment Crisis in Ireland*. Cork University Press.

Kennedy, S. (1985) *But Where Can I Go? Homeless Women in Dublin*. Arlen House.

Kennedy, S. (1987) Children and Young People Out-of-Home in Ireland. In Kennedy, S. (Ed) *Streetwise. Homelessness among the Young in Ireland and Abroad*. Glendale Press.

Kenny, B. (2023) *Máirín de Burca – Activist, Feminist, Socialist*. Lettertec.

Kenny, S. and McLaughlin, E. (2022) Political Economy of Secession: Lessons from the Early Years of the Irish Free State. *National Institute Economic Review* 261: 48–78.

Keogh, D. (1994) *Twentieth-Century Ireland: Nation and State*. Gill and Macmillan.

Kilgannon, D. (2023) *Intellectual Disability and Ireland, 1947–1996: Towards a Fuller Life?* Liverpool University Press.

Kilkenny, P. (2019) *Trends Analysis: Housing Assistance Payment (2014–2019)*. Department of Public Expenditure and Reform, Government of Ireland.

King, L. (2015) 'Guinness Is Good for You': Experiments in Workers Housing and Public Amenities by the Guinness Brewery and Guinness/Iveagh Trust, 1872–1915. In Geary, L. M. and Walsh, O. (Eds) *Philanthropy in Nineteenth Century Ireland*. Four Courts Press.

Kinsella, E. (2023) *The Irish Defence Forces, 1922–2022*. Four Courts Press.

Kitchin, R., O'Callaghan, C. and Gleeson, J. (2014) The New Ruins of Ireland? Unfinished Estates in the Post-Celtic Tiger Era. *International Journal of Urban and Regional Research*, 38: 1069–1080.

Kolbert, C. F. and O'Brien, T. (1975) *Land Reform in Ireland: A Legal History of the Irish Land Problem and Settlement*. University of Cambridge Department of Land Economy: Occasional paper No. 3.

Kuhn, R. and Culhane, D. P. (1998) Applying Cluster Analysis to Test a Typology of Homelessness by Pattern of Shelter Utilization: Results from the Analysis of Administrative Data. *American Journal of Community Psychology* 26(2): 207–232.

Law Reform Commission (1985) *Report on Vagrancy and Related Offences*. Law Reform Commission.

Leach, D. (2009) *Fugitive Ireland: European Minority Nationalists and Irish Political Asylum, 1937–2008*. Four Courts Press.

Leahy, A. (1974) *Medical Care for the Vagrant in Ireland*. Simon Ireland.

Leahy, A. (2018) *The Stars are Our Only Warmth: A Memoir*. O'Brien Press.

Leahy, A. and Dempsey, A. (1995) *Not Just a Bed for the Night: The Story of Trust*. Marino Books.

Leahy, A. and Magee, D. (1976) *Report on Broad Medical Service for Single Homeless People in the City of Dublin*. Trust.

Lee, J. J. (1979) Aspects of Corporatist Thought in Ireland: The Commission on Vocational Organisation, 1939–43. In Cosgrove, A. and McCartney, D. (Eds) *Studies in Irish History – Presented to R. Dudley Edwards*. University College Dublin.

Lee, J. J. (1989) *Ireland 1912–1985: Politics and Society*. Cambridge University Press.

Lee, J. J. (2008) From Empire to Europe: The Irish State 1922–73. In Adshead, M., Kirby, P. and Millar, M. (Eds) *Contesting the State: Lessons from the Irish State*. Manchester University Press, pp 25–49.

Lee, J. J. (2017) The Irish Free State. In Crowley, J., O Drisceoil, D. and Murphy, M. (Eds) *Atlas of the Irish Revolution*. Cork University Press.

Leonard, L. (1992a) Voluntary-Statutory Partnership in the Housing Area: The Experience of the Simon Community. *Co-options – Journal of the Community Workers Co-operative* Spring: 79–84.

Leonard, L. (1992b) Official Homelessness Figures Show Only Tip of Iceberg. *Simon Community Newsletter* No. 180. Simon Community National Office.

Leonard, L. (1994) Official Homelessness Results Published – Simon Questions New Assessments. *Simon Community Newsletter* No. 198. Simon Community National Office.

Levinson, B. M. (1966) Subcultural Studies of Homeless Men. *Transactions of the New York Academy of Sciences* 29(December): 165–182.

Lewis, E. (2019) *Social Housing Policy in Ireland: New Directions*. Institute of Public Administration.

Lima, V. (2021) *The Impact of the Pandemic on Services Oriented Towards Single Homeless Persons*. UCD Geary Institute. Available at: https://publicpolicy.ie/papers/the-impact-of-the-pandemic-on-services-oriented-towards-single-homeless-persons/

Lima, V. (2025) *Housing Challenges and Needs of Migrants in Ireland*. Dublin City University and Housing Agency.

Lindsay, D. (1990) *Dublin's Oldest Charity: The Sick and Indigent Roomkeepers Society 1879–1990*. Anniversary Press.

Local Government Board (1906) *Annual Report of the Local Government Board for Ireland for the Year ending 31st March, 1906*. Stationery Office.

Local Government Board (1908) *Annual Report of the Local Government Board for Ireland for the Year ending 31st March, 1908*. Stationery Office.

Lodge-Patch, I. C. (1970) Homeless Men: A London Survey. *Proceedings of the Royal Society of Medicine* 63: 437–446.

Long, A. E., Sheridan, S., Gambi, L. and Hoey, D. (2019) *Family Homelessness in Dublin: Causes, Housing Histories, and Finding a Home*. Focus Ireland.

Lord Mayor's Commission on Housing (1993) *Report*. Dublin Corporation.

Lucey, D. S. (2015) *The End of the Irish Poor Law? Welfare and Healthcare Reform in Revolutionary and Independent Ireland*. Manchester University Press.

Lucey, S. D. (2024) Poor Law Reform in Revolutionary and Independent Ireland. In O'Keefe, H., Crowley, J., O Drisceoil, D., Borgonovo, J. and Murphy, M. (Eds) *Atlas of the Irish Civil War: New Perspectives*. Cork University Press.

Mac Riocaird, C. (1989) Galway Simon Community 1979–1989: The Early Days. *Simon Community Newsletter*, No. 154, October, pp 1–6.

Maher, C. and Allen, M. (2014) What Is Preventing Us from Preventing Homelessness? A Review of the Irish National Preventative Strategy. *European Journal of Homelessness* 8(2).

Maher, I. (1989) Grafting the Homeless on to the Housing Code. *The Irish Jurist* (NS) 24(2): 182–197.

Mahoney, P. (2016) *Grim Bastilles of Despair: The Poor Law Union Workhouses in Ireland*. Quinnipiac University Press.

Maître, B., Russell, H. and Whelan, C. (2014) *Trends in Economic Stress and the Great Recession in Ireland: An Analysis of the CSO Survey on Income and Living Conditions (SILC)*. Department of Social Protection.

Mansergh, N. (2024) *The Irish Construction Cycle 1970–2023: Policies and Escape Routes*. Eastwood Books.

Maphosa, P. (2024) *New Families Entering Emergency Accommodation in the Dublin region, years 2020–2023*. Dublin Region Homeless Executive.

Maphosa, P. and Mayock, P. (2025) *Youth Homelessness in the Dublin Region, 2023*. Dublin Region Homeless Executive.

Matthews, Z. (2022) *A Profile of Families Experiencing Homelessness in the Dublin Region, 2019*. Dublin Region Homeless Executive.

May, S. (1944) Two Dublin Slums. *The Bell* 7(4): 351–356.

Mayock, P. and O'Sullivan, E. (2007) *Lives in Crisis: Homeless Young People in Dublin*. Liffey Press.

Mayock, P. and Neary, F. (2021) *Domestic Violence and Family Homelessness*. Focus Ireland.

Mayock, P. and Sheridan, S. (2020) Women Negotiating Power and Control as they 'Journey' through Homelessness: A Feminist Poststructuralist Perspective. *European Journal of Homelessness* 14(2): 17–47.

Mayock, P., Sheridan, S. and Parker, S. (2012) Migrant Women and Homelessness: The Role of Gender-based Violence. *European Journal of Homelessness* 6(1): 59–82.

References

Mayock, P., Sheridan, S. and Parker, S. (2015) *The Dynamics of Long-term Homelessness among Women in Ireland*. Dublin Regional Homeless Executive.

Mazars (2015) *Independent Review of Homeless Services*. Department of Environment, Community and Local Government.

McCabe, C. (2018) *Begging, Charity and Religion in Pre-Famine Ireland*. Liverpool University Press.

McCarthy, P. and Conlon, E. (1988) *A National Survey on Young People Out of Home in Ireland*. Streetwise National Coalition.

McCashin, A. (1982) Social Policy: 1957–82. In Litton, F. (Ed) *Unequal Achievement: The Irish Experience 1957–1982*. Institute of Public Administration.

McCashin, A. (2019) *Continuity and Change in the Welfare State: Social Security in the Republic of Ireland*. Palgrave Macmillan.

McCook, J. J. (1893) A Tramp Census and Its Revelations. *Forum* 15: 753–766.

McCullagh, D. (1998) *A Makeshift Majority: The First Inter-Party Government, 1948–51*. Institute of Public Administration.

McDowell, R. B. (1964) *The Irish Administration 1801–1914*. Routledge & Kegan Paul.

McEneaney, S. (2019) Home Sweet Home? Housing Activism and Political Commemoration in Sixties Ireland. *History Workshop Journal* 87: 5–26.

McGarry, F. (2016) Independent Ireland. In Bourke, R. and McBride, I. (Eds) *The Princeton History of Modern Ireland*. Princeton University Press.

McGee, H. (2020, 9 February) Election 2020 Analysis: Exit Polls Confirms Health, Housing, Homelessness of Most Concern to Voters. *The Irish Times*. Available at: https://www.irishtimes.com/news/politics/election-2020-exit-poll-confirms-health-housing-homelessness-of-most-concern-to-voters-1.4167030

McGinnity, F., Privalko, I., Russell, H., Curristan, S., Stapleton, A. and Laurence, J. (2022) *Origin and Integration: Housing and Family Among Migrants in the 2016 Irish Census*. Economic and Social Research Institute.

McMahon, D. (1984) *Republicans and Imperialists: Anglo-Irish Relations in the 1930s*. Yale University Press.

McManus, L. (2011) The Homeless Agency: A Model for Partnership. *Cornerstone* 44: 13–14.

McManus, R. (2002) *Dublin, 1910–1940: Shaping the City and Suburbs*. Four Courts Press.

McManus, R. (2003) Blue Collars, 'Red Forts', and Green Fields: Working-Class Housing in Ireland in the Twentieth Century. *International Labor and Working-Class History* 64: 38–54.

McManus, R. (2018) Dublin's Lodger Phenomenon in the Early Twentieth Century. *Irish Economic and Social History* 45(1): 23–46.

McManus, R. (2019) Tackling the Urban Housing Problem in the Irish Free State, 1922–1940. *Urban History* 46(1): 62–81.

Meagher, G. A. (1959) Housing: Finance. *Administration* 7(2): 191–202.

Medico-Social Research Board (1979) *Annual Report for 1979*. Medico-Social Research Board.

Meehan, C. (2013) *A Just Society for Ireland? 1964–1987*. Palgrave Macmillan.

Meghan, P. J. (1963) *Housing in Ireland*. Institute of Public Administration.

Mills, F., Smyth, E., Walsh, F. with Tovey, H. and Walsh, J. (1991) *Scheme of Last Resort? A Review of the Supplementary Welfare Allowance*. Combat Poverty.

Ministry of Local Government (1924) *Rules and Regulations for the Administration of Home Assistance entitled The County Boards of Health (Assistance) Order, 1924*. Stationery Office.

Monahan, P. (1959) Housing: The Social Background. *Administration* 7(2): 166–177.

Montgomery, A. E., Metraux, S. and Culhane, M. P. (2013) Rethinking Homelessness Prevention among Persons with Serious Mental Illness. *Social Issues and Policy Review* 7(1): 58–82.

Moore, J. (1994) *B&B in Focus: The Use of Bed and Breakfast Accommodation for Homeless Adults in Dublin*. Focus Point.

Morrin, H. (2019) *A Profile of Families Experiencing Homelessness in the Dublin Region: 2016–2018 Families*. Dublin Region Homeless Executive.

Morrissey, P. (1988) Current Policy and Future Plans as Related to Marginal Groups. In Blackwell, J. and Kennedy, S. (Eds) *Focus on Homelessness: A New Look at Housing Policy*. Columba Press, pp 77–80.

Murphy-Lawless, J. and Dillon, B. (1992) *Promises, Promises. An Assessment of the Effectiveness of the Housing Act 1988, in Housing Homeless People in Ireland*. Nexus/National Campaign for the Homeless.

Murphy, E. (2024) *Running from Office: Confessions of Ambition and Failure in Politics*. Eriu.

Murphy, F. (1984) Dublin Slums in the 1930s. *Dublin Historical Record* 37(3–4): 104–111.

Murphy, G. (2009) *In Search of the Promised Land: The Politics of Post-War Ireland*. Mercier Press.

Murphy, J. A. (1975) *Ireland in the Twentieth Century*. Gill and Macmillan.

Murphy, P. and Kennedy, S. (1988) *A Part in Dublin: Accommodation for People Out of Home, 1986 and 1988*. Focus Point.

Murray, J. (1989) It was Twenty Years Ago Today: The Early Days of the Simon Community. *Simon Community Newsletter* No. 148, 3–6.

Murray, P. and Feeney, M. (2017) *Church, State and Social Science in Ireland: Knowledge Institutions and the Rebalancing of Power, 1937–73*. Manchester University Press.

Murtagh, T. (2020) *Henrietta Street: Grandeur and Decline, 1800–1922*. Dublin City Council.

Murtagh, T. (2023) *Spectral Mansions: The Making of a Dublin Tenement, 1800–1914*. Four Courts Press.

National Campaign for the Homeless (1985) *Ireland's Young Homeless*. Dublin.

National Campaign for the Homeless (1986) *Homelessness in the European Community*. Report of the First EEC Commission Seminar on Poverty and Homelessness held in Cork, Ireland, 13–15 September 1985.

National Committee on Pilot Schemes to Combat Poverty (1980) *Final Report*. National Committee on Pilot Schemes to Combat Poverty.

National Economic and Social Council (1976a) *Towards a Social Report*. National Economic and Social Council.

National Economic and Social Council (1976b) *Report on Housing Subsidies*. National Economic and Social Council.

National Economic and Social Council (1988) *A Review of Housing Policy*. National Economic and Social Council Report No. 87.

National Economic and Social Council (1990) *A Strategy for the Nineties: Economic Stability and Structural Change*. National Economic and Social Council.

National Economic and Social Council (2004) *Housing in Ireland: Performance and Policy*. Report No. 112. National Economic and Social Development Office.

National Economic and Social Council (2005) *The Developmental Welfare State*. Report No. 113. National Economic and Social Development Office.

National Economic and Social Council (2015) *Ireland's Private Rental Sector: Pathways to Secure Occupancy and Affordable Supply*. National Economic and Social Council.

National Oversight and Audit Commission (2021) *NOAC Performance Indicator Report 2020*. National Oversight and Audit Commission.

Naughtie, A. (2023, 13 May) Far-Right Anti-Immigration Activists Take Credit for Burning Dublin Refugee Camp. *The Irish Times*. Available at: https://www.euronews.com/2023/05/13/far-right-anti-immigration-activists-take-credit-for-burning-dublin-refugee-camp

Ni Chearbhaill, M. B. (2008) *The Society of St Vincent de Paul in Dublin, 1926–1975* (Unpublished PhD thesis). National University of Ireland, Maynooth.

Nicholls, G. (1836) *First Report of George Nicholls: Poor Laws Ireland*. Her Majesty's Stationery Office.

Nicholls, G. (1838) *Poor Laws – Ireland: Three Reports by George Nicholls, Esq to Her Majesty's Principal Secretary of State for the Home Department*. Stationery Office.

Nolan, B., Whelan, C. T. and Williams, J. (1998) *Where Are Poor Households: The Spatial Distribution of Poverty and Distribution in Ireland*. Oak Tree Press.

Norris, M. (2001) Regenerating Run Down Public Housing Estates: A Review of the Operation of the Remedial Works Scheme since 1985. *Administration* 49(1): 25–45.

Norris, M. (2003) Housing. In Callanan, M. and Keogan, J. (Eds) *Local Government in Ireland: Inside Out*. Institute of Public Administration, pp 165–189.

Norris, M. (2016) *Property, Family and the Irish Welfare State*. Palgrave.

Norris, M. (2019) *Financing the Golden Age of Irish Social Housing, 1932–1956 (and the Dark Ages Which Followed)*. Geary Institute Work Paper WP2019/01.

Norris, M. and Hayden, A. (2018) *The Future of Council Housing: An Analysis of the Financial Sustainability of Local Authority Provided Social Housing*. The Community Foundation for Ireland.

Norris, M. and Fahey, T. (2011) From Asset Based Welfare to Welfare Housing? The Changing Function of Social Housing in Ireland. *Housing Studies* 26(3): 495–464.

Norris, M. and Byrne, M. (2021) The Political Economy of Housing in Ireland. In Farrell, D. M. and Hardiman, N. (Eds) *The Oxford Handbook of Irish Politics*. Oxford University Press.

Norris, M. and Shiels, P. (2007) Housing affordability in the Republic of Ireland: Is Planning Part of the Problem or Part of the Solution? *Housing Studies* 22(1): 57–58.

Nowicki, M., Brickell, K. and Harris, E. (2019) The Hotelisation of the Housing Crisis: Experiences of Family Homelessness in Dublin Hotels. *The Geographical Journal* 185: 313–324.

Ó Broin, E. (2019) *Home: Why Public Housing is the Answer*. Merrion Press.

Ó Broin, E. and McCann, M. (2025) *Flats and Cottages: Herbert Simms and the Housing of Dublin's Working Class 1932–1948*. Merrion Press.

Ó Broin, L. (1982) *Frank Duff: A Biography*. Gill and Macmillan.

Ó Cinneide, S. (1969) The Development of the Home Assistance Scheme. *Administration* 17(3): 284–308.

Ó Cinneide, S. (1970) *A Law for the Poor: A Study of Home Assistance in Ireland*. Institute of Public Administration.

Ó Cinneide, S. (Ed) (1992) *Social Europe: EC Social Policy and Europe*. Institute of European Affairs.

Ó Cinneide, S. and Mooney, P. (1972) *Simon Survey of the Homeless*. The Simon Community supported by the Medico-Social Research Board.

Ó Ciosáin, N. (2014) *Ireland in Official Print Culture 1800–1850: A New Reading of the Poor Inquiry*. Oxford University Press.

Ó Corrain, D. (2024) The Catholic Church and the Irish State, 1916–1973. In Ganiel, G. and Holmes, A. R. (Eds) *The Oxford Handbook of Religion in Modern Ireland*. Oxford University Press.

Ó Grada, C. (1997) *A Rocky Road: The Irish Economy since the 1920s*. Manchester University Press.

Ó hUiginn, P. (1960) Some Social and Economic Aspects of Housing: An International Comparison. *Administration* 8(1): 43–71.

Ó Riain, S. (2014) *The Rise and Fall of Ireland's Celtic Tiger: Liberalism, Boom and Bust*. Cambridge University Press.

Ó Tuathaigh, G. (2024) Leadership and Independent Ireland's Performance since 1922: A Historiographical perspective on Lee's Assessment. In Nyhan Grey, M. (Ed) *A Tract for Our Times: A Retrospective on Joe Lee's Ireland 1912–1985*. Dublin University Press.

O'Brien, G. (1936) Patrick Hogan: Minister for Agriculture 1922–1932. *Studies* 25(99): 353–368.

O'Brien, J. (1979) *Criminal Neglect – Some Aspects of Law Enforcement as it Affects the Single Homeless. A Submission from the Simon Community (National Office) to the Commission of Enquiry into the Irish Penal System*. Simon Community (National Office).

O'Brien, J. (1981) Poverty and Homelessness. In Kennedy, S. (Ed) *One Million Poor? The Challenge of Irish Inequality*. Turoe Press.

O'Brien, L. and Dillon, B. (1982) *Private Rented: The Forgotten Sector*. Threshold.

O'Carroll, A. (2021) *Interim Report on Mortality in Single Homeless Population, 2020*. Dublin Region Homeless Executive.

O'Carroll, A., Duffin, T. and Collins, J. (2020) *Saving Lives in the Time of COVID-19: Case Study of Harm Reduction, Homelessness and Drug Use in Dublin, Ireland*. London School of Economics and Political Science.

O'Connell, C. (1993) Housing Trends and Issues: The Role of Social Housing. *Administration* 41(3): 249–261.

O'Connell, C. (1994) Housing in The Republic of Ireland: A Review of Recent Trends and Recent Policy Measures. *Administration* 42(2): 159–169.

O'Connell, C. (1998) Tenant Involvement in Local Authority Estate Management: A New Panacea for Policy Failure? *Administration* 46(2): 25–46.

O'Connell, C. (1999) Local Authorities as Landlords. In Fahey, T. (Ed) *Social Housing in Ireland: A Study of Success, Failure and Lessons Learned*. Oak Tree Press), pp 57–79.

O'Connell, C. and Fahey, T. (1999) Local Authority Housing in Ireland. In Fahey, T. (Ed) *Social Housing in Ireland: A Study of Success, Failure and Lessons Learned*. Oak Tree Press, pp 35–56.

O'Connell, P. J. and Rottman, D. B. (1992) The Irish Welfare State in Comparative Perspective. In Goldthorpe, J. H. and Whelan, C. T. (Eds) *The Development of Industrial Society in Ireland*. Oxford University Press.

O'Connor, J. (1995) *The Workhouses of Ireland: The Fate of Ireland's Poor*. Anvil Books.

O'Connor, N. (2008) Can we Agree the Number of People who are Homeless (and does it really matter?). In Downey, D. (Ed) *Perspectives on Irish Homelessness: Past, Present and Future*. Homeless Agency.

O'Donnell, I. and O'Sullivan, E. (2020) 'Coercive Confinement': An Idea Whose Time Has Come? *Incarceration: An International Journal of Imprisonment, Detention and Coercive Confinement.* DOI.ORG/10.1177/ 2632666320936440

O'Donnell, J. (2020) Estimating Annual Homelessness. *Demographic Research* 43: 1–34.

O'Donnell, R. (1998) *Ireland's Economic Transformation: Industrial Policy, European Integration and Social Partnership.* University of Pittsburgh, Working Paper No. 2.

O'Donnell, R. (2000) Public Policy and Social Partnership. In Dunne, J., Ingram, A., Litton, F. and O'Connor, F. (Eds) *Questioning Ireland: Debates in Political Philosophy and Public Policy.* Institute of Public Administration.

O'Donnell, R. and O'Reardon, C. (1996) The Irish Experiment. *New Economy* 3(1): 33–38.

O'Donovan, J. (1899) Irish Workhouse Reform. *Irish Ecclesiastical Record* Ser. 4, V: 248–260.

O'Driscoll, F. (2000) Social Catholicism and the Social Question in Independent Ireland: The Challenge to the Fiscal System. In Cronin, M. and Regan, J. M. (Eds) *Ireland: The Politics of Independence, 1922–49.* Macmillan Press Ltd.

O'Hagan, J. (2018) The Irish Economy 1973 to 2016. In Bartlett, T. (Ed) *The Cambridge History of Ireland: 1880 to the Present, Vol. 4.* Cambridge University Press.

O'Halloran, M. (2020) *The Lost Gaeltacht: The Land Commission Migration - Clonbur, Co. Galway to Allenstown, County Meath.* Homefarm Publications.

O'Leary, D. (2000) *Vocationalism and Social Catholicism in Twentieth-Century Ireland.* Irish Academic Press.

O'Meara, L. (2014) *From Richmond Barracks to Keogh Square.* Riposte Books.

O'Neill, B., Devlin, E. and J. Prunty (2014) Our Lady's Henrietta Street, Dublin: Accommodation for Discharged Female Prisoners. In Prunty, J. and O'Sullivan, L. (Eds) *The Daughters of Charity of St Vincent De Paul in Ireland: The Early Years.* Columba Press.

O'Neill, C. (2024) *Power and Powerlessness in Ireland: Life in a Palliative State.* Oxford University Press.

O'Rourke, K. H. (1991) Burn Everything British But Their Coal: The Anglo-Irish Economic War of the 1930s. *The Journal of Economic History* 51(2): 357–366.

O'Rourke, K. H. (2017) Independent Ireland in Comparative Perspective. *Irish Economic and Social History* 44(1): 19–45.

O'Shea, J. (1983) *Priest, Politics and Society in Post-famine Ireland: A Study of County Tipperary 1850–1891.* Wolfhound Press.

References

O'Sullivan, A. (1988) The Allocation of Dwellings by Dublin Corporation, Particularly to Homeless People. In Blackwell, J. and Kennedy, S. (Eds) *Focus on Homelessness: A New Look at Housing Policy*. Columba Press, pp 85–89.

O'Sullivan, E. (1995) Section 5 of the Child Care Act 1991 and Youth Homelessness. In Ferguson, H. and Kenny, P. (Eds) *On Behalf of the Child: Child Welfare, Child Protection and the Child Care Act 1991*. A & A Farmar, pp 84–104.

O'Sullivan, E. (1998) Aspects of youth homelessness in the Republic of Ireland. In D. Avramov (Ed) *Youth Homelessness in the European Union*. FEANTSA, pp 250–261.

O'Sullivan, E. (2009) *Residential Child Welfare in Ireland: An Outline of Policy, Legislation and Practice, Commission to Inquire into Child Abuse Report Vol 4*. Stationery Office.

O'Sullivan, E. (2012) *Ending Homelessness – A Housing-Led Approach*. Department of the Environment, Heritage and Local Government.

O'Sullivan, E. (2014) Child Welfare Services, 1970–80: From the Kennedy Committee to the Task Force. In Luddy, M. and Smith, J. (Eds) *Children, Childhood and Irish Society: 1500 to the Present*. Four Courts Press.

O'Sullivan, E. (2016) Homeless Women: A Historical Perspective. In Mayock, P. and Bretheton, J. (Eds) *Homeless Women in Europe*. Palgrave Macmillan.

O'Sullivan, E. (2017) International Commentary: Family Options Study Observations from the Periphery of Europe. Cityscape: *A Journal of Policy Development and Research* 19(3): 207–213.

O'Sullivan, E. (2020) *Reimagining Homelessness*. Policy Press.

O'Sullivan, E. (2023) Histories of Homelessness. In Place, N. and Bretherton, J. (Eds) *The Routledge Handbook of Homelessness*. Routledge.

O'Sullivan, E. and I. O'Donnell, (2012) (eds) *Patients, Prisoners and Penitents: Coercive Confinement in Ireland*, Manchester University Press.

O'Sullivan, E., Byrne, E. and Allen, M. (2021) *Focus on Homelessness: A Decade of Homelessness Data-Significant Developments in Homelessness 2014–2023*. Focus Ireland.

O'Sullivan, E., Byrne, E. and Allen, M. (2023) *Public Expenditure on Services for Households Experiencing Homelessness*. Focus Ireland.

O'Sullivan, E. and Mayock, P. (2008) Youth Homelessness in Ireland: The Emergence of a Social Problem. *Youth Studies Ireland* 3(1): 15–29.

O'Sullivan, E., Pleace, N., Busch-Geertsema, V. and Hrast, M. F. (2000) Distorting Tendencies in Understanding Homelessness in Europe. *European Journal of Homelessness* 14(3): 109–135.

O'Sullivan, E. and Tsemberis, S. (2024) *Peer Review on Implementation of Housing First Approach to Tackle Long Term Homelessness of People with Complex Needs*. Publications Office of the European Union.

O'Sullivan, E., Curran, H., Byrne, E. and Allen, M. (2024) COVID-19 and Trends in Homelessness in Ireland. In Johnson, G., Culhane, D., Fitzpatrick, S., Metraux, S. and O'Sullivan E. (Eds) *Research Handbook on Homelessness*. Edward Elgar.

O'Sullivan, E., Palcic, D. and Reeves, E. (2025) A Century of Housing Privatisation: The Case of Ireland. In Greve, C., Hodge, G. and Reeves, E. (Eds) *Research Handbook on Privatization*. Edward Elgar, pp 213–228.

O'Sullivan, E., Reidy, A. and Allen, M. (2021a) *Focus on Homelessness: Adult-Only Households, Vol. 4*. Focus Ireland.

O'Sullivan, E., Reidy, A. and Allen, M. (2021b) *Focus on Homelessness: Significant Developments in Homelessness 2014–2021*. Focus Ireland.

OECD (2024) HC3.1. Homeless Population. Available at: https://www.oecd.org/els/family/HC3-1-Homeless-population.pdf

Office of the Comptroller and Auditor General (2024) *Report on the Accounts of the Public Services 2023 – Exceptional State funding of the Peter McVerry Trust*. Office of the Comptroller and Auditor General.

Oliver, E. (2025) *Irish Nation Building: Government, Business and Power, 1922–1958*. Palgrave Macmillan.

Ombudsman (2025) *An Investigation by the Ombudsman into the Administration of the Housing Assistance Payment Scheme*. Office of the Ombudsman.

Organisation for Economic Co-operation and Development (1964) *Ireland*. Organisation for Economic Co-operation and Development.

Owen, R. and Matthiessen, M. (2021) COVID-19 Response and Homelessness in the EU. *European Journal of Homelessness* 15(1): 161–184.

Parker, S. (2021) *The Dynamics of Family Homelessness in Ireland: A Mixed Methods Study* (Doctoral Dissertation). Available at: http://www.tara.tcd.ie/handle/2262/97200

Parliamentary Budget Office (2024) *Social Housing: Ongoing Needs 2023*. Houses of the Oireachtas.

Parsell, C. (2018) *The Homeless Person in Contemporary Society*. Routledge.

Parsell, C. (2023) *Homelessness*. Polity Press.

Parsell, C. and Watts, B. (2017) Charity and Justice: A Reflection on New Forms of Homeless Provision in Australia. *European Journal of Homelessness* 11(2): 65–76.

Pfretzschner, P. A. (1965) *The Dynamics of Irish Housing*. Institute of Public Administration.

Phelan, E. and Norris, M. (2008) Neo-Corporatist Governance of Homeless Services in Dublin: Reconceptualization, Incorporation and Exclusion. *Critical Social Policy* 28(1): 51–73.

Pleace, N. and Hermans, K. (2020) Counting all Homelessness in Europe: The Case for Ending the Separate Enumeration of 'Hidden Homelessness'. *European Journal of Homelessness* 14: 35–62.

Pleace, N., Baptista, I., Benjaminsen, L. and Busch-Geertsema, V. (2018) *Homeless Services in Europe*. European Observatory on Homelessness.

Pleace, N., Baptista, I., Benjaminsen, L., Busch Geertsema, V., O'Sullivan, E. and Teller, N. (2021) *European Homelessness and COVID-19*. European Observatory on Homelessness.

Potter, M. (2018) Municipal Social Housing in Ireland, 1866–1914. In Laragy, G., Purdue, O. and Wright, J. J. (Eds) *Urban Spaces in Nineteenth-Century Ireland*. Liverpool University Press.

Power, A. (1993) *Hovels to High Rise: State Housing in Europe since 1850*. Routledge.

Power, A. (1997) *Estates on the Edge: The Social Consequences of Mass Housing in Northern Europe*. Macmillan Press.

Prunty, J. (1998) *Dublin Slums 1800–1925: A Study in Urban Geography*. Academic Press.

Prunty, J. (2017) *The Monasteries, Magdalen Asylums and Reformatory Schools of Our Lady of Charity in Ireland, 1853–1973*. Columba Press.

Puirseil, N. (2007) *The Irish Labour Party 1922–73*. UCD Press.

Quadragesimo Anno (1931) Encyclical of Pope Pius xi on reconstruction of the social order to our venerable brethren, the patriarchs, primates, archbishops, bishops, and other ordinaries in peace and communion with the apostolic see, and likewise to all the faithful of the Catholic world. https://www.vatican.va/content/pius-xi/en/encyclicals/documents/hf_p-xi_enc_19310515_quadragesimo-anno.html

Quinlivan, A. (2006) *Philip Monahan – A Man Apart: The Life and Times of Ireland's First Local Authority Manager*. Institute of Public Administration.

Redmond, D. and Kernan, G. (2005) Housing Policy, Homeownership and the Provision of Affordable Housing. In Moore, N. and Scott, M. (Eds) *Renewing Urban Communities: Environment, Citizenship and Sustainability in Ireland*. Ashgate, pp 235–252.

Redmond, D. and Norris, M. (2014) Social Housing in the Republic of Ireland. In Scanlon, K., Whitehead, C. and Fernandez, A. (Eds) *Social Housing in Europe*. Wiley Blackwell.

Redmond, D., Hegarty, O. and Reynolds, M. (2021) *Planning Gain and Obligations: Promise and Performance of Part V*. Clúid Housing.

Rental Tenancies Board (various years) *The Rent Index*. RTB. [Online]. Available at: https://rtb.ie/data-insights/rtb-research-reports/rtb-esri-rent-index/

Rents and Leaseholds Commission (1952) *Report on Rent Control*. Stationery Office.

Report of Dublin Corporation Lord Mayor's Commission on Housing (March 1993). Stationery Office.

Report of the Inter-Departmental Committee on Issues Relating to Possible Transfer of Administration of Rent and Mortgage Interest Supplementation from Health Boards to Local Authorities (1999). *Report*. Stationery Office.

Rerum Novarum: Encyclical of Pope Leo XIII on Capital and Labour (1891) Available at: https://www.vatican.va/content/leo-xiii/en/encyclicals/documents/hf_l-xiii_enc_15051891_rerum-novarum.html

Residential Tenancies Board (2017) *The RTB Rent Index Quarter 4 2016*. Residential Tenancies Board.

Residential Tenancies Board (2021a) *Small Landlords Report*. Residential Tenancies Board.

Residential Tenancies Board (2021b) *Annual Report 2020*. Residential Tenancies Board.

Review Group on the Role of Supplementary Welfare Allowance in Relation to Housing (1995) *Report to the Minister for Social Welfare*. Stationery Office.

Richards, M. (1998) *Single Issue*. Poolbeg Press.

Ridge, M. (1992) Local Government Finance and Equalisation: The Case of Ireland. *Fiscal Studies* 13(3): 54–73.

Riordan, S. (2000) 'A Political Blackthorn': Seán MacEntee, the Dignan Plan and the Principle of Ministerial Responsibility. *Irish Economic and Social History* 27: 44–62.

Robins, J. (Ed) (1997) *Reflections on Health: Commemorating Fifty Years of the Department of Health 1947–1997*. Department of Health.

Roche, D. (1982) *Local Government in Ireland*. Institute of Public Administration.

Roche, W. K., O'Connell, P. J. and Proythero, A. (Eds) (2016) *Austerity and Recovery in Ireland: Europe's Poster Child and the Great Recession*. Oxford University Press.

Royal Commission on the Poor Laws and Relief of Distress (1909) *Report on Ireland*. Stationery Office.

Russell, H., Privalko, I., McGinnity, G. and Enright, S. (2021) *Monitoring Adequate Housing in Ireland*. ESRI.

Ryan, J. (2022) *Gerald O'Donovan, A Life: 1871–1942*. Liverpool University Press.

Ryan, L. (1967) Social Dynamite: A Study of Early School Leavers. *Christus Rex* 21(1): 7–44.

Saorstat Eireann (1933) *Final Report of the Commission of Inquiry into the Sale of Cottages and Plots Provided under the Labourers (Ireland) Acts*. Stationery Office.

Sassi, J., Farrell, S., Leonard, R. and Hedderman, A. (2025) Housing. In Gilmore, O. and Landy D. (Eds) *Fragments of Victory: The Contemporary Irish Left*. Pluto.

SCSI (2023) *Tender Price Index, August 2023*. Chartered Property Land and Construction Surveyors.

Scutella, R. and Wood, G. A. (2024) The Dynamics of Homelessness. In Johnson, G., Culhane, D., Fitzpatrick, S., Metraux, S. and O'Sullivan, E. (Eds) *Research Handbook on Homelessness*. Edward Elgar.

Select Committee on Crime, Lawlessness and Vandalism (1986) *Ninth Report – Report on Certain offences under the Vagrancy Acts*. Dáil Eireann.

References

Serme-Morin, C. and Coupechoux, S. (2019) *Fourth Overview of Housing Exclusion in Europe, 2019.* FAP/FEANTSA.

Shannon, D. (1988) The History and Future of the Housing (Miscellaneous Provisions) Bill, 1985. In Kennedy, S. and Blackwell, J. (Eds) *Focus on Homelessness: A New Look at Housing Policy.* Columba Press, pp 127–143.

Sheridan, S. (2022) *Evaluation of Focus Ireland Shielding Service.* Focus Ireland.

Sheridan, S. and Parker, S. (2023) Ireland and Homelessness. In Place, N. and Bretherton, J. (Eds) *The Routledge Handbook of Homelessness.* Routledge.

Shinn, M. and Khadduri, J. (2020) *In the Midst of Plenty: Homelessness and What to do About it.* Wiley-Blackwell.

Simon Community (1986) *Comments by the Simon Community on the Housing (Miscellaneous Provisions) Bill, 1985.* Simon Community – National Office.

Simon Community Newsletter (1988) Housing Bill 1988, March, Number 136, pp 1–3.

Society of St. Vincent de Paul (1981) *Towards a National Social Policy.* Society of St. Vincent de Paul.

Somerville-Woodward, R. (2002) *Ballymun, A History: Volumes 1 & 2 Synopsis.* Ballymun Regeneration Ltd.

Stanley, W. and Allen, M. (2018) Family Homelessness End of Year Review 2017. Focus Ireland. Available at: https://www.focusireland.ie/wp-content/uploads/2021/09/Stanley-and-Allen-2018-Insights-into-Family-Homelessness-No-13-Family-Homelessness-End-of-Year-Review-2017.pdf

Sweetman, M. (1972) *Housing.* Veritas.

Swift, R. and Campbell, S. (2017) The Irish in Britain. In Biagini, E. F. and Daly, M. E. (Eds) *The Cambridge Social History of Modern Ireland.* Cambridge University Press.

The Housing Assistance Payment (HAP): Making the Right Impact? 2019 Society of St Vincent De Pau and Threshold. Available at: https://www.svp.ie/wp-content/uploads/2019/07/HAP-Report2019.pdf

Thomas, S., Johnston, B., Barry, S., Siersbaek, R. and Burke, S. (2021) Sláintecare Implementation Status in 2020: Limited Progress with Entitlement Expansion. *Health Policy* 125(3): 277–283.

Threshold (1987) *Policy Consequences: A Study of the £5,000 Surrender Grant in the Dublin Housing Area.* Threshold.

Threshold (2021) *HAP and Rent Supplement Discrimination.* Threshold.

Tsemberis, S. (2010) *Housing First: The Pathways Model to End Homelessness for People with Mental Illness and Addiction.* Hazelden Press.

Tubridy, F. (2024) Militant Research in the Housing Movement: The Community Action Tenants Union Rent Strike History Project. *Antipode: A Radical Journal of Geography* 56(3): 1027–1046.

Viney, M. (1962) *Mental Illness: An Inquiry.* Irish Times.

Viney, M. (1964) *No Birthright: A Study of the Irish Unmarried Mother and her Child*. Irish Times.

Viney, M. (1966) The Young Offenders – Patterns of Crime. *Irish Times*, 28 April, p 10.

Viney, M. (1970) *The Broken Marriage: A Study in Depth of a Growing Irish Social Problem*. Irish Times.

Wafer, U. (2006) *Counted In, 2005*. Homeless Agency.

Waldron, R. (2022a) Experiencing Housing Precarity in the Private Rental Sector During the COVID-19 Pandemic: The Case of Ireland. *Housing Studies* 38(1): 84–106.

Waldron, R. (2022b) Responding to Housing Precarity: The Coping Strategies of Generation Rent. *Housing Studies* 39(1): 124–145.

Waldron, R., O'Donoghue-Hynes, B. and Redmond, D. (2019) Emergency Homeless Shelter Use in the Dublin Region 2012–2016: Utilizing a Cluster Analysis of Administrative Data. *Cities* 94: 143–152.

Waldron, R., Redmond, D. and O'Donoghue-Hynes, B. (2024) Understanding the Emergency Accommodation Use Patterns of Homeless Families. *Cities* 155.

Wallich-Clifford, A. (1976) *Caring on Skid Row*. Veritas.

Walsh, A.-M. (1999) Root Them in the Land: Cottage Schemes for Agricultural Labourers. In Augusteijn, J. (Ed) *Ireland in the 1930s*. Four Courts Press.

Walsh, D. (2015) Psychiatric Deinstitutionalisation in Ireland 1960–2013. *Irish Journal of Psychological Medicine* 32(4): 347–352.

Walsh, D. and Daly, A. (2004) *Mental Illness in Ireland 1750–2002: Reflections on the Rise and Fall of Institutional Care*. Health Research Board.

Walsh, K. and Harvey, B. (2015) *Family Experiences of Pathways into Homelessness*. Focus Ireland.

Walsh, K. and Harvey, B. (2017) *Finding a Home: Families' Journeys out of Homelessness*. Focus Ireland.

Washbrook, R. A. (1970) The Homeless Offender: An English Study of 200 Cases. *International Journal of Offender Therapy* 14(3): 176–184.

Watson, D. and Corrigan, E. (2019) Social Housing in the Irish Housing Market. *The Economic and Social Review* 50(1): 213–248.

Watson, D., Maître, B., Grotti, R. and Whelan, C. (2018) *Poverty Dynamics of Social Risk Groups in the EU: An analysis of the EU Statistics on Income and Living Conditions, 2005–2014*. ESRI.

Whelan, M., Nolan, W. and Duffy, P. J. (2004) State-Sponsored Migrations to the East Midlands in the Twentieth Century. In Duffy, P. J. (Ed) *To and From Ireland: Planned Migration Schemes c.1600–2000*. Geography Publications.

Whitaker, T. K. (1956) Capital Formation, Saving and Economic Progress. *Statistical and Social Society of Ireland* 19: 184–209.

Whyte, G. (2002) *Social Inclusion and the Legal System: Public Interest Law in Ireland*. Institute of Public Administration.
Whyte, G. (2020) Begging and Irish Law. *Irish Jurist NS* 64: 153–166.
Williams, J. and Gorby, S. (2002) *Counted in 2002: The Report of the Assessment of Homelessness in Dublin*. Homeless Agency/Economic and Social Research Institute.
Williams, J. and O'Connor, M. (1999) *Counted In: The Report of the 1999 Assessment of Homelessness in Dublin, Kildare and Wicklow*. Economic and Social Research Institute/Homeless Initiative.
Wills, C. (2007) *That Neutral Island: A Cultural History of Ireland During the Second World War*. Faber and Faber.
Woods, A. (1998) *Dublin Outsiders: A History of the Mendicity Institute, 1818–1998*. A&A Farmar.
Yeates, P. (2000) *Lockout: Dublin 1913*. Gill and Macmillan.

Index

1836 Poor Law Inquiry 2
1906 Report of the Vice-Regal Commission on Poor Law Reform in Ireland 6, 46

A

Aalen, F. H. A. 10, 32
An Act to make Provision for the Punishment of Vagrants and Persons offending against the Laws in force for the Relief of the destitute Poor in Ireland (1847) 4–5
Action Plan to Address Homelessness (DECLG, 2014) 170
activism 187–189, 203–204, 228–229
Ad-Hoc Committee on the Homeless 95, 97, 98–100, 102, 247
Adane, Elias 207
affordable housing 66, 136, 158, 182, 209, 215
agricultural labourers 20
agriculture 17–18
  bloodless revolution 19
  importance of 18
  small-scale farming 19
  see also land
AHBs 89, 111, 121, 122, 136, 184–186
  acceptance or rejection of nominations 123–124
  government financing 160
  increased role of 136, 160
  new builds 220
  regulatory remit of RTB 191
  social housing output 90, 118, 135, 161, 185, 220, 221
Allen et al 261
Allen, Mike 172
ALONE 78
Anglo-Irish economic war 19
Anglo-Irish Treaty 15–16
anti-immigration groups 224, 230
Apollo House 187–188, 203
apprenticeships 159
Approved Housing Bodies (AHBs) *see* AHBs
Approved Housing Bodies Regulatory Authority (ABHRA) 220, 229
Arensberg, Conrad 36
Assessment of Homelessness 114, 146–147
Assessment of Housing Needs 114, 146, 148
asylum seekers 216
asylum system 8, 60

austerity 131, 151, 154, 155–157
  Budget 2011 155
  Budget 2012 155
  government spending cuts 155
  impact on housing system 157–158, 179
  limited civil society protest 157
  poverty 155–156
  social welfare expenditure 156
  welfare cuts to lone parents 156
  welfare cuts to young adults 156
Austria 258, 259

B

Ballymun 57, 92
banking system, failures 151, 157
Barry, Frank 16
bed-and-breakfast accommodation 115–116, 147, 175
begging 49, 62–63, 263n2
blackguards 48, 49
Blackwell, John 91
Blaney, Neil 71
Boards of Guardians 4
Boland, Kevin 73
Bolton Street 41, 56
bovine economy 17
Boyle et al 129
Broderick, John 109–110, 250
Browne, Noel 42, 43–44, 47, 48, 52–53
Brownlee, Andrew 144
Brú Chaoimhín shelter 85–86
Bruton, John 112
budgets *see* Government: Budgets
Burton, Joan 154
buy-to-let (BTL) mortgages 158, 190
Byrne, Linda 56
Byrne, Michael and Norris, Michelle 165

C

Cabinet Sub-Committee on Social Inclusion 130, 133, 141
Campaign for Public Housing 203
Canavan, Fr J. E. 31
Capital Assistance Scheme (CAS) 121, 122
Capital Investment Advisory Committee 50–51, 54–55, 76
Capuchin Franciscan Friars 70
Cashman, Bob 235
casual vacancies 91
Casual Wards 3, 21, 43, 95
  closure of 59–60, 109–110
Casuals 1, 4, 6, 43–47
  as blackguards 49
  definition 6

Index

exclusion from County Homes 25–26, 45, 59
inclusion in County Homes 46–47
Catholic Church 18
  active participation in social justice issues 64–65
  ideas for societal reorganisation 20
  social science perspective 65
  social teaching on subsidiarity 20, 39–40
  spread of Catholicism 37
Ceallaigh, Sean T. O. 32
Celtic Tiger economy 107, 132, 148, 149, 151
Censuses 22, 30, 53–54, 78, 174, 175, 255, 256
Central Bank Code of Conduct on Mortgage Arrears (2013) 158
Central Implementation Unit 168
Central Statistics Office (CSO) 194
charitable organisations 8–9, 228–229, 237
Cherish 64
Child Care Act (1991) 88, 116, 129
Chopra, Ajai 155
Citizens Housing Council 31–32, 33–34
  Report on Slum Clearance in Dublin (1938) 31, 33–34
civic society 64–65, 87–88, 95, 143–144, 156, 237
Civil War 15–16
Clann Na Poblachta 41–42
Cluskey, Frank 80
co-operative housing 121–122
Colivet, Michael P. 34
Collins, Barbara and McKeown, Kieran 114
Collins, John 24, 35
Collis, Robert 31
Commission of Inquiry into Banking, Currency and Credit 20
Commission of Inquiry into the Sale of Cottages and Plots provided under the Labourers' Acts 35
Commission of Inquiry on Mental Illness 60
Commission on Emigration and Other Population Problems 42
Commission on Housing 227–228, 240
Commission on Itinerancy 63
Commission on the Private Rented Sector 138
Commission on the Relief of the Sick and Destitute Poor, including the Insane Poor 22–23, 25–26, 235
  report (1927) 22, 25, 46
Commission on Vocational Organisation 20, 50
Committee on the Price of Building Land 73–74
  Majority report 73, 74
  Minority report 73–74
common lodging houses 9
Communist Party of Ireland 68
Community Action Tenants Union 229
Community and Voluntary Pillar 127
Condon, Colm SC 56
Congested Districts Board 10, 18
congregate shelters 24
Conroy, Judge John 54
construction industry
  Celtic Tiger era 151
  collapse of 151, 157–159, 160, 179
  construction workers 159
  ghost estates 154, 157–158, 158–159, 170
  migrant workers 149
  social housing 53, 58, 77, 105–106, 117–119
  structural constraints 181
Construction Industry Federation (CIF) 127
Corish, Brendan 63
Cork Corporation 32
Corporation Buildings 12
Corporation Place 'the Cages' 57
Corrie, Jonathan 169, 179, 250
Cosgrave, Liam 58
Cost Rental Tenant In Situ (CRTiS) Scheme 215
Costello, John A. 42
Costello, M. J. 51
County Homes 21, 22, 109–110, 234
  able-bodied Casuals 48
  Casual Wards *see* Casual Wards
  exclusion of Casuals 25–26, 45, 59
  inclusion of Casuals 46–47
  Inter-Departmental Committee 44–46, 47
  obligation to work 48
  primitive accommodation 22
  reform 43–44, 46, 47
  residents 44–45
Coveney, Simon 183, 187, 188, 201, 247
COVID-19 pandemic 208, 210–212, 213, 220, 230
  emergency measures 210–212
  lockdowns 210
  vaccinations 210
crime 5, 48, 49, 119
  see also begging; prison; vagrancy; vagrants
crisis 163, 233, 249–251
  homelessness 180–207, 250
  housing 180–207, 208–231
  responses to 250
  role of 249–251
  see also global financial crisis (GFC)

299

Crisis (UK charity) 67
Cross-Departmental Team on
  Homelessness 130, 133, 141, 146, 168
Crossman, Virginia 3, 4
Crowley, Br Kevin 64
Cumann na nGaedheal 15, 16
Curran, John 181, 186–187

D

Dalton, Rev R. J. 32
Daly, Mary 15, 32, 34, 38
  Capital Investment Advisory Committee
    reports 51
  Celtic Tiger 132
  contribution of Irish emigrants 37
  financial crisis 180
  Irish housing market 182
  Irish membership of the EEC 52
Dawson, Charles 7
De Bromhead, A. and Lyons, R. C. 36
De Rossa, Prionsias 65
De Valera, Eamonn 42
Deeney, Dr James 262n1
deinstitutionalisation 60–61
Delany, A. P. 22
Delivering Homes, Sustaining
  Communities (2007) 137
Denmark 159, 258, 259, 260, 261
Dennehy, Denis and Mary 65
Department of the Environment 94, 100,
  113, 114, 122, 133
Department of the Environment,
  Community and Local Government
  (DECLG) 167, 168–169, 169–170,
  176–177
Department of the Environment, Heritage
  and Local Government 141
Department of Finance 17, 44, 45, 51
Department of Health 44, 47, 97, 98,
  133, 218
Department of Housing, Local
  Government and Heritage 111,
  120–121, 173, 199, 237, 243, 256
  funding provision 131, 218, 239
Department of Justice 97
Department of Lands and the Gaeltacht 29
Department of Local Government and
  Public Health 21
Department of Social Welfare 17, 49, 50,
  80, 124
Departmental Committee on Vagrancy 7
detention colonies 7
Dickson, David 32
differential rents 33–35, 39, 76, 106, 158,
  193, 241
Dignan, Rev John, Bishop of
  Clonfert 24, 50
Direct Provision Centres (DPCs) 255

discrimination 192
District and Auxiliary Mental Hospitals 8
domestic rates 77–78
Dooley, Terence 20
dualist profit-rental system 158
Dublin 12
  emergency accommodation 154, 199,
    200, 211, 214, 244
  families in shelters 200
  ghettos 57
  homelessness 84, 148–149
  increase housing supply 91
  Pathway to Home: The Homeless
    Action Plan Framework for Dublin,
    2014–2016 (2014) 172
  poor housing conditions 12–13
  positive case study during
    COVID-19 211
  Report of Inquiry into the Housing of
    the Working Classes of the City of
    Dublin, 1939–43 (1943) 32
  Report on Slum Clearance in Dublin
    (1938) 31, 33–34
  rough sleepers 197–198, 216, 217
  single homeless persons 149
Dublin Artisans Dwellings
  Company 11, 121
Dublin City Council (DCC) 147, 172,
  176, 202, 212, 236
Dublin Corporation 12, 32, 33, 87,
  91, 128
  housing 56–57
  Housing Forum 127
Dublin County Borough 123
Dublin Diocesan Welfare
  Committee 70
Dublin Flatdwellers Association 78
Dublin Homeless Initiative 133, 134
Dublin House of Industry 24
Dublin Housing Action Committee
  (DHAC) 65–66, 82, 87
Dublin Housing First Demonstration
  Project (DHFDP) 171–172
Dublin Housing First scheme 201
Dublin Housing Inquiry Commission 34
Dublin Lockout 13
Dublin Region Homeless Executive
  (DRHE) 171, 172, 174, 206,
  229, 263n2
  emergency accommodation during
    COVID-19 211
  HAP scheme 164–165
  National Quality Standards 204
  Place Finder service 165
Dublin Shelter for Men 9
Dublin Simon Community 9, 84
Duff, Frank 26–27, 47, 234–235, 262n3
dump estates 57

Index

E

Earner-Byrne, Lindsey 61, 66
Eason, Charles 7
Eastern Health Board (EHB) 116, 127, 128
Economic and Social Research Institute (ESRI) 70, 77, 114, 148–149
'The Emergency' 30, 37
emergency accommodation 142, 154, 169, 173–174, 180, 188, 189
  adult-only households 214, 215
  during COVID-19 208, 213
  in Dublin 154, 199, 200, 211, 214, 244
  entering 155, 190, 191, 199, 200, 213, 244
  exiting 199, 200, 213, 214, 244
  expansion of infrastructure 201
  expenditure on 173, 218
  families 200–201, 213–215
  family hubs 175, 202
  hotels 224
  interagency collaboration during COVID-19 211–212
Emergency Measures in the Public Interest (COVID-19) Act (2020) 210–211
emigration 27, 36–38, 42–43, 56, 80, 91, 126
  returning Irish emigrants 80, 126, 204
England 258, 259
Equal Status Acts (2000–2018) 192
European Central Bank 151
European Commission 151, 222
European Consensus Conference on Homelessness (2010) 167
European Observatory on Homelessness 88
European Platform against Poverty and Social Exclusion 167
European Platform for Combatting Homelessness (EPOCH) 225
European Social Fund (ESF) 225
European Typology of Homelessness and Housing Exclusion (ETHOS) 173, 254

F

Fahey, Tony 10, 17, 119
faith-based organisations 43–44, 47, 64, 234, 235–236
  see also voluntary housing agencies/bodies
family economy 17–20
family hubs 175, 202, 237
far-right movement 208, 224, 230
farming *see* agriculture
FEANTSA 88, 167
Fearon, John 67
Fédération Européenne d'Associations Nationales Travaillant avec les Sans Abris *see* FEANTSA
Feeney et al 61–62
Feery, Patsy 127, 250
Fenian Street 41, 56
Ferriter, Diarmaid 152
Fianna Fáil 16, 41–42, 58, 111–112, 132, 209, 249
  abolition of domestic rates 77–78
  decline in social housing 53
  in government *see* governments
  Housing Act (1988) 84, 103–105, 113
  land annuities 19
  public housing programme 28–29
  Social Partnership Agreement 106–107
  spending on social welfare 65
  State welfare services 17
  support for minority government 183
  tenant purchase scheme 35
Fine Gael 153–154, 156, 179, 181, 183, 209
  in government *see* governments
  Housing (Miscellaneous Provisions) Bill (1985) 100–103
  just society approach 65
Finland 159, 258, 259, 260, 261
FitzGerald, Garret 82, 83
fixed rent 33–34
Flannery, Fr Austin 64, 65–66
Flynn, Anthony 228–229
Flynn, Padraig 103–104, 113
Focus Housing 122
Focus Ireland 112, 122, 143, 172
Focus Point (later Focus Ireland) 87, 88, 116
forced labour farms 7
for-profit providers 202–203, 210, 236, 237
furnished dwellings 30
Future of Health Services (1966) 71

G

Garvin, Tom 15, 18
General Prisons Board 7
ghost estates 154, 157–158, 158–159, 170
global financial crisis (GFC) 131, 134, 136–137, 149, 151, 152, 155, 160
  impact on housing system 157–159, 160, 179
Glynn, Sir Joseph 31
Gmelch, George 62–63
Gmelch, Sharon Bohn 62–63
Government plans to address homelessness
  Action Plan to Address Homelessness (DECLG, 2014) 170
  Homeless Policy Statement (2013) 167, 174
  Homeless Strategy - Implementation Plan (2009) 145–146
  Homelessness: A Preventative Strategy (2002) 140, 141

Homelessness: An Integrated Strategy (2000) 131, 133, 140
Homelessness Oversight Group Report (2013) 168, 255–256
Housing First Implementation Plan 2018–2021 (2018) 184, 201
Housing First National Implementation Plan 2022–2026 (2022) 226–227
Housing for All – A New Housing Plan for Ireland (2021) 224, 225–228
Implementation Plan on the State's Response to Homelessness (DECLG, 2014) 168–169, 174
Progress Reports on the Implementation Plan on the State's Response to Homelessness (DECLG, 2014) 169
Rebuilding Ireland: Action Plan for Housing and Homelessness (2016) see Rebuilding Ireland: Action Plan for Housing and Homelessness (2016)
Rebuilding Ireland: Homelessness Pillar (2016) 183–184, 190
Report of the Homelessness Inter-Agency Group (2018) 189–190
The Way Home: A Strategy to Address Adult Homelessness in Ireland 2008–2013 (2008) 131, 133–134, 144–146
Government, the
  Budget 2011 155
  Budget 2012 155
  Budget 2016 165
  Budget 2024 218
  'confidence and supply' arrangement 181, 183, 187, 194–195, 263n1
  ideology of 248–249
  see also State
governments
  (1922–32) Cumann na nGaedheal 15, 16
  (1932–1948) Fianna Fáil 15, 16, 17, 19
  (1948–1951) First Inter-Party Government 42
  (1954–1957) Fine Gael/Labour Party coalition 42
  (1957–1959) Fianna Fáil 42
  (1959–1966) Fianna Fáil 42, 58
  (1966–1973) Fianna Fáil 58
  (1973–1977) Fine Gael/Labour Party coalition 58
  (1977–1981) Fianna Fáil 58, 77
  (1981–1982) Fine Gael/Labour Party coalition 82, 83
  (1982–1987) Fine Gael/Labour Party coalition 83, 100–103
  (1987–1992) Fianna Fáil/Progressive Democrats 83–84, 103, 111–112, 113
  (1992–1994) Fianna Fáil/Labour Party coalition 112, 113
  (1994–1997) Fine Gael/Labour/Democratic Left coalition 'Rainbow Coalition' 112, 132
  (1997–2008) Fianna Fáil/Progressive Democrats coalition 132
  (2008–2011) Fianna Fáil/Green Party coalition 132, 155
  (2011–2016) Fine Gael/Labour Party coalition 153–154, 156, 179
  (2016–2020) Fine Gael minority government 181
  (2020-present, 2025) Fianna Fáil/Fine Gael coalition 209–210
Great Famine 3
Green Party 132, 209
  in government see governments
Griffith Barracks 56
Guidance for Homeless and Vulnerable Groups (2020) 211

H

Habitual Residence Condition 246
Hanna, Erika 56
Hannan, Damian F. 36
Hannan, Damian F. and Commins, Patrick 18, 20
Hansard, Glen 188
HAP scheme 163–165, 180, 184, 226
  administrative inefficiencies 194
  changing profile of tenants 194
  criticisms of 194–196
  dearth of available properties 195
  differential rent 193
  discretionary uplift payments 195
  discrimination against tenants 192
  expansion of 193–194
  expenditure on 196–201
  Homeless HAP (HHAP) scheme see Homeless HAP (HHAP) scheme
  increased rates 195
  lack of security for tenants 196
  landlord guarantee 195
  mainstreaming of 192–193
  ongoing need for social housing 220
  preventative Homeless HAP 192
  replacement of RS 193
Harris, Simon 209
Hart, Peter 69
Harvey, Brian 104
Haughey, Charles 55, 58, 82, 84, 112, 113
Hayden, Aideen 93
Health Act (1953) 47–49, 94, 238
Health Act (2004) 239–240
health authorities 99–100
Health Boards 71, 88, 94, 98–99, 100, 116–117, 141, 238
Health Impact Assessment 143
Health Service Executive (HSE) 144, 211

Index

Hickey et al 140
hidden homeless persons 85
hidden homeless women 85, 86–87
Higgins, Mary 104, 128–129, 133, 134, 251
High Court 116–117
high support accommodation 147
Hogan, Patrick 18, 20
Hogan, Phil 154
Holohan, Carole 66
Holyfield Building 57
Home Assistance 22–23, 79–80
  able-bodied applicants 23
  discretion and eligibility 23
Home Assistance Officers 23
Home Sweet Home 188
Homeless: A Preventative Strategy (2002) 140, 141
homeless action plans 140, 142
Homeless Agency (later DRHE) 149, 251, 263n2
Homeless HAP (HHAP) scheme 164–165, 195
  HAP cap 164, 193
  Place Finder service 193
Homeless Initiative (later Homeless Agency) 111, 128–129, 130, 133, 148–149, 263n2
  partnership 251
homeless NGOs see NGOs
homeless persons 26
  adults 68–71
  Census profile 174
  composition of 47
  description of 70–71
  emergency accommodation 175
  families 66–67, 68, 155, 169, 174, 174–175
  financial assistance 100, 101
  hidden 85, 86–87
  Housing First approach 154
  increased social housing allocations 91–92
  Irish emigrants in America 38
  Irish emigrants in England 38
  permanent, standard housing for 167
  rough sleepers see sleeping rough
  single 68, 71, 98–99, 113, 114, 136, 149
  'on-street' services 188–189, 204
  women 62, 85, 86–87, 174
  see also vagrants
homeless policy
  housing-led 166–169
  ideology of Government 248–249
  role of crisis 249–251
Homeless Policy Statement (2013) 167, 174

homeless services expenditure 176–177, 202–203, 218–219
homeless women 26, 83, 84–87, 174, 256
  begging 62–63
  hidden 85, 86–87
  imprisonment 62
  labour colonies 7
  Magdalen Asylums 61
  refuges/shelters 9, 24–25, 27, 85, 86–87
  understanding of 245
  see also County Homes
homelessness
  acceleration of 155
  active role for Central Government 146
  association with dysfunctional alcoholic men 61–62
  attitudes to 61–63
  campaigning activities 95
  consensus on commitment to ending 143–144
  'Counted In' survey 172
  dedicated health service 70
  definition in legislation 95–96, 102, 104
  definitions 66–67, 243
  dynamics of 243
  'eviction to sell' 213–214, 215
  extent of 146–148
  fluidity of 242–246
  funding for 144–145
  gendered nature of 245
  Government review of strategies 141–143
  health or housing question 94, 95, 183, 238–240
  hidden homeless women 85, 86–87
  housing-led policy shift 166–169
  inconsistency of approach and organisation 142
  long-term patterns 234
  measuring 217–218, 254–257
  measuring (2011–2016) 172–173
  measuring, time frames for 243
  milestones 143, 152, 167
  Monthly Reports 173
  'national crisis' (2016–20) 180–181
  national strategic approach 133–134
  in the early 1970s 68–71
  in the 1980s 84–87
  in the 1990s, local authority assessment 113–115
  optimism 154–155
  'panic or ignore' dichotomy 250
  policy debate 94–95
  policy developments 224–228
  post-2014 increases 174–176
  pre-2014 scale of 173–174
  preventative strategy for 140–141
  primary causes of 190–192

303

prior to Independence 1–8
priority issue for 2020 election 209
projects/services 145
and psychiatric deinstitutionalisation 60–61
public debate 203
residential services 84–85
responsibility for 234–240
rise of 169–172
robust and comprehensive data 155
social partnership 126–129
statutory rules 146
successes 252–253
survey 68–70
trends 258–261
trends (2014–2019) 196–201
trends (2020–2024) 212–216
'wandering abroad' offence 104
see also vagrancy
Homelessness: An Integrated Strategy (2000) 131, 133, 140
Homelessness Inter-Agency Group 189–190
Homelessness Oversight Group 168–169, 175, 179, 187, 241–242, 247
report 168, 255–256
Homelessness Policy Implementation Team 168
Homelessness Policy Statement (2013) 169, 173, 179
homeownership 53–54, 73
help for 182
see also private housing
HOPE 63–64
hostel-type accommodation 147
hotel accommodation 175, 184, 202, 224
housing 10–11
  capital investment 50–52
  changing priorities of 50–52
  dangerous buildings scare 56
  demolitions 56–57
  dysfunctional market 181
  emigration 42–43
  falling supply of 28
  ghost estates 154, 157–158, 158–159, 170
  Government referendum commitment 228
  housing market collapse 151, 156–157, 179
  housing policy 71, 72–73
  housing policy objectives 72–73
  impact of COVID-19 220
  impact of global financial crisis 157–159, 160, 179
  increased supply 91–92
  long-term approach 227
  mortgage arrears 158

needs met, view 50–52
negative equity 158
overheated property market 151
paying for 240–242
priority issue for 2020 election 209
problems 10, 66
repossessions 158
White Papers 38–39
see also affordable housing; private housing; private rented housing; public housing; social housing
Housing Act (1966) 33, 72, 74, 76, 80, 94, 238
Housing Act (1988) 83, 84, 103–105, 114, 117, 129, 238
DoE review 113
impact of 112–113
see also Section 10 funding (Housing Act, 1988)
Housing Act (2009) 251
Housing Agency 187
Housing (Amendment) Act (1958) 51
housing and homelessness activism 187–189, 203–204, 228–229
Housing Assistance Payment (HAP) *see* HAP
Housing Board 34
Housing (Building Facilities) Act (1924) 28
Housing Commission (2024) 242
Housing (Financial and Miscellaneous Provisions) Act (1932) 28, 31
Housing First 167–168, 182
Housing First Implementation Plan (2018–2021) 184, 201
Housing First in Ireland 170–172, 184, 201, 226
Housing First National Implementation Plan 2022–2026 (2022) 226–227
Housing for All - A New Housing Plan for Ireland (2021) 209, 224, 225–228
Housing (Homeless Persons) Act (1977) 96
Housing (Homeless Persons) Bill (1983) 95–98, 99, 102
Housing Management Group 120
Housing (Miscellaneous Provisions) Act (1931) 28
Housing (Miscellaneous Provisions) Act (2014) 163, 164
Housing (Miscellaneous Provisions) Bill (1985) 102
Housing Needs Assessment (HNA) 147, 255
(1999) 133
(2013) 154
Housing of the Working Classes Act (1890) 11, 13

Index

Housing of the Working Classes Acts 11, 12, 29
Housing of the Working Classes (Ireland) Act (1908) 11
Housing (Private Rented Dwellings) Act (1982) 79
Housing Procurement Agency 182
Housing Strategic Policy Committee 212
Housing Subsidies (NESC, 1976) 77
housing tenure 53–55

I

immigration 151
  see also migration
Implementation Plan (2009) 145–146
Implementation Plan on the State's Response to Homelessness (DECLG, 2014) 168–169, 174
Independence
  homelessness, public assistance and institutional provision 20–25
  private rented housing 30–31
  public rental housing 27–30
Indoor Relief 3, 6
Industrial Schools 8, 47, 61
Inner City Helping Homeless 189, 228, 238
institutional landlords 196
Integrated Strategy (2000) 141–142
intentional homelessness 96, 97, 100, 102, 103, 176, 249
Inter-Departmental Committee on County Homes 44–46, 47, 59, 138–139
  recommendations 45–46
  Report (1949) 44–45
  Report (1951) 59
Interdepartmental Committee on the Administration of the Rent Supplement Scheme 124
  Report (1999) 139
Interdepartmental Committee on the Care of the Aged 60
  Report (1968) 109
International Monetary Fund (IMF) 151
International Protection Accommodation Services (IPAS) offices 216–218, 222
International Protection Applicants (IPAs) 216, 222
Ireland
  austerity see austerity
  demographic changes 220–224
  economic growth 132, 222
  economic restructuring 155
  fall in inequality 156
  GDP 151
  GNP 156
  government debt 151
  government departments see individual departments
  membership of the EEC 52, 59
  neutrality in World War II 30
  record of vagrancy 62
  Ukrainian refugees 222, 224
  youth unemployment 151
  see also Celtic Tiger economy; Irish Free State
Ireland 1912–1985 (Lee) 231
Ireland's Private Rental Sector: Pathways to Secure Occupancy and Affordable Supply (2015) 165
Irish Communist Organisation (ICO) 67–68
Irish Congress of Trade Unions (ICTU) 203
Irish Free State 15, 16, 58
  coercive confinement 27
  economic performance 16–17
  interventionism 27
  maintaining the status quo 20
  prioritising agriculture 17–18
  private enterprise 17
  rural fundamentalist ideology 18, 32
  social housing programme 28
  see also Independence
Irish Home Builders Association 136
Irish Lunatic Asylums for the Poor Act (1817) 8
Irish Poor Law Act (1838) 1, 2–3
Irish Republican Army (IRA) 8
The Irish Times 176
Irish Workers' Party 67
Iveagh Hostel 9, 11, 121
Iveagh Trust 9, 11, 70, 121

J

Job Seekers Allowance (JSA) 222–224
Johnston, Tom 28, 249

K

Kaim-Caudle, Peter 52, 56, 72–73
Kavanagh, Liam 101
Kearns, Kevin C. 63
Keenan-Thomson, Tara 66
Kelleher, Patricia 112
Kelly, Alan 154, 169–170, 175, 176, 187, 247
Kennedy, Finola. 31, 52
Kennedy, Sr Stanislaus 85, 87, 88–89, 104
Kenny, Enda 153, 183, 189
Kenny, John 73–74
Kenny Report 73–74, 248
Keogh Square 'the Dungeons' 57

L

Labour Party 65, 83, 100–103, 112, 153–154, 156, 179, 181, 249
  in government see governments

Labourers' Acts 12, 29, 53, 54
  (1893) 13
  (1936) 35, 76
labourers' cottages 10
Labourers' Ireland Act (1883) 10, 11
land 17–20
  division and redistribution of 18, 19–20
  see also agriculture
Land Act (1923) 19, 20
Land Act (1933) 19
land annuities 19
Land Commission 10, 18, 19, 152
  housebuilding programme 29
  powers of compulsory acquisition 19
Land Development Agency 186
landlord class 3
landlords 51, 190
  'buy-to-rent' investors 138
  eviction of tenants 184
  no-fault evictions 191, 215
  RAS payments 139
  selling up 190–191, 215
  vacant possession 138
Law Reform Commission 104
Leahy, Alice 70
Leahy, Alice and Magee, David 69–70
Lee, Joe 16, 17, 21, 231
Legion of Mary 24, 39–40, 45, 46, 48, 127–128, 234, 237
Lehman Brothers bank 151
Lemass, Sean 19, 42, 58
Leonard, Liz 112–113
Leonard, Pauline 127, 250
Lisbon Declaration on the European Platform on Combatting Homelessness (2021) 224–225, 226
local authorities 25, 28
  allocations 91, 113
  arbitrary policy-making 113
  assessment of housing needs 101, 104, 147–148
  central government grants 105
  centrality of housing provision 72
  differential rents 33–35, 39, 76, 106
  discretionary powers 103, 104
  HAP caps 164
  housebuilding programmes 74–75, 105
  housing problems 74
  implementation of the Housing Act (1988) 113
  maintenance issues 120
  new duties and funding 100–101, 104
  performance and financial reports 173, 177, 199
  provision of public housing 11, 12
  provision of social housing 52–53, 56
  records 147, 148
  reduced role for social housing 120–121
  rental income 123
  residualisation of housing 117–120
  responsibility for homelessness 238
  responsibility for reasonable and suitable accommodation 96
  ring-fencing allocations 182, 247
  sales policy 76–77
  social housing acquisition programmes 162
  social housing completions 74–75
  social housing expenditure 123
  statutory duties 96, 99–100, 104
  subsidies and funding 11, 28, 29–30, 31
  temporary accommodation responsibility 96
  tenant purchase scheme 35–36
local connection rules 96, 246
Local Government (Financial Provisions) Act (1978) 77
local government, funding sources 77–78
Local Government (Temporary Provisions) Act (1923) 22, 25
Local Loans Fund 29–30
London, homeless Irish emigrants 38
long-term accommodation 147
Longford County Home 44
Lord Mayor's Commission on Housing in Dublin (1993) 121
low-income households 163, 166
Lynch, Jack 58
Lynch, Patrick 50–51
Lyons, Danny 127

M

Magdalen Asylums 8, 25, 61
MakeRoom 143, 145, 152
marginality 8, 27
Marrowbone Lane 31
Marshalsea Barracks/Prison complex 57
Martin, Micheál 209
Matthews, Zach 205
Mayock, Paula 61, 63, 174, 199, 202, 245, 256
May, Sheila 32
McCashin, Anthony 49–50, 66
McEntee, Seán 50
McManus, Liz 127–128
McQuaid, Archbishop 66
Medico-Social Research Board 68–69
Meghan, P. J. 36
Memorandum on the Preparation of A Statement of Policy on Housing Management (1993) 121, 122–123
Mendicity Institution 9
mental health services 156
middle-income households 156

Index

migration 107–109, 124–126, 149–150, 177, 204–206, 245–246
  inward migration 137, 149–150, 218, 222, 245–246
    EEA/UK and Non-EEA citizens 218
  net inward migration 177, 180, 204
  net migration 91, 150, 151, 178, 222
    (1926–1948) 36, 37
    (1926–1963) 43
    (1926–1981) 81
    (1926–1988) 108
    (1926–1996) 125
    (1926–2020) 204–205
    (1926–2024) 223
  net outward migration 43, 80, 91, 107–109
  outward migration 149, 151, 177
  see also emigration
Millennium Tenant Purchase Scheme 93
minority government (2016–2020) 181–183
Mitchell, Gay 127
Model Lodging House 9, 56, 84
Molloy, Bobby 73
Monahan, Philip 28, 34
Morino Garden suburb 28
Morning Star Hostel 24, 27, 46
mortgage arrears 158
Mother and Baby Scheme 44, 47, 52, 61
Mount Pleasant Buildings 57
Murphy, Eoghan 189, 197, 209, 239
Murphy, John 189
Murphy, John A. 16
Murphy-Lawless, J. and Dillon, B. 112
Murphy, Tim 42
Murray, Jim 68

N

NAMA (National Assets Management Agency) 182, 187, 188, 264n7
National Army 16
National Association of Tenants Organisations (NATO) 76
National Building Agency 57
National Campaign for the Homeless 86, 87–88, 95, 112, 116, 143
National Economic and Social Council (NESC) 69, 77, 93–94, 94, 107, 186, 263n5
  Ireland's Private Rental Sector: Pathways to Secure Occupancy and Affordable Supply (2015) 165
  life-cycle approach 137
  reports on housing 121–122, 158
National Homeless Action Committee (NHAC) 226
National Homeless and Housing Coalition 203

National Homelessness Consultative Committee (NHCC) 142–143, 168, 172, 189
National Recovery Programme (NRP) 151
National Youth Homelessness Strategy (2022) 210
negative equity 158
Netherlands 258, 259
NGOs 112, 152, 157, 202, 212, 237
  coalition 143, 152
  'The Poor Can't Pay' campaign 157
  responsibility for homelessness 237
  see also individual NGOs
Nicholls, George 2
night lodgers 4, 6
night shelters 9, 70
no-fault evictions 191, 215
Nolan et al 120
Norris, Michelle 32–33
Norris, Michelle and Byrne, Michael 109
Norris, Michelle and Fahey, Tony 105–106
Norris, Michelle and Hayden, Aideen 241, 242
North Dublin Union Workhouse complex 24
Norton, William 42
Norway 258, 259
Nusight magazine 61–62

O

Ó Cinneide, Seamus 79–80
Ó hUiginn, Pádraig 51
Ó Tuathaigh, Gearoid 231
O'Brien, Darragh 209
O'Brien, George 18
O'Brien, Justin 62, 70–71
O'Connell, Cathal 119
O'Connor, Charles 25
O'Donnell, Rory 107, 239
O'Donovan, Fr Gerald 7
Office of the Ombudsman 194, 195, 196
Ogle, Brendan 188
O'Leary, Don 20
O'Meara, Michael 250
One Parent Family Payment (OFP) 156
opiate substitution therapy (OST) 212
O'Riordan, Michael 65
O'Sullivan, Jan 154, 167, 169
O'Sullivan, Eoin and Tsemberis, Sam 168
O'Sullivan, Eoin 172
Outdoor Relief (later Home Assistance) 2, 3, 4, 22, 79

P

Parker, Sarah 200
Parliamentary Committee on Crime, Lawlessness and Vandalism 104
Part V policy 136–137, 160–162

Partnership 2000 for Inclusion, Employment and Competitiveness (1996) 126–127
partnership, role of 251–252
In Partnership with Youth (1985) 88
PASS system (Pathway Accommodation & Support System) 171, 172, 198–199, 200, 254, 256–257
Pathway to Home: The Homeless Action Plan Framework for Dublin, 2014–2016 (2014) 172
Pathways to Housing First model 168, 171
Penrose, Willie 154
performance principle 231
Personal Public Service numbers 222
Peter McVerry Trust 172, 229
Pfretzschner, Paul 55, 120
Phelan, Elaine and Norris, Michelle 129
Place Finder service 165
Plan for Social Housing (1991) 111, 120–121
Planning Act (2000) 242
Planning and Development Acts (2000–2020) 136, 139–140
Planning Group on the Local Authority Rent Assistance 139
point-in-time count 197–198, 216, 217, 243, 244, 247, 254
Policy and Procedural Guidance for Housing Authorities in Relation to Assisting Victims of Domestic Violence with Emergency and Long-term Accommodation Needs 256
Poor Laws 21–24, 245
poor relief 1–3
  see also workhouses
Poor Relief (Ireland) Act (1847) 79
possessor principle 231
Potter, Matthew 10
poverty 1–2, 66, 74, 155–156, 157
Poverty Impact Assessment 143
Power, Anne 92
Preventative Strategy 142
Prevention of Crime Act (1871) 5, 62
Prison Service 140
prisons 8, 25, 49, 62–63, 69
Private Emergency Accommodation (PEA) 202–203
private housing 28, 53–54
  housing policy 72–73
  impact of global financial crisis 157–158
  public subsidies 28
  State Aid 73
  see also homeownership
private property 16–17
private rented housing 51, 78–80, 82, 137–140
  affordability 192

barriers to entry 192
decline 54, 78–79, 137–138
flux and changes 190
growth 138
market pressure 166
post-Independence 30–31
reliance on 193
rent supplements 124
social housing provision 170, 193
Private Residential Tenancies Act (2004) 138
Programme for Competitiveness and Work 1994–96 (1994) 126
Programme for Economic and Social Progress (PESP) (1991) 117, 126
Programme for Economic Development (1958) 41, 51, 52, 55, 58
Programme for Economic Expansion (1958) 52, 55
Programme for Economic Progress (1958) 51–52
Programme for Government: Our Shared Future (2020) 209, 227, 228
Programme for National Recovery (1987–1990) 106, 107
Programme for Prosperity and Fairness (2000) 107
Programme for the Homeless 70
Programme on Economic and Social Progress (1991) 126
Progressive Democrats 112, 132
  in government see governments
property-based welfare state 17
property rights 248
psychiatric hospitals 60–61, 70
The Psychiatric Services: Planning for the Future (1984) 60–61
Public Assistance Act (1939) 24, 79
public housing see social housing
public protest 157, 188, 203, 230, 237
public rental housing 27–30

Q

Quadragesmio Anno (1931) 20
Quarterly Financial Reports 173, 177, 257
Quarterly Performance Reports 173, 199, 257
Quinn, Ruairi 97–98

R

Radharc 65
Raidió Teilifís Éireann (RTÉ) 65
Raise the Roof 203, 229
Rapid Build Housing 183, 263n2
Rebuilding Ireland: Action Plan for Housing and Homelessness (2016) 183–187, 202
  appraisal of progress 184–186

Index

criticisms of 186–187
distinct approach 186–187
Homeless Pillar 183–184, 190
Housing First 184
improving the rental sector 184
pillars 183–184, 190, 206
private rental sector 186
Rapid Build Housing 183–184
Report of the Oireachtas Committee on Housing and Homelessness 186–187
roll out of HAP 192–193
Reformatory Schools 8, 61
refugees 222, 224, 255–256
Regina Coeli Hostel 24, 27, 39, 85
Regional Homeless Fora 145, 152
Rent Allowance 79
rent control 30–31, 54–55, 78, 79
see also differential rent
rent increases 166, 193, 195
rent levels 35, 76, 138, 154, 166, 192, 230
Rent Pressure Zones (RPZ) 184
Rent Restrictions Act (1946) 31, 55, 79
Rent Restrictions Act (1960) 55, 79
rent strike 76
rent subsidy schemes 194
Rent Supplement 79, 124, 138, 139, 163, 193
Rent Tribunal 79
Rental Accommodation Scheme (RAS) 139, 163–164, 226
Rental Subsidy Scheme (RSS) 122
Rents and Leaseholds Commission 54
Report of Inquiry into the Housing of the Working Classes of the City of Dublin, 1939–43 (1943) 32
Report of the Commission on Itinerancy (1963) 63
Report of the Departmental Committee appointed by the Local Government Board for Ireland to Inquire into the Housing Conditions of the Working Classes in the City of Dublin (1914) 12–13
Report of the Departmental Committee on Vagrancy (1906) 6
Report of the Inter-Departmental Working Group on Mortgage Arrears (2011) 158
Report of the Oireachtas Committee on Housing and Homelessness (2016) 181–183, 186–187
Report on Slum Clearance in Dublin (1938) 31
repossessions, housing 55
Rerum Novarum (1891) 20
Residential Property Price Index (RPPI) 215
residential services 84–85, 89

Residential Tenancies Acts 184, 191, 211
(2004) 138
(2014) 191
(Amendment, 2016) 191
Residential Tenancies Board (RTB) *see* RTB
Revolutionary Housing League 229
Reynolds, Albert 112
Richmond Asylum 24
Richmond Penitentiary 24
Roberts, Ruaidhri 51
Robinson, Mary 86
Roche, Desmond 35
rough sleepers *see* sleeping rough
Royal Commission of Inquiry into the Conditions of the Poorer Classes in Ireland (1836) 2, 3
Royal Commission on the Poor Laws and Relief of Distress (1909) 7
RTB 166, 191
Annual Report (2020) 191
Rules and Regulations for the Administration of Home Assistance (1924) 23
rural fundamentalism 18, 32
rural Ireland 17, 20, 41, 42, 50
political concerns 18
public housing 10, 11, 35, 38
social housing 28, 93
tenant purchase scheme 53, 76, 93
Ryan, Brendan 82, 95, 97, 104–105, 238, 249
Ryan, Dr James 39, 47–48, 49
Ryan, Louden 50–51, 74

S

Salvation Army 9
Scheme of National Health Insurance 50
Schickle, Win 63–64
Scotland 258, 259
Sean McDermott Street Magdalen 24–25
Section 10 funding (Housing Act, 1988) 104, 131, 173, 177, 188, 199, 239, 254
emergency and temporary accommodation 199, 213
responsibilities of housing authorities 104
Service Level Agreements (SLAs) 236, 237
7 Days 66
shelter beds 127
shelters 84, 200
Sheridan, Jim 188
Sick and Indigent Roomkeepers Society 9
Simms, Herbert George 33
Simon Community 68, 69, 71, 87, 102, 104, 143
Cork 95
Dublin 9, 84

single homeless persons 68, 71, 98–99, 113, 114, 136, 149
   in Dublin 149
Sinn Féin 15, 65, 68, 209, 230, 249
Skid Row 38
Sláintecare strategy 187
sleep outs 203
sleeping rough 69, 70, 84, 134, 149, 170, 171, 174
   deaths 198
   in Dublin 197–198, 216, 217
   point-in-time count 197–198, 216, 217
   responses to recurring crises 251
   unique individuals 216
   Winter Rough Sleeping Count (2016) 197
slum clearances 17, 28, 31, 33
'slum-dwelling' households 241
slums 13, 31
   see also urban slums
small landlords 190
social exclusion 157
social housing 10–14, 27, 54
   allocations to homeless households 175–176, 187
   capital funding 166
   Central Government capital funding 160
   construction 242
   counterbalance within housing market 165–166
   decline in output 53, 116, 117–119, 134–136
   differential rents 33–35, 106, 241
   emergency allocations during COVID-19 212
   funding 29–30
   funding for 105–106, 166, 182
   impact of global financial crisis 157, 160
   increase in 28–29
   increased availability of 89–91
   lack of professional management 120
   local authorities 11, 13
   'Million Pound Scheme' 28
   mixed economy of 160–162, 165–166
   needs assessment 220
   needs basis 246
   new builds and completions 53, 75, 89, 90, 105, 106, 170
   output 29, 131, 135, 161, 185, 220, 221
   policy change in the early 1990s 105
   property speculators and developments 28–29
   queue jumping 101–102, 176, 247
   range of options 152
   reduced role for local authorities 120–121
   rental income 106
   residualisation of 117–120, 158

rural 10
sales to tenants 162–163
selling to tenants 248–249
social segregation 122, 158
source of employment 28
spending cuts 105–106
state funding 83, 89, 105, 106
stigmatisation of 119
tenant dissatisfaction 123
tenant purchases 36, 93
transfer list 164
urban 11
voids 168–169, 175, 187, 241–242, 247
waiting list 85, 91, 114, 115, 117, 119, 129, 137, 164, 246–247
see also Part V policy
Social Housing - The Way Ahead (1995) 111, 115, 121
Social Housing Strategy 2020 (DECLG, 2014) 170, 193
social movements 64–65, 87–88
Social Partners 142–143
Social Partnership Agreement 106–107, 130, 239, 250, 251, 252
   in the homelessness sector 126–129, 152, 239
   Programme for Competitiveness and Work 1994–1996 (1994) 126
   Programme for Economic and Social Progress (PESP) (1991) 117, 126
   Programme for National Recovery (1987) 106, 107
social security system 17, 49–50
Social Welfare Act (1952) 49
Society of St Vincent de Paul 39–40, 45, 48, 62, 95, 143
Special Committee on Housing and Homelessness 181–182
   report and recommendations 181–183
Special Report on Homeless Persons in Ireland (CSO, 2012) 174
Spring, Dick 96–97
Squatter 67
St. Brendan's Psychiatric Hospital 70
St Joseph's Night Shelter 9
Stabilising Rents, Boosting Supply: A Package to Deliver Rent Certainty and Housing Supply (DECLG, 2015) 166
Stagg, Emmet 127, 250–251
Staples, Leo and Mary 56
State, the
   emergency accommodation 201
   HAP scheme *see* HAP scheme
   'Million Pound Scheme' 28
   responsibility for homelessness 62, 234–235, 235, 236, 249
   responsibility for social housing 11, 30, 41, 170, 186

Index

sale of housing stock 162
subject subsidies 100
subsidies for homeownership 73
see also local authorities
'A Strategy for the Nineties' (NESC) 93–94
Strategy for the Rental Sector (2016) 184
street-based services 188–189
on-street services 188–189, 204
'Streetwise' conference (1987) 88, 89
Streetwise National Coalition 89, 116, 143
Summit on Homelessness 169–170
Supplementary Welfare Allowance Act (1975) 80
Supplementary Welfare Allowance scheme 80, 87, 124
Supported Temporary Accommodation 232
Surrender Grant Scheme 89, 91–92, 119
Sweden 258, 259
Sweetman, Fr Michael 64, 65, 66

T

Task Force on Child Care Services 63
TB (tuberculosis) 52–53
Temporary Protection Directive (EC) 222
Tenant in Situ Scheme 215
tenant purchase schemes 35–36, 39, 53, 54, 76–78, 162
  alignment of urban and rural schemes 93
  decline in social housing stock 162
  impact of 119, 162
tenants
  emergency protection during COVID-19 210–211
  help for 182
  increased termination notice periods 192
  insecurity of tenure 184
  preventative Homeless Hap 192
tenements 11–12, 12–13
  classes of 13
  collapse of 56
Thatcher, Margaret 93, 248
Third Report of the Royal Commission on the Housing of the Working Classes (1885) 11–12
Three Reports by George Nicholls, Esq (1838) 3
Threshold 78, 91–92, 143
time on list system 247
Towards 2016 (2006) 142–143
tramps 1, 6
transitional accommodation 147
Traveller community 26, 62–63
Troika 151, 157, 159
Trust 70
Tuairim 64
Tusla – The Child and Family Agency 255, 256

U

Ukrainian refugees 222, 224
unemployment 74, 84, 112, 163, 179, 180
  emigration 80, 87, 103, 149
  global financial crisis 151, 163
  homelessness 70
  Rent Supplement 124, 138–139
  residualisation of social housing 119–120
  Surrender Grant 92, 119
Unfinished Housing Developments 159
unfurnished dwellings 30, 54
UNICEF 88
United States, homelessness 38
unsheltered homelessness (2020–2024) 216–218
urban housing 11, 11–13
urban slums 31–35
  Citizens Housing Council report 31, 33–34
  differential rents 33–35, 241
  government failure to tackle 32
  living conditions 31

V

vagabonds 1
vagrancy 245–246
  association with disorder 5
  Irish record of 62
  limited discussion about 26–27
  vagrant question 5–8
Vagrancy Acts 49, 62, 104
  (1824) 5, 62, 104
  (1986) 104
  committals under 62
  offences 62
Vagrancy and Related Offences (1985) 104
Vagrancy in Ireland (memo, 1906) 6
vagrants 1, 3–8
  'down and out class' 26–27
  hostility towards 8
  prosecutions and convictions 4, 5
  weaknesses of 61–62
Varadkar, Leo 189, 197, 209
Vardy, Marion 56
Vice-Regal Commission (1906) 6, 7, 46
Viney, Michael 57, 64
voids 168–169, 187
  renovation of 175, 241–242, 247
voluntary housing 121, 122
voluntary housing agencies/bodies 46, 48–49, 59, 64, 70, 114, 121, 144, 237–238
  fear of obsolescence 144
  financial auditing of 229
  government funding 71, 94, 122, 126
  greater role for 123
  hostels 71

responsibility for homelessness 236
social partnership 126–127
spending cutbacks 156
see also Approved Housing Bodies (ABHs); faith-based organisations; Legion of Mary; Society of St Vincent de Paul

W

Wallich-Clifford, Anton 68
War of Independence 15–16
water charges protests 157, 179
The Way Home: A Strategy to Address Adult Homelessness in Ireland 2008–2013 (2008) 131, 133–134, 144–146
welfare system
　advanced 13
　expenditure 156
Whately, Richard 2
Whitaker, T. K. 51
White Papers
　The Health Services and their Further Development (1966) 59, 238
　Housing - Progress and Prospects (1964) 71–73, 78
　Housing: A Review of Past Operations and Immediate Requirements (1948) 38–39
　Housing in the Seventies (1969) 73–74, 78
　On the Reconstruction and Improvement of County Homes (1951) 45
　Social Security (1949) 49
Winter Rough Sleeping Count (2016) 197
women, homeless *see* homeless women
Women's Liberation Movement 64
workhouses 1–2, 234
　abolition proposals 21
　casuals 6
　denunciation of 21
　eligibility principle 2–3
　funding for 3
　modelled on English system 2
　official view of 21
　opposition to 2
　rules and regulations 6
　vagrants 3–5, 6
　see also County Homes
Working Group on Homeless (1992) 127
Working Group on the Implementation of the Provisions relating to the Homeless (1985) 102–103

Y

youth homelessness 63–64
　Child Care Act (1991) 116–117
　growing visibility in the 1980s 88–89
　legislation 88–89
Youth Homelessness Strategy 2023–2025 (2022) 228

www.ingramcontent.com/pod-product-compliance
Lightning Source LLC
Chambersburg PA
CBHW051527020426
42333CB00016B/1816